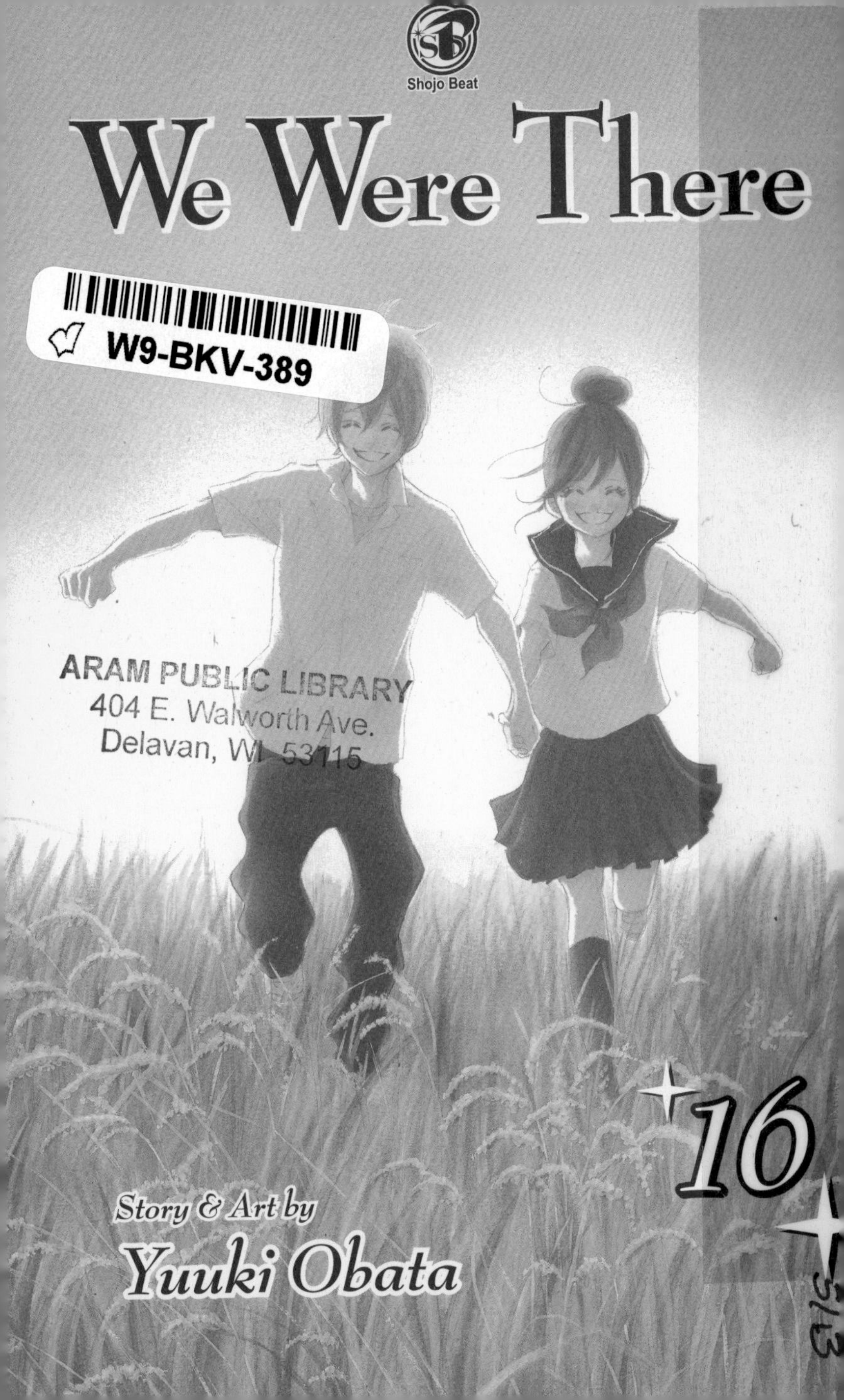
Shojo Beat
We Were There
16
Story & Art by
Yuuki Obata

Contents

Characters

Masafumi Takeuchi
Yano's best friend. He works for a foreign finance company. He asked Nanami to marry him but was rejected.

Nanami Takahashi
Nanami works at a publishing company in Tokyo. She is unable to forget her feelings for Yano.

Motoharu Yano
Nanami's ex-boyfriend. He works for an architecture and design firm. He is currently living with Yuri.

Story

After Takeuchi tells Nanami to pursue the kind of relationship with Yano that she thinks is right, Nanami starts planning a way to approach Yano. After staying with Yuri in her mother's last moments, Yano and Yuri are able to move on from their pasts and say goodbye. Yano finds peace with what happened with his mother and with Nana. Where will Nanami and Yano's feelings lead them now?

Chapter 65

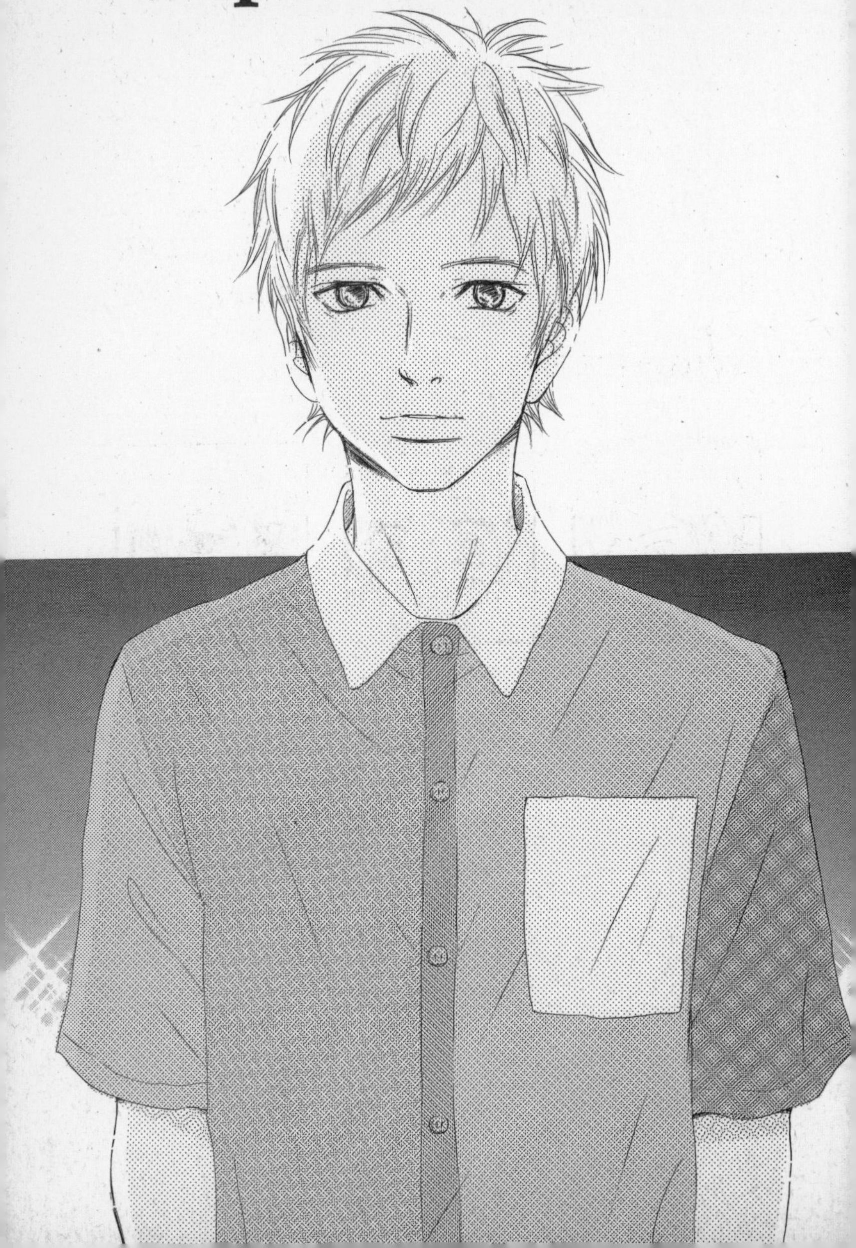

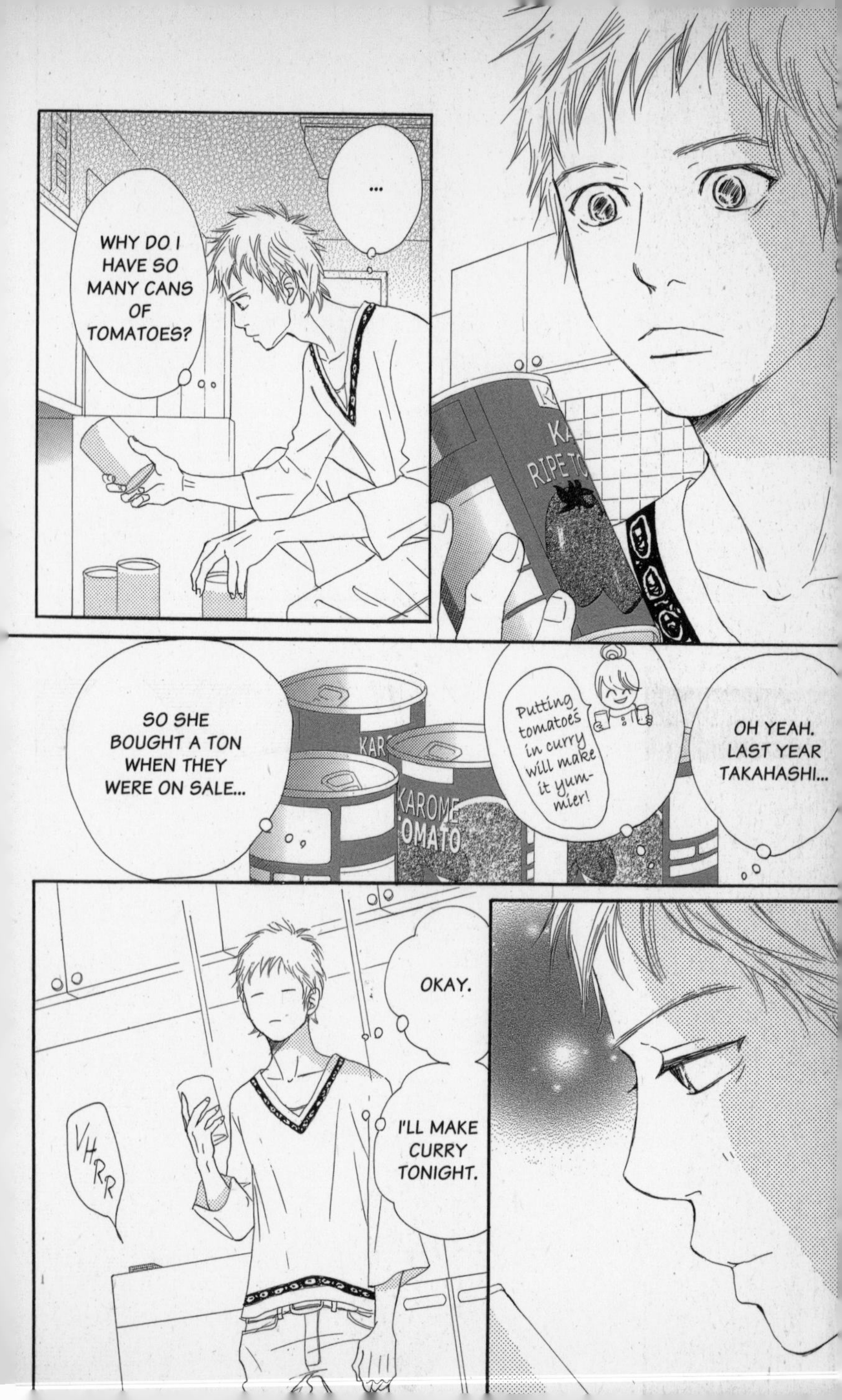
...
WHY DO I HAVE SO MANY CANS OF TOMATOES?
OH YEAH. LAST YEAR TAKAHASHI...
Putting tomatoes in curry will make it yummier!
SO SHE BOUGHT A TON WHEN THEY WERE ON SALE...
OKAY.
I'LL MAKE CURRY TONIGHT.
VHRR

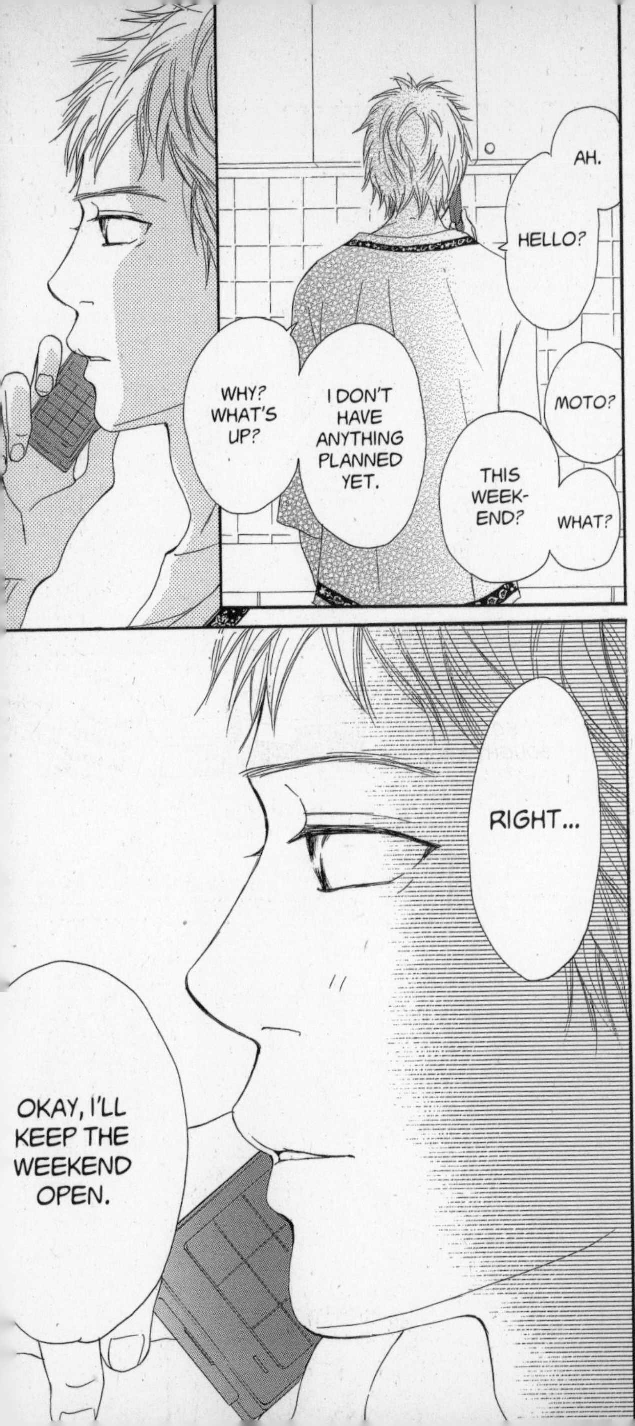
AH.
HELLO?
MOTO?
WHAT?
THIS WEEK-END?
I DON'T HAVE ANYTHING PLANNED YET.
WHY? WHAT'S UP?
RIGHT...
OKAY, I'LL KEEP THE WEEKEND OPEN.

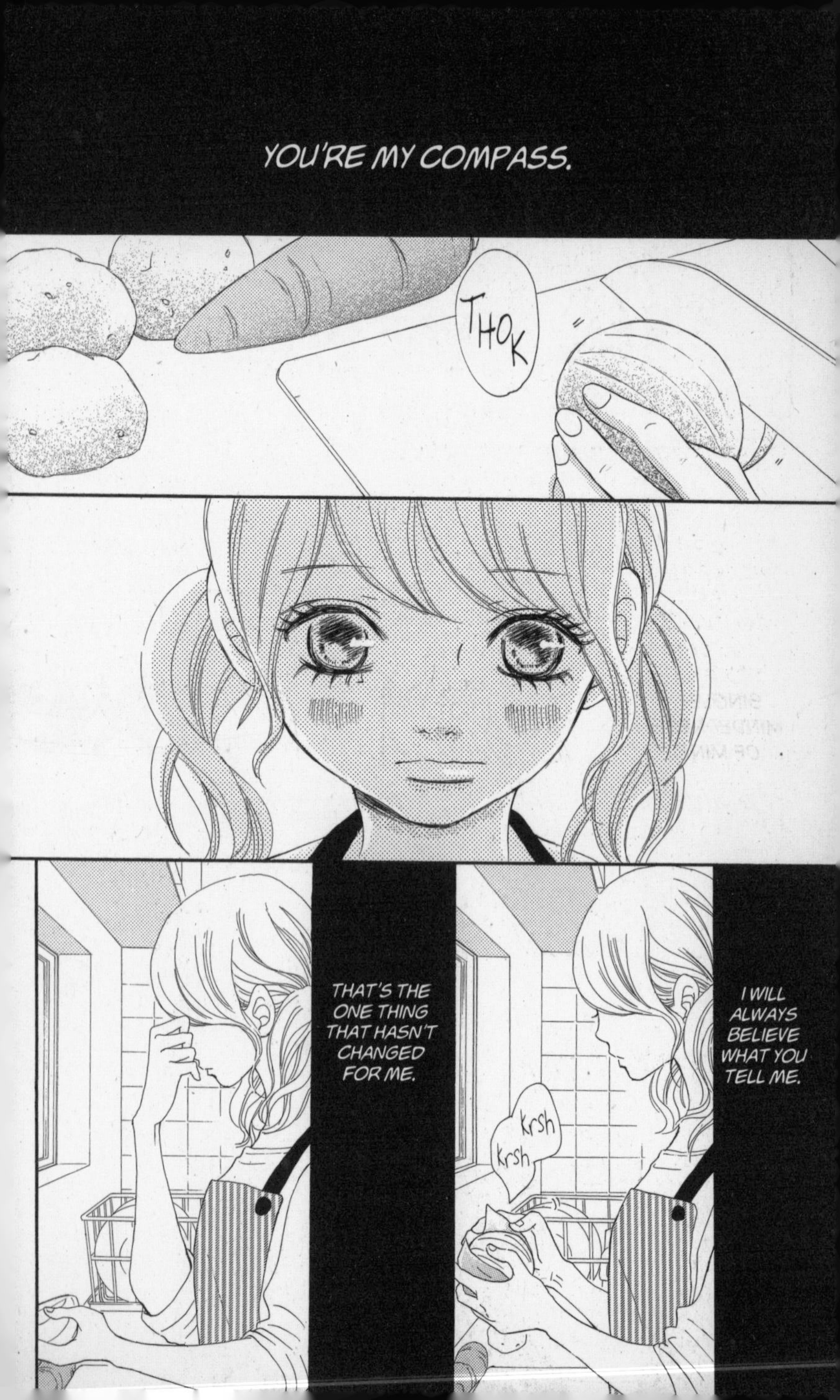
YOU'RE MY COMPASS.
THOK
I WILL ALWAYS BELIEVE WHAT YOU TELL ME.
krsh
krsh
THAT'S THE ONE THING THAT HASN'T CHANGED FOR ME.

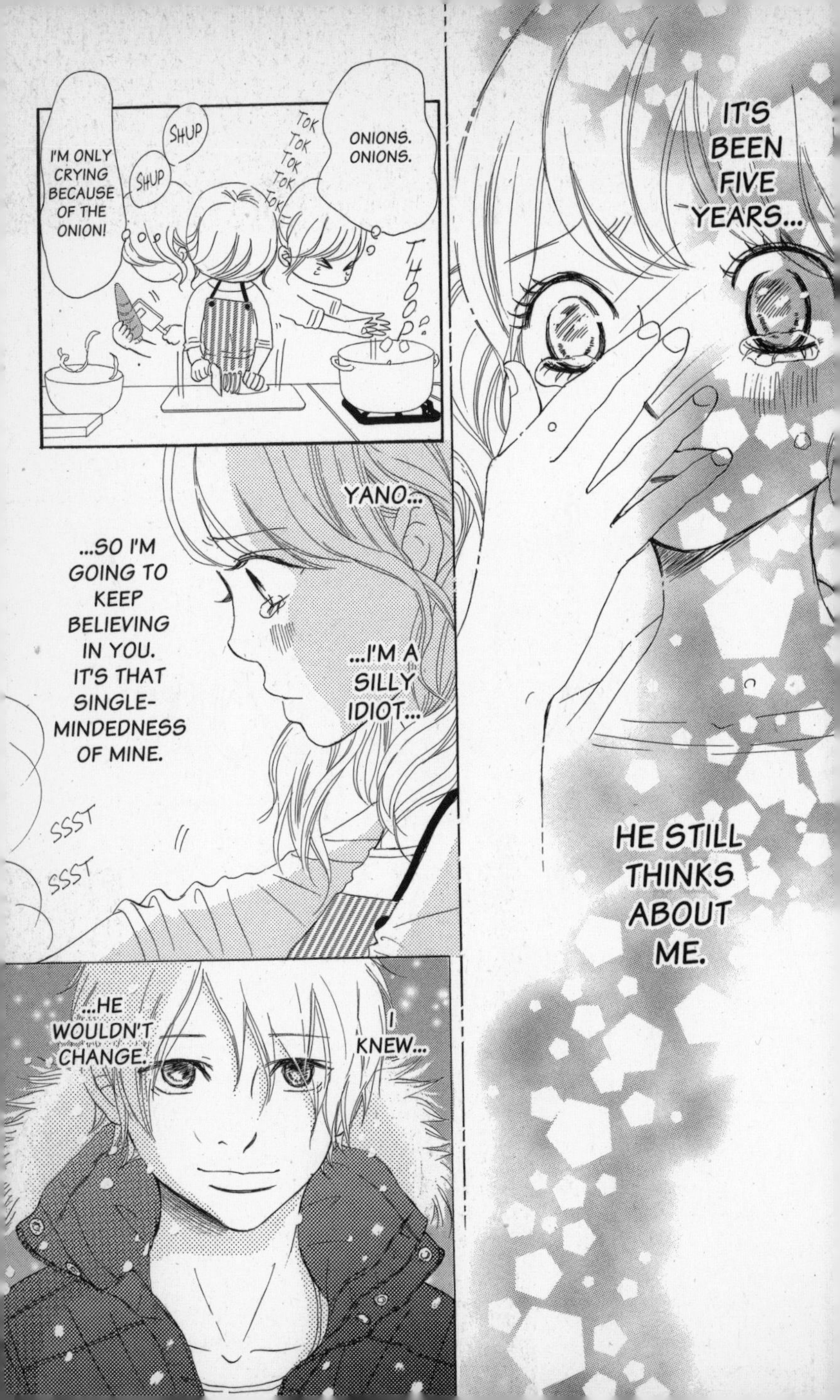
IT'S BEEN FIVE YEARS...
HE STILL THINKS ABOUT ME.
ONIONS. ONIONS.
TOK TOK TOK TOK TOK
THOOP
SHUP
SHUP
I'M ONLY CRYING BECAUSE OF THE ONION!
YANO...
...I'M A SILLY IDIOT...
...SO I'M GOING TO KEEP BELIEVING IN YOU. IT'S THAT SINGLE-MINDEDNESS OF MINE.
SSST
SSST
I KNEW...
...HE WOULDN'T CHANGE.

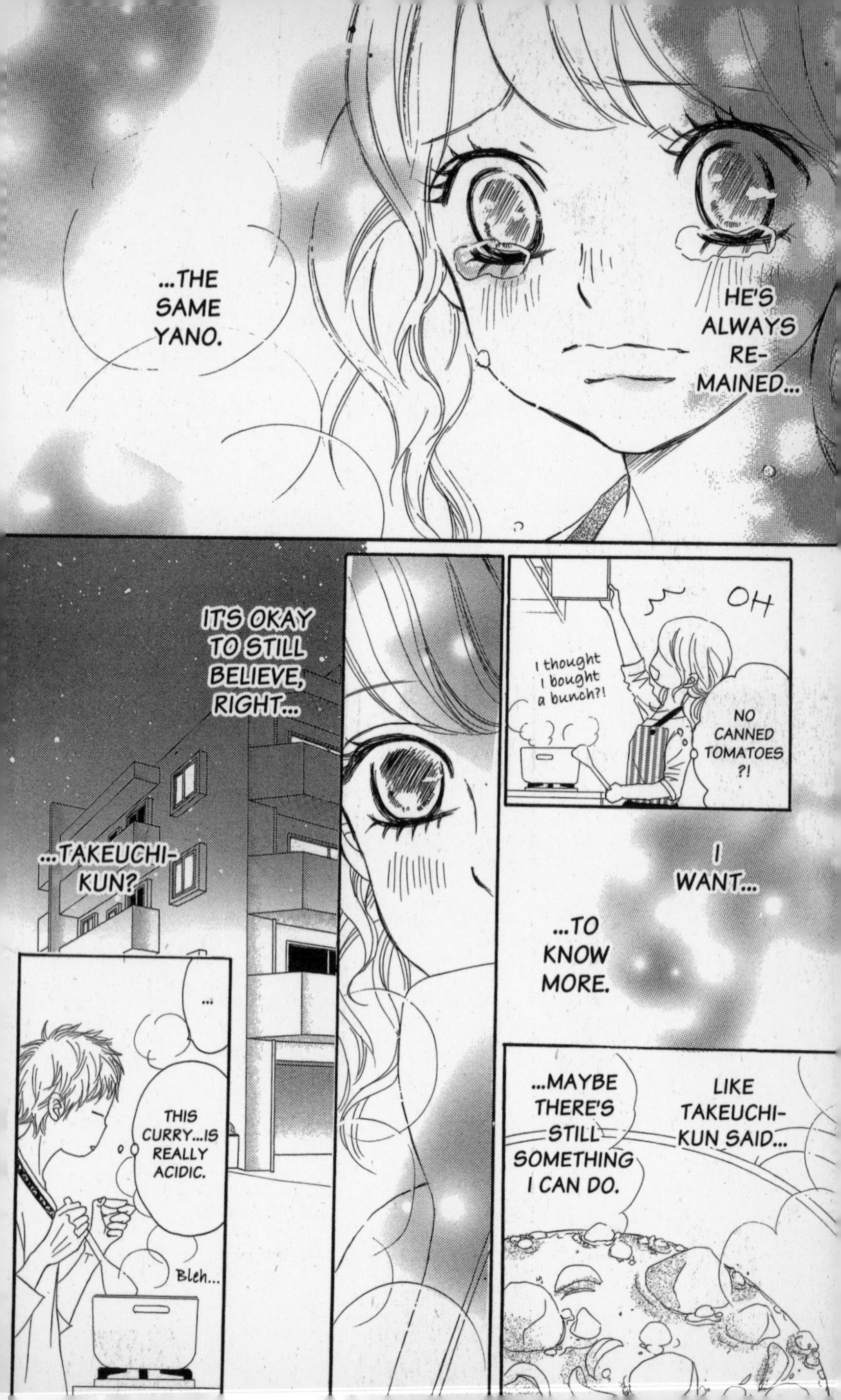
HE'S ALWAYS RE-MAINED...
...THE SAME YANO.
OH
NO CANNED TOMATOES?!
I thought I bought a bunch?!
I WANT...
...TO KNOW MORE.
LIKE TAKEUCHI-KUN SAID...
...MAYBE THERE'S STILL SOMETHING I CAN DO.
IT'S OKAY TO STILL BELIEVE, RIGHT...
...TAKEUCHI-KUN?
...
THIS CURRY...IS REALLY ACIDIC.
Bleh...

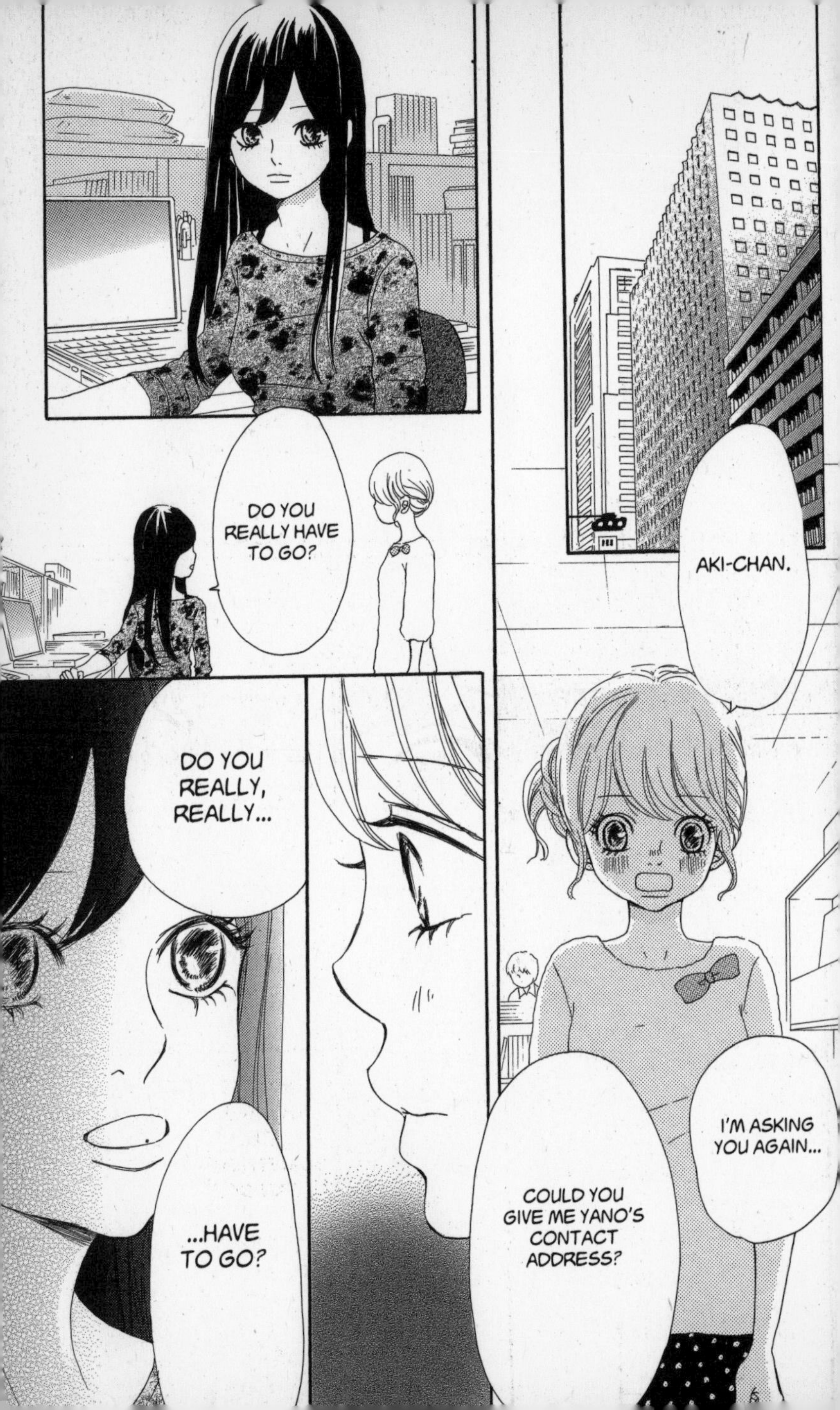
AKI-CHAN.
I'M ASKING YOU AGAIN...
COULD YOU GIVE ME YANO'S CONTACT ADDRESS?
DO YOU REALLY HAVE TO GO?
DO YOU REALLY, REALLY...
...HAVE TO GO?

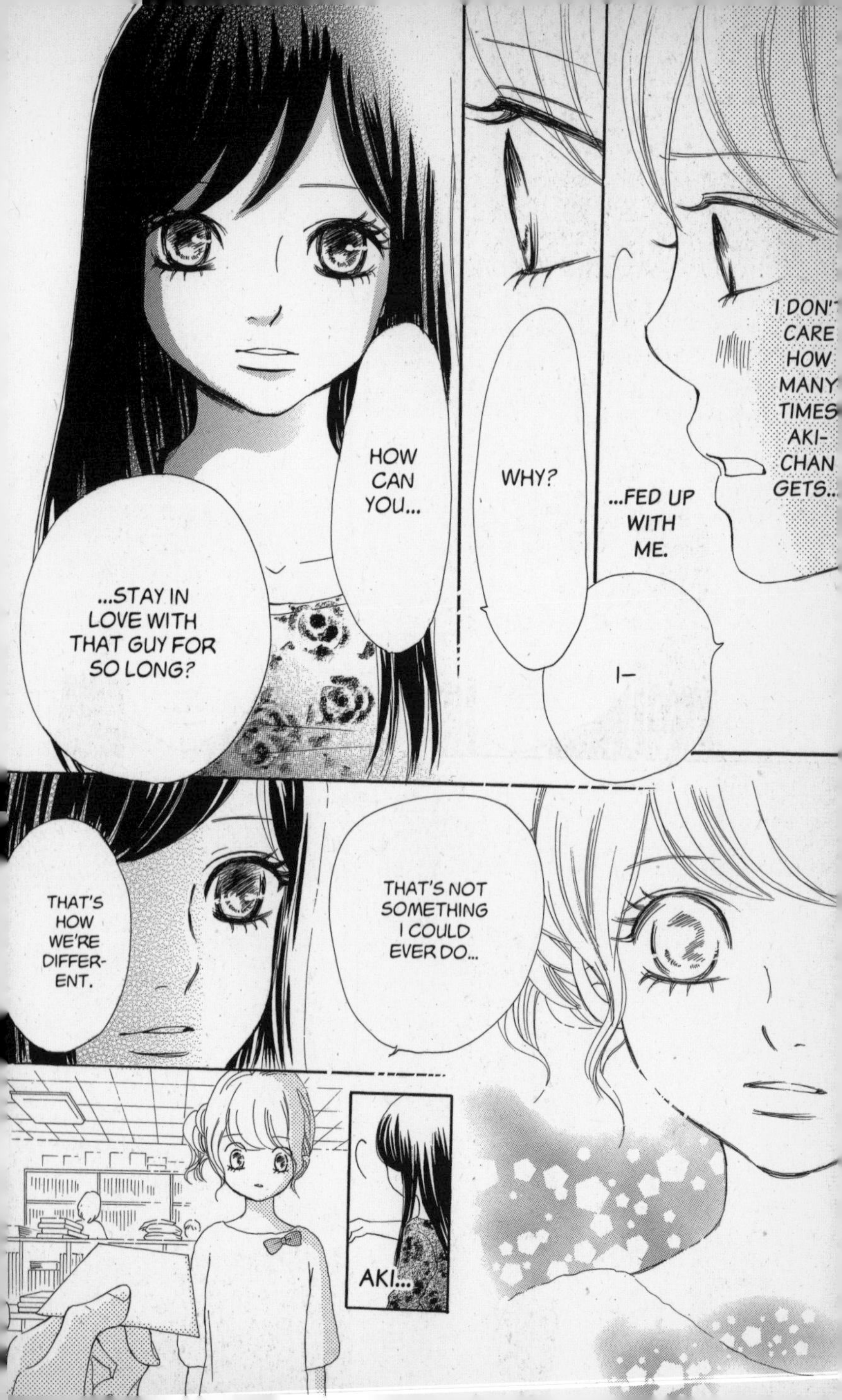
I DON'T CARE HOW MANY TIMES AKI-CHAN GETS...
...FED UP WITH ME.
I—
WHY?
HOW CAN YOU...
...STAY IN LOVE WITH THAT GUY FOR SO LONG?
THAT'S NOT SOMETHING I COULD EVER DO...
THAT'S HOW WE'RE DIFFER-ENT.
AKI...

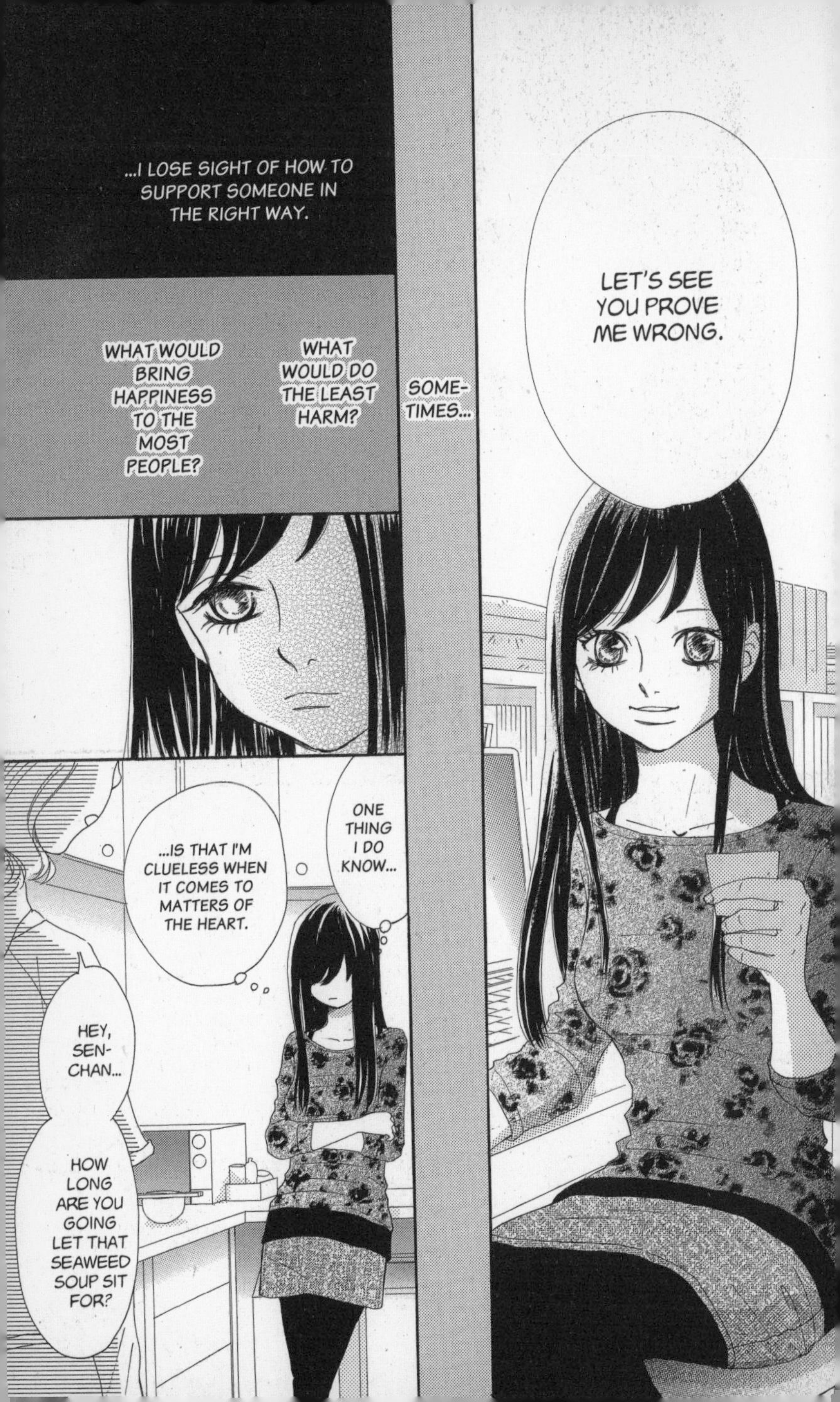
LET'S SEE YOU PROVE ME WRONG.
...I LOSE SIGHT OF HOW TO SUPPORT SOMEONE IN THE RIGHT WAY.
SOME-TIMES...
WHAT WOULD DO THE LEAST HARM?
WHAT WOULD BRING HAPPINESS TO THE MOST PEOPLE?
ONE THING I DO KNOW...
...IS THAT I'M CLUELESS WHEN IT COMES TO MATTERS OF THE HEART.
HEY, SEN-CHAN...
HOW LONG ARE YOU GOING LET THAT SEAWEED SOUP SIT FOR?

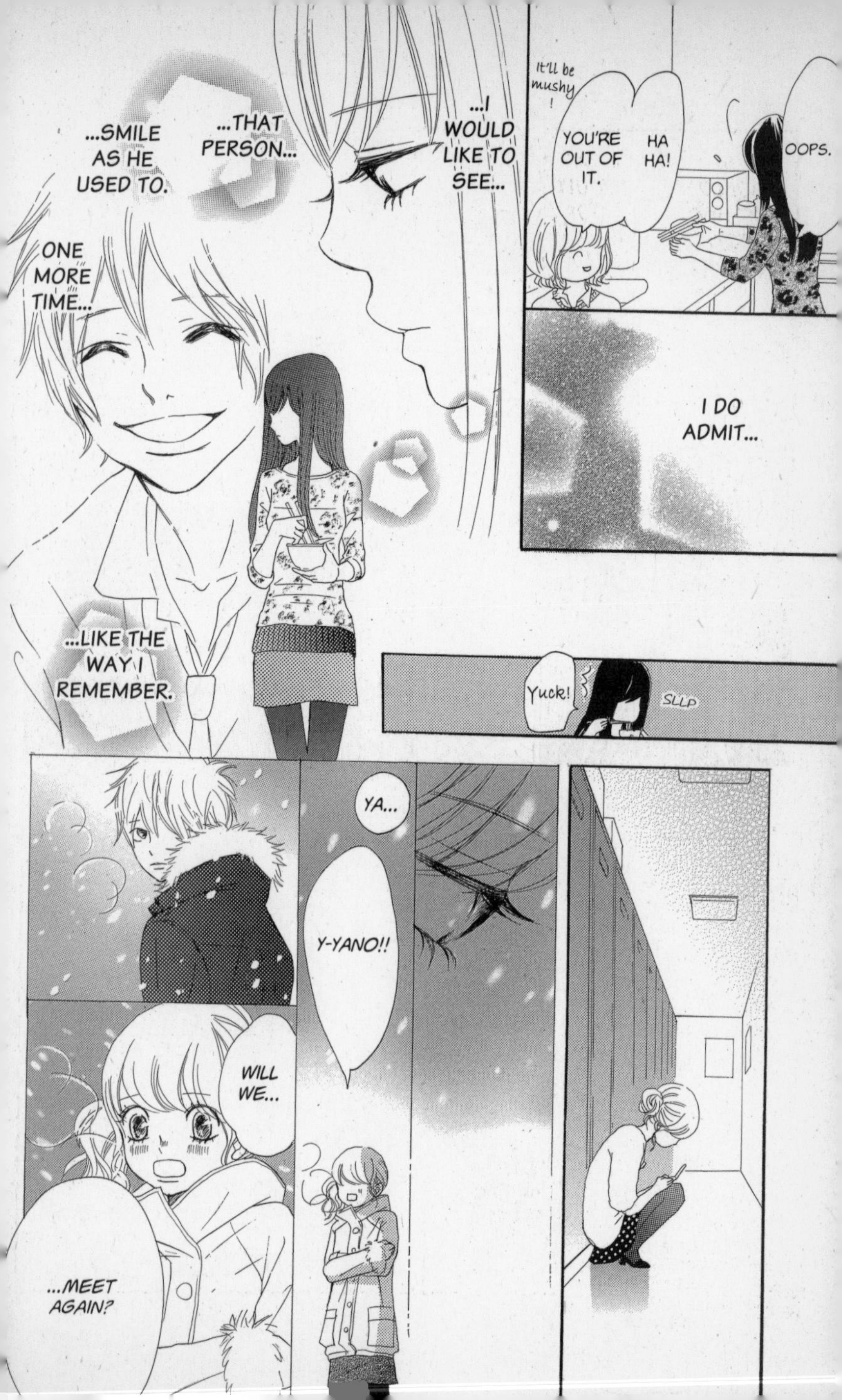
OOPS.
HA HA!
YOU'RE OUT OF IT.
It'll be mushy!
I DO ADMIT...
Yuck!
SLLP
...I WOULD LIKE TO SEE...
...THAT PERSON...
...SMILE AS HE USED TO.
ONE MORE TIME...
...LIKE THE WAY I REMEMBER.
YA...
Y-YANO!!
WILL WE...
...MEET AGAIN?

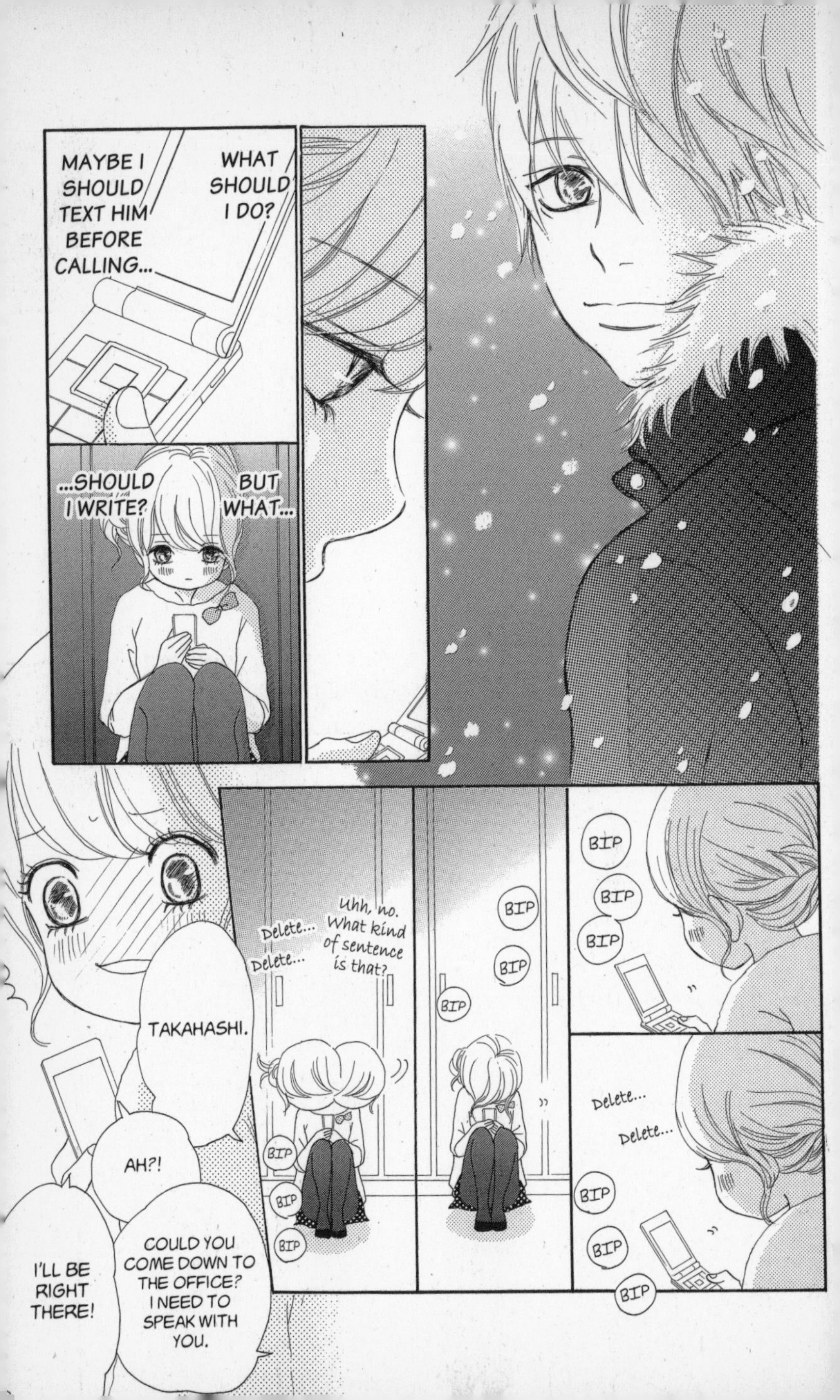
WHAT SHOULD I DO?
MAYBE I SHOULD TEXT HIM BEFORE CALLING...
BUT WHAT...
...SHOULD I WRITE?
BIP
BIP
BIP
Delete...
Delete...
BIP
BIP
BIP
BIP
BIP
BIP
Uhh, no. What kind of sentence is that?
Delete...
Delete...
BIP
BIP
BIP
TAKAHASHI.
AH?!
COULD YOU COME DOWN TO THE OFFICE? I NEED TO SPEAK WITH YOU.
I'LL BE RIGHT THERE!

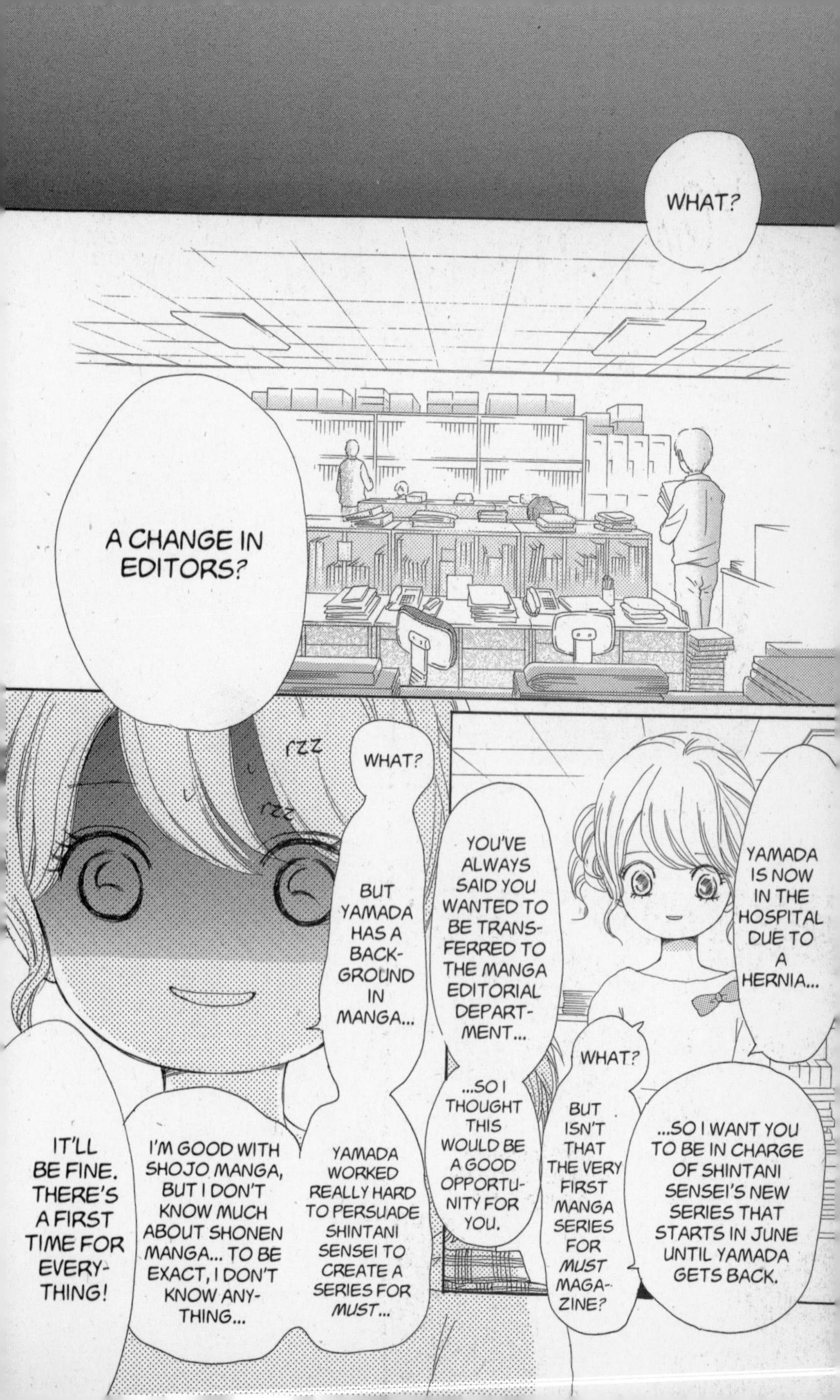
WHAT?
A CHANGE IN EDITORS?
YAMADA IS NOW IN THE HOSPITAL DUE TO A HERNIA...
...SO I WANT YOU TO BE IN CHARGE OF SHINTANI SENSEI'S NEW SERIES THAT STARTS IN JUNE UNTIL YAMADA GETS BACK.
WHAT?
BUT ISN'T THAT THE VERY FIRST MANGA SERIES FOR *MUST* MAGAZINE?
YOU'VE ALWAYS SAID YOU WANTED TO BE TRANSFERRED TO THE MANGA EDITORIAL DEPARTMENT...
...SO I THOUGHT THIS WOULD BE A GOOD OPPORTUNITY FOR YOU.
WHAT?
BUT YAMADA HAS A BACKGROUND IN MANGA...
YAMADA WORKED REALLY HARD TO PERSUADE SHINTANI SENSEI TO CREATE A SERIES FOR *MUST*...
I'M GOOD WITH SHOJO MANGA, BUT I DON'T KNOW MUCH ABOUT SHONEN MANGA... TO BE EXACT, I DON'T KNOW ANYTHING...
IT'LL BE FINE. THERE'S A FIRST TIME FOR EVERYTHING!

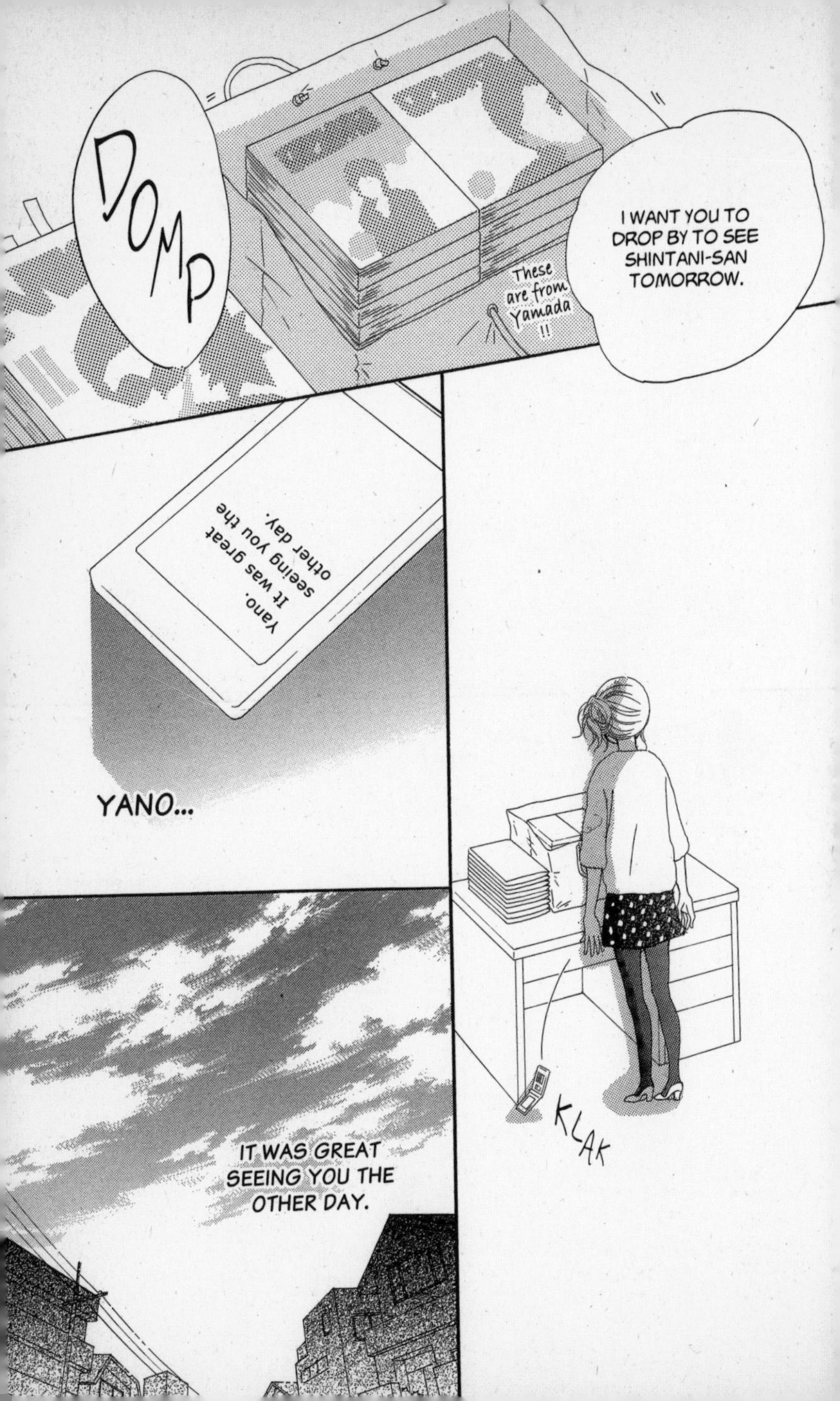
I WANT YOU TO DROP BY TO SEE SHINTANI-SAN TOMORROW.
These are from Yamada !!
DOMP
KLAK
Yano, It was great seeing you the other day.
YANO...
IT WAS GREAT SEEING YOU THE OTHER DAY.

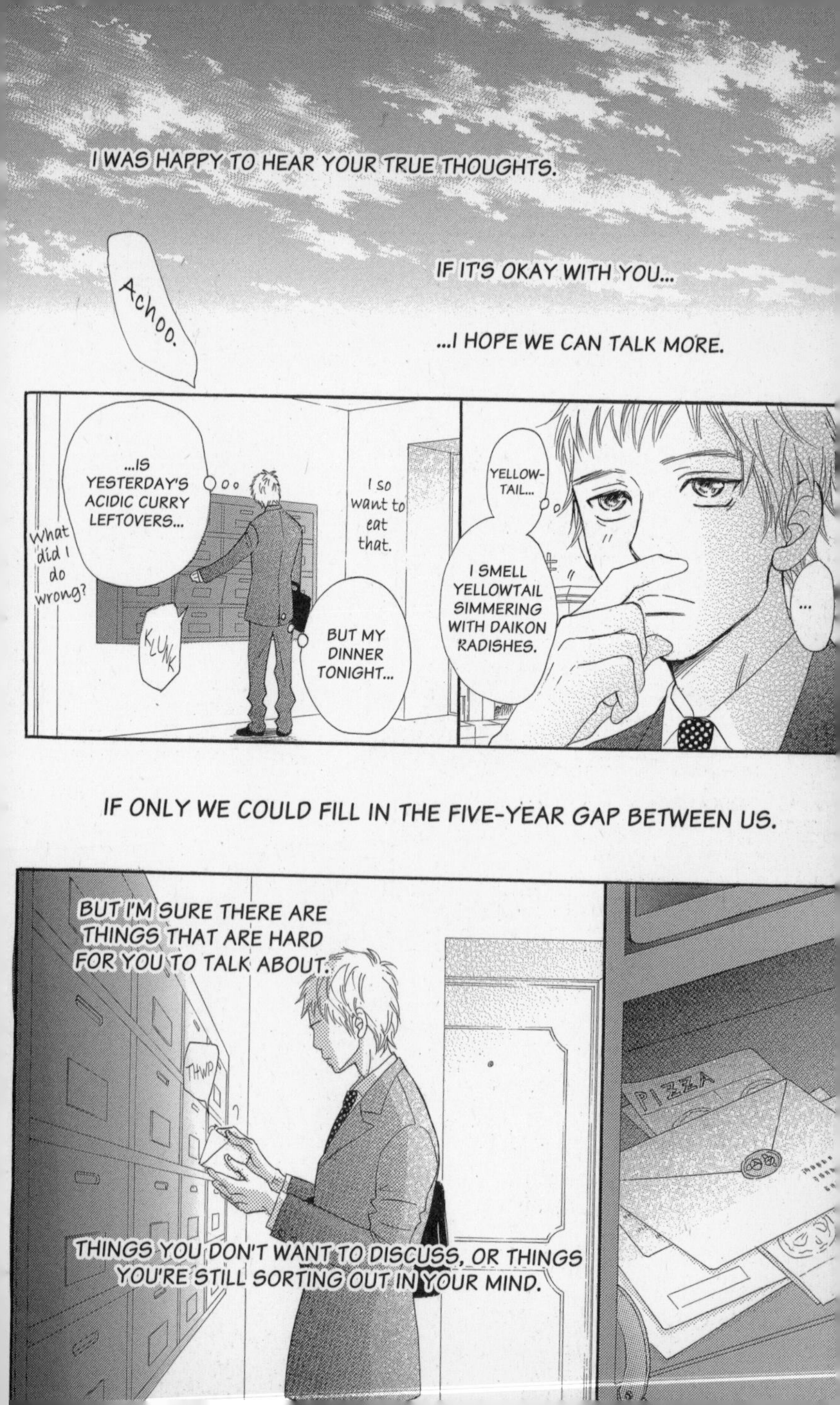

I WAS HAPPY TO HEAR YOUR TRUE THOUGHTS.
IF IT'S OKAY WITH YOU...
Achoo.
...I HOPE WE CAN TALK MORE.
YELLOW-TAIL...
I SMELL YELLOWTAIL SIMMERING WITH DAIKON RADISHES.
...
I so want to eat that.
BUT MY DINNER TONIGHT...
...IS YESTERDAY'S ACIDIC CURRY LEFTOVERS...
What did I do wrong?
KLUNK
IF ONLY WE COULD FILL IN THE FIVE-YEAR GAP BETWEEN US.
PIZZA
BUT I'M SURE THERE ARE THINGS THAT ARE HARD FOR YOU TO TALK ABOUT.
THWP
THINGS YOU DON'T WANT TO DISCUSS, OR THINGS YOU'RE STILL SORTING OUT IN YOUR MIND.

I WON'T FORCE YOU TO TELL ME.

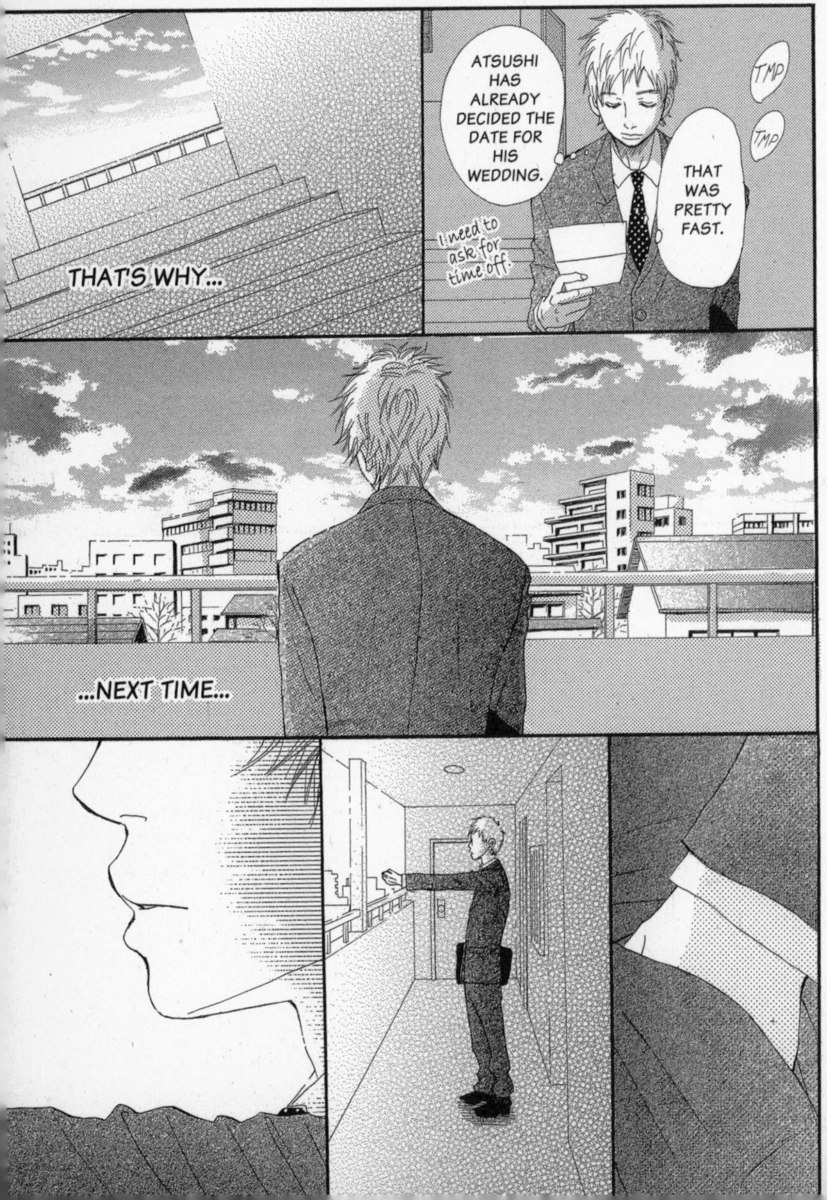

ATSUSHI HAS ALREADY DECIDED THE DATE FOR HIS WEDDING.
TMP
TMP
THAT WAS PRETTY FAST.
I need to ask for time off.
THAT'S WHY...
...NEXT TIME...

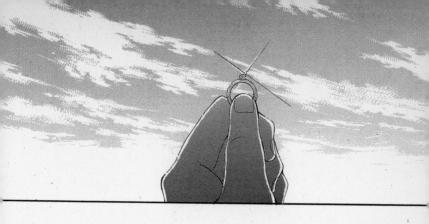

...WOULD YOU LISTEN...

...TO WHAT I WANT TO
SAY TO YOU?

Chapter 66

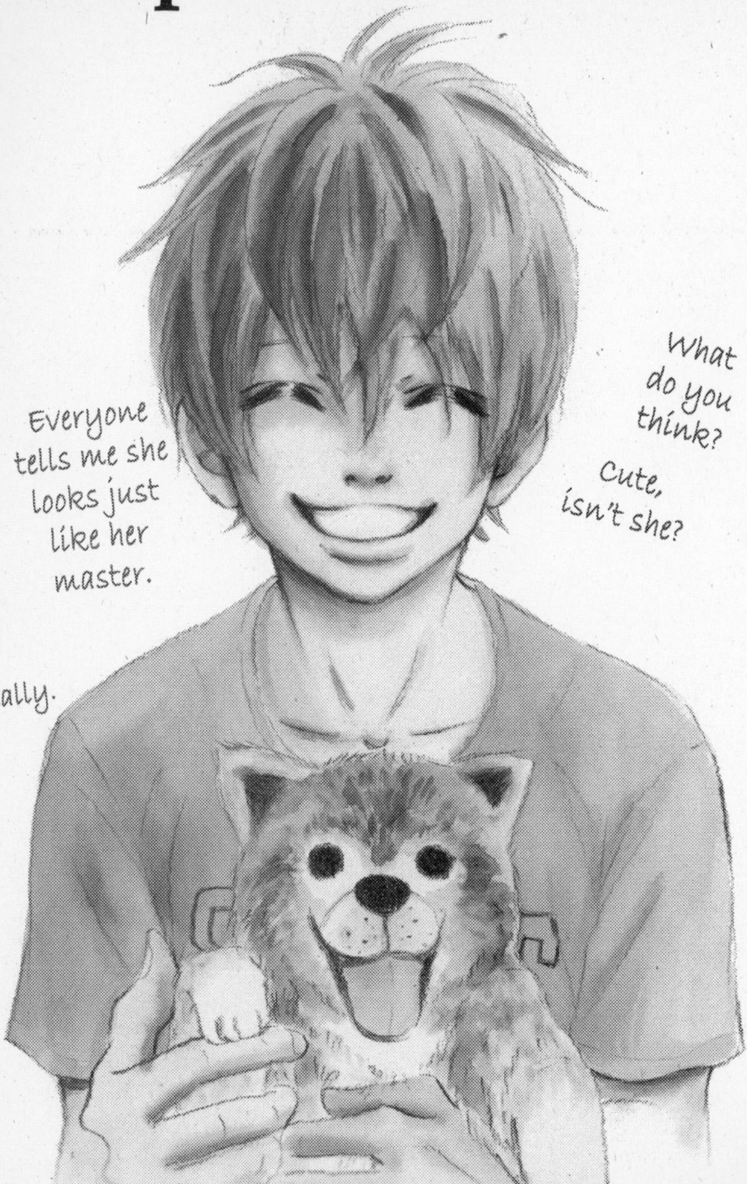
What do you think?
Cute, isn't she?
Everyone tells me she looks just like her master.
Really.

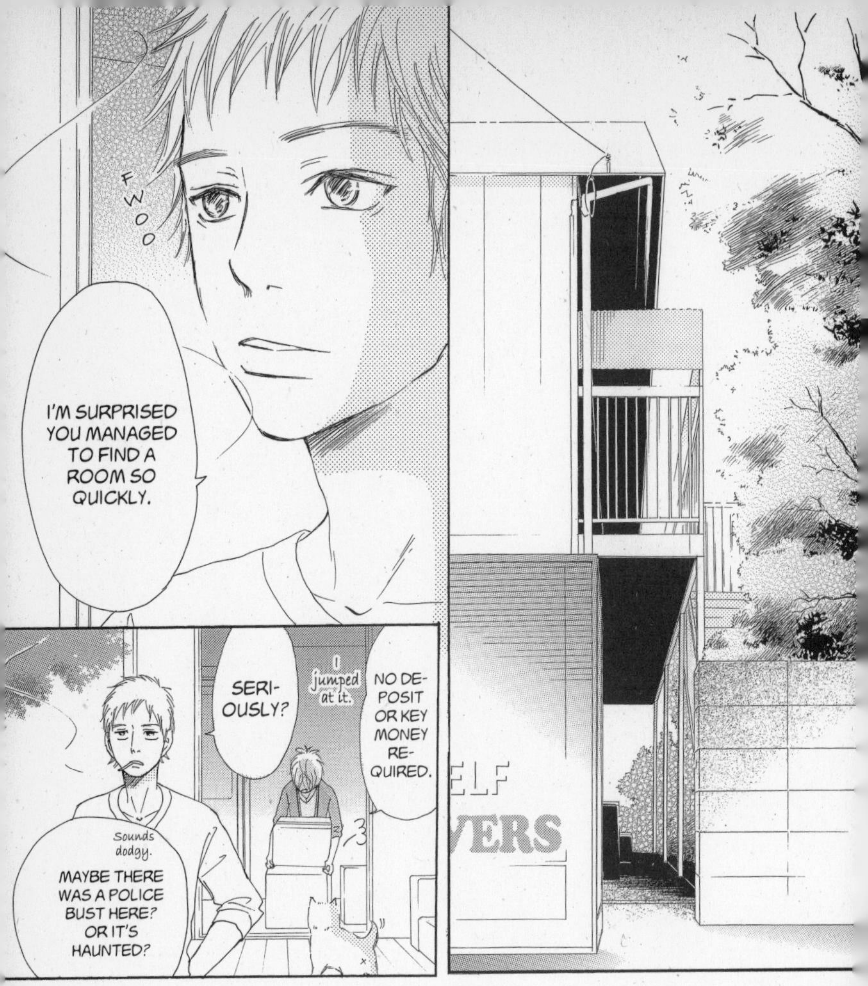

ELF
VERS
FWOO
I'M SURPRISED YOU MANAGED TO FIND A ROOM SO QUICKLY.
NO DEPOSIT OR KEY MONEY REQUIRED.
I jumped at it.
SERIOUSLY?
Sounds dodgy.
MAYBE THERE WAS A POLICE BUST HERE? OR IT'S HAUNTED?

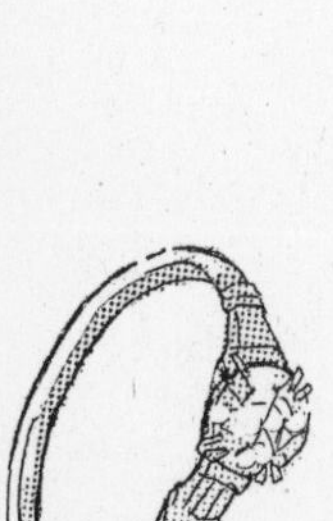

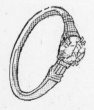

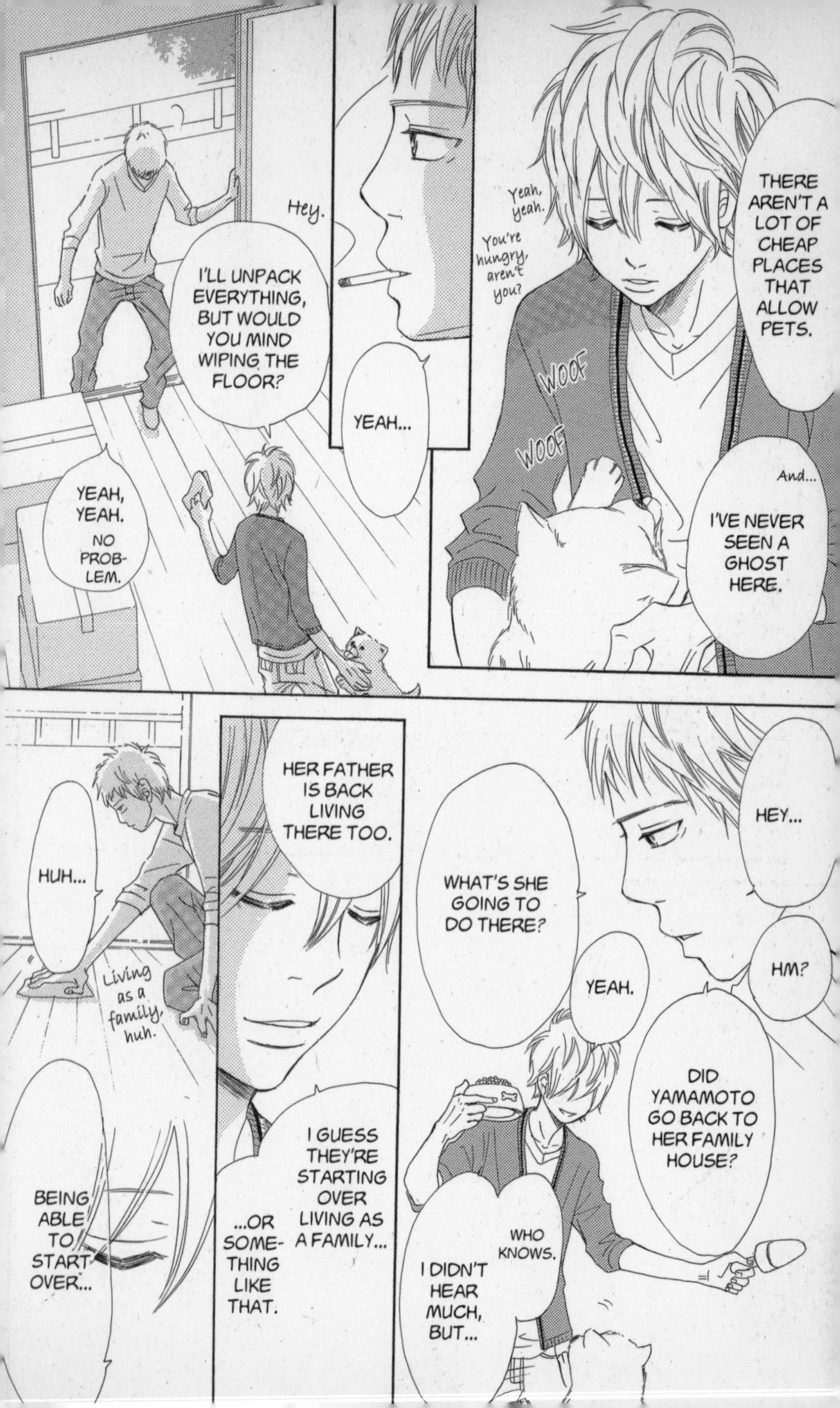
THERE AREN'T A LOT OF CHEAP PLACES THAT ALLOW PETS.
Yeah, yeah.
You're hungry, aren't you?
WOOF
WOOF
And...
I'VE NEVER SEEN A GHOST HERE.
Hey.
YEAH...
I'LL UNPACK EVERYTHING, BUT WOULD YOU MIND WIPING THE FLOOR?
YEAH, YEAH.
NO PROBLEM.
HEY...
HM?
DID YAMAMOTO GO BACK TO HER FAMILY HOUSE?
YEAH.
WHAT'S SHE GOING TO DO THERE?
WHO KNOWS.
I DIDN'T HEAR MUCH, BUT...
HER FATHER IS BACK LIVING THERE TOO.
I GUESS THEY'RE STARTING OVER LIVING AS A FAMILY...
...OR SOMETHING LIKE THAT.
HUH...
Living as a family, huh.
BEING ABLE TO START OVER...

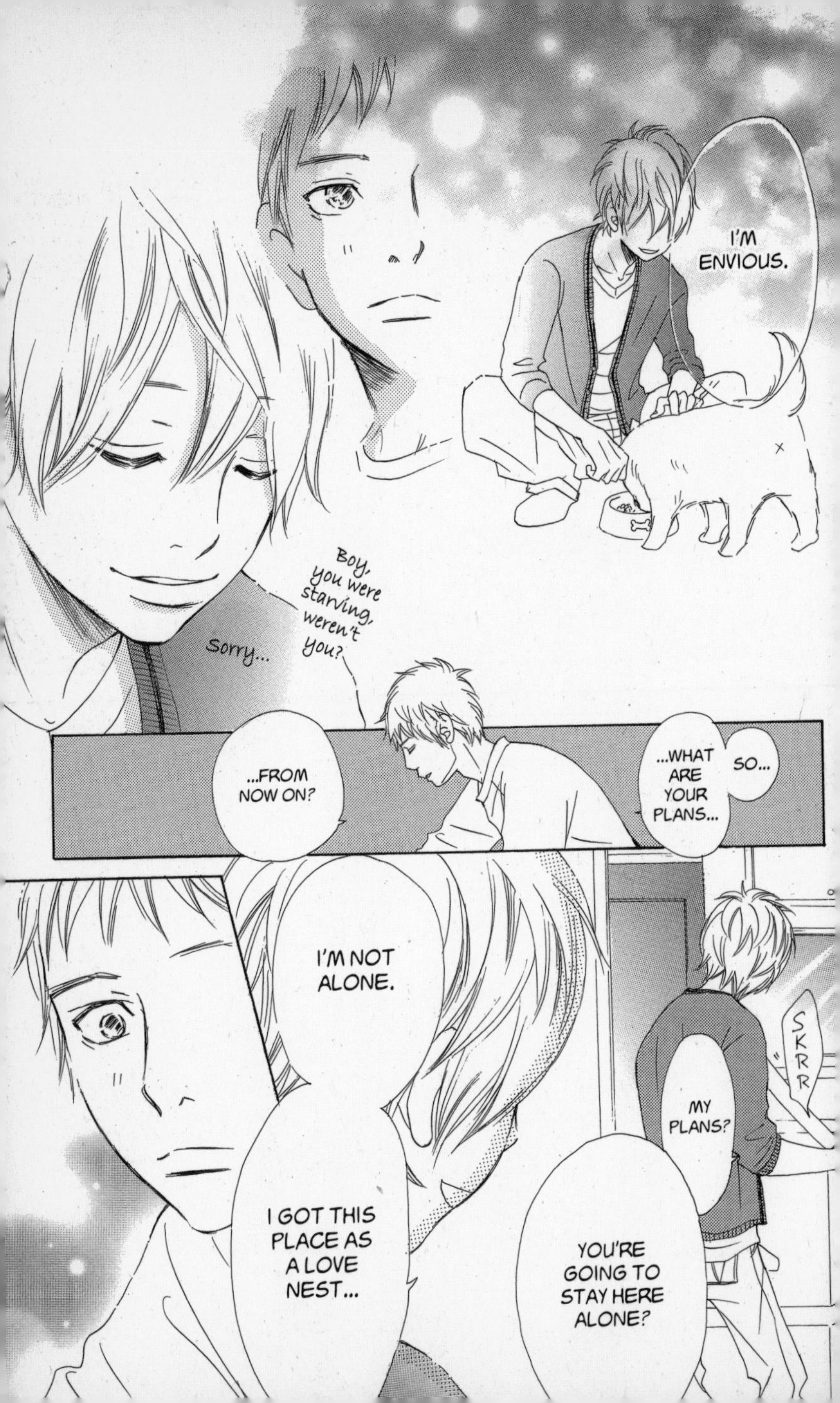
I'M ENVIOUS.
Boy, you were starving, weren't you?
Sorry...
SO...
...WHAT ARE YOUR PLANS...
...FROM NOW ON?
SKRR
MY PLANS?
YOU'RE GOING TO STAY HERE ALONE?
I'M NOT ALONE.
I GOT THIS PLACE AS A LOVE NEST...

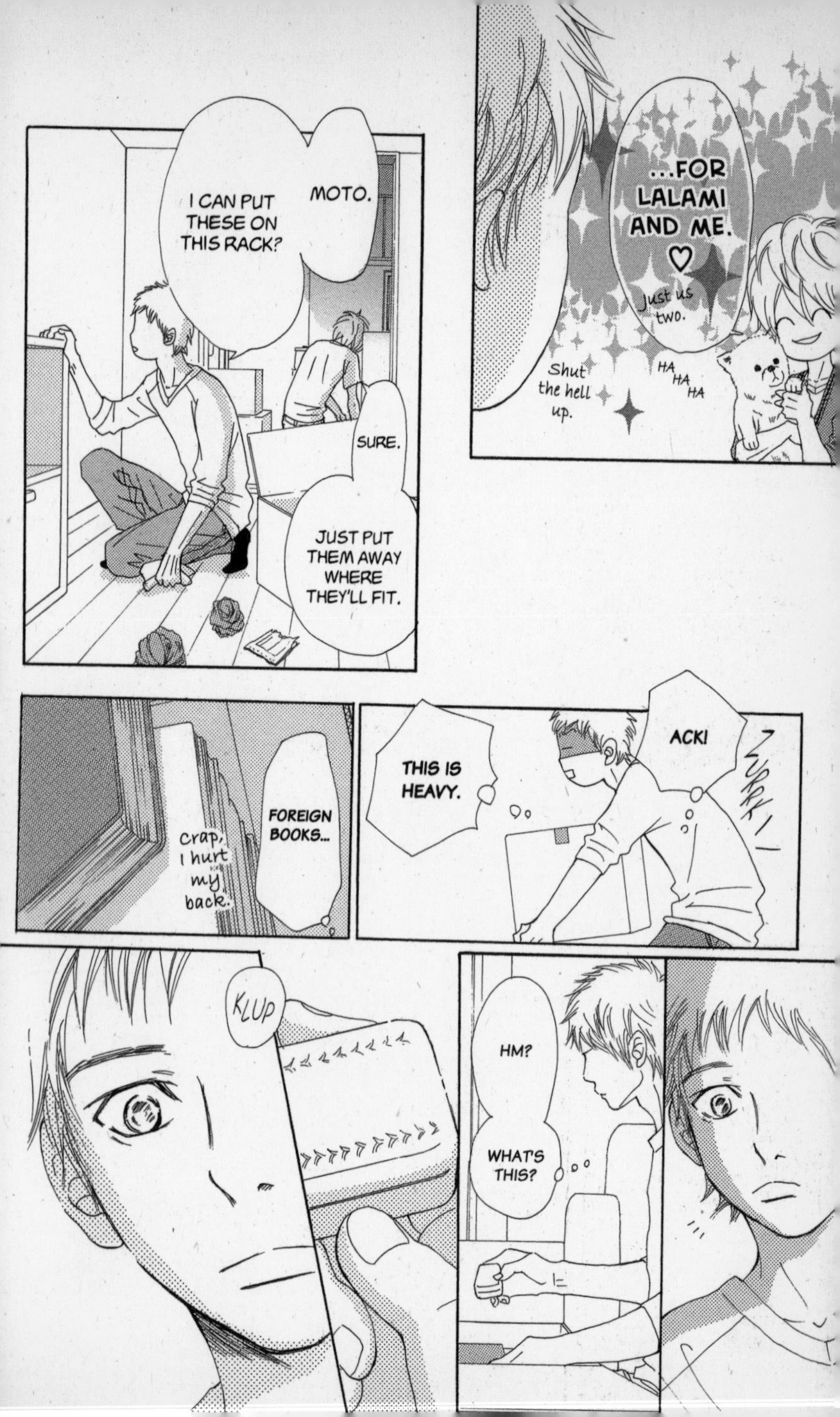
...FOR LALAMI AND ME. ♡
Just us two.
HA HA HA
Shut the hell up.
MOTO.
I CAN PUT THESE ON THIS RACK?
SURE.
JUST PUT THEM AWAY WHERE THEY'LL FIT.
ACK!
ZURRK!
THIS IS HEAVY.
FOREIGN BOOKS...
Crap, I hurt my back.
HM?
WHAT'S THIS?
KLUP

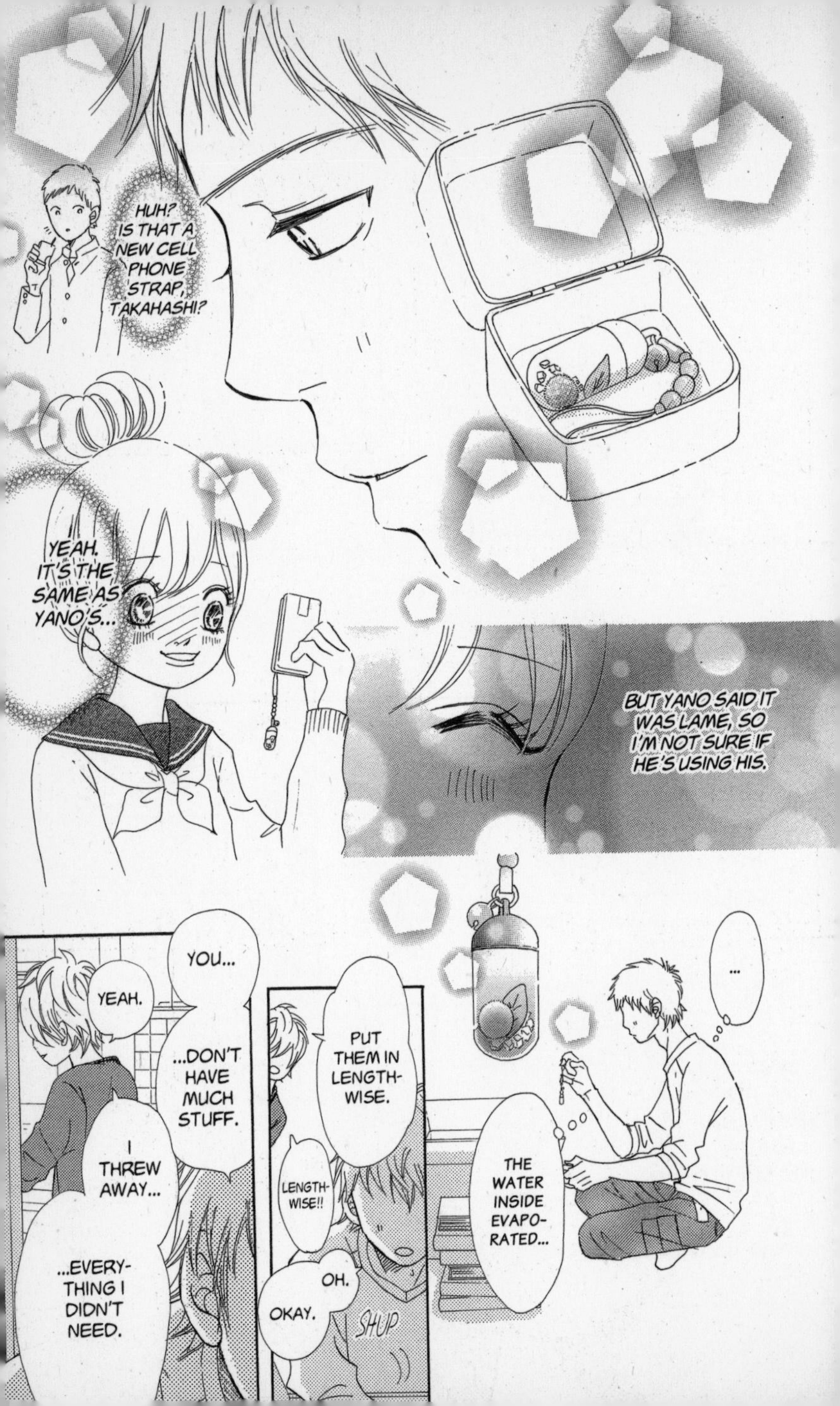
HUH? IS THAT A NEW CELL PHONE STRAP, TAKAHASHI?
YEAH. IT'S THE SAME AS YANO'S...
BUT YANO SAID IT WAS LAME, SO I'M NOT SURE IF HE'S USING HIS.
...
THE WATER INSIDE EVAPO-RATED...
PUT THEM IN LENGTH-WISE.
LENGTH-WISE!!
OH.
OKAY.
SHUP
YOU...
YEAH.
...DON'T HAVE MUCH STUFF.
I THREW AWAY...
...EVERY-THING I DIDN'T NEED.

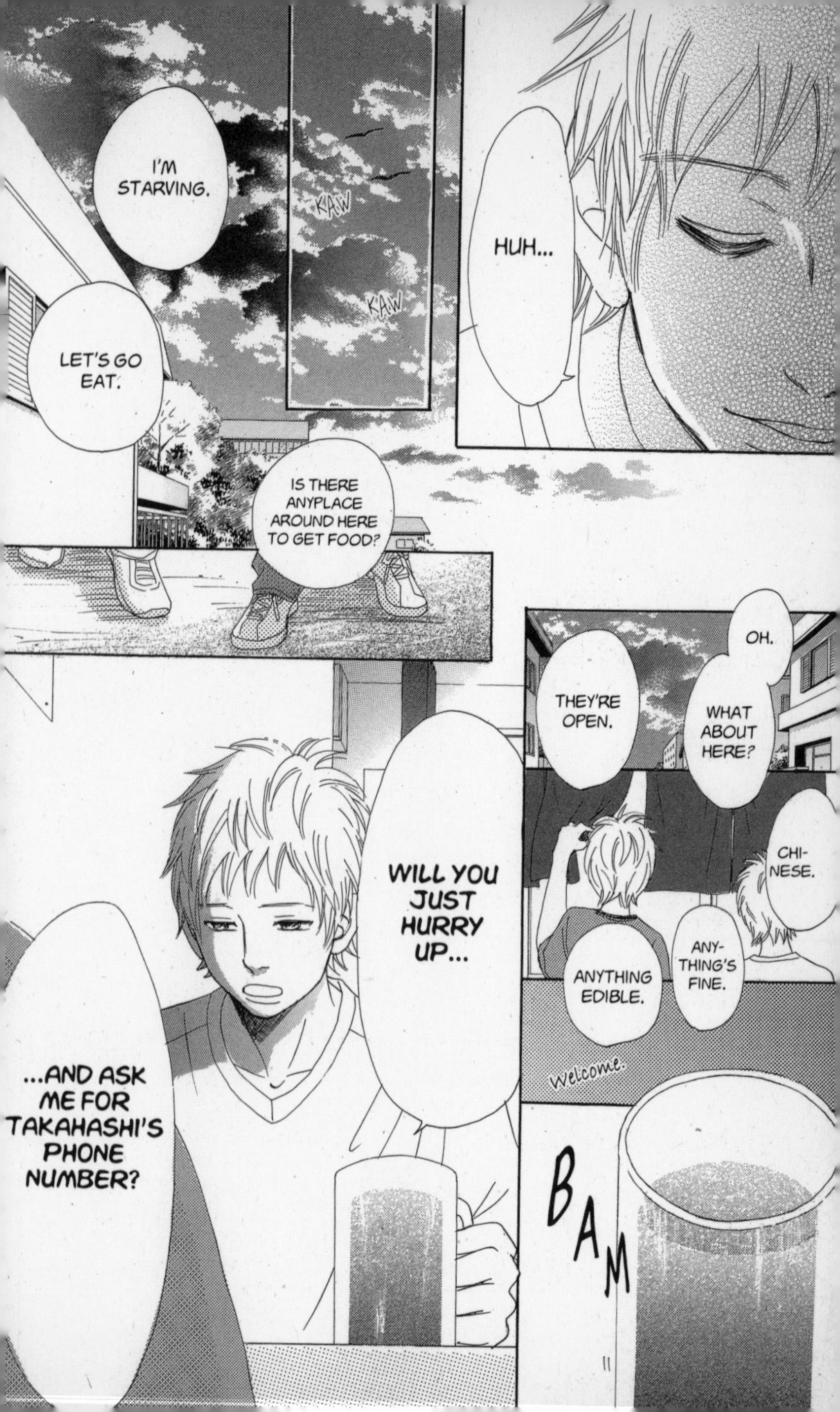
HUH...
I'M STARVING.
KAW
KAW
LET'S GO EAT.
IS THERE ANYPLACE AROUND HERE TO GET FOOD?
OH.
WHAT ABOUT HERE?
THEY'RE OPEN.
CHI-NESE.
ANY-THING'S FINE.
ANYTHING EDIBLE.
Welcome.
BAM
WILL YOU JUST HURRY UP...
...AND ASK ME FOR TAKAHASHI'S PHONE NUMBER?

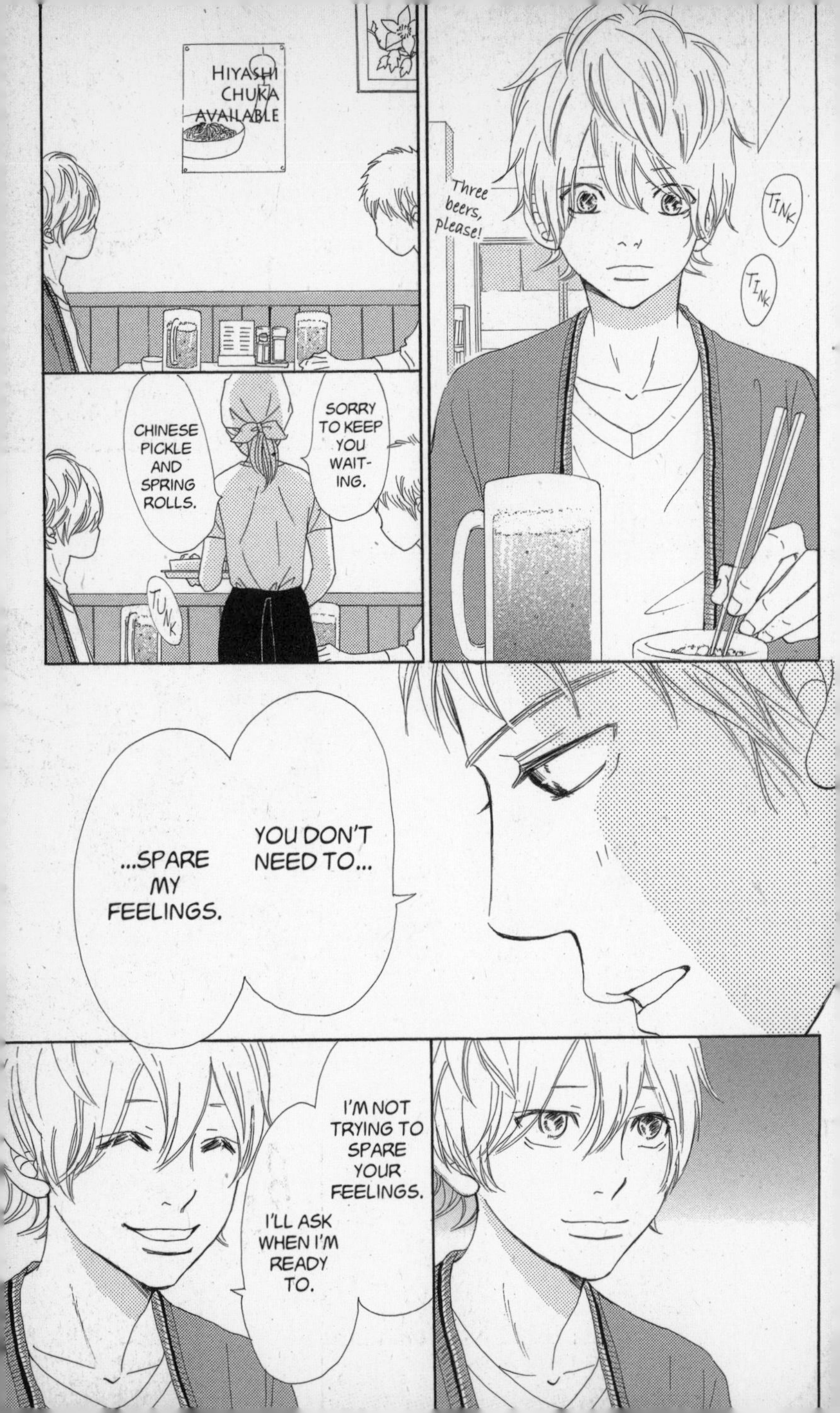
Three beers, please!
TINK
TINK
HIYASHI CHUKA AVAILABLE
SORRY TO KEEP YOU WAIT-ING.
CHINESE PICKLE AND SPRING ROLLS.
TUNK
YOU DON'T NEED TO...
...SPARE MY FEELINGS.
I'M NOT TRYING TO SPARE YOUR FEELINGS.
I'LL ASK WHEN I'M READY TO.

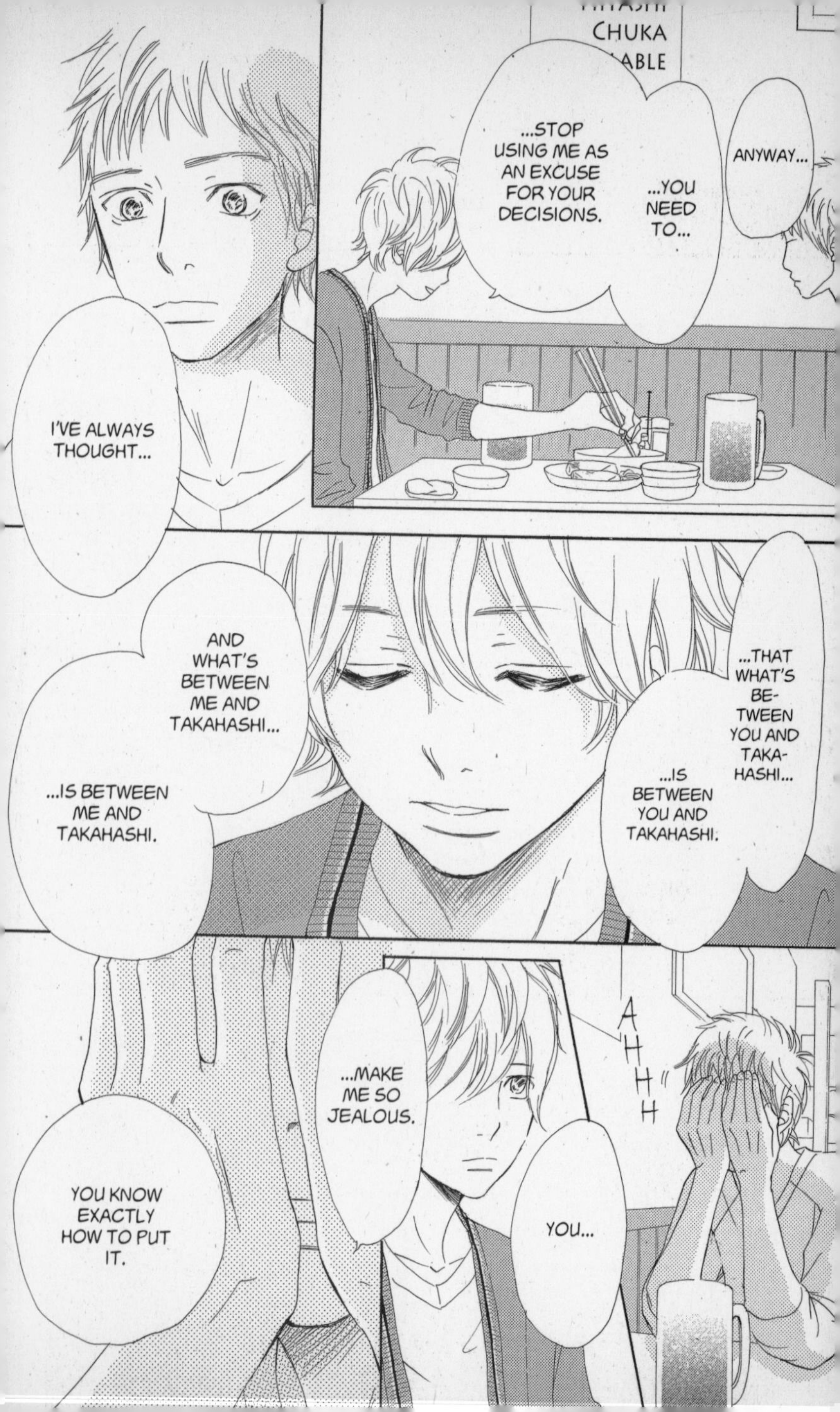
CHUKA
ANYWAY...
...YOU NEED TO...
...STOP USING ME AS AN EXCUSE FOR YOUR DECISIONS.
I'VE ALWAYS THOUGHT...
...THAT WHAT'S BE- TWEEN YOU AND TAKA- HASHI...
...IS BETWEEN YOU AND TAKAHASHI.
AND WHAT'S BETWEEN ME AND TAKAHASHI...
...IS BETWEEN ME AND TAKAHASHI.
AHHH
YOU...
...MAKE ME SO JEALOUS.
YOU KNOW EXACTLY HOW TO PUT IT.

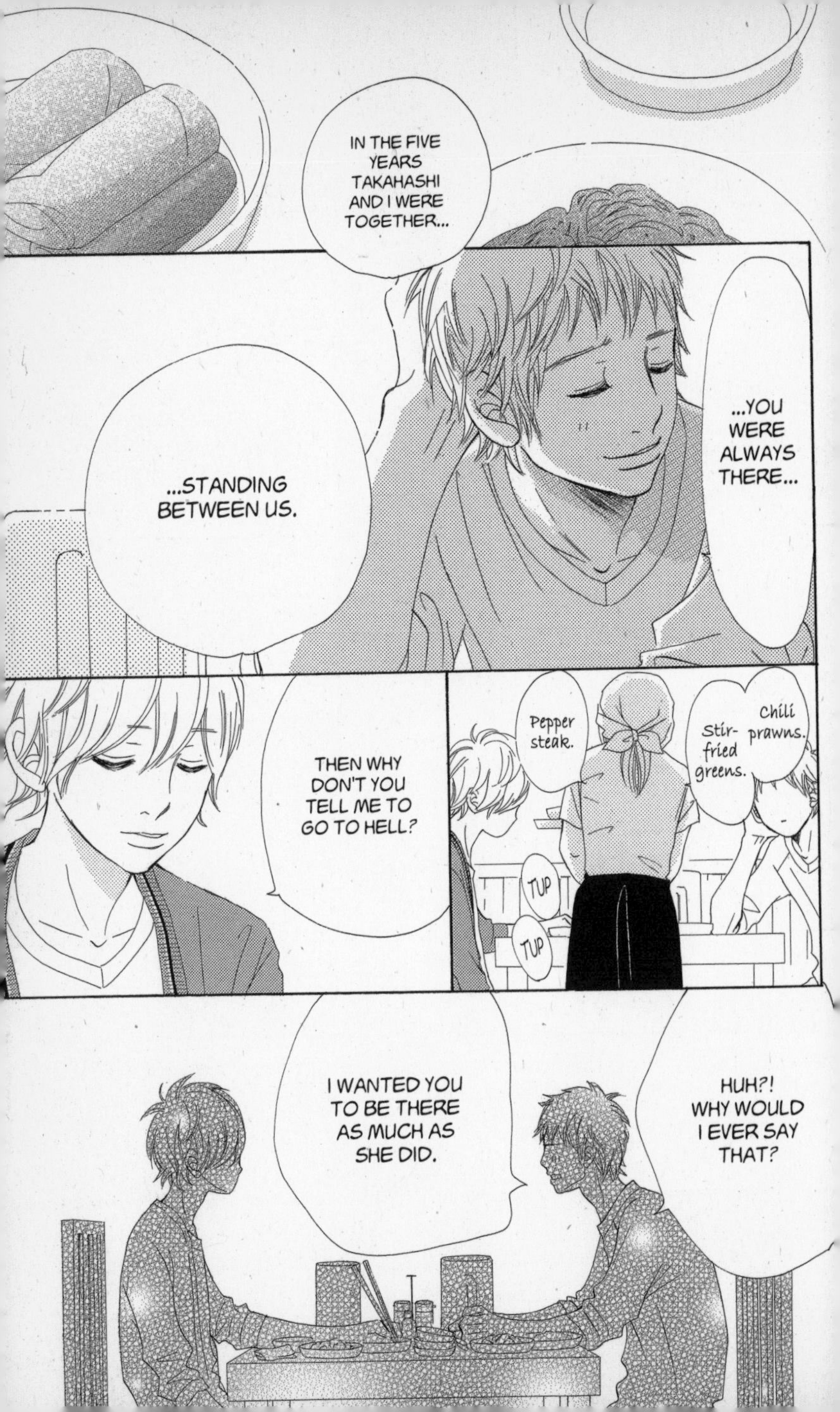
IN THE FIVE YEARS TAKAHASHI AND I WERE TOGETHER...
...YOU WERE ALWAYS THERE...
...STANDING BETWEEN US.
Chili prawns.
Stir-fried greens.
Pepper steak.
TUP
TUP
THEN WHY DON'T YOU TELL ME TO GO TO HELL?
HUH?! WHY WOULD I EVER SAY THAT?
I WANTED YOU TO BE THERE AS MUCH AS SHE DID.

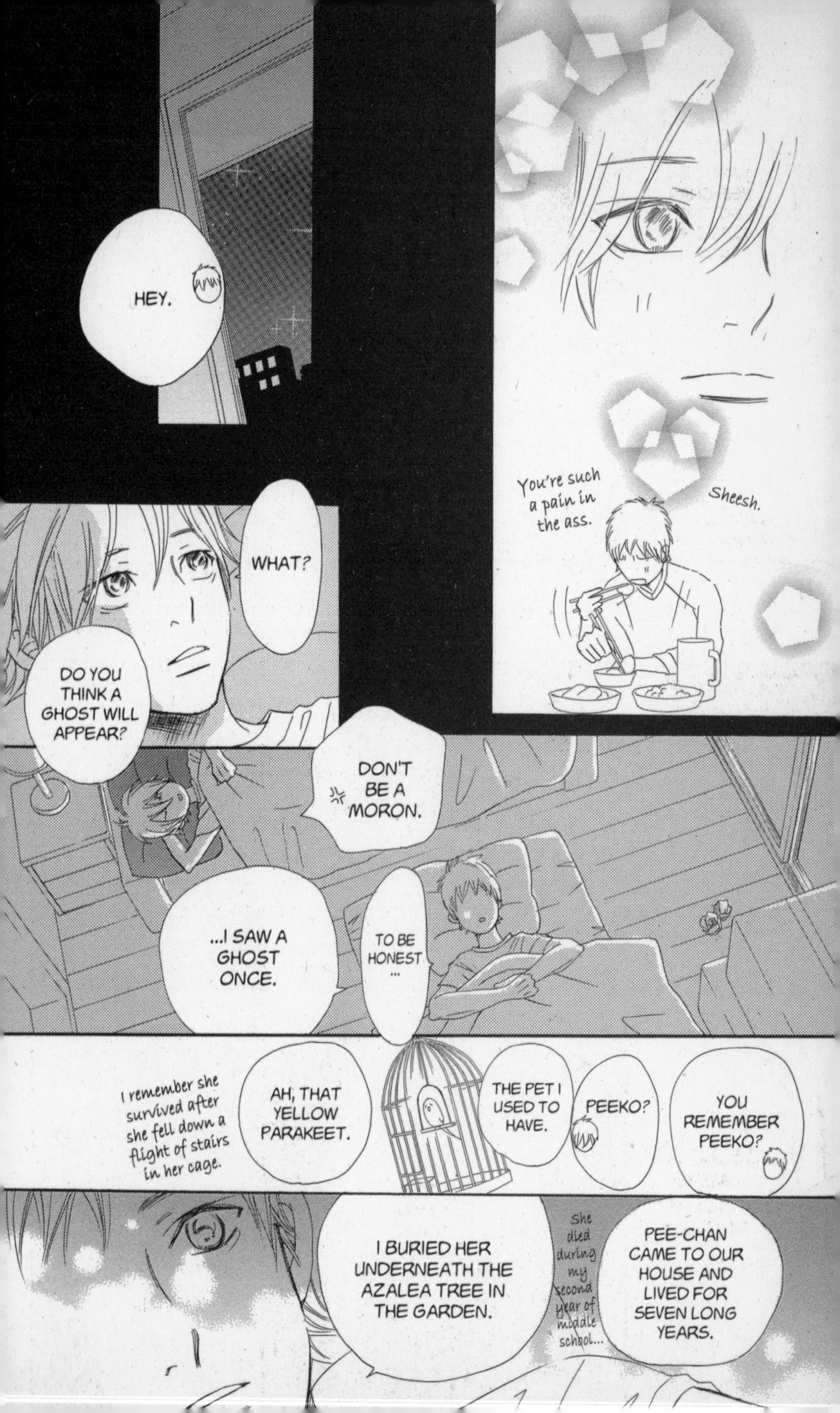
Sheesh.
You're such a pain in the ass.
HEY.
WHAT?
DO YOU THINK A GHOST WILL APPEAR?
DON'T BE A MORON.
TO BE HONEST...
...I SAW A GHOST ONCE.
YOU REMEMBER PEEKO?
PEEKO?
THE PET I USED TO HAVE.
AH, THAT YELLOW PARAKEET.
I remember she survived after she fell down a flight of stairs in her cage.
PEE-CHAN CAME TO OUR HOUSE AND LIVED FOR SEVEN LONG YEARS.
She died during my second year of middle school...
I BURIED HER UNDERNEATH THE AZALEA TREE IN THE GARDEN.

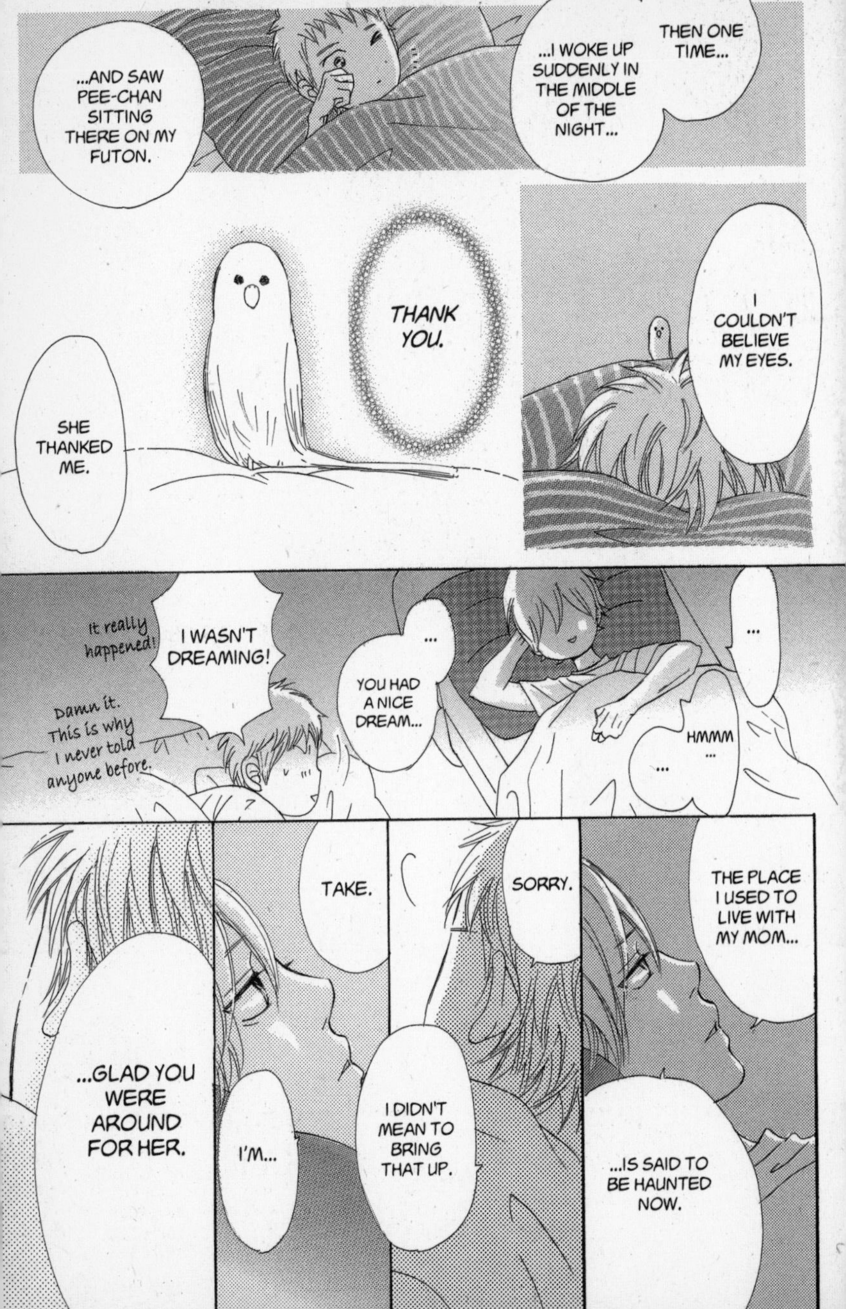
THEN ONE TIME...
...I WOKE UP SUDDENLY IN THE MIDDLE OF THE NIGHT...
...AND SAW PEE-CHAN SITTING THERE ON MY FUTON.
I COULDN'T BELIEVE MY EYES.
THANK YOU.
SHE THANKED ME.
...
HMMM ... ...
...
YOU HAD A NICE DREAM...
I WASN'T DREAMING!
It really happened!
Damn it. This is why I never told anyone before.
THE PLACE I USED TO LIVE WITH MY MOM...
...IS SAID TO BE HAUNTED NOW.
SORRY.
I DIDN'T MEAN TO BRING THAT UP.
TAKE.
I'M...
...GLAD YOU WERE AROUND FOR HER.

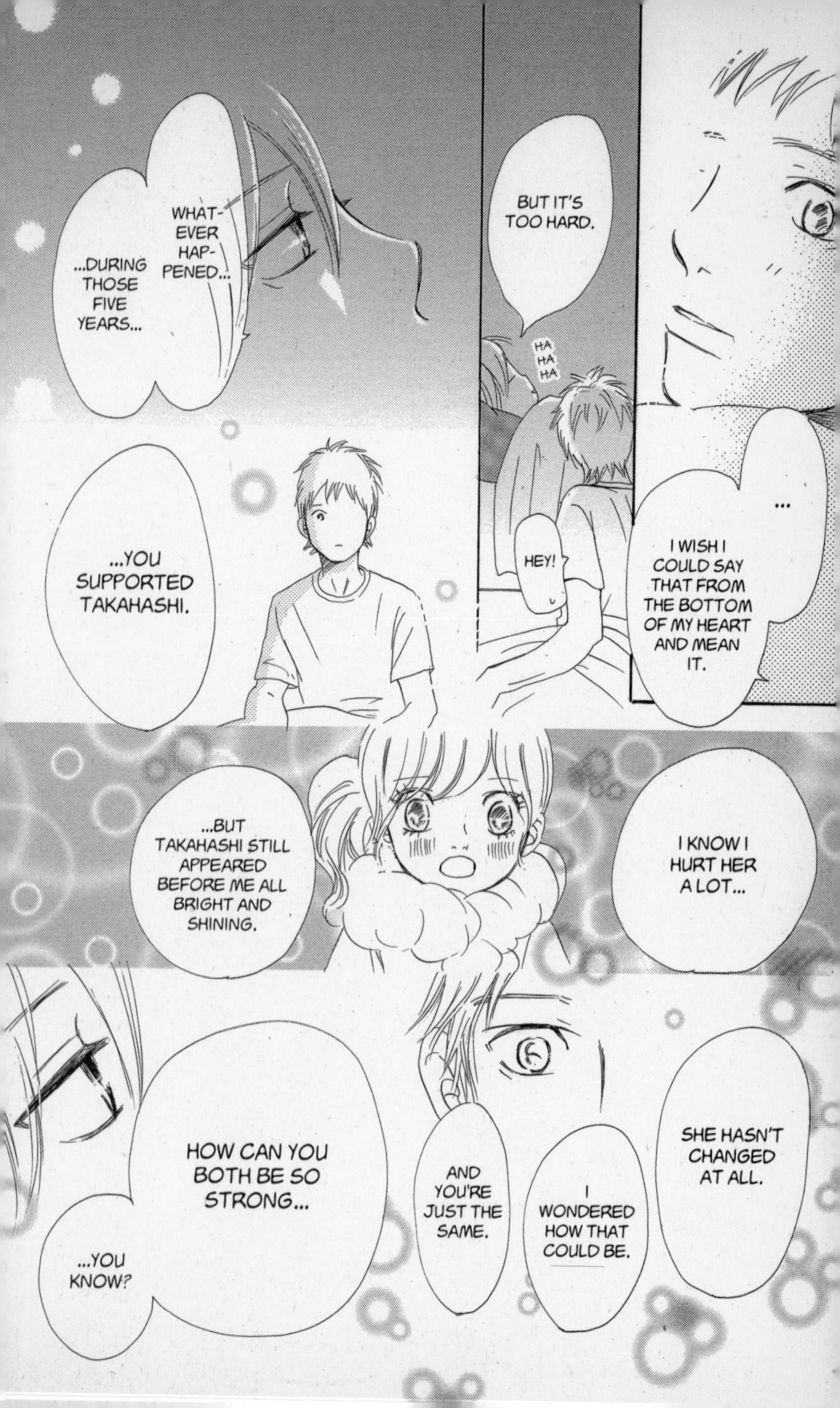
...
I WISH I COULD SAY THAT FROM THE BOTTOM OF MY HEART AND MEAN IT.
BUT IT'S TOO HARD.
HA HA HA
HEY!
WHAT-EVER HAP-PENED...
...DURING THOSE FIVE YEARS...
...YOU SUPPORTED TAKAHASHI.
I KNOW I HURT HER A LOT...
...BUT TAKAHASHI STILL APPEARED BEFORE ME ALL BRIGHT AND SHINING.
SHE HASN'T CHANGED AT ALL.
I WONDERED HOW THAT COULD BE.
AND YOU'RE JUST THE SAME.
HOW CAN YOU BOTH BE SO STRONG...
...YOU KNOW?

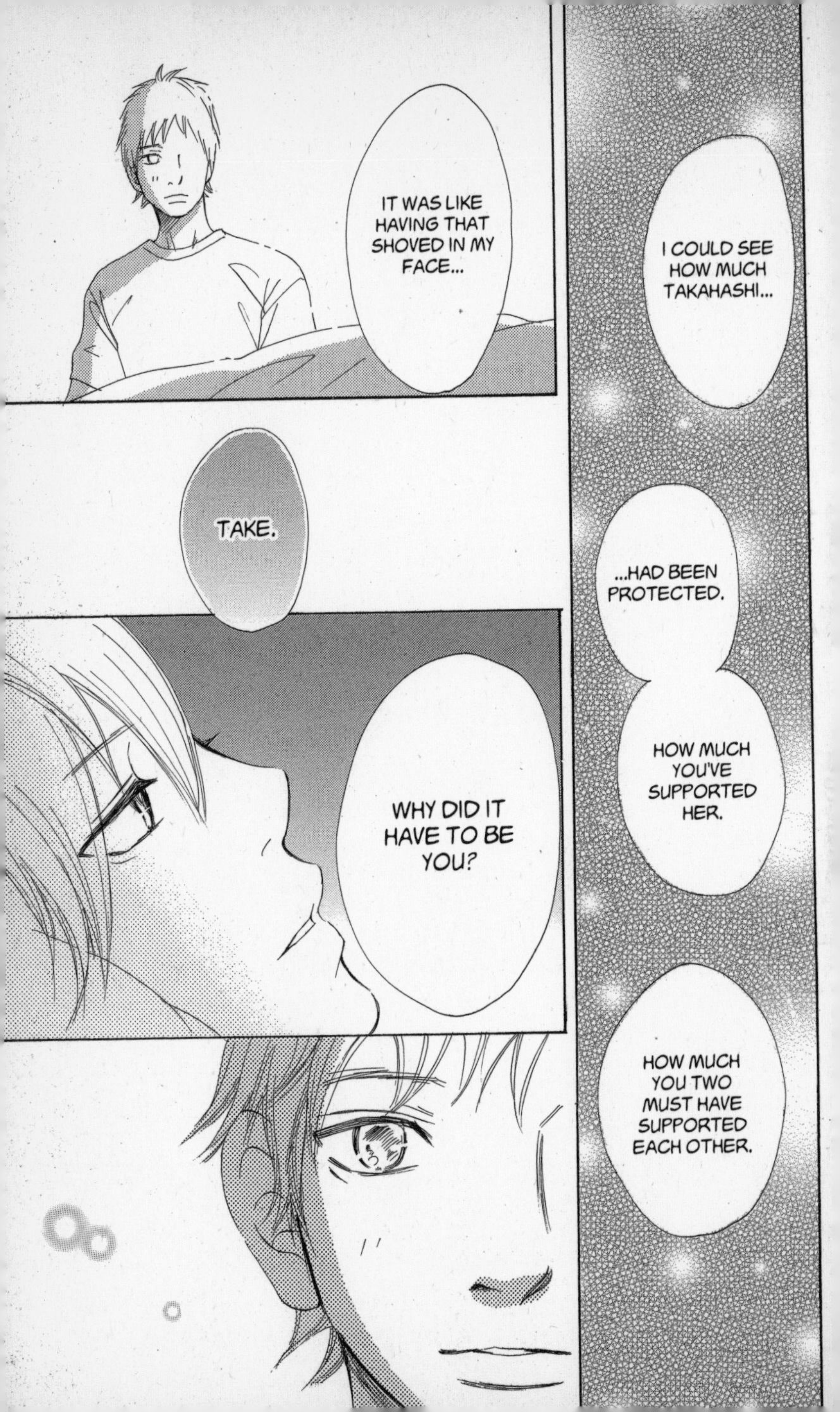
I COULD SEE HOW MUCH TAKAHASHI...
...HAD BEEN PROTECTED.
HOW MUCH YOU'VE SUPPORTED HER.
HOW MUCH YOU TWO MUST HAVE SUPPORTED EACH OTHER.
IT WAS LIKE HAVING THAT SHOVED IN MY FACE...
TAKE.
WHY DID IT HAVE TO BE YOU?

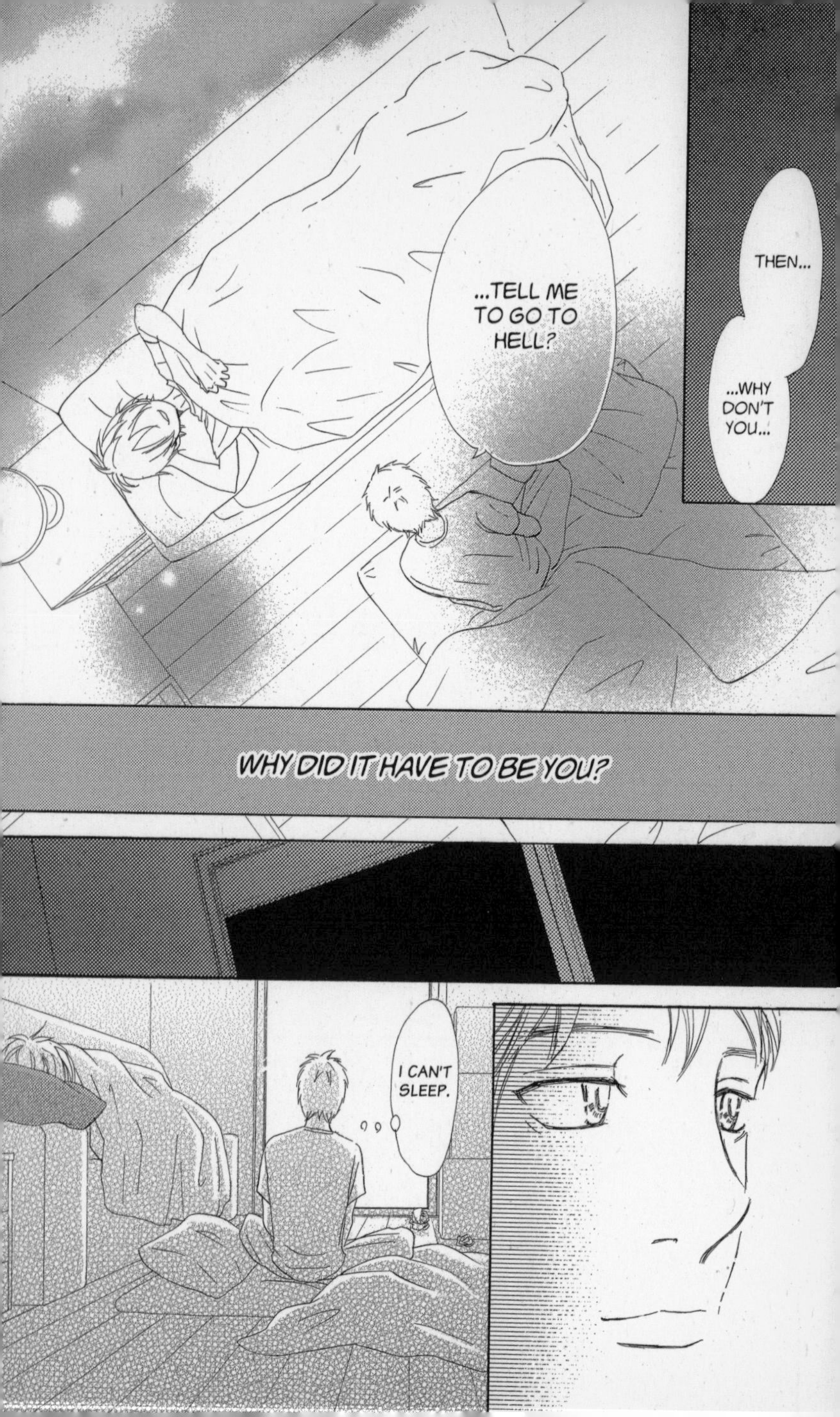
THEN...
...WHY DON'T YOU...
...TELL ME TO GO TO HELL?
WHY DID IT HAVE TO BE YOU?
I CAN'T SLEEP.

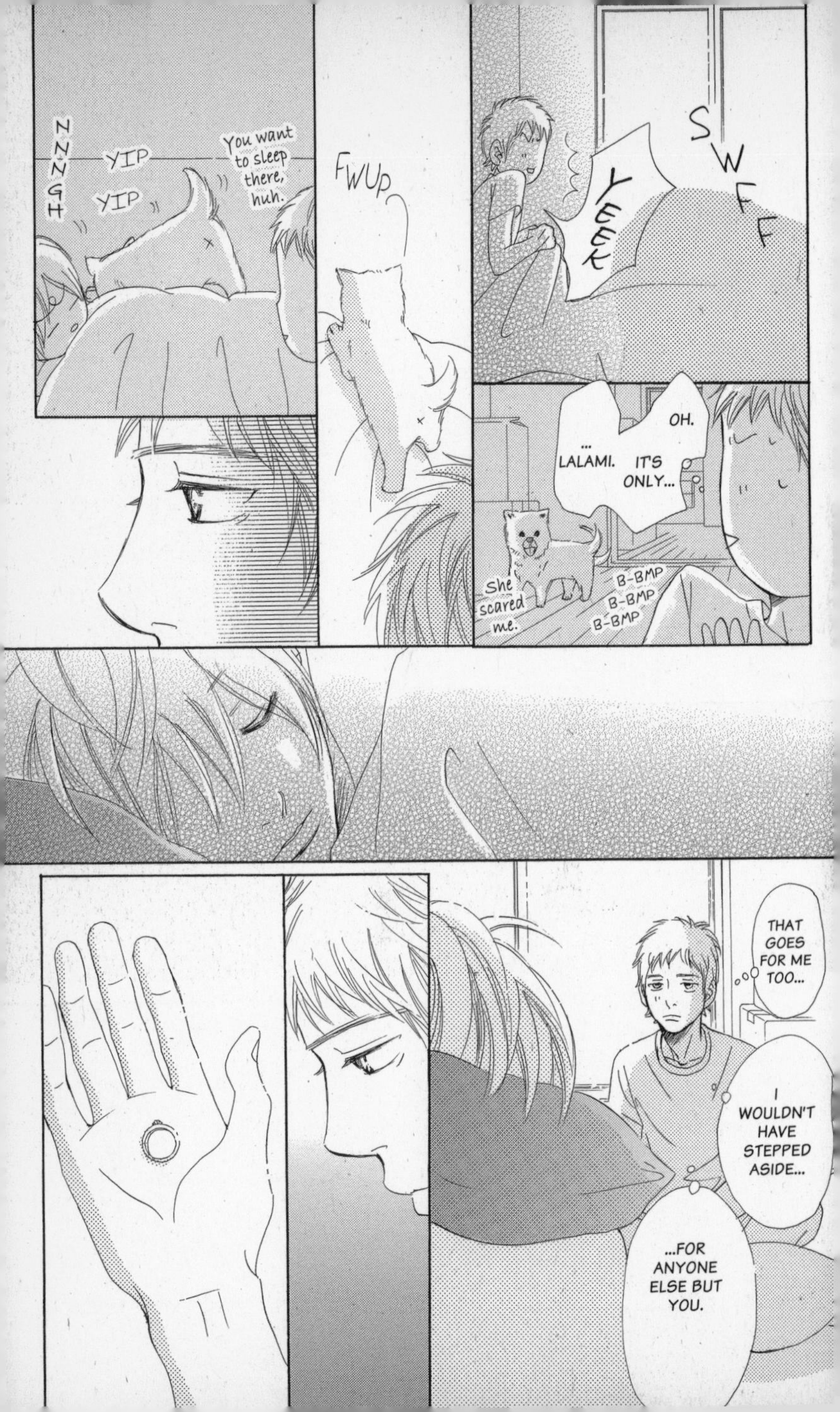
SWFF
YEEK
OH. IT'S ONLY...
...LALAMI.
B-BMP B-BMP B-BMP
She scared me.
FWUP
You want to sleep there, huh.
YIP
YIP
NNNGH
THAT GOES FOR ME TOO...
I WOULDN'T HAVE STEPPED ASIDE...
...FOR ANYONE ELSE BUT YOU.

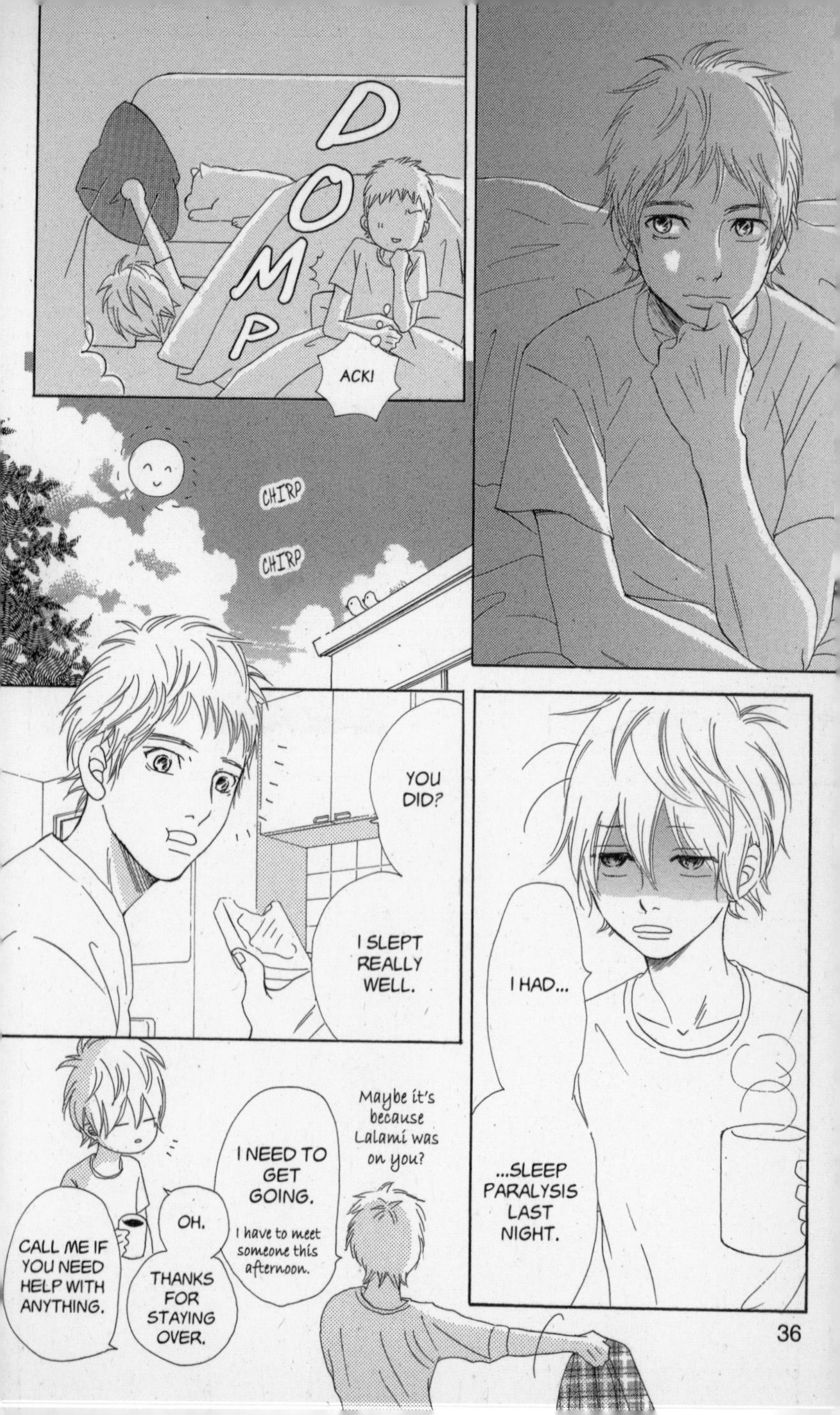
DOMP
ACK!
CHIRP
CHIRP
I HAD...
...SLEEP PARALYSIS LAST NIGHT.
YOU DID?
I SLEPT REALLY WELL.
Maybe it's because Lalami was on you?
I NEED TO GET GOING.
I have to meet someone this afternoon.
OH.
THANKS FOR STAYING OVER.
CALL ME IF YOU NEED HELP WITH ANYTHING.

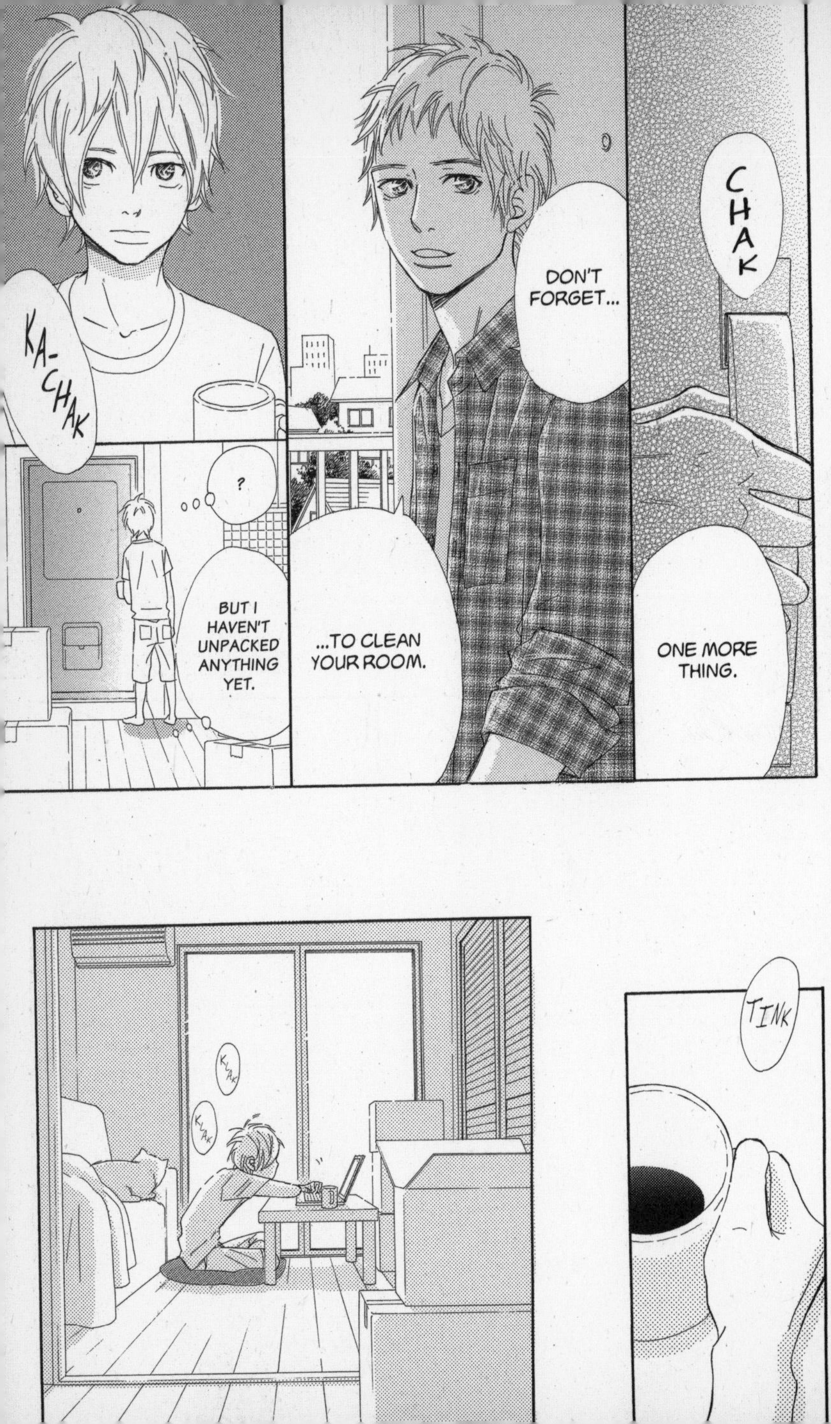
CHAK
ONE MORE THING.
DON'T FORGET...
...TO CLEAN YOUR ROOM.
KA-CHAK
?
BUT I HAVEN'T UNPACKED ANYTHING YET.
TINK
KLAK
KLAK

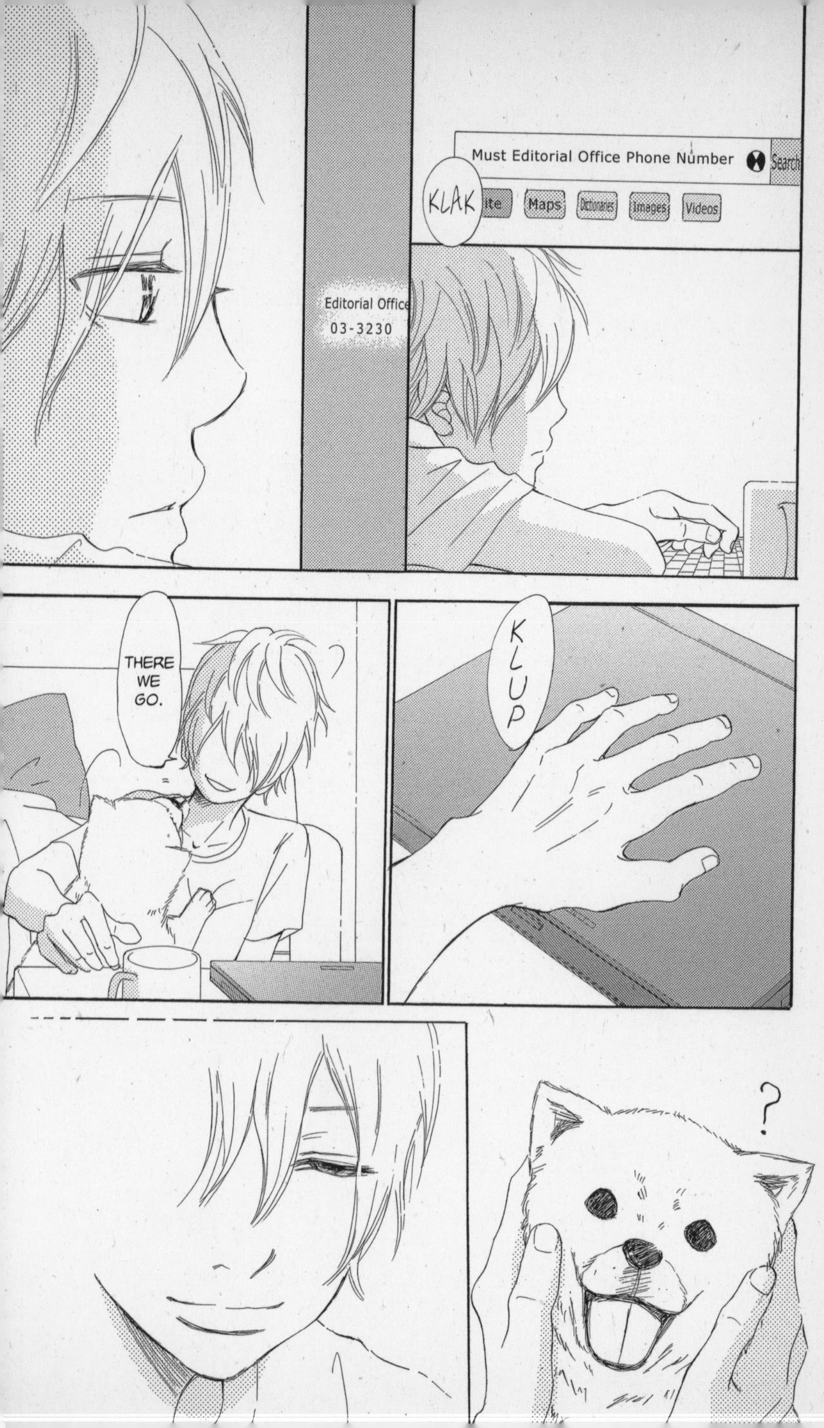
Must Editorial Office Phone Number
Search
KLAK
ite
Maps
Dictionaries
Images
Videos
Editorial Office
03-3230
KLUP
THERE WE GO.
?

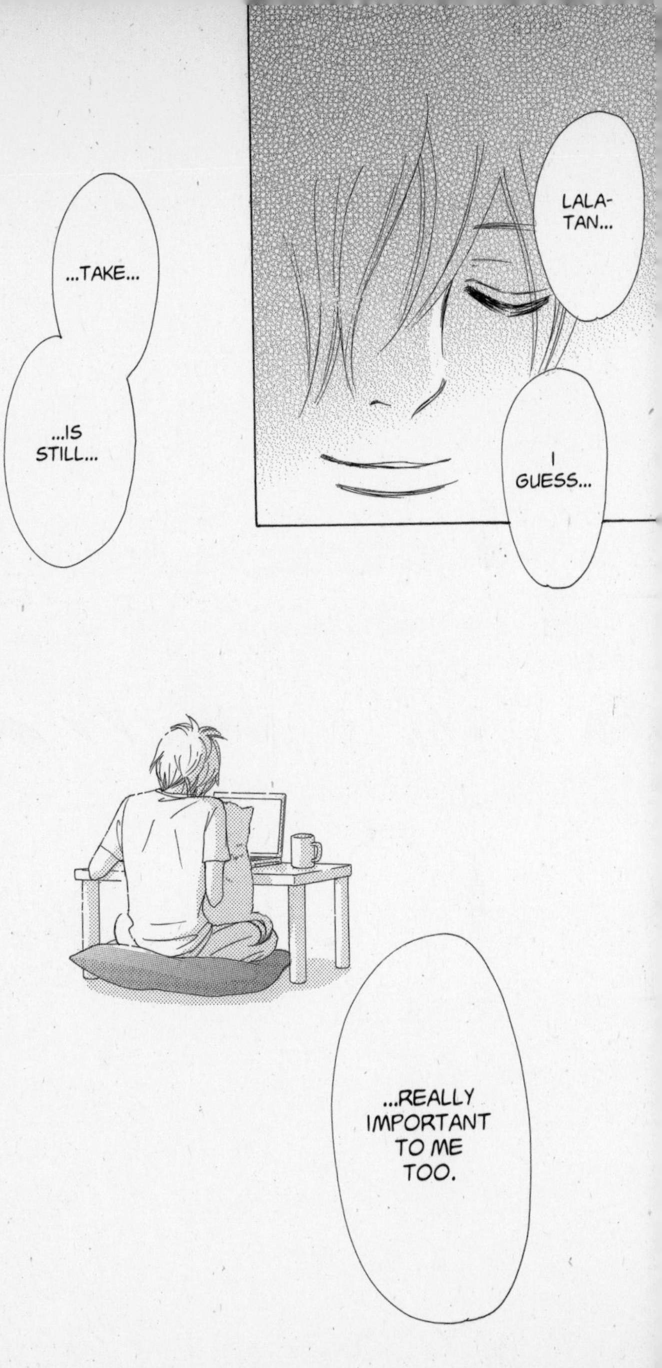
LALA-TAN...
I GUESS...
...TAKE...
...IS STILL...
...REALLY IMPORTANT TO ME TOO.

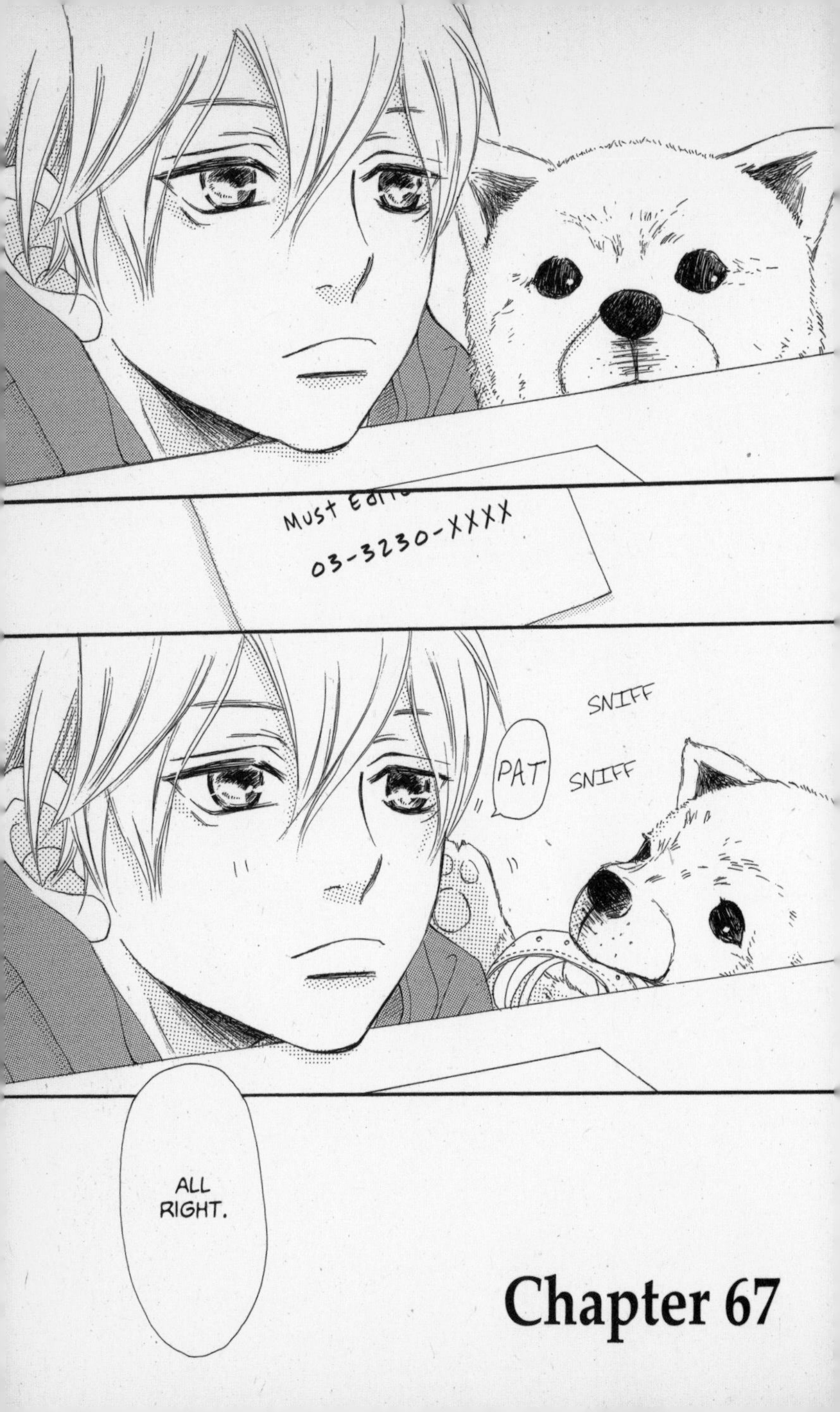
Must Edit
03-3230-XXXX
SNIFF
SNIFF
PAT
ALL RIGHT.
Chapter 67

Chapter 67

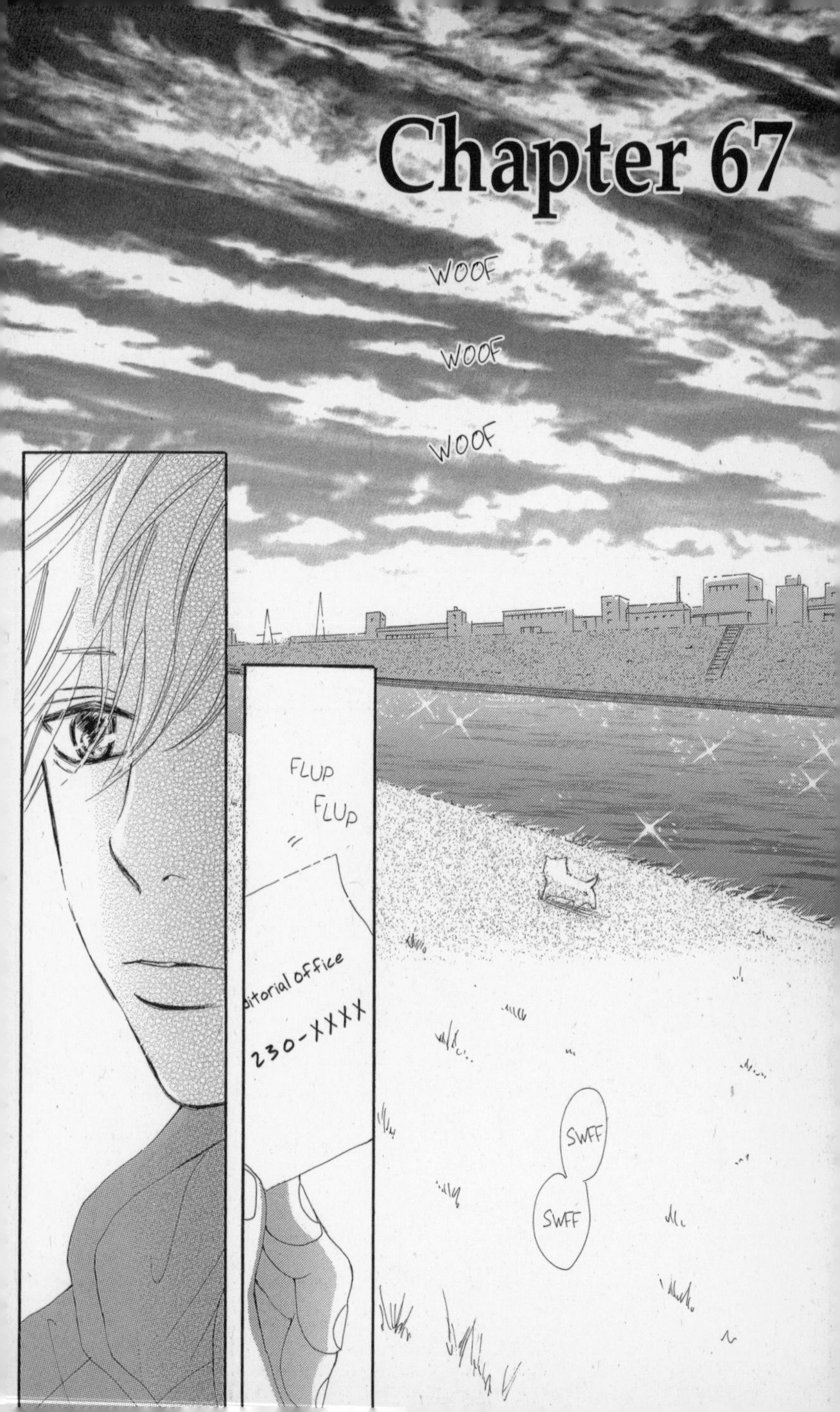
WOOF
WOOF
WOOF
SWFF
SWFF
FLUP
FLUP
ditorial office
230-XXXX

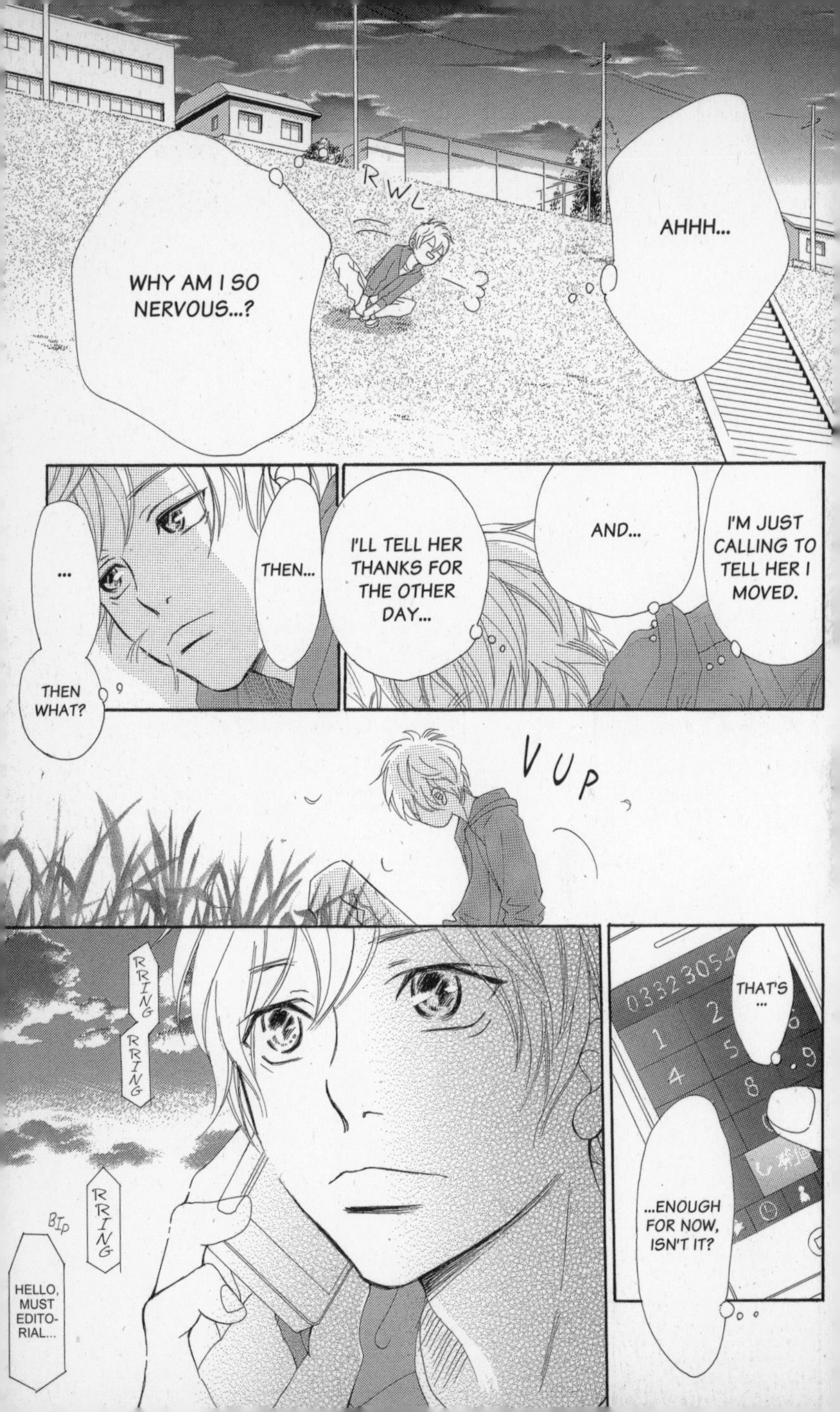
AHHH...
RWL
WHY AM I SO NERVOUS...?
I'M JUST CALLING TO TELL HER I MOVED.
AND...
I'LL TELL HER THANKS FOR THE OTHER DAY...
THEN...
...
THEN WHAT?
VUP
THAT'S ...
...ENOUGH FOR NOW, ISN'T IT?
RRING
RRING
RRING
BIP
HELLO, MUST EDITORIAL...

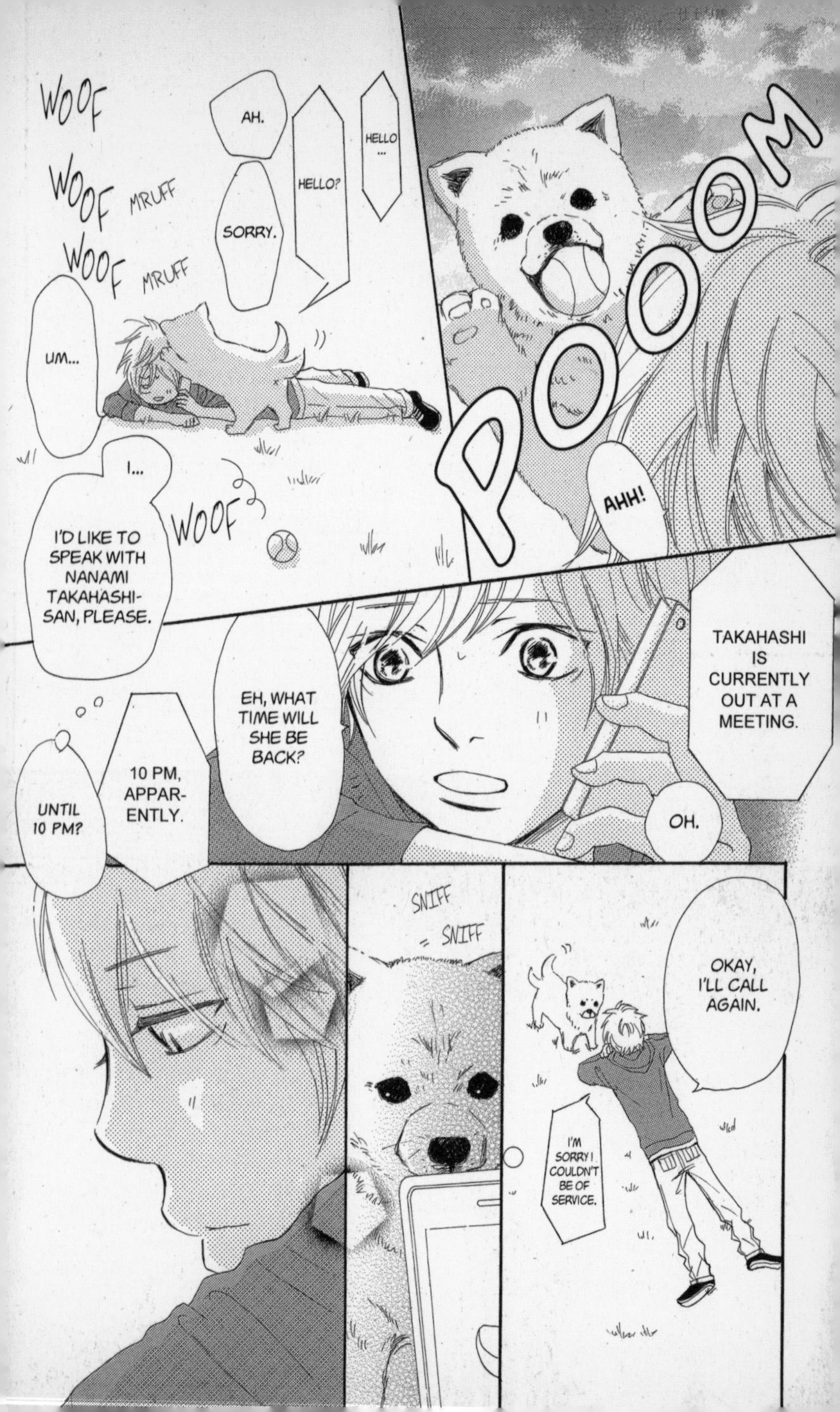
POOOOM
AHH!
HELLO...
HELLO?
AH.
SORRY.
WOOF
WOOF MRUFF
WOOF MRUFF
UM...
I...
I'D LIKE TO SPEAK WITH NANAMI TAKAHASHI-SAN, PLEASE.
WOOF
TAKAHASHI IS CURRENTLY OUT AT A MEETING.
OH.
EH, WHAT TIME WILL SHE BE BACK?
10 PM, APPARENTLY.
UNTIL 10 PM?
OKAY, I'LL CALL AGAIN.
I'M SORRY I COULDN'T BE OF SERVICE.
SNIFF
SNIFF

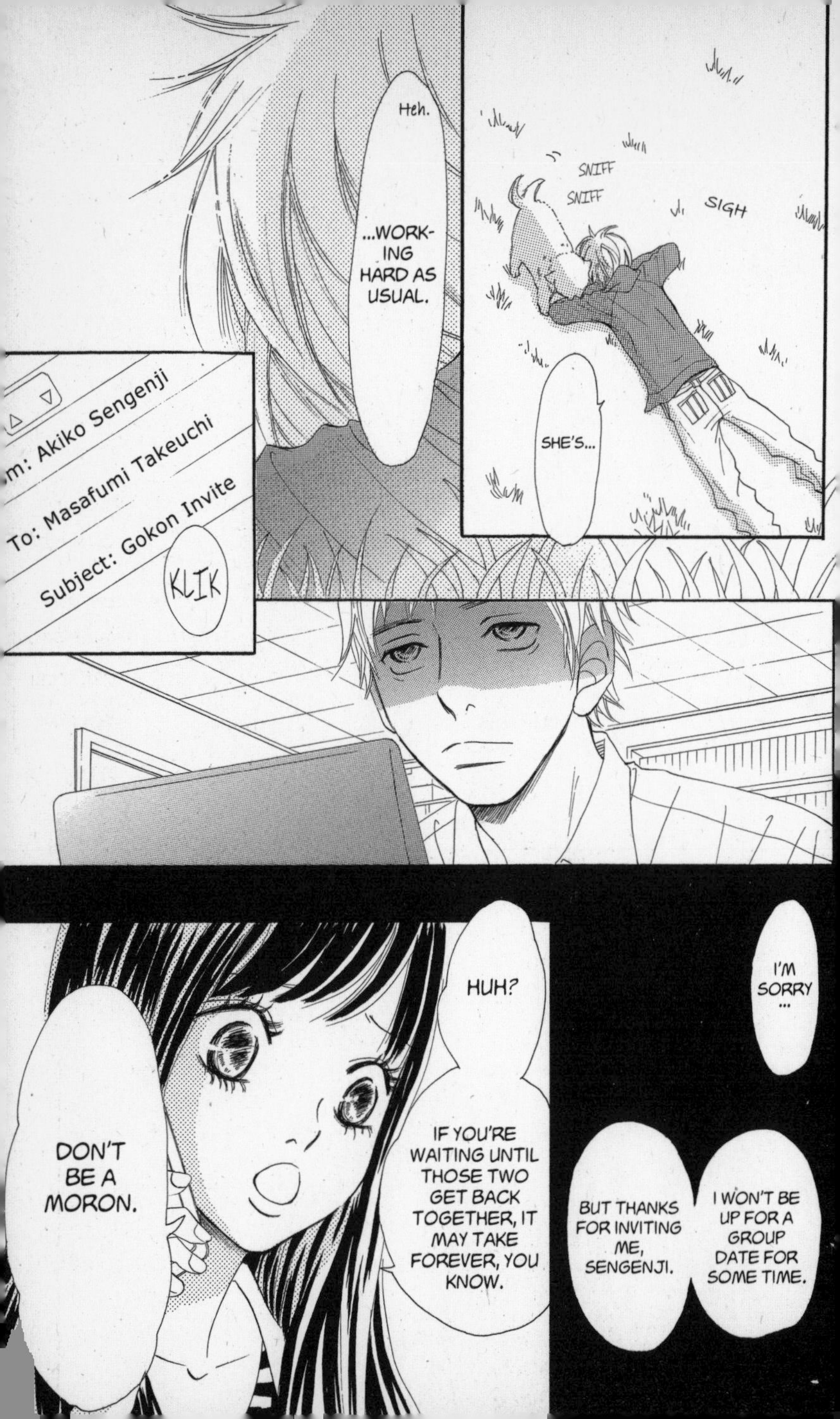
SNIFF
SNIFF
SIGH
SHE'S...
Heh.
...WORKING-ING HARD AS USUAL.
m: Akiko Sengenji
To: Masafumi Takeuchi
Subject: Gokon Invite
KLIK
I'M SORRY...
I WON'T BE UP FOR A GROUP DATE FOR SOME TIME.
BUT THANKS FOR INVITING ME, SENGENJI.
HUH?
IF YOU'RE WAITING UNTIL THOSE TWO GET BACK TOGETHER, IT MAY TAKE FOREVER, YOU KNOW.
DON'T BE A MORON.

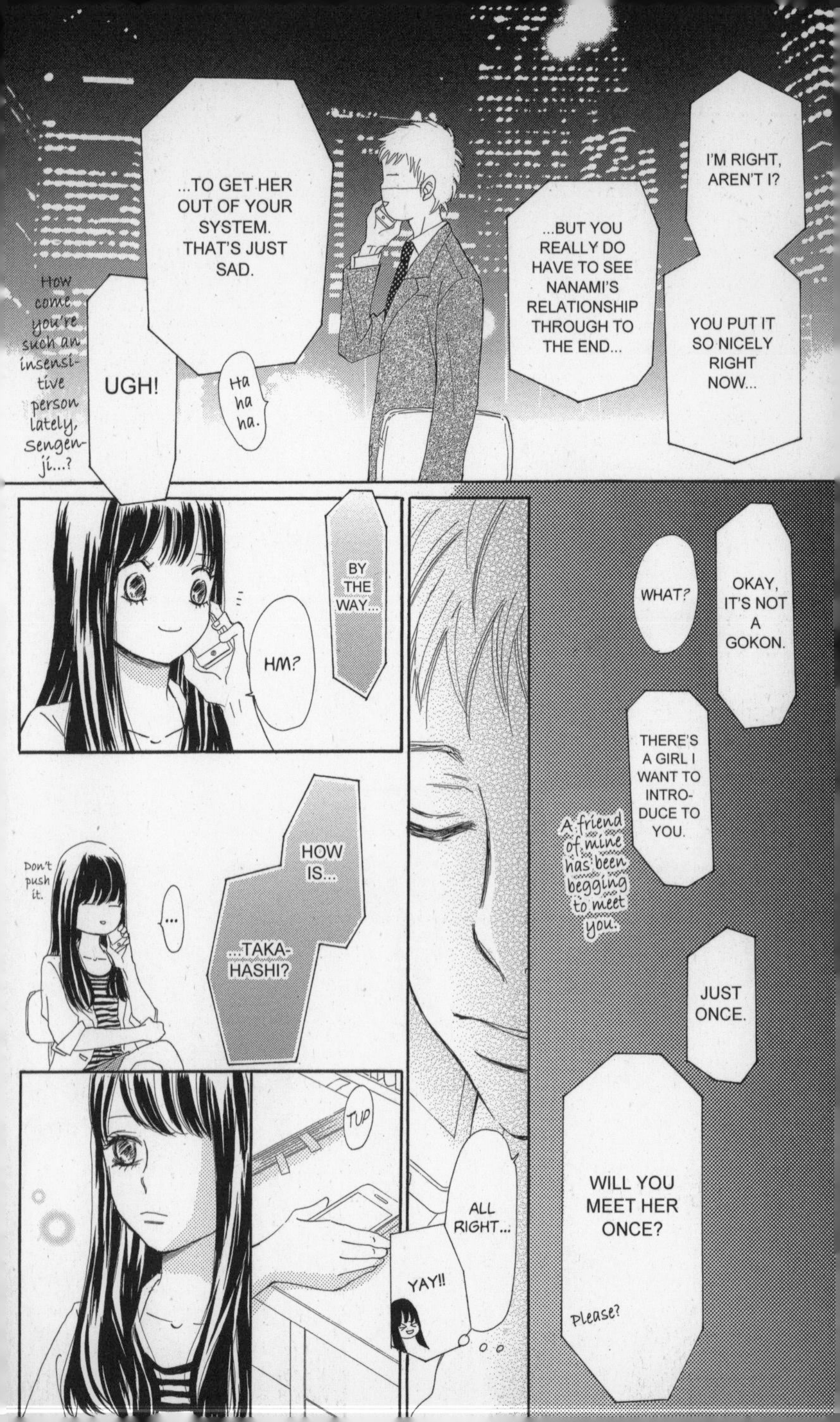
I'M RIGHT, AREN'T I?
YOU PUT IT SO NICELY RIGHT NOW...
...BUT YOU REALLY DO HAVE TO SEE NANAMI'S RELATIONSHIP THROUGH TO THE END...
...TO GET HER OUT OF YOUR SYSTEM. THAT'S JUST SAD.
Ha ha ha.
UGH!
How come you're such an insensitive person lately, Sengenji...?
OKAY, IT'S NOT A GOKON.
WHAT?
THERE'S A GIRL I WANT TO INTRODUCE TO YOU.
A friend of mine has been begging to meet you.
JUST ONCE.
WILL YOU MEET HER ONCE?
Please?
ALL RIGHT...
YAY!!
BY THE WAY...
HM?
HOW IS...
...TAKAHASHI?
...
Don't push it.
TUP

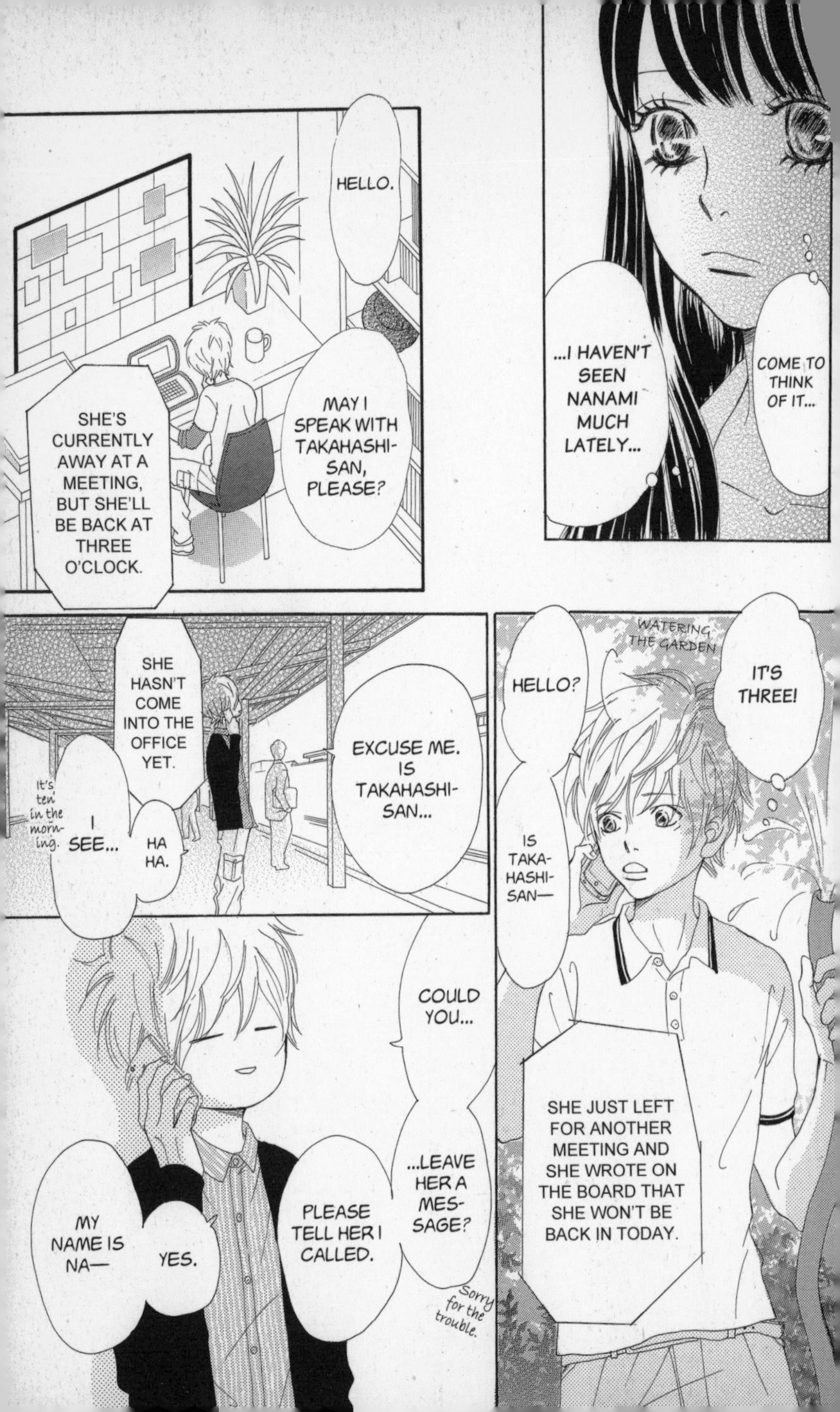
COME TO THINK OF IT...
...I HAVEN'T SEEN NANAMI MUCH LATELY...
HELLO.
MAY I SPEAK WITH TAKAHASHI-SAN, PLEASE?
SHE'S CURRENTLY AWAY AT A MEETING, BUT SHE'LL BE BACK AT THREE O'CLOCK.
WATERING THE GARDEN
IT'S THREE!
HELLO?
IS TAKA-HASHI-SAN—
SHE JUST LEFT FOR ANOTHER MEETING AND SHE WROTE ON THE BOARD THAT SHE WON'T BE BACK IN TODAY.
EXCUSE ME. IS TAKAHASHI-SAN...
SHE HASN'T COME INTO THE OFFICE YET.
HA HA.
I SEE...
It's ten in the morn-ing.
COULD YOU...
...LEAVE HER A MES-SAGE?
Sorry for the trouble.
PLEASE TELL HER I CALLED.
YES.
MY NAME IS NA—

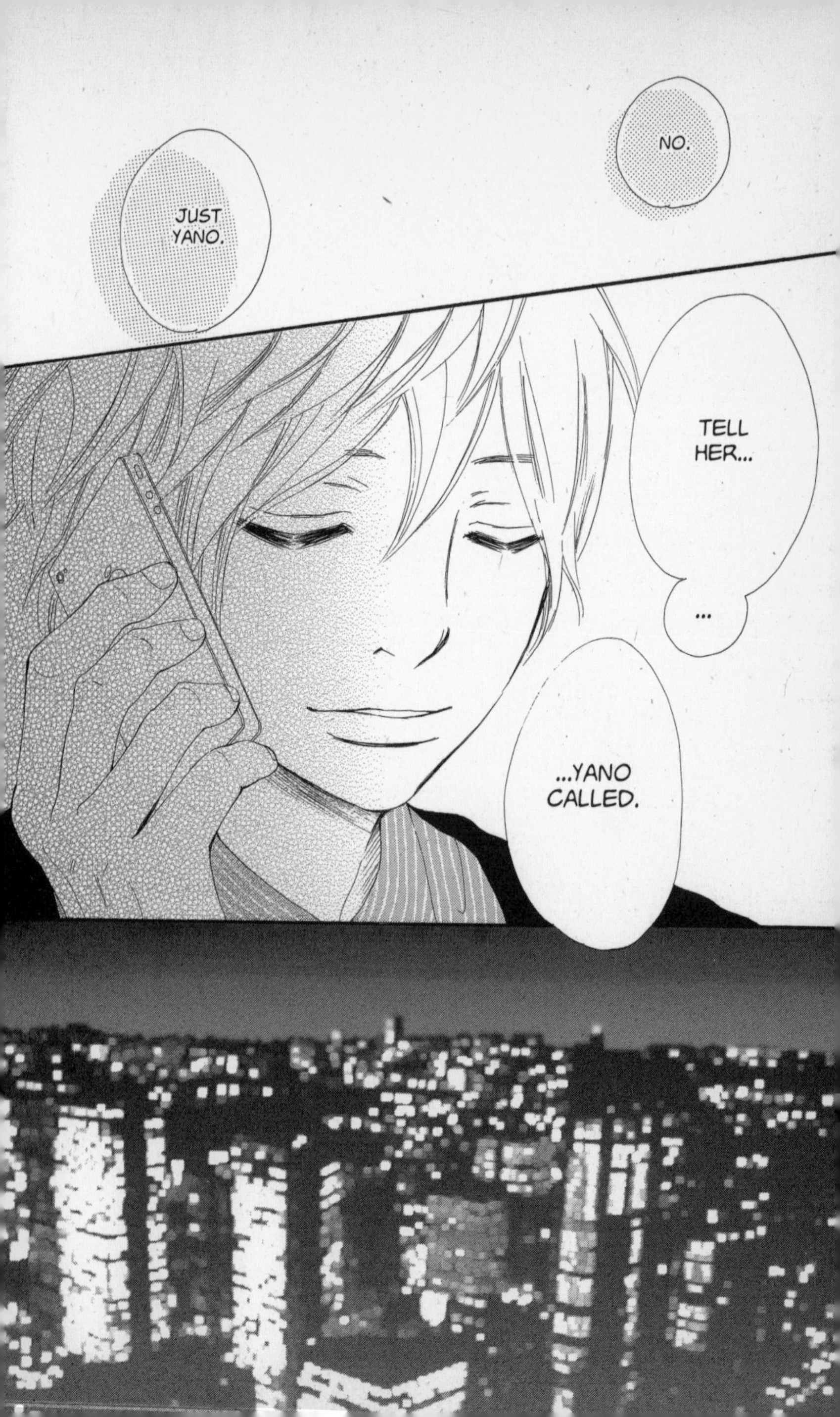
NO.
JUST YANO.
TELL HER...
...
...YANO CALLED.

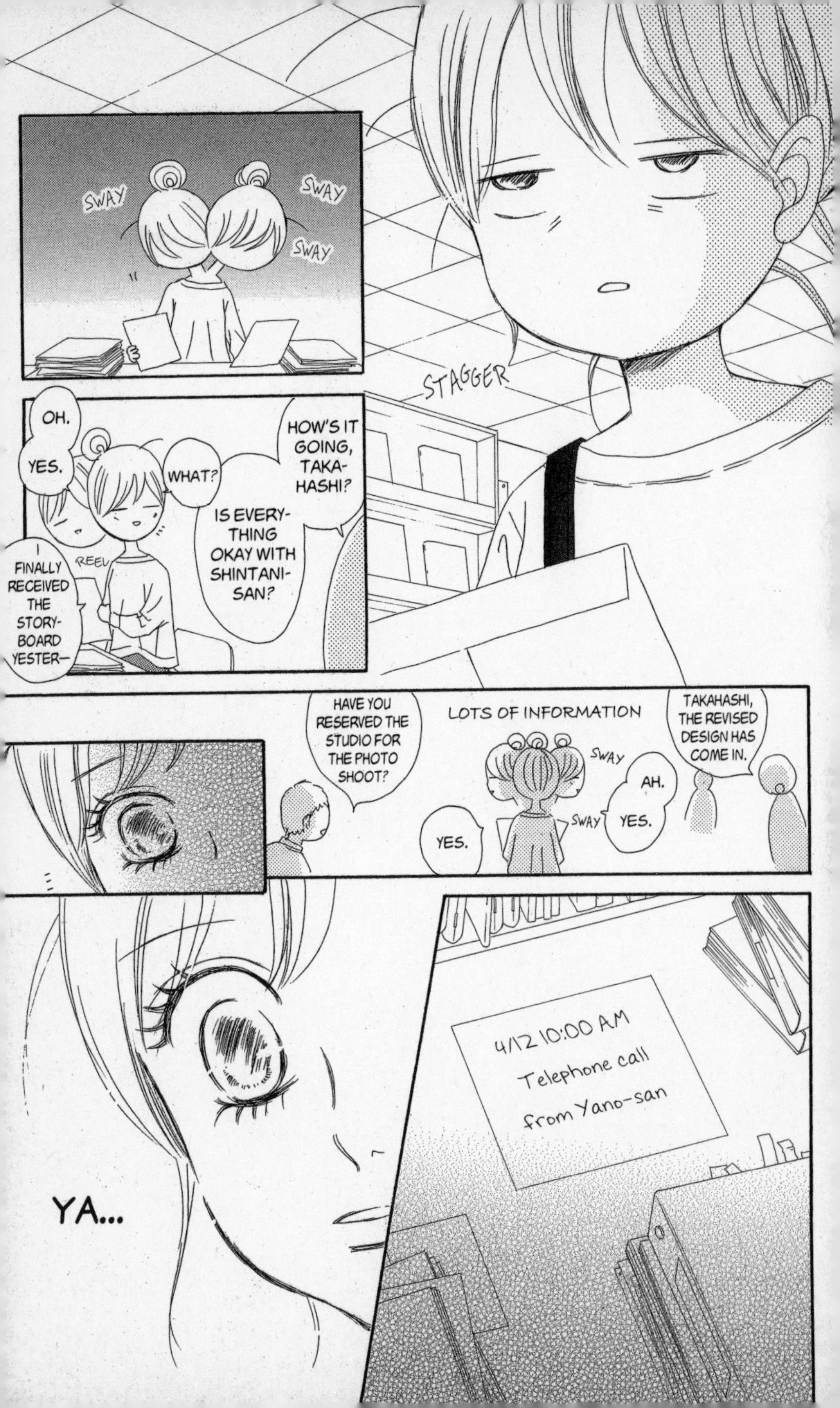
STAGGER
SWAY
SWAY
SWAY
HOW'S IT GOING, TAKAHASHI?
IS EVERYTHING OKAY WITH SHINTANI-SAN?
WHAT?
OH.
YES.
REEL
I FINALLY RECEIVED THE STORYBOARD YESTER—
TAKAHASHI, THE REVISED DESIGN HAS COME IN.
SWAY
AH.
YES.
SWAY
LOTS OF INFORMATION
YES.
HAVE YOU RESERVED THE STUDIO FOR THE PHOTO SHOOT?
4/12 10:00 AM
Telephone call
from Yano-san
YA...

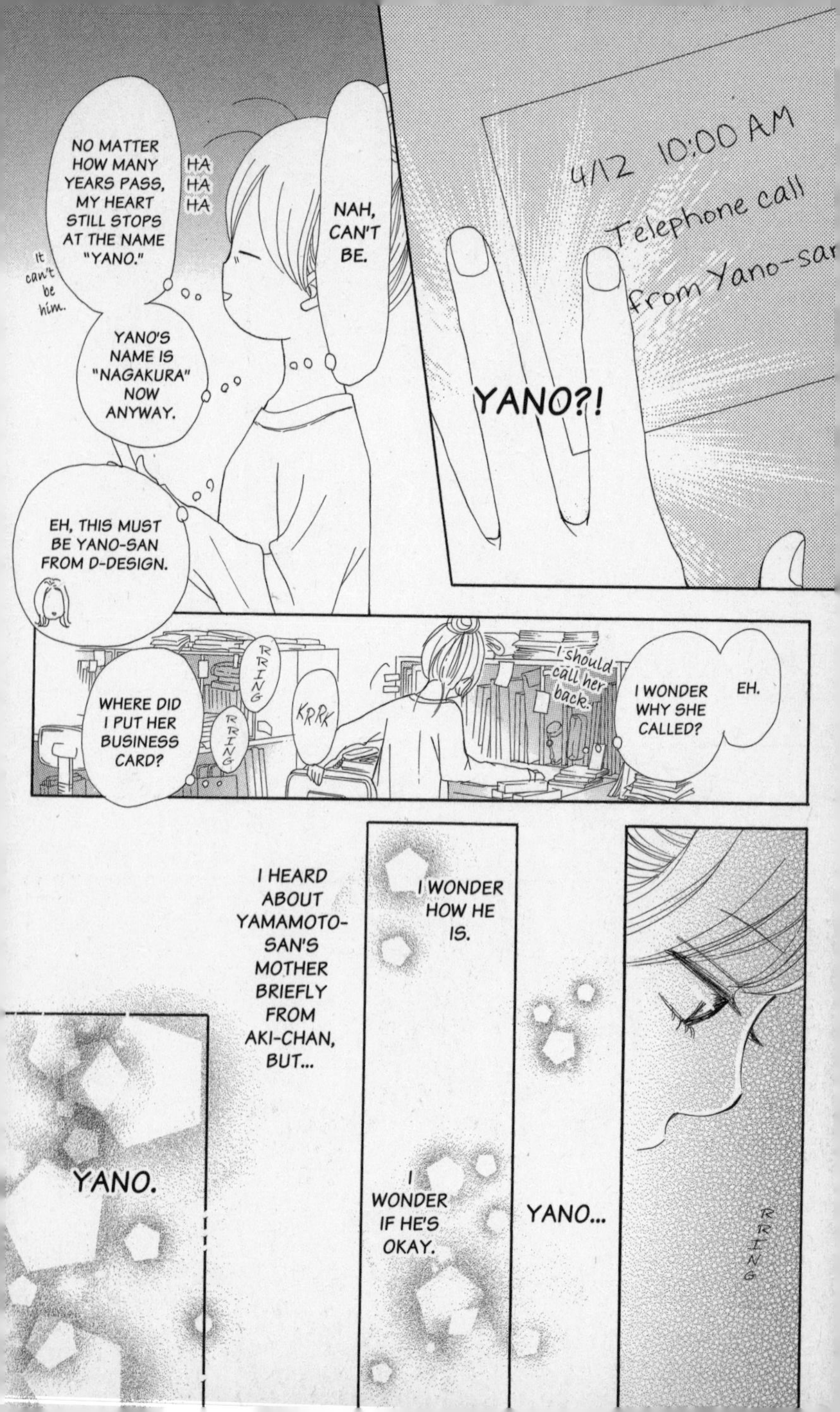
4/12 10:00 AM
Telephone call from Yano-san
YANO?!
NAH, CAN'T BE.
HA HA HA
NO MATTER HOW MANY YEARS PASS, MY HEART STILL STOPS AT THE NAME "YANO."
It can't be him.
YANO'S NAME IS "NAGAKURA" NOW ANYWAY.
EH, THIS MUST BE YANO-SAN FROM D-DESIGN.
EH.
I WONDER WHY SHE CALLED?
I should call her back.
KRRK
RRING
RRING
WHERE DID I PUT HER BUSINESS CARD?
RRING
YANO...
I WONDER HOW HE IS.
I WONDER IF HE'S OKAY.
I HEARD ABOUT YAMAMOTO-SAN'S MOTHER BRIEFLY FROM AKI-CHAN, BUT...
YANO.

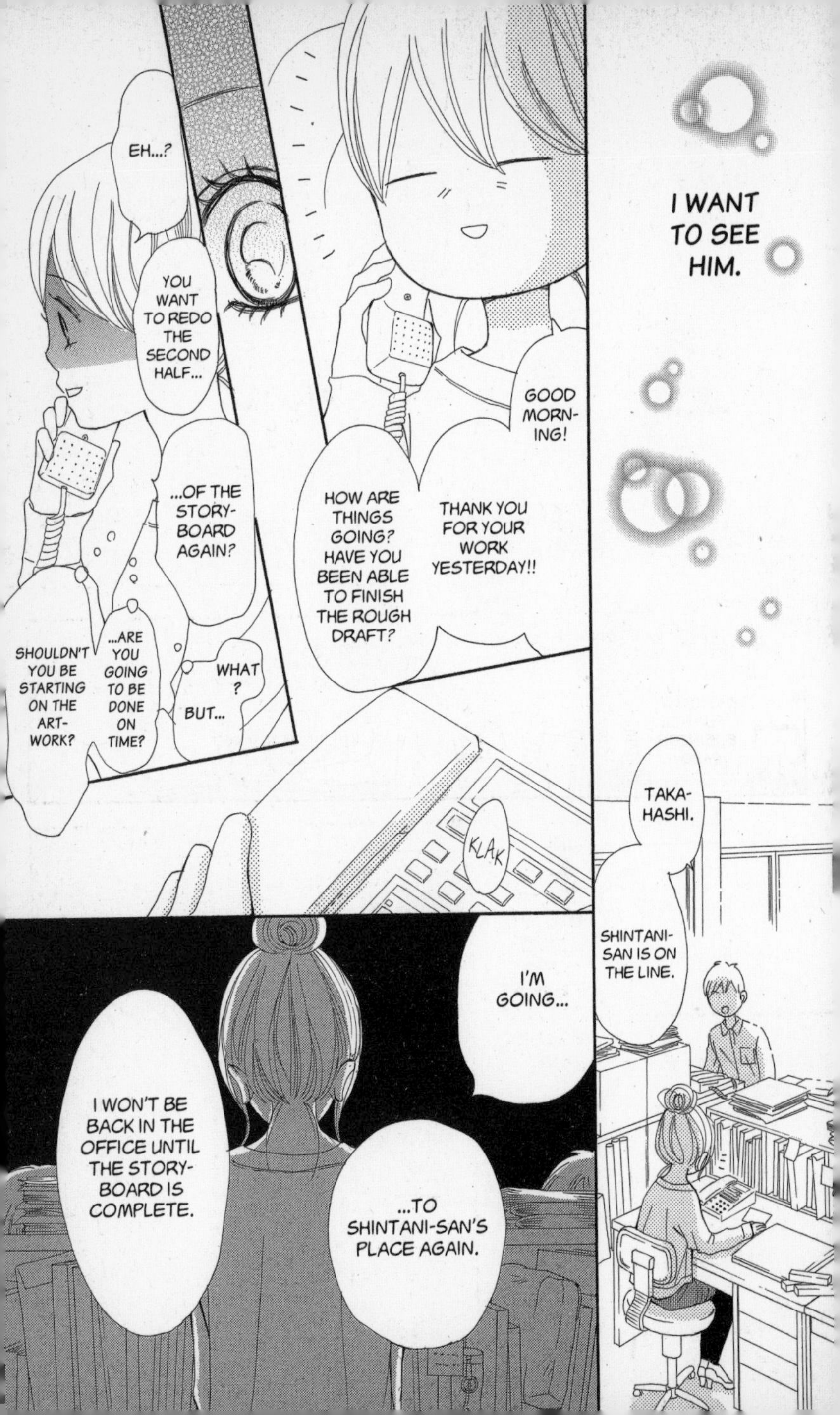
I WANT TO SEE HIM.
TAKA-HASHI.
SHINTANI-SAN IS ON THE LINE.
GOOD MORN-ING!
THANK YOU FOR YOUR WORK YESTERDAY!!
HOW ARE THINGS GOING? HAVE YOU BEEN ABLE TO FINISH THE ROUGH DRAFT?
KLAK
EH...?
YOU WANT TO REDO THE SECOND HALF...
...OF THE STORY-BOARD AGAIN?
WHAT?
BUT...
...ARE YOU GOING TO BE DONE ON TIME?
SHOULDN'T YOU BE STARTING ON THE ART-WORK?
I'M GOING...
...TO SHINTANI-SAN'S PLACE AGAIN.
I WON'T BE BACK IN THE OFFICE UNTIL THE STORY-BOARD IS COMPLETE.

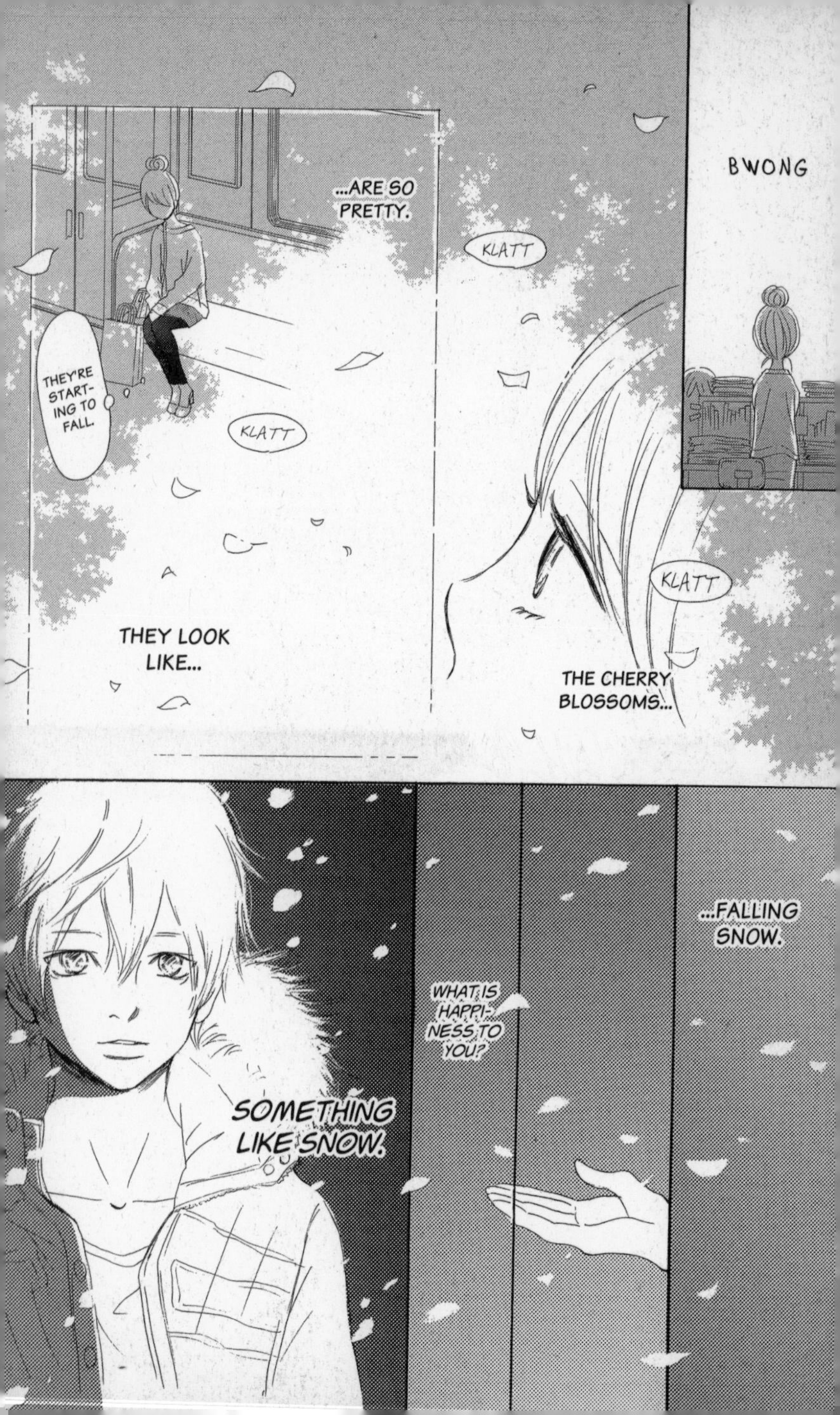

BWONG
KLATT
KLATT
THE CHERRY BLOSSOMS...
...ARE SO PRETTY.
THEY'RE STARTING TO FALL.
KLATT
THEY LOOK LIKE...
...FALLING SNOW.
WHAT IS HAPPINESS TO YOU?
SOMETHING LIKE SNOW.

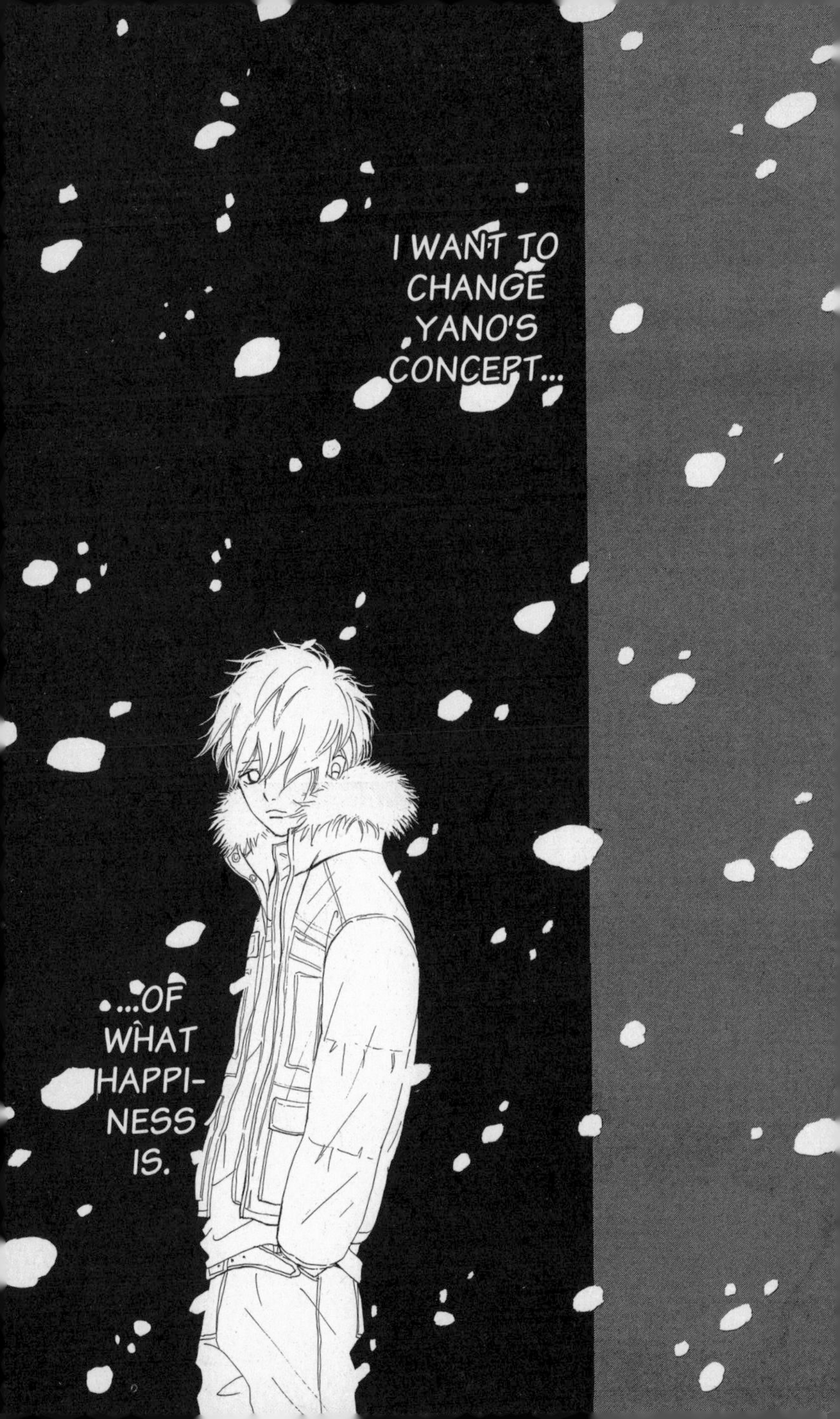
I WANT TO CHANGE YANO'S CONCEPT...
...OF WHAT HAPPI-NESS IS.

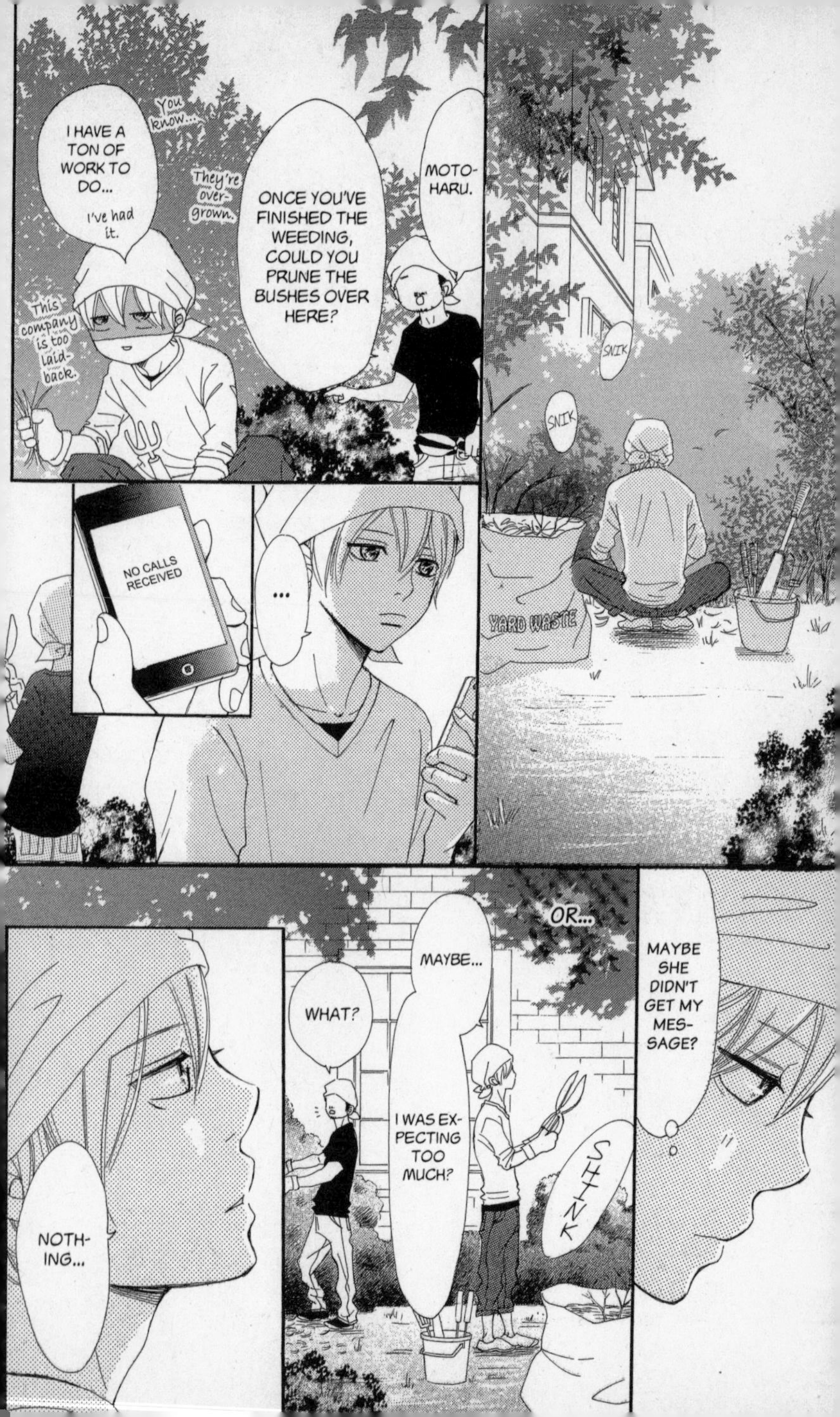
SNIK
SNIK
MOTO-HARU.
ONCE YOU'VE FINISHED THE WEEDING, COULD YOU PRUNE THE BUSHES OVER HERE?
You know...
They're over-grown.
I HAVE A TON OF WORK TO DO...
I've had it.
This company is too laid-back.
YARD WASTE
...
NO CALLS RECEIVED
MAYBE SHE DIDN'T GET MY MES-SAGE?
OR...
MAYBE...
I WAS EX-PECTING TOO MUCH?
SHINK
WHAT?
NOTH-ING...

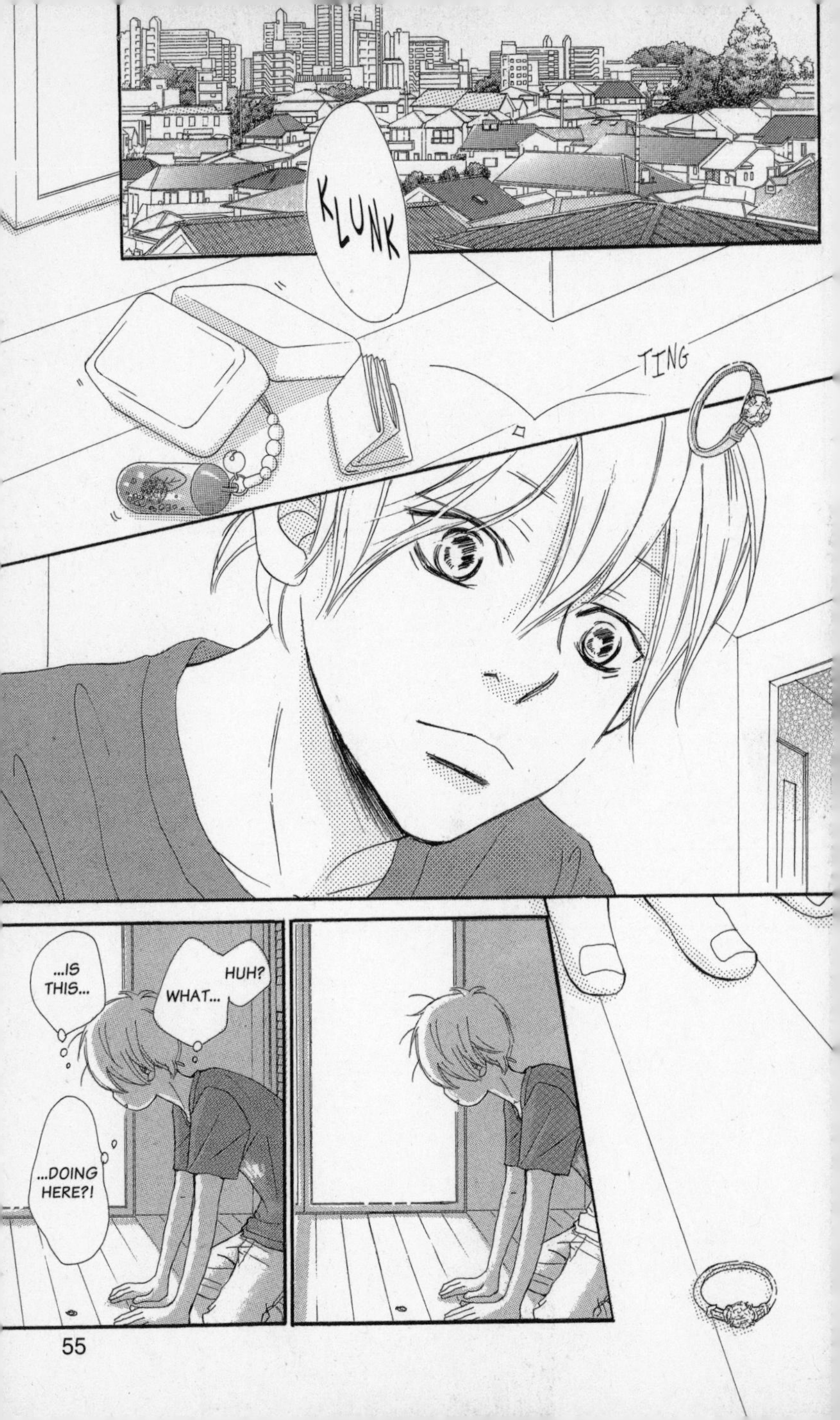
KLUNK
TING
HUH?
WHAT...
...IS THIS...
...DOING HERE?!

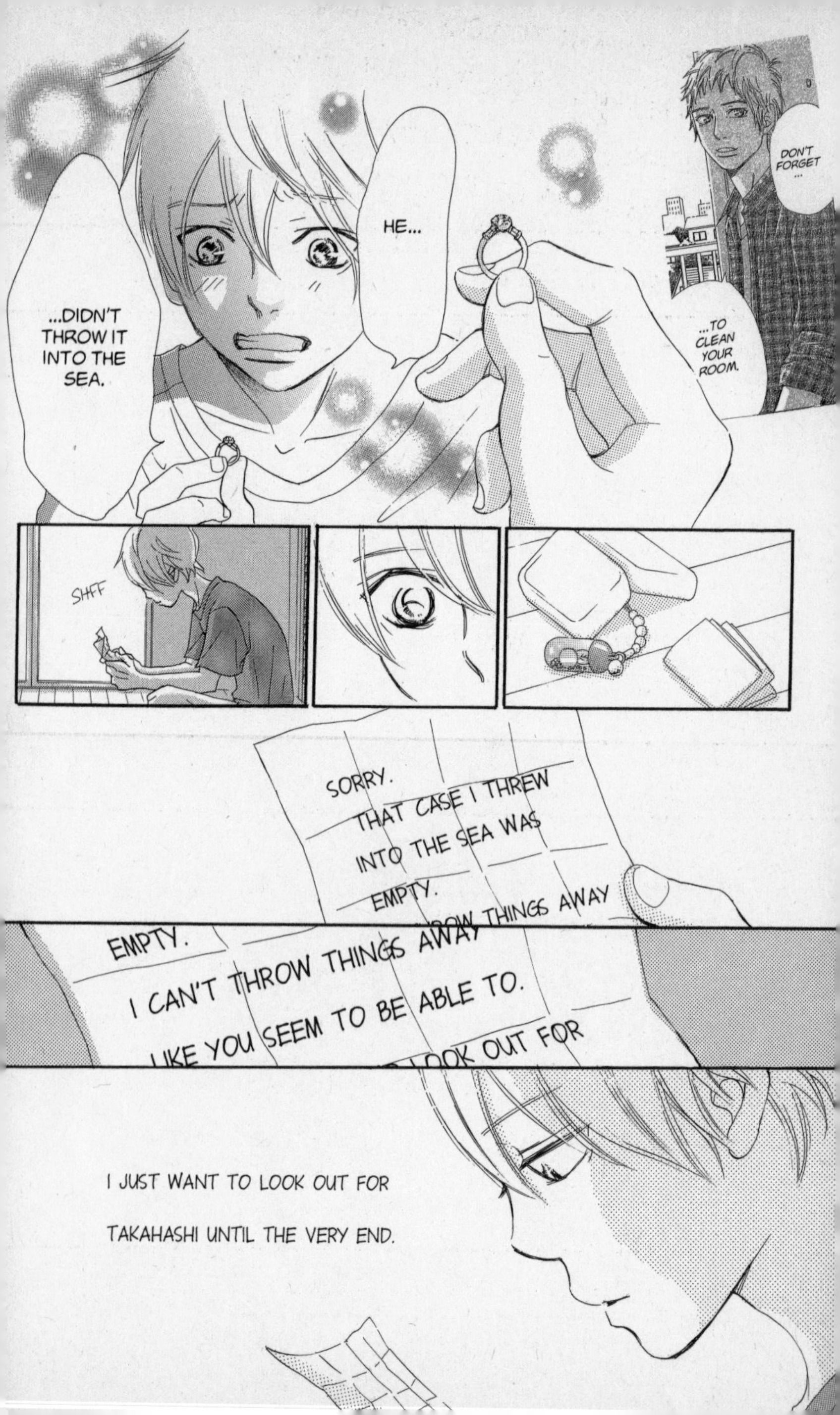
DON'T FORGET...
...TO CLEAN YOUR ROOM.
HE...
...DIDN'T THROW IT INTO THE SEA.
SHFF
SORRY.
THAT CASE I THREW
INTO THE SEA WAS
EMPTY.
THINGS AWAY
EMPTY.
I CAN'T THROW THINGS AWAY
LIKE YOU SEEM TO BE ABLE TO.
LOOK OUT FOR
I JUST WANT TO LOOK OUT FOR
TAKAHASHI UNTIL THE VERY END.

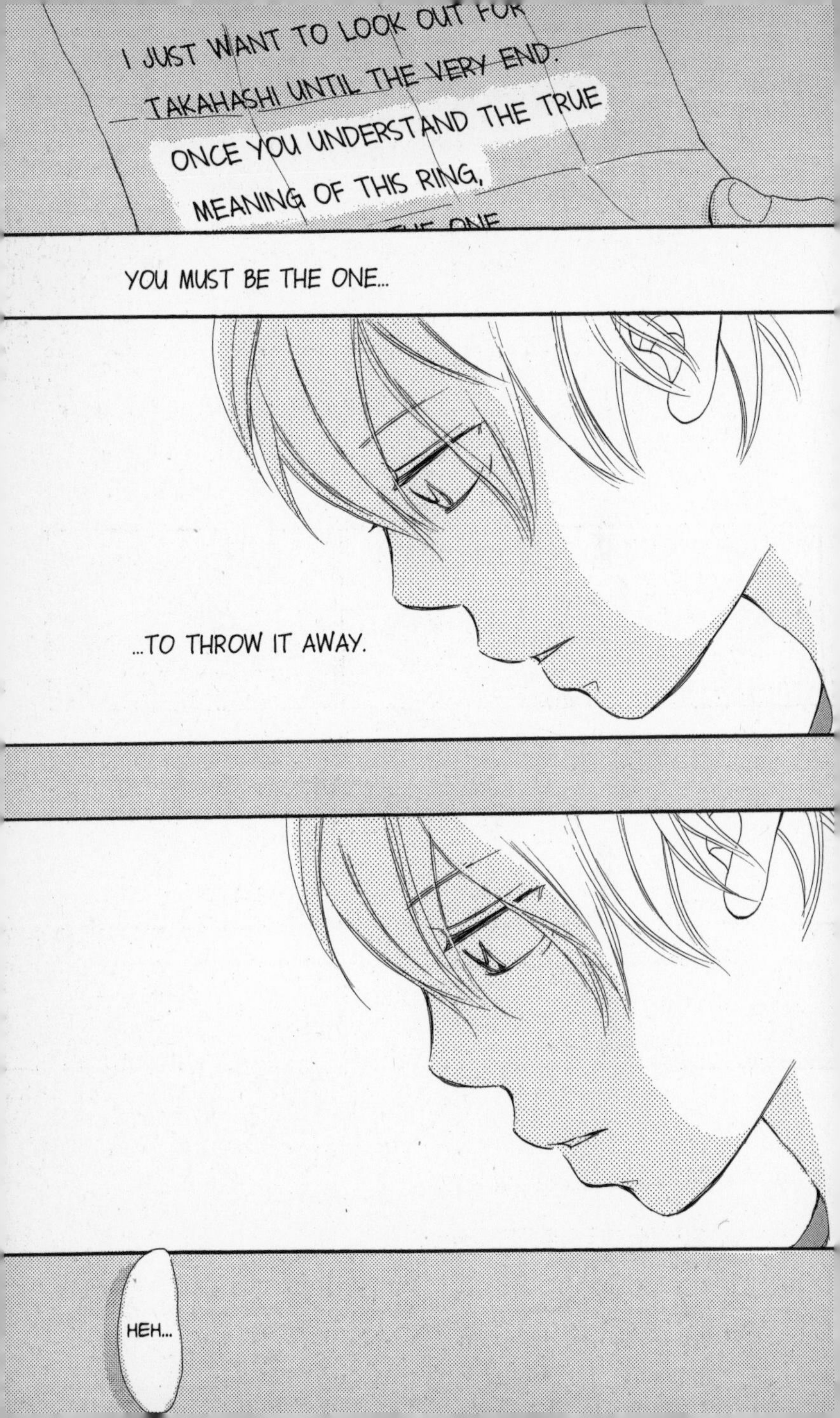
I JUST WANT TO LOOK OUT FOR
TAKAHASHI UNTIL THE VERY END.
ONCE YOU UNDERSTAND THE TRUE
MEANING OF THIS RING,
YOU MUST BE THE ONE...
...TO THROW IT AWAY.
HEH...

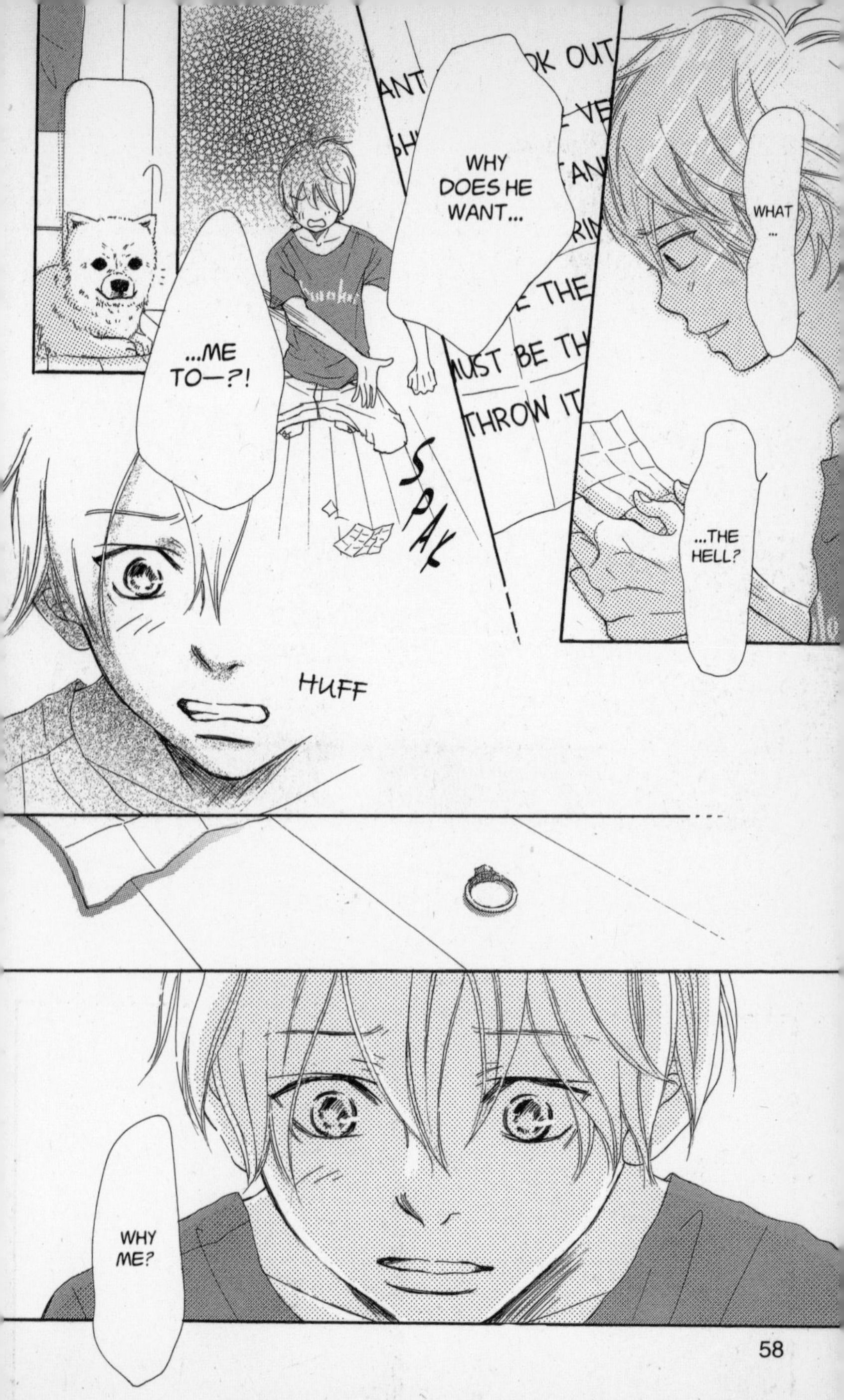
WHAT ...
...THE HELL?
WHY DOES HE WANT...
...ME TO—?!
SPAK
HUFF
WHY ME?

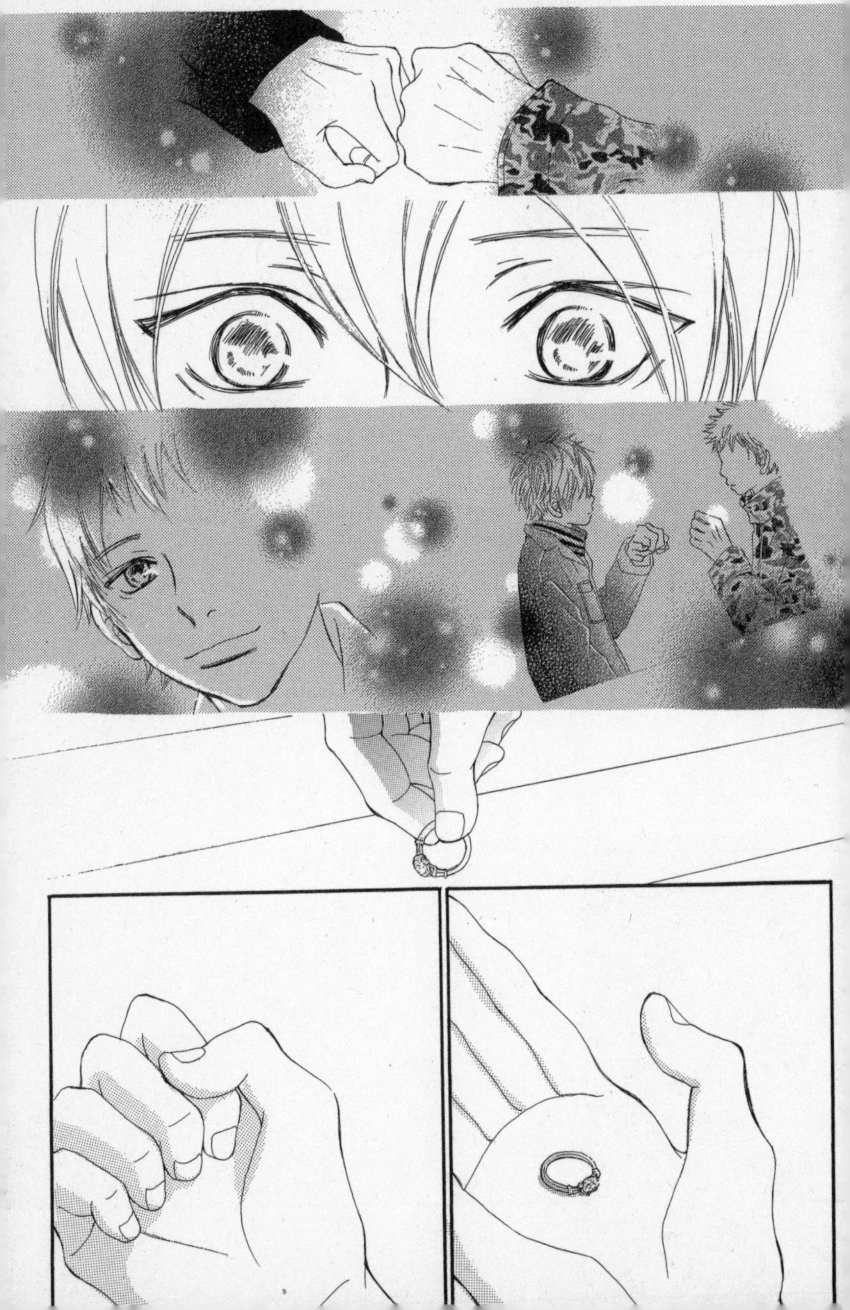

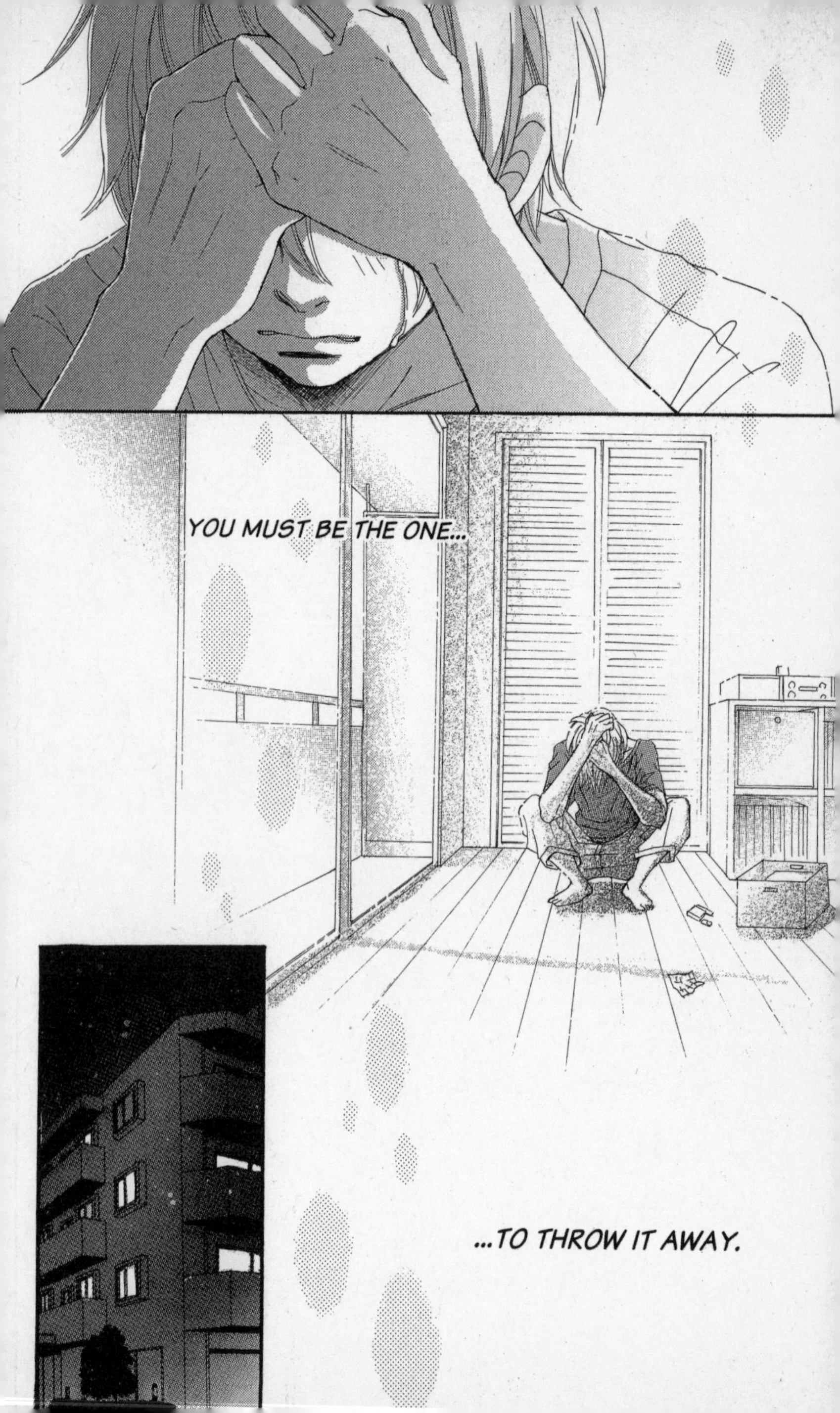
YOU MUST BE THE ONE...
...TO THROW IT AWAY.

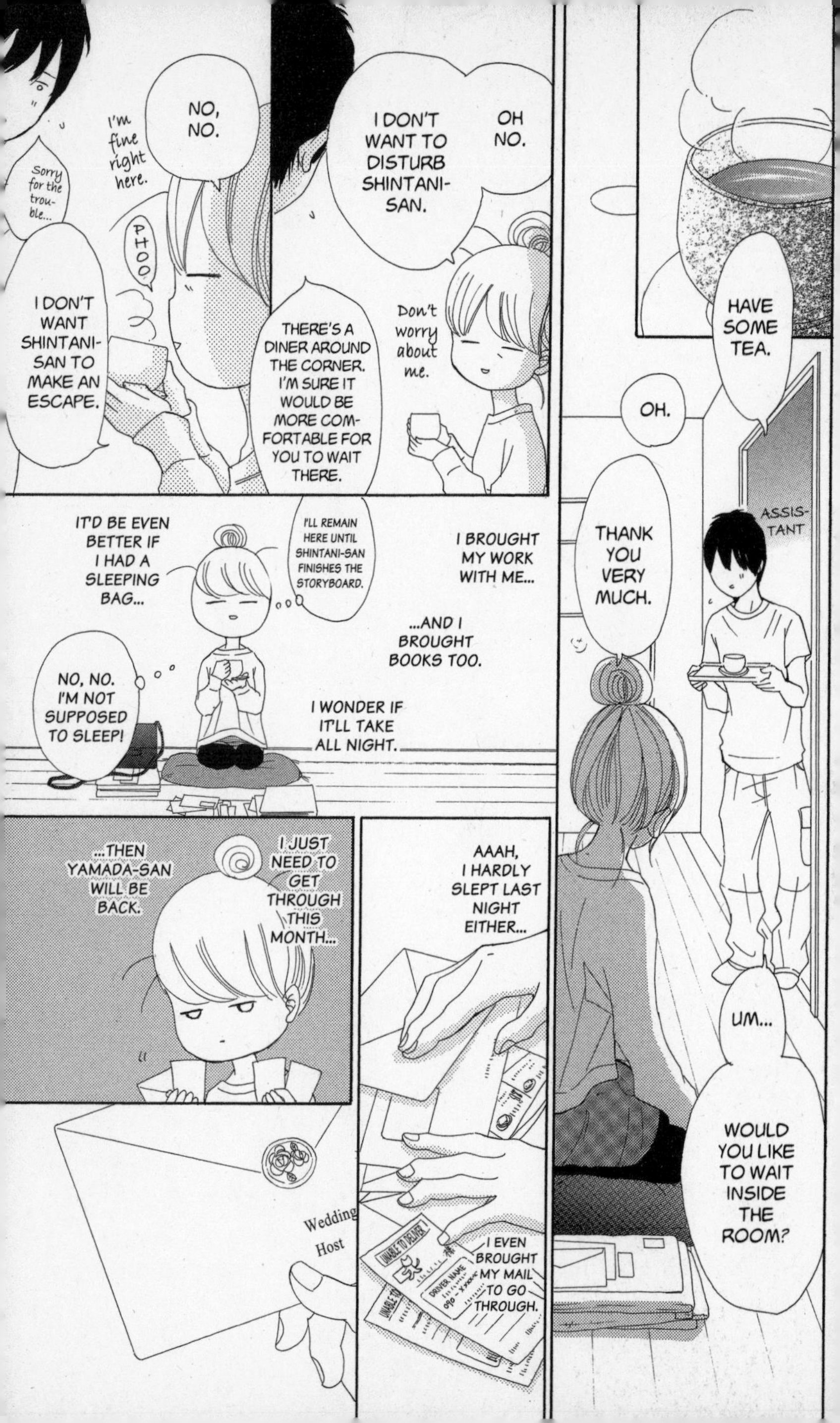
HAVE SOME TEA.
OH.
ASSISTANT
THANK YOU VERY MUCH.
UM...
WOULD YOU LIKE TO WAIT INSIDE THE ROOM?
OH NO.
I DON'T WANT TO DISTURB SHINTANI-SAN.
Don't worry about me.
THERE'S A DINER AROUND THE CORNER. I'M SURE IT WOULD BE MORE COMFORTABLE FOR YOU TO WAIT THERE.
NO, NO.
I'm fine right here.
Sorry for the trouble...
PHOO
I DON'T WANT SHINTANI-SAN TO MAKE AN ESCAPE.
I BROUGHT MY WORK WITH ME...
...AND I BROUGHT BOOKS TOO.
I'LL REMAIN HERE UNTIL SHINTANI-SAN FINISHES THE STORYBOARD.
IT'D BE EVEN BETTER IF I HAD A SLEEPING BAG...
I WONDER IF IT'LL TAKE ALL NIGHT.
NO, NO. I'M NOT SUPPOSED TO SLEEP!
AAAH, I HARDLY SLEPT LAST NIGHT EITHER...
I EVEN BROUGHT MY MAIL TO GO THROUGH.
UNABLE TO DELIVER
DRIVER NAME
I JUST NEED TO GET THROUGH THIS MONTH...
...THEN YAMADA-SAN WILL BE BACK.
Wedding Host

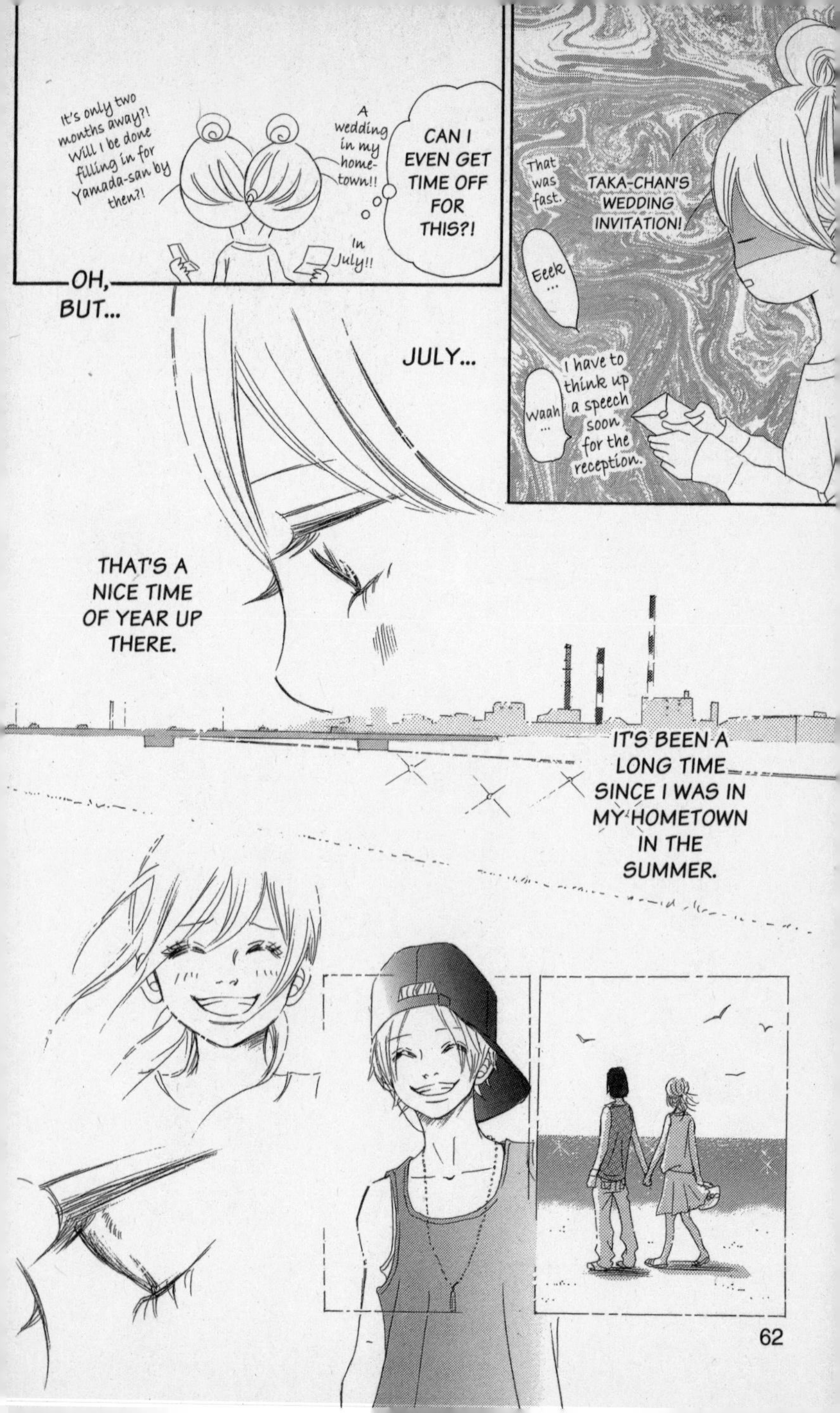
TAKA-CHAN'S WEDDING INVITATION!
That was fast.
Eeek...
I have to think up a speech soon for the reception.
Waah...
CAN I EVEN GET TIME OFF FOR THIS?!
A wedding in my hometown!!
In July!!
It's only two months away?! Will I be done filling in for Yamada-san by then?!
OH, BUT...
JULY...
THAT'S A NICE TIME OF YEAR UP THERE.
IT'S BEEN A LONG TIME SINCE I WAS IN MY HOMETOWN IN THE SUMMER.

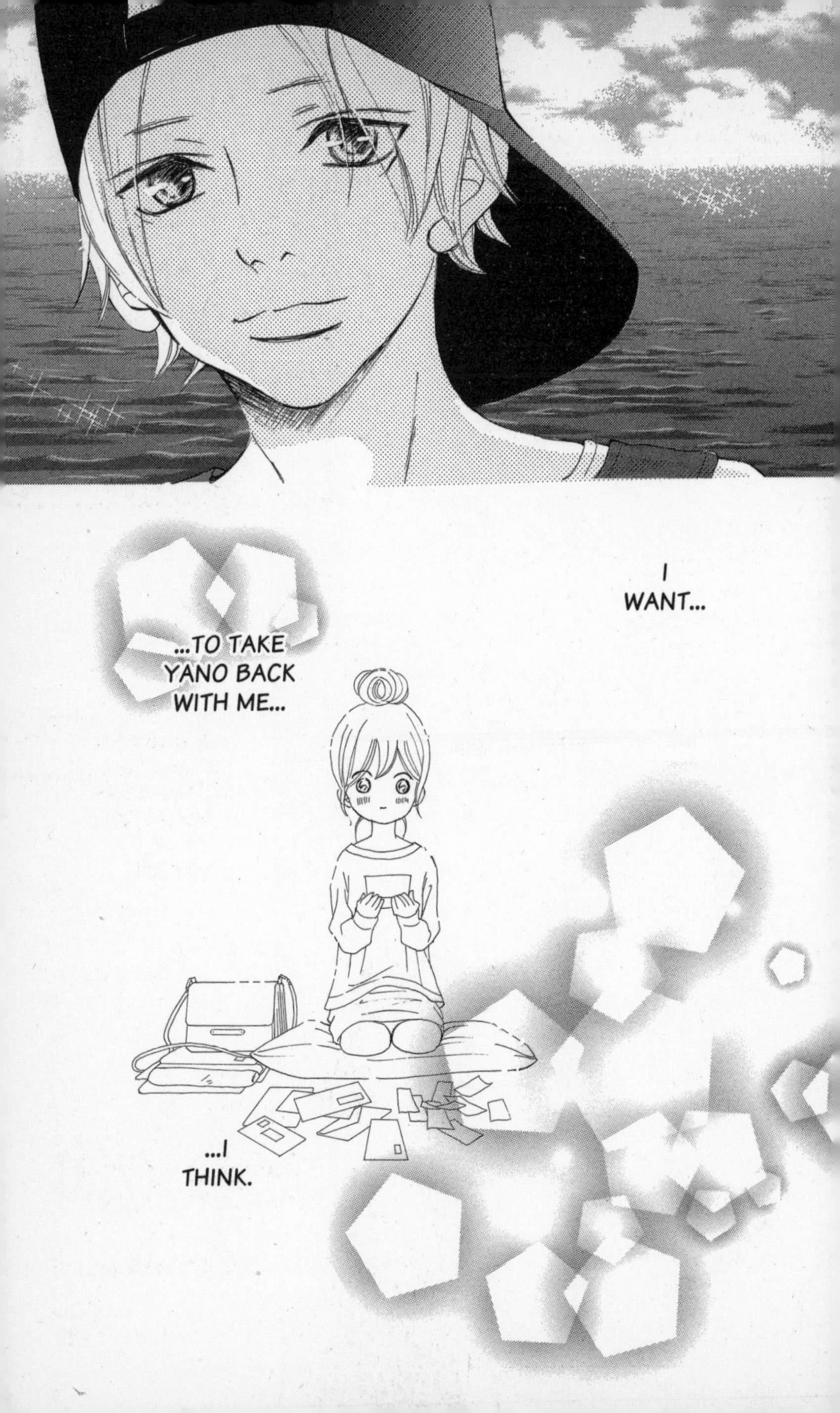
I WANT...
...TO TAKE YANO BACK WITH ME...
...I THINK.

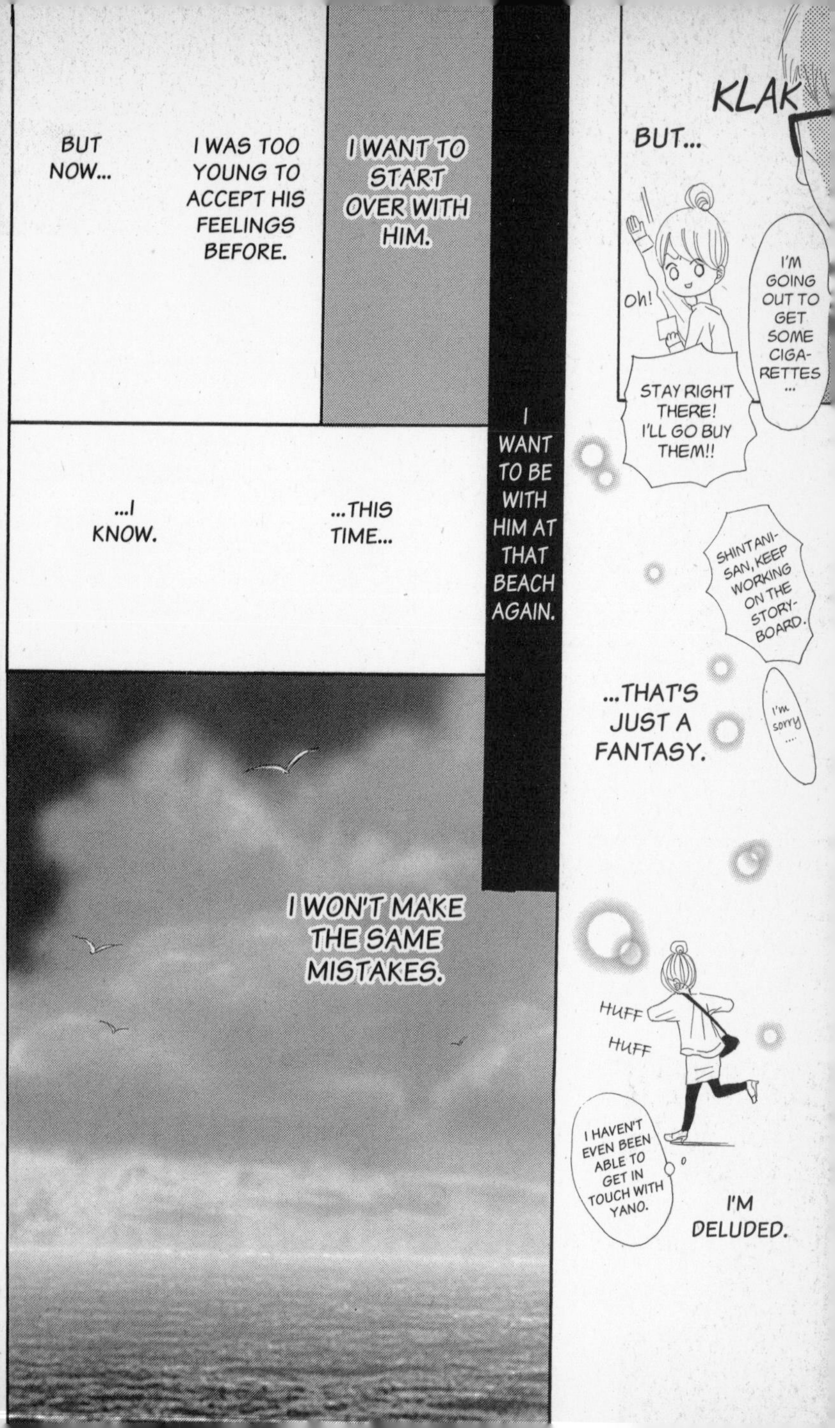
KLAK
I'M GOING OUT TO GET SOME CIGARETTES...
BUT...
Oh!
STAY RIGHT THERE! I'LL GO BUY THEM!!
SHINTANI-SAN, KEEP WORKING ON THE STORYBOARD.
I'm sorry....
...THAT'S JUST A FANTASY.
HUFF
HUFF
I HAVEN'T EVEN BEEN ABLE TO GET IN TOUCH WITH YANO.
I'M DELUDED.
I WANT TO BE WITH HIM AT THAT BEACH AGAIN.
I WANT TO START OVER WITH HIM.
I WAS TOO YOUNG TO ACCEPT HIS FEELINGS BEFORE.
BUT NOW...
...THIS TIME...
...I KNOW.
I WON'T MAKE THE SAME MISTAKES.

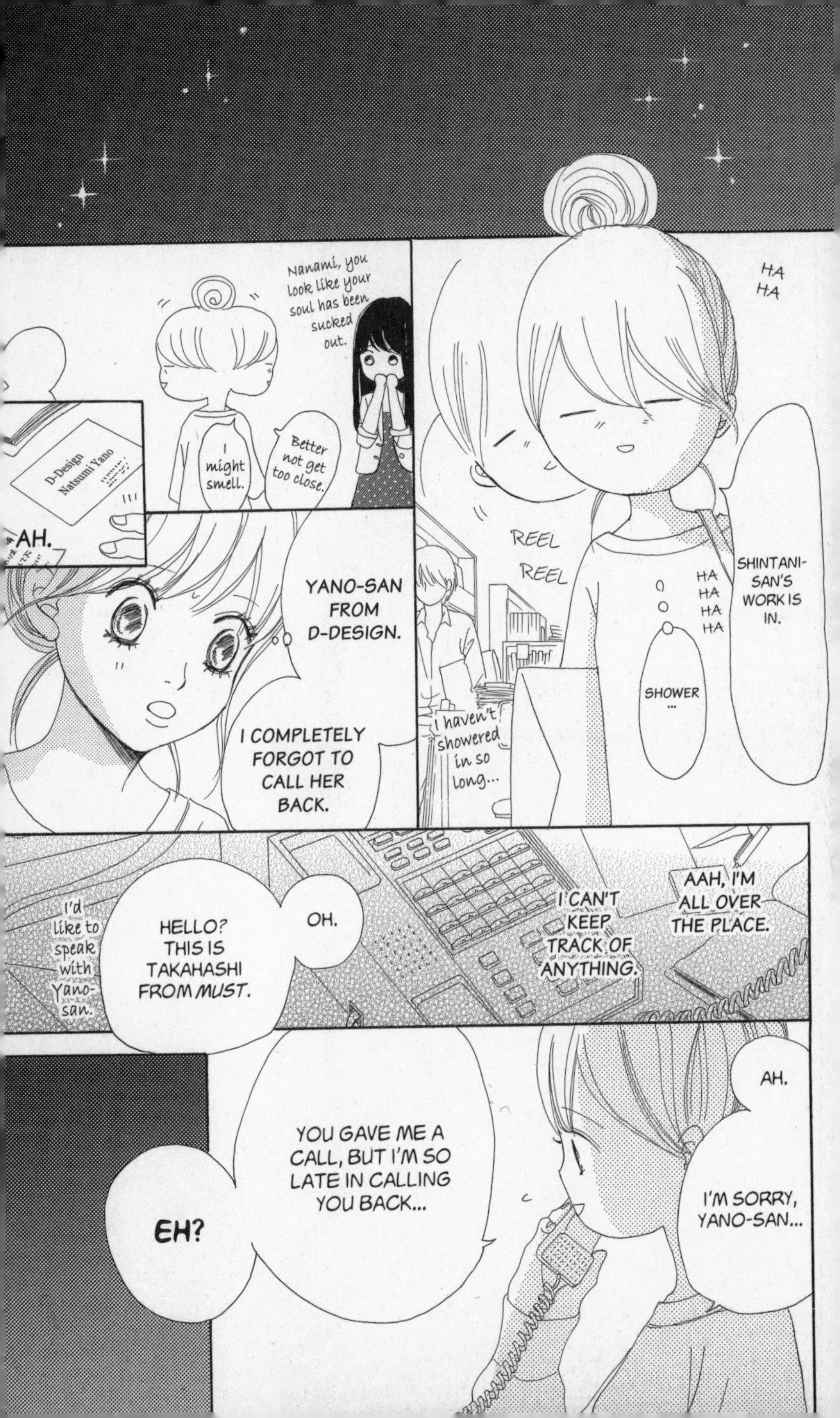
HA HA
SHINTANI-SAN'S WORK IS IN.
HA HA HA HA
SHOWER...
REEL REEL
I haven't showered in so long...
Nanami, you look like your soul has been sucked out.
Better not get too close.
I might smell.
D-Design Natsumi Yano
AH.
YANO-SAN FROM D-DESIGN.
I COMPLETELY FORGOT TO CALL HER BACK.
AAH, I'M ALL OVER THE PLACE.
I CAN'T KEEP TRACK OF ANYTHING.
OH.
HELLO? THIS IS TAKAHASHI FROM MUST.
I'd like to speak with Yano-san.
AH.
I'M SORRY, YANO-SAN...
YOU GAVE ME A CALL, BUT I'M SO LATE IN CALLING YOU BACK...
EH?

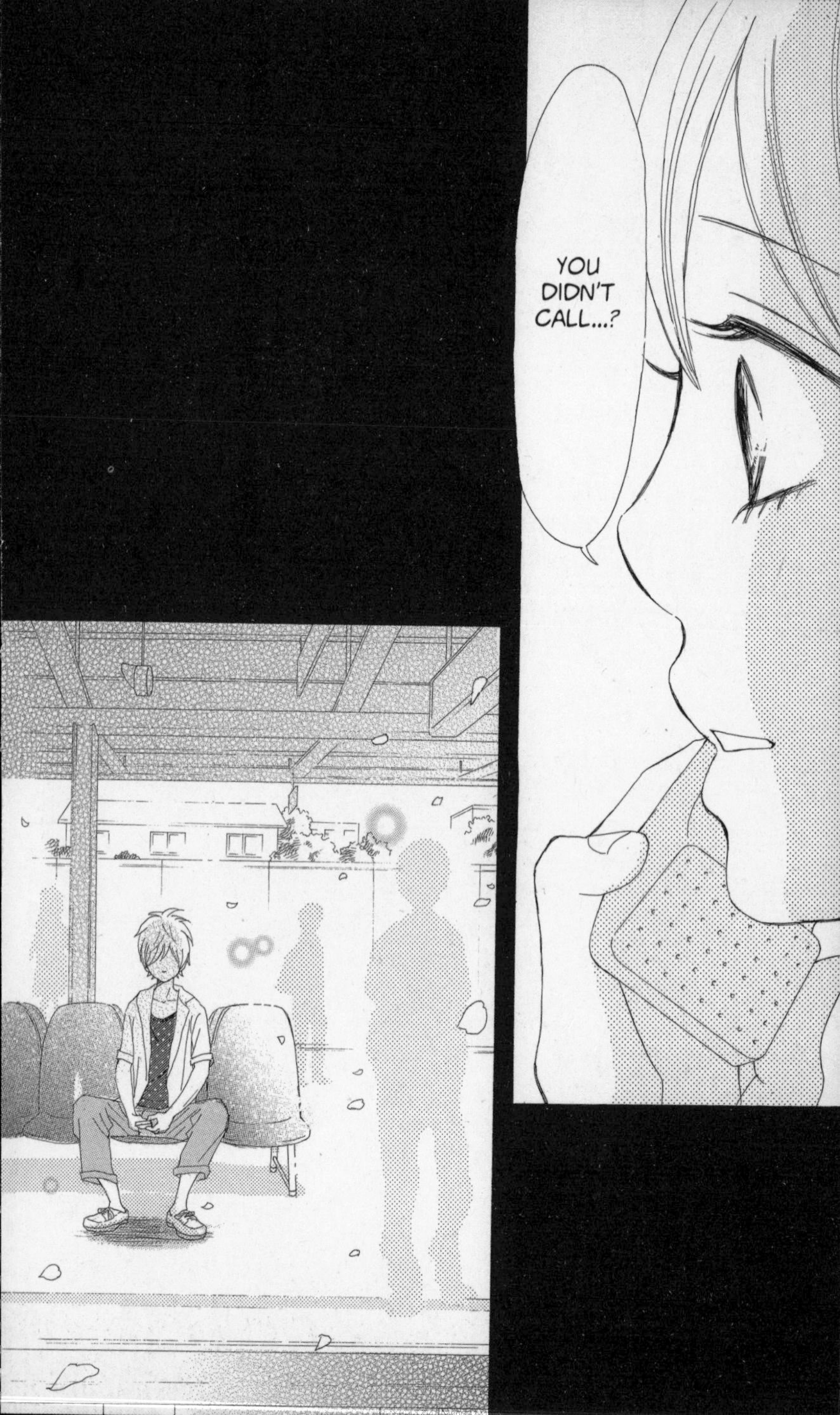
YOU DIDN'T CALL...?

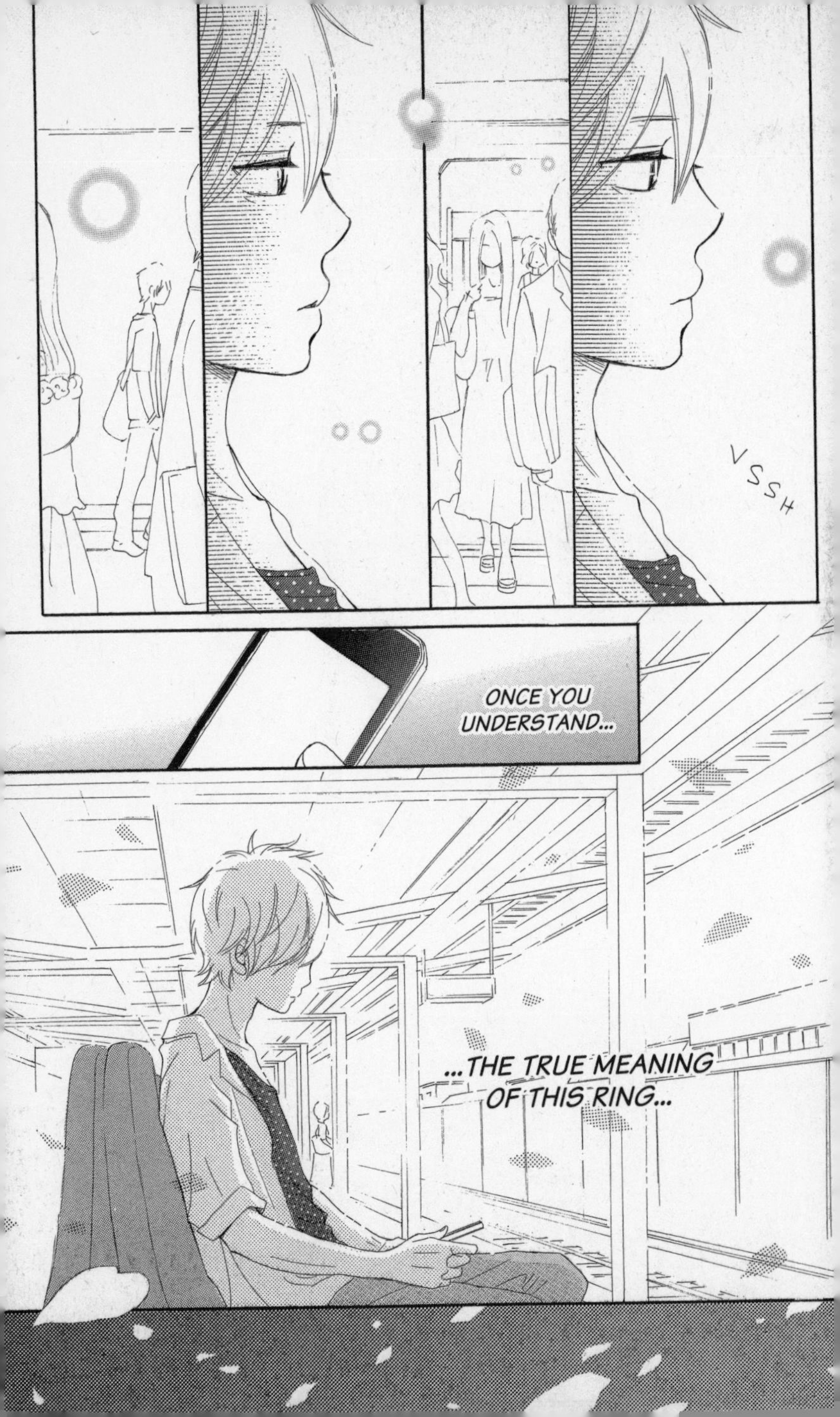
VSSH
ONCE YOU UNDERSTAND...
...THE TRUE MEANING OF THIS RING...

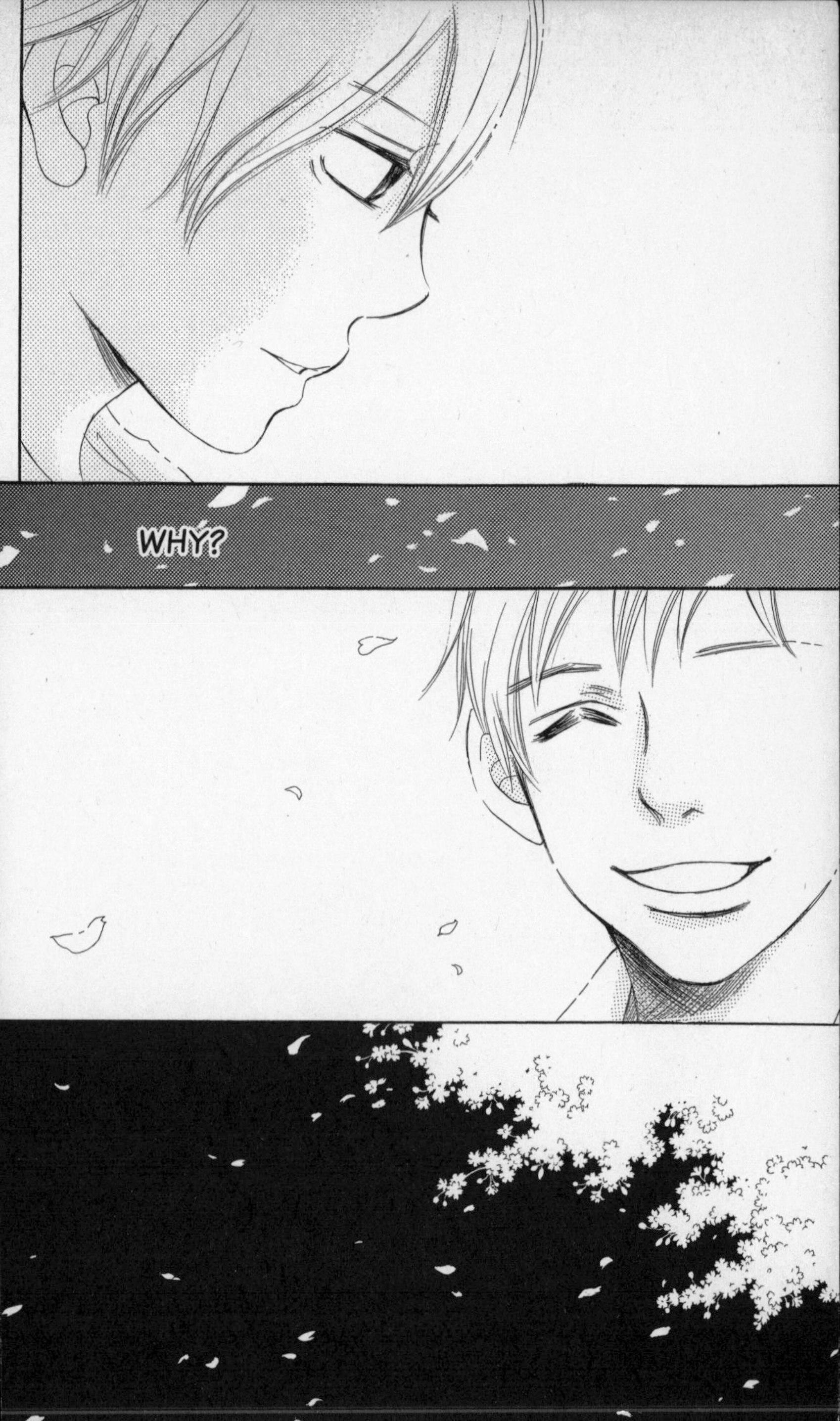
WHY?

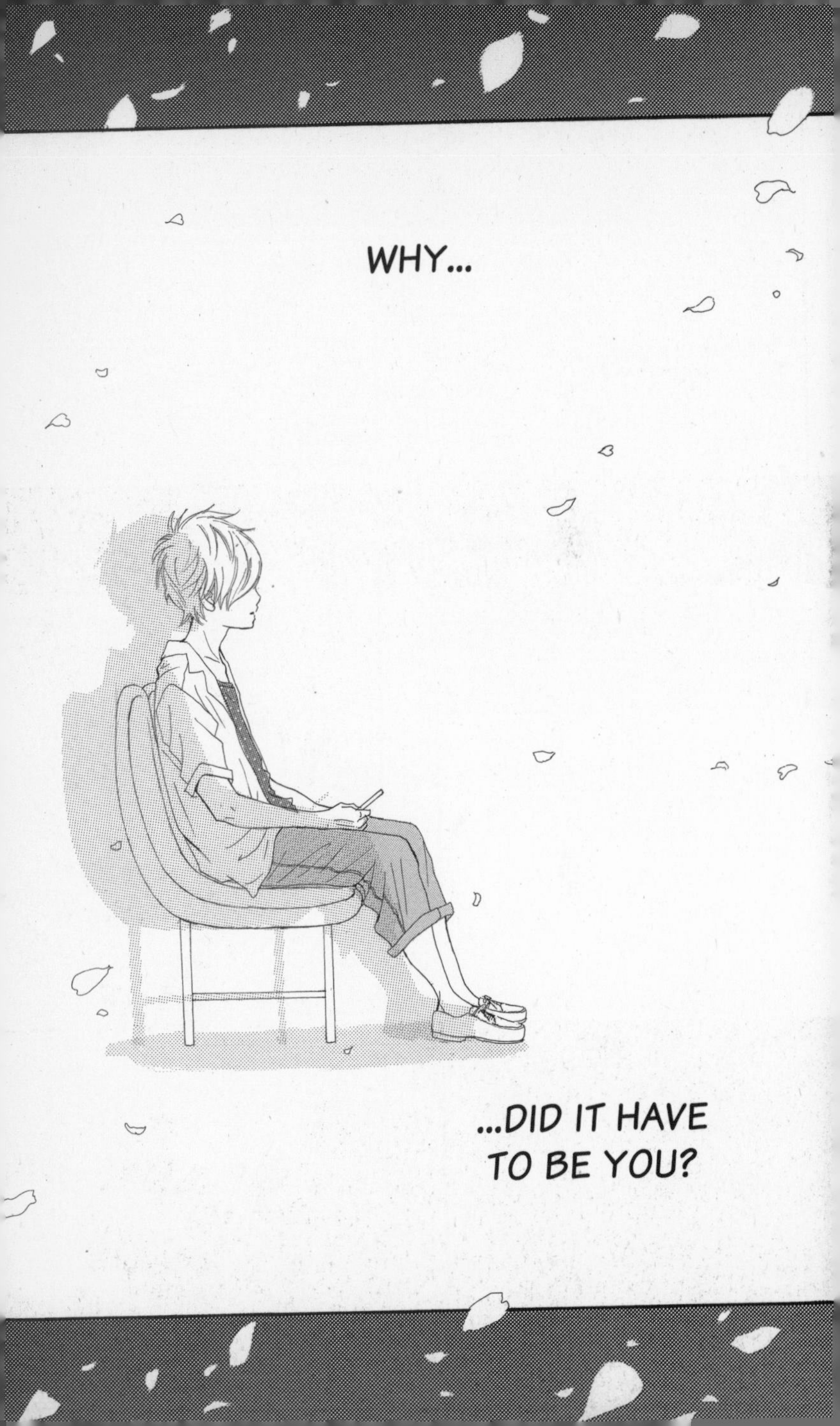
WHY...
...DID IT HAVE TO BE YOU?

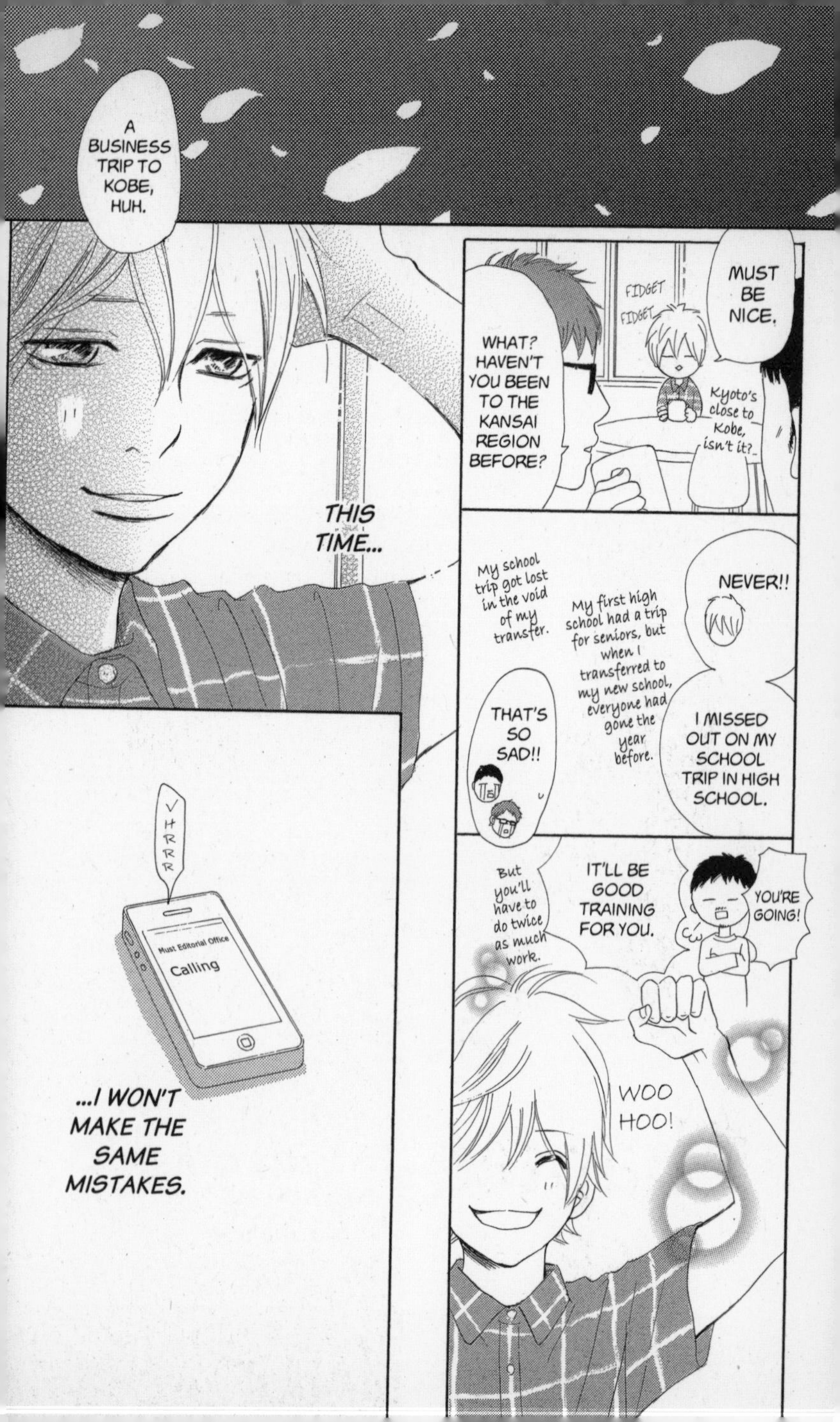
A BUSINESS TRIP TO KOBE, HUH.
MUST BE NICE.
FIDGET FIDGET
Kyoto's close to Kobe, isn't it?
WHAT? HAVEN'T YOU BEEN TO THE KANSAI REGION BEFORE?
NEVER!!
I MISSED OUT ON MY SCHOOL TRIP IN HIGH SCHOOL.
My first high school had a trip for seniors, but when I transferred to my new school, everyone had gone the year before.
My school trip got lost in the void of my transfer.
THAT'S SO SAD!!
YOU'RE GOING!
IT'LL BE GOOD TRAINING FOR YOU.
But you'll have to do twice as much work.
WOO HOO!
THIS TIME...
VHRRR
Must Editorial Office
Calling
...I WON'T MAKE THE SAME MISTAKES.

Seriously?

Only three more chapters!

Chapter 68

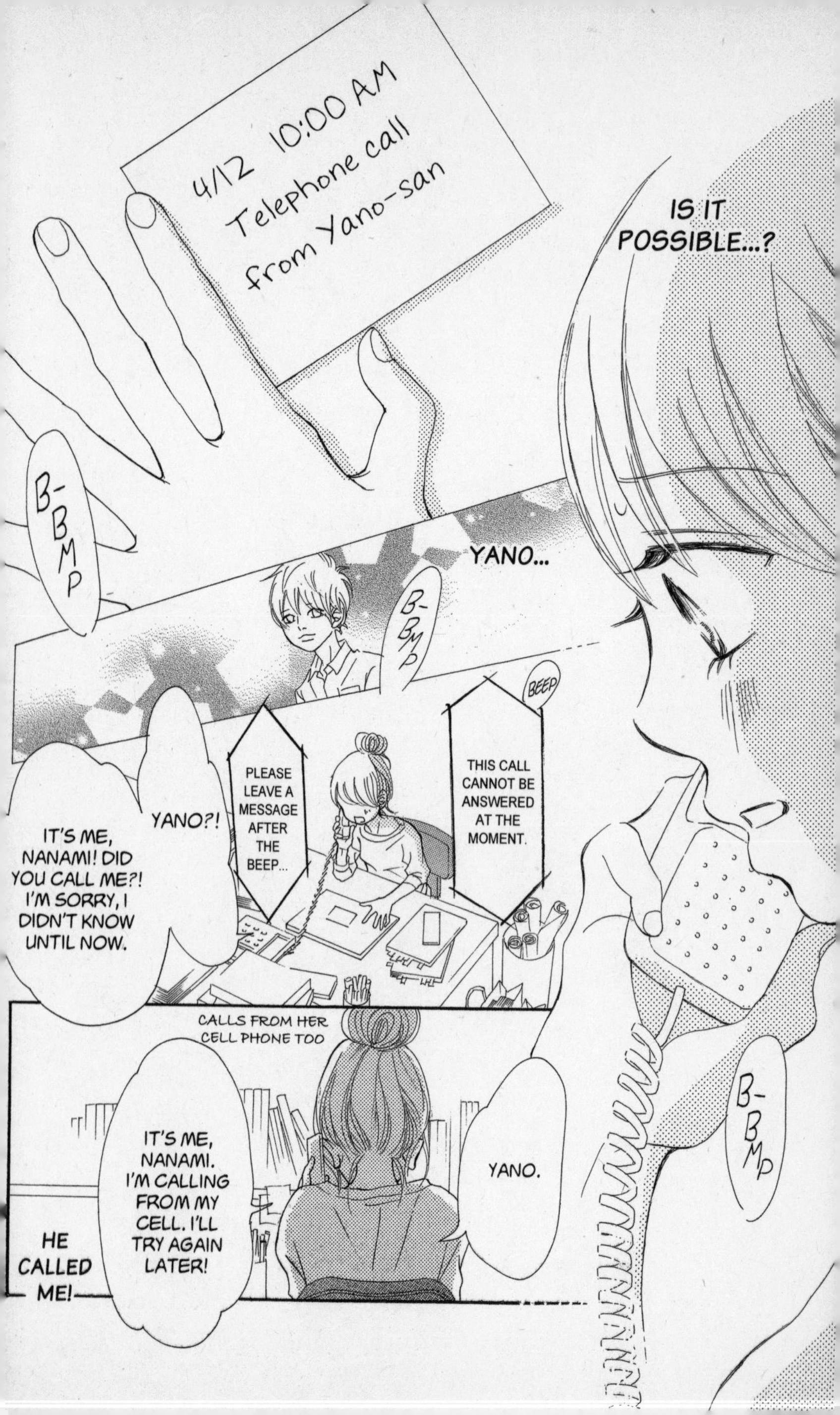
4/12 10:00 AM Telephone call from Yano-san
B-BMP
IS IT POSSIBLE...?
YANO...
B-BMP
BEEP
THIS CALL CANNOT BE ANSWERED AT THE MOMENT.
PLEASE LEAVE A MESSAGE AFTER THE BEEP...
YANO?!
IT'S ME, NANAMI! DID YOU CALL ME?! I'M SORRY, I DIDN'T KNOW UNTIL NOW.
B-BMP
YANO.
CALLS FROM HER CELL PHONE TOO
IT'S ME, NANAMI. I'M CALLING FROM MY CELL. I'LL TRY AGAIN LATER!
HE CALLED ME!

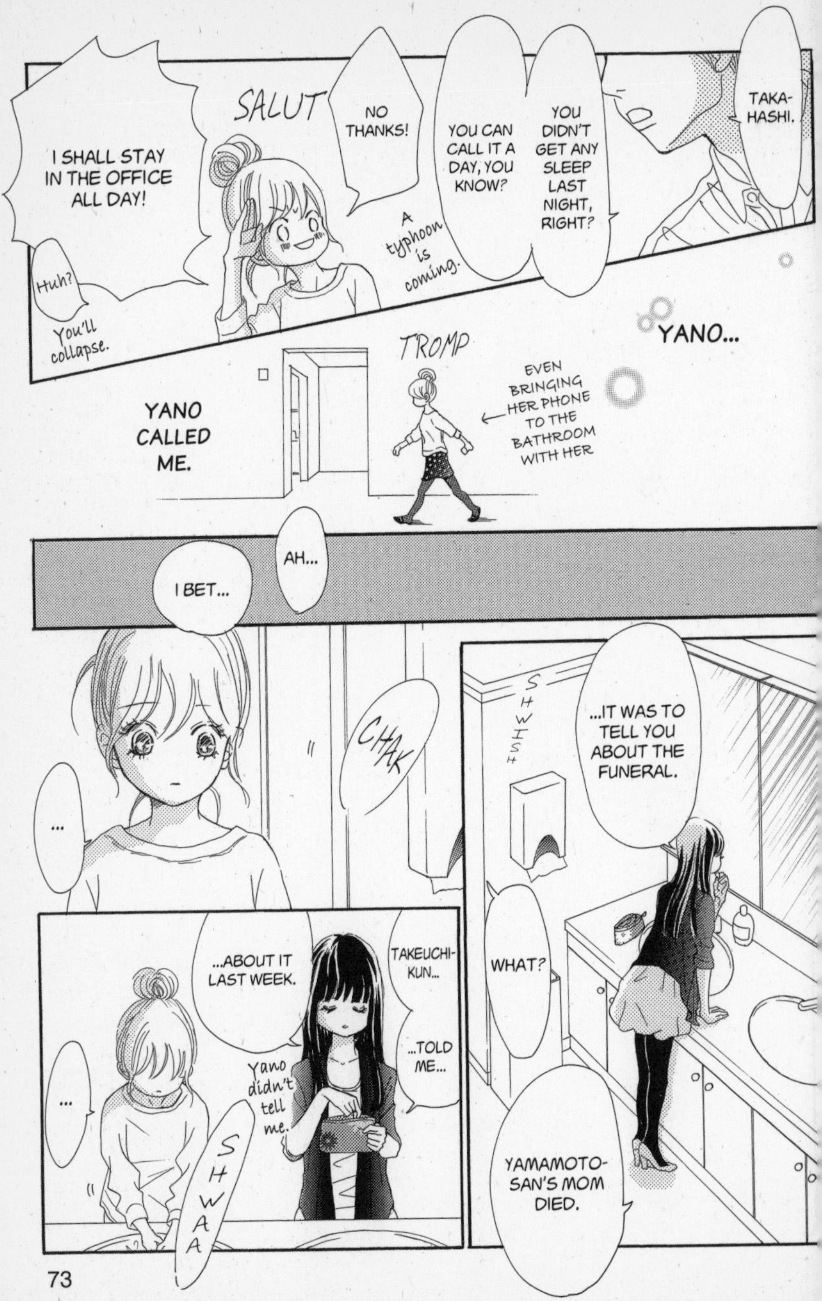
TAKA-HASHI.
YOU DIDN'T GET ANY SLEEP LAST NIGHT, RIGHT?
YOU CAN CALL IT A DAY, YOU KNOW?
A typhoon is coming.
NO THANKS!
SALUT
I SHALL STAY IN THE OFFICE ALL DAY!
Huh?
You'll collapse.
YANO...
EVEN BRINGING HER PHONE TO THE BATHROOM WITH HER
TROMP
YANO CALLED ME.
AH...
I BET...
...IT WAS TO TELL YOU ABOUT THE FUNERAL.
SHWISH
WHAT?
YAMAMOTO-SAN'S MOM DIED.
CHAK
...
TAKEUCHI-KUN...
...TOLD ME...
...ABOUT IT LAST WEEK.
Yano didn't tell me.
SHWAA
...

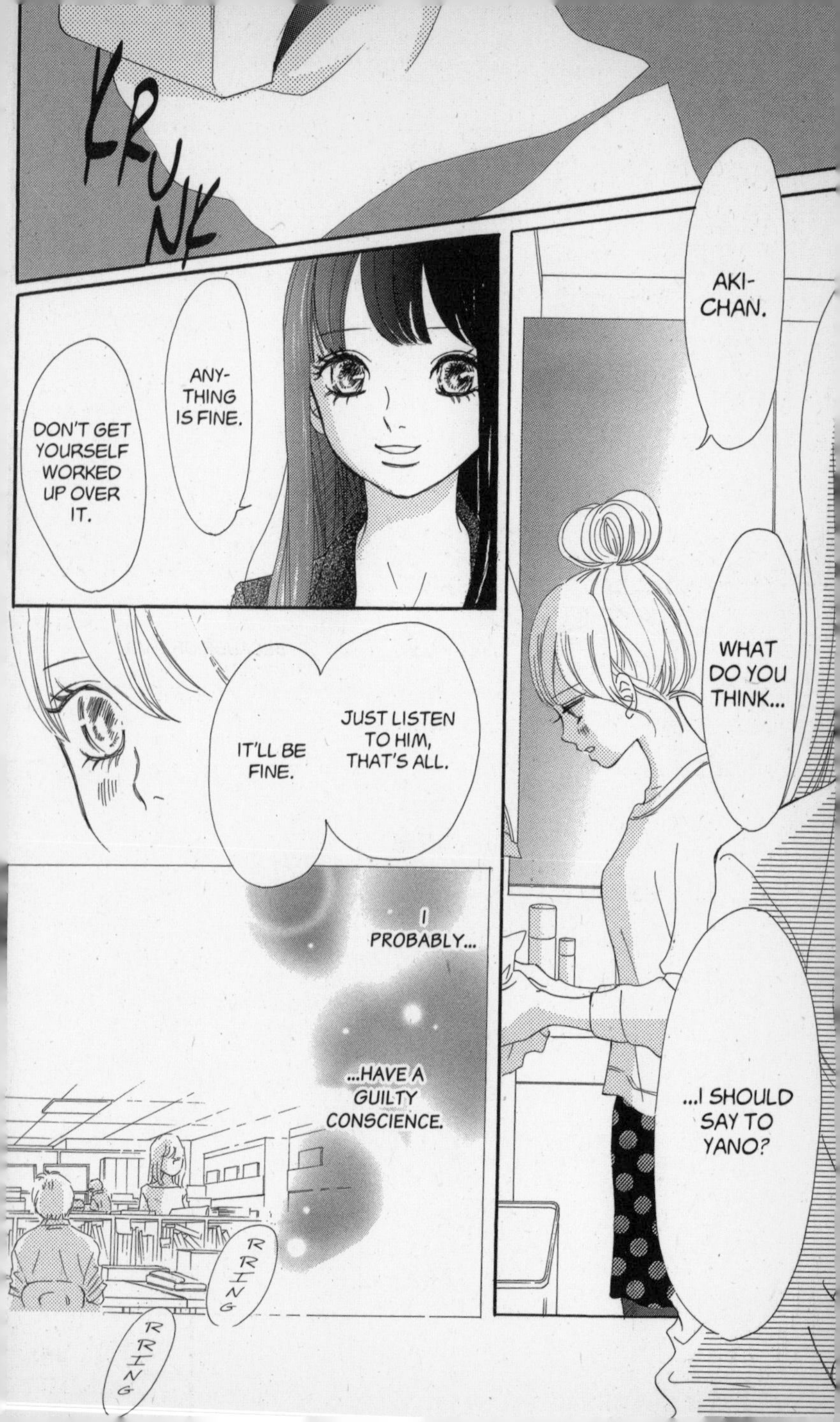
KRUNK
AKI-CHAN.
WHAT DO YOU THINK...
...I SHOULD SAY TO YANO?
ANY-THING IS FINE.
DON'T GET YOURSELF WORKED UP OVER IT.
JUST LISTEN TO HIM, THAT'S ALL.
IT'LL BE FINE.
I PROBABLY...
...HAVE A GUILTY CONSCIENCE.
RRING
RRING

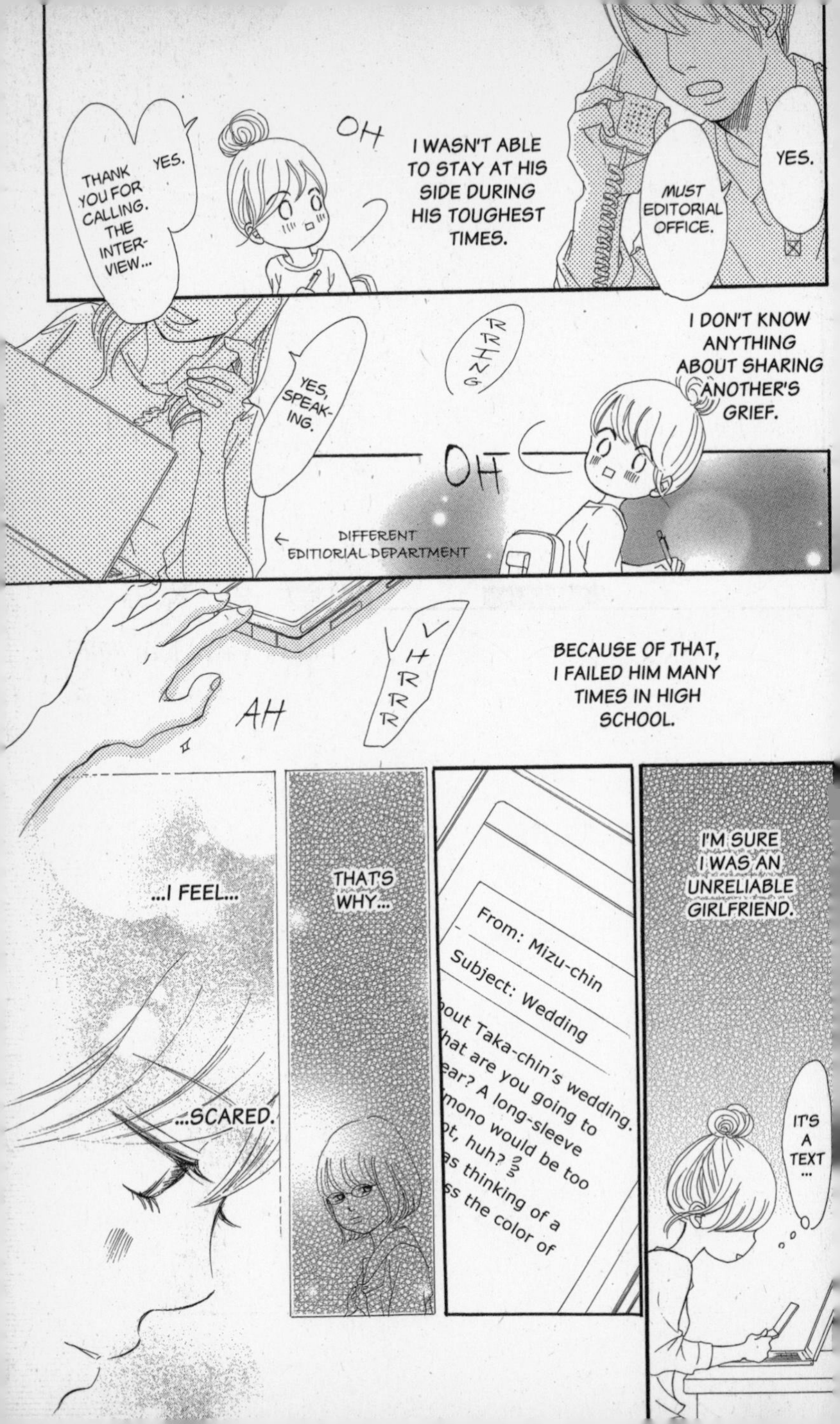
YES.
MUST EDITORIAL OFFICE.
I WASN'T ABLE TO STAY AT HIS SIDE DURING HIS TOUGHEST TIMES.
OH
YES.
THANK YOU FOR CALLING. THE INTER-VIEW...
I DON'T KNOW ANYTHING ABOUT SHARING ANOTHER'S GRIEF.
OH
RRING
YES, SPEAK-ING.
← DIFFERENT EDITIORIAL DEPARTMENT
BECAUSE OF THAT, I FAILED HIM MANY TIMES IN HIGH SCHOOL.
VHRRR
AH
I'M SURE I WAS AN UNRELIABLE GIRLFRIEND.
IT'S A TEXT...
From: Mizu-chin
Subject: Wedding
bout Taka-chin's wedding.
hat are you going to
ear? A long-sleeve
mono would be too
ot, huh?
as thinking of a
ss the color of
THAT'S WHY...
...I FEEL...
...SCARED.

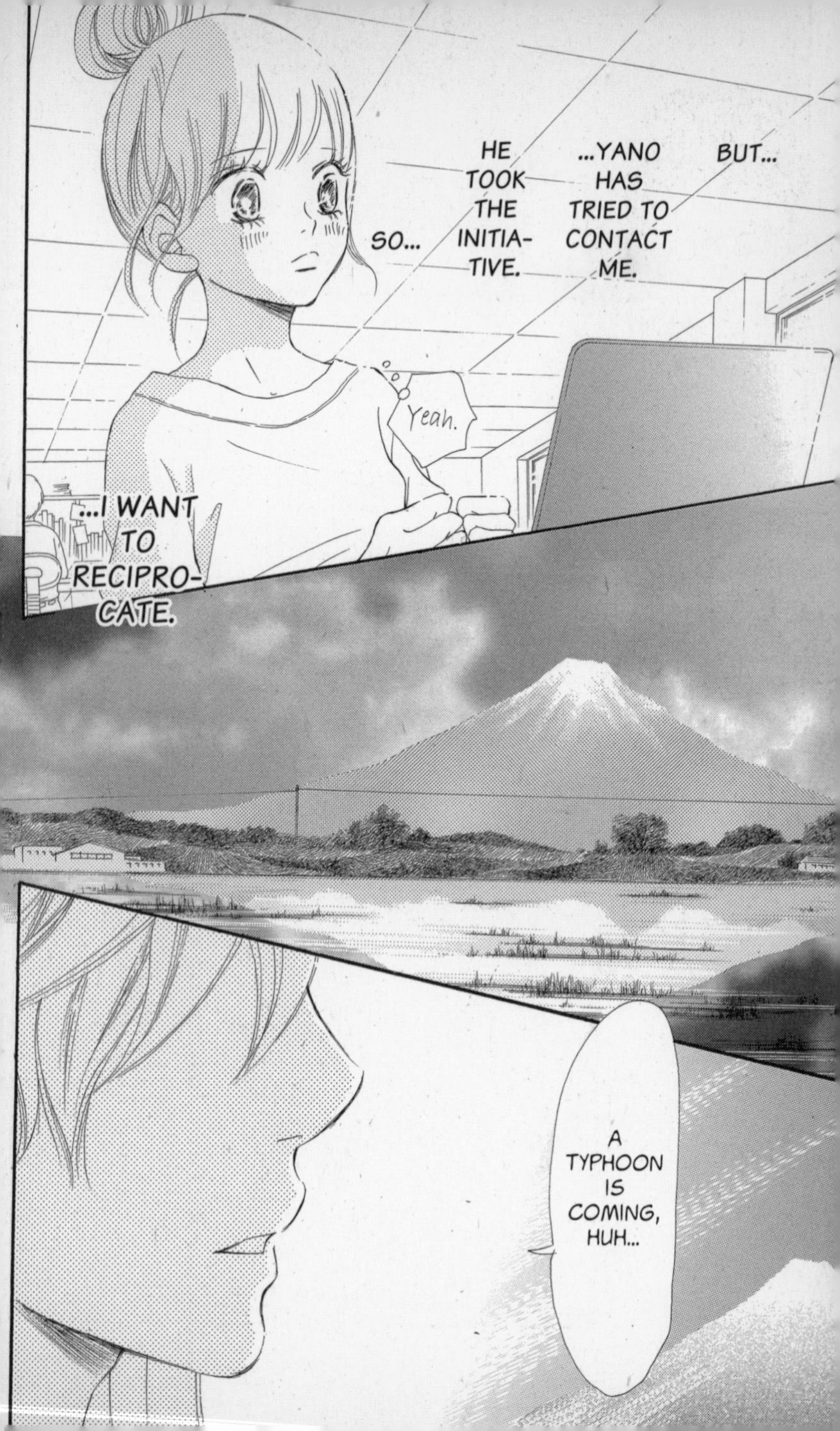
BUT...
...YANO HAS TRIED TO CONTACT ME.
HE TOOK THE INITIA-TIVE.
SO...
Yeah.
...I WANT TO RECIPRO-CATE.
A TYPHOON IS COMING, HUH...

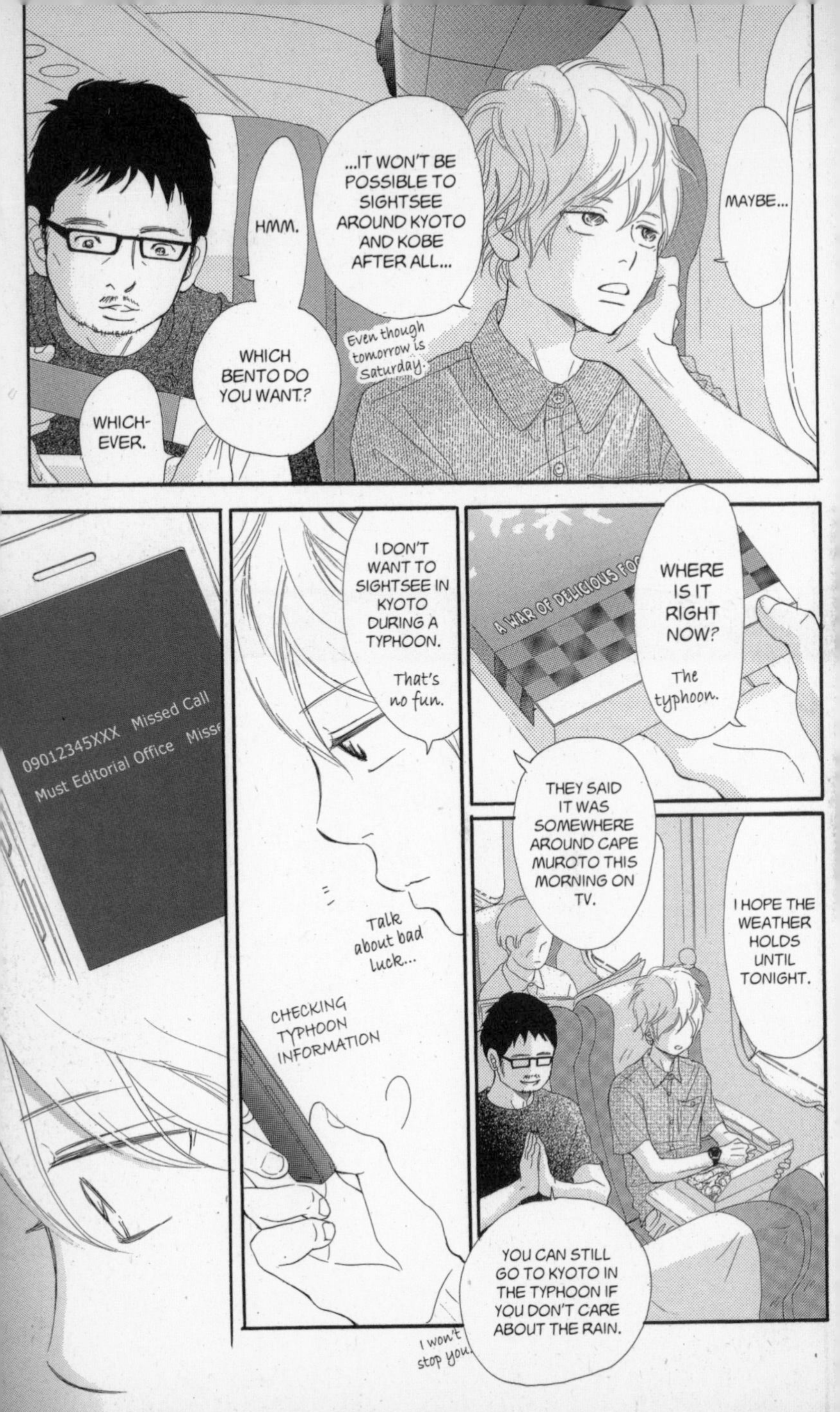
MAYBE...
...IT WON'T BE POSSIBLE TO SIGHTSEE AROUND KYOTO AND KOBE AFTER ALL...
Even though tomorrow is Saturday.
HMM.
WHICH BENTO DO YOU WANT?
WHICH-EVER.
WHERE IS IT RIGHT NOW?
The typhoon.
A WAR OF DELICIOUS FO
THEY SAID IT WAS SOMEWHERE AROUND CAPE MUROTO THIS MORNING ON TV.
I HOPE THE WEATHER HOLDS UNTIL TONIGHT.
YOU CAN STILL GO TO KYOTO IN THE TYPHOON IF YOU DON'T CARE ABOUT THE RAIN.
I won't stop you.
I DON'T WANT TO SIGHTSEE IN KYOTO DURING A TYPHOON.
That's no fun.
Talk about bad luck...
CHECKING TYPHOON INFORMATION
09012345XXX Missed Call
Must Editorial Office

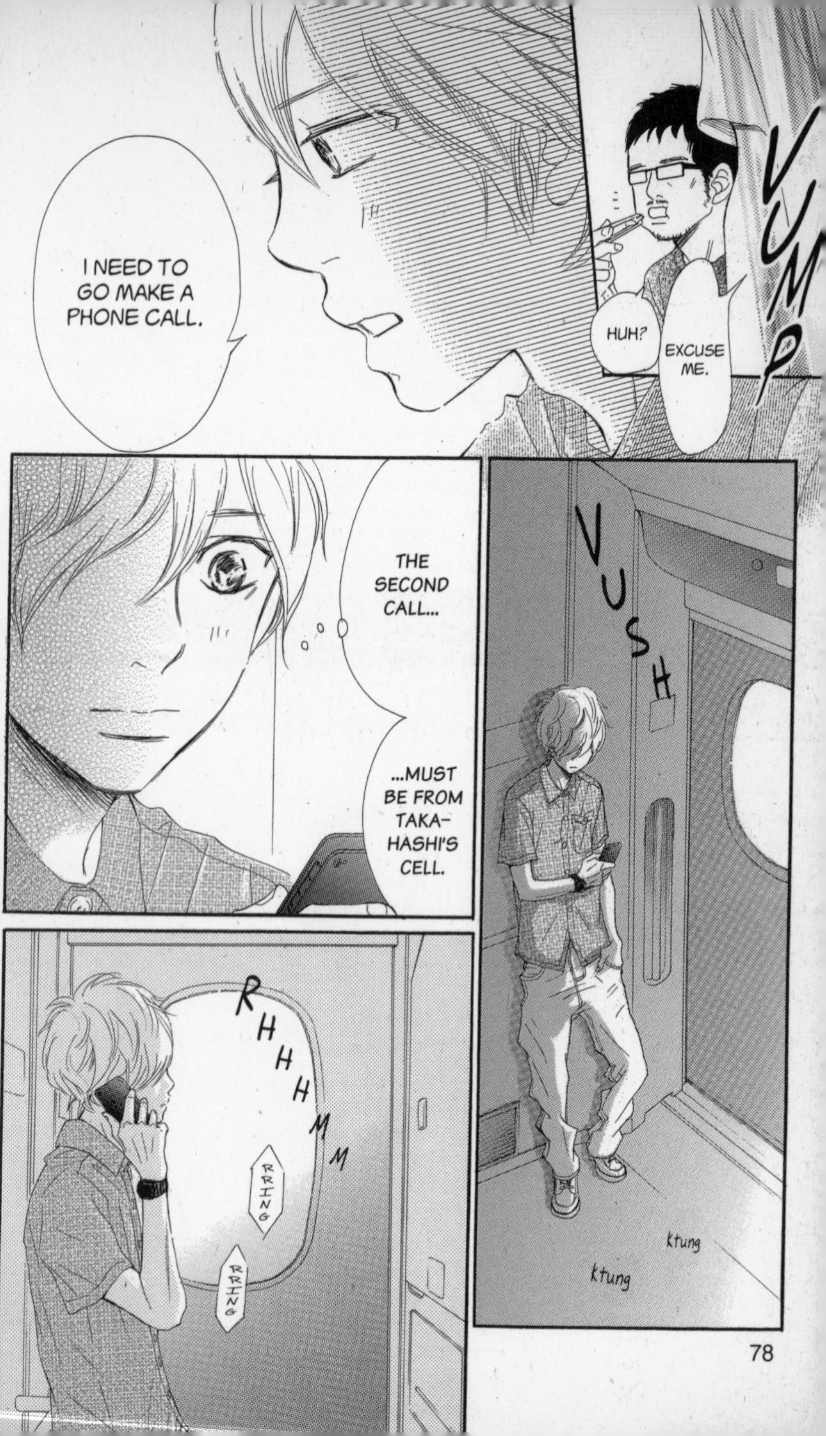
VUMP
HUH?
EXCUSE ME.
I NEED TO GO MAKE A PHONE CALL.
VUSH
ktung
ktung
THE SECOND CALL...
...MUST BE FROM TAKA-HASHI'S CELL.
RHHHMM
RRING
RRING

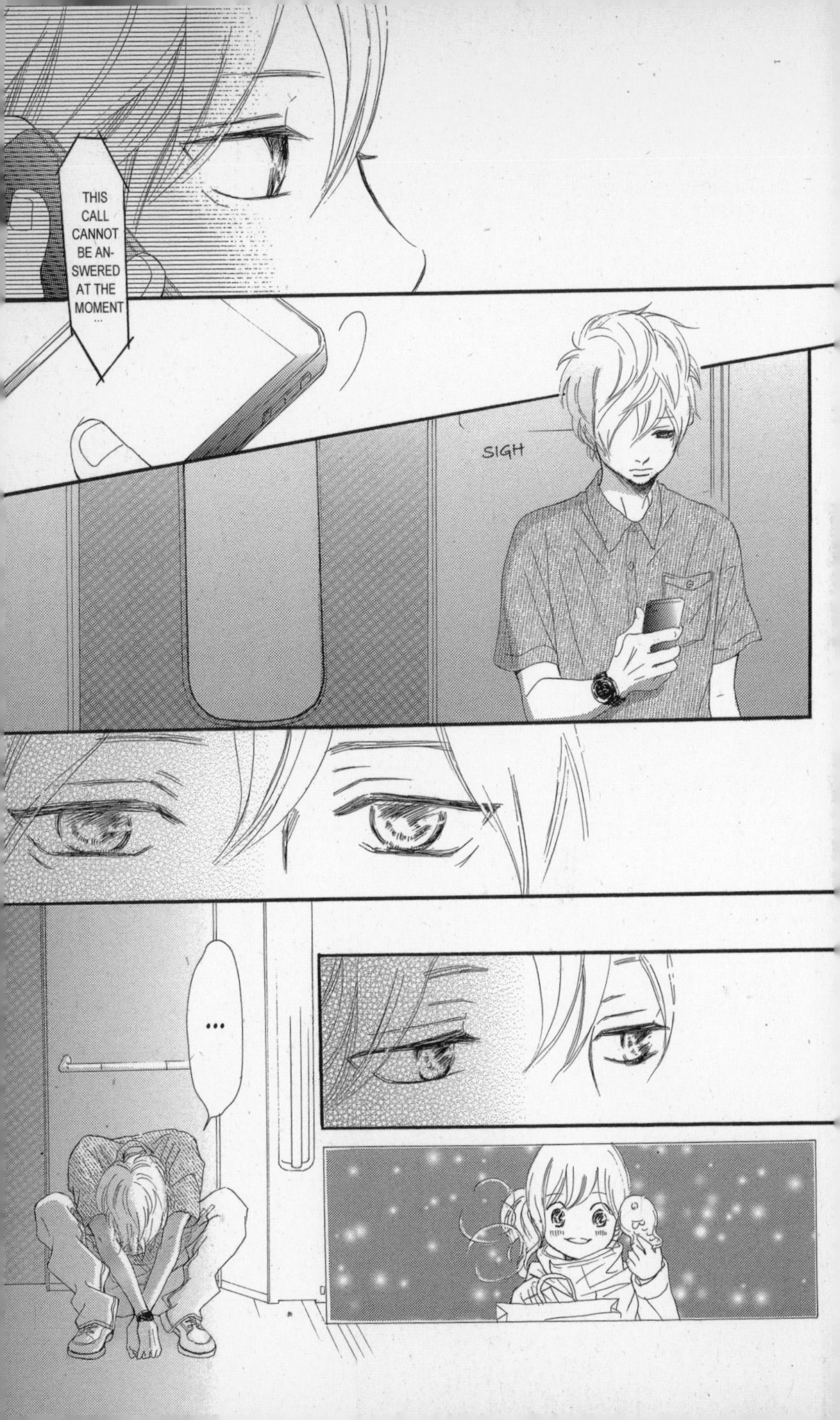
THIS CALL CANNOT BE AN-SWERED AT THE MOMENT ...
SIGH
...

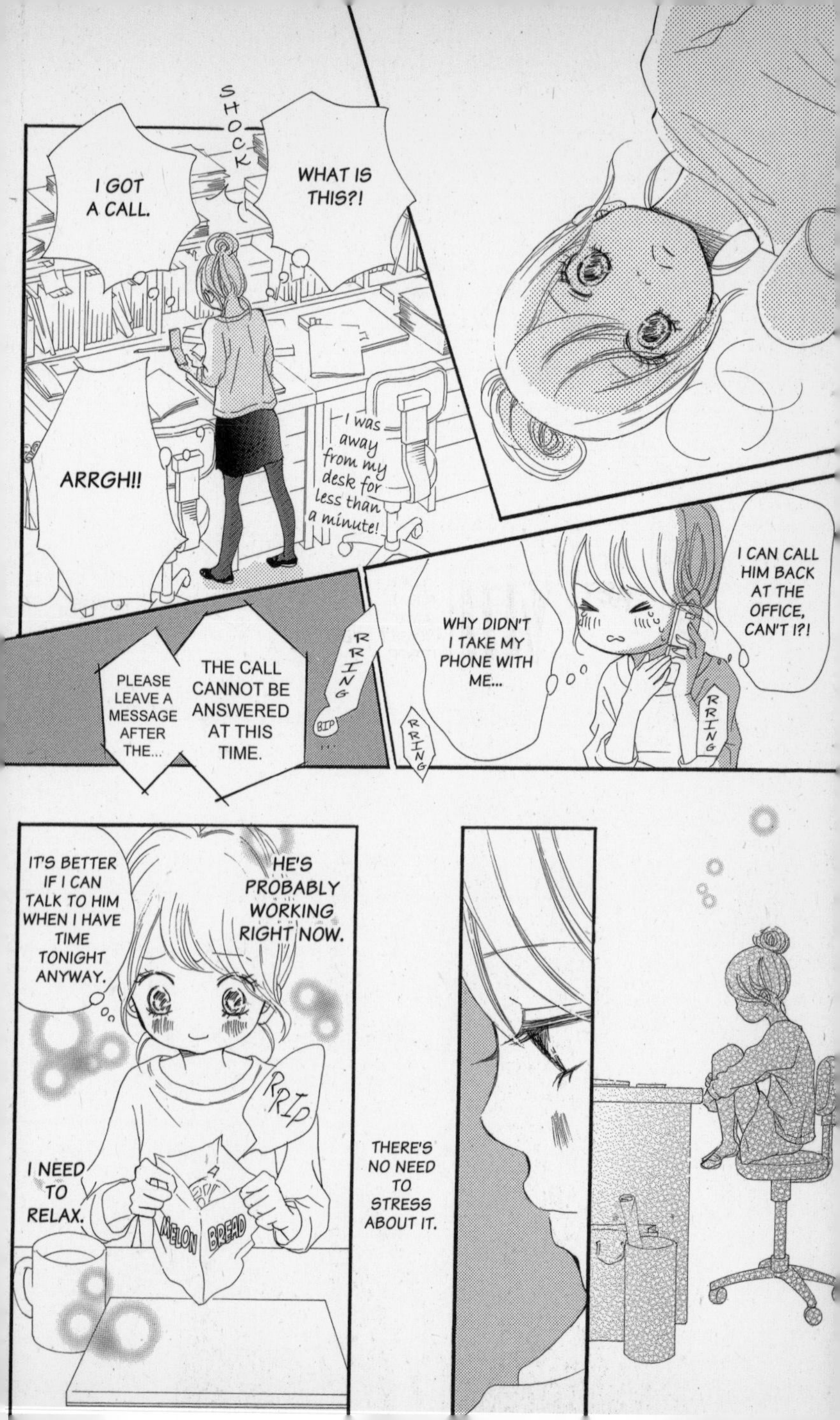
SHOCK
WHAT IS THIS?!
I GOT A CALL.
I was away from my desk for less than a minute!
ARRGH!!
I CAN CALL HIM BACK AT THE OFFICE, CAN'T I?!
RRING
WHY DIDN'T I TAKE MY PHONE WITH ME...
RRING
RRING
BIP
THE CALL CANNOT BE ANSWERED AT THIS TIME.
PLEASE LEAVE A MESSAGE AFTER THE...
THERE'S NO NEED TO STRESS ABOUT IT.
HE'S PROBABLY WORKING RIGHT NOW.
IT'S BETTER IF I CAN TALK TO HIM WHEN I HAVE TIME TONIGHT ANYWAY.
RRIP
I NEED TO RELAX.
MELON BREAD

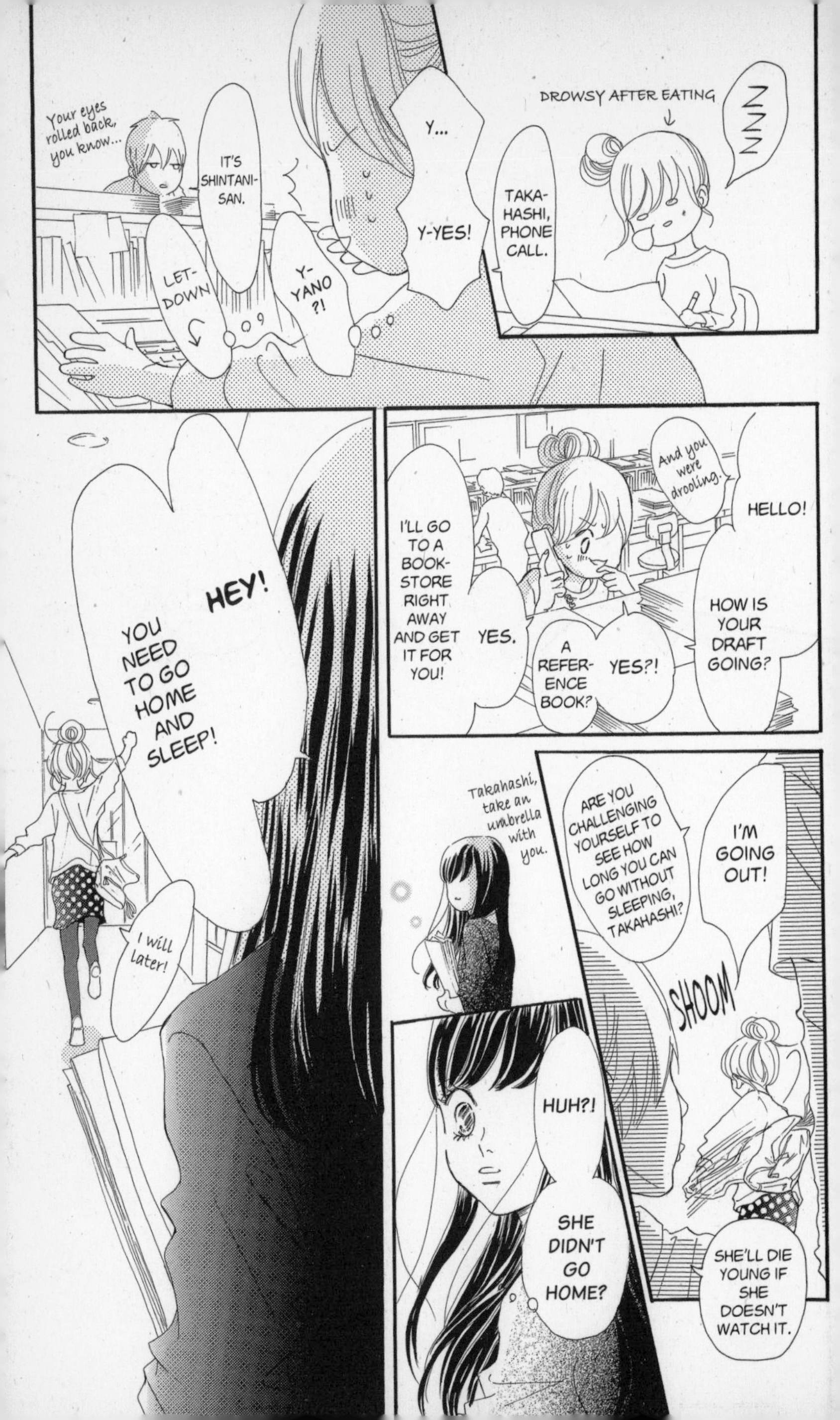
DROWSY AFTER EATING
ZZZ
TAKAHASHI, PHONE CALL.
Y-YES!
Y...
Y-YANO?!
IT'S SHINTANI-SAN.
LET-DOWN
Your eyes rolled back, you know...
HELLO!
And you were drooling.
HOW IS YOUR DRAFT GOING?
YES?!
A REFERENCE BOOK?
YES.
I'LL GO TO A BOOKSTORE RIGHT AWAY AND GET IT FOR YOU!
I'M GOING OUT!
ARE YOU CHALLENGING YOURSELF TO SEE HOW LONG YOU CAN GO WITHOUT SLEEPING, TAKAHASHI?
Takahashi, take an umbrella with you.
SHOOM
SHE'LL DIE YOUNG IF SHE DOESN'T WATCH IT.
HUH?!
SHE DIDN'T GO HOME?
HEY!
YOU NEED TO GO HOME AND SLEEP!
I will later!

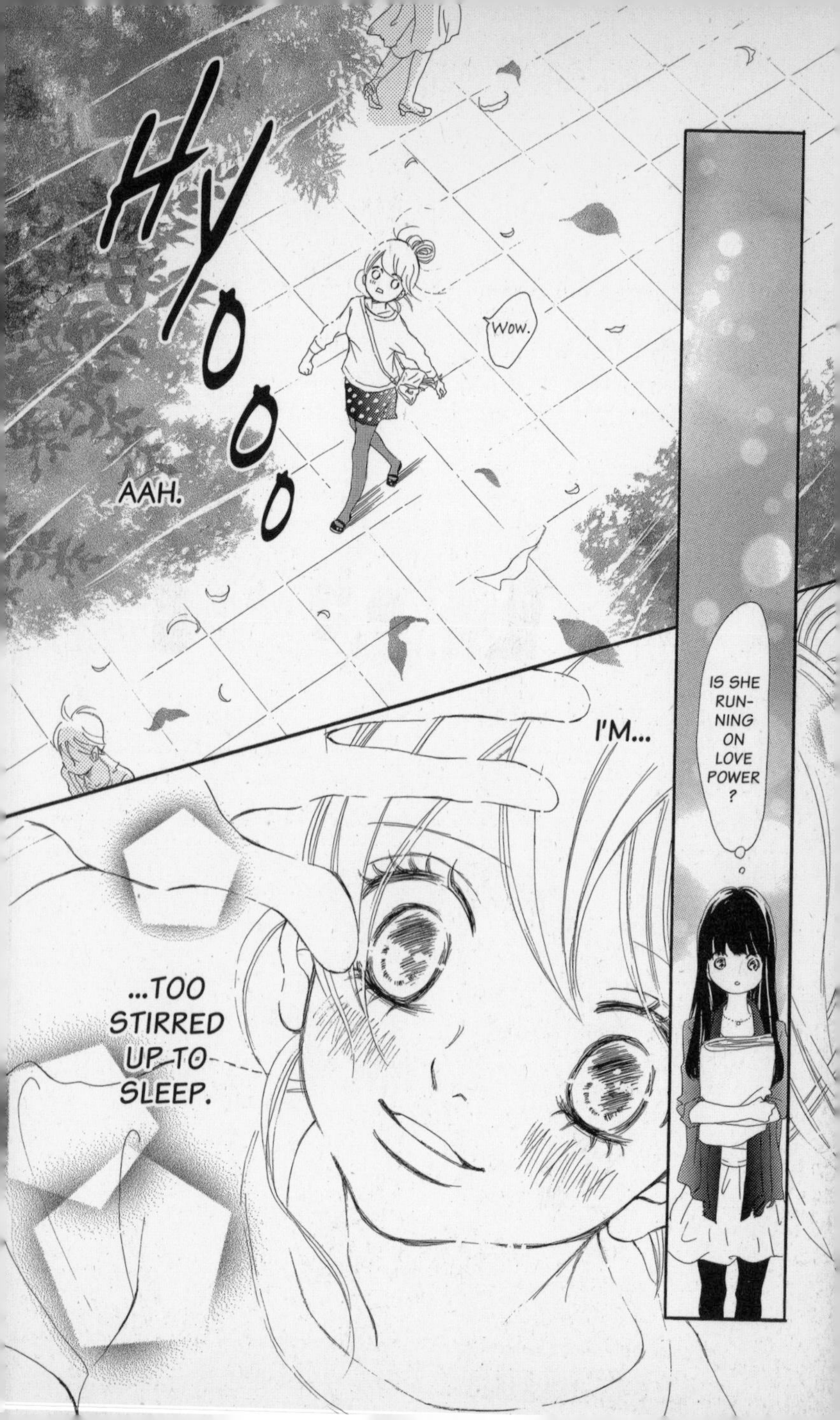
IS SHE RUNNING ON LOVE POWER?
HYOOOO
AAH.
Wow.
I'M...
...TOO STIRRED UP TO SLEEP.

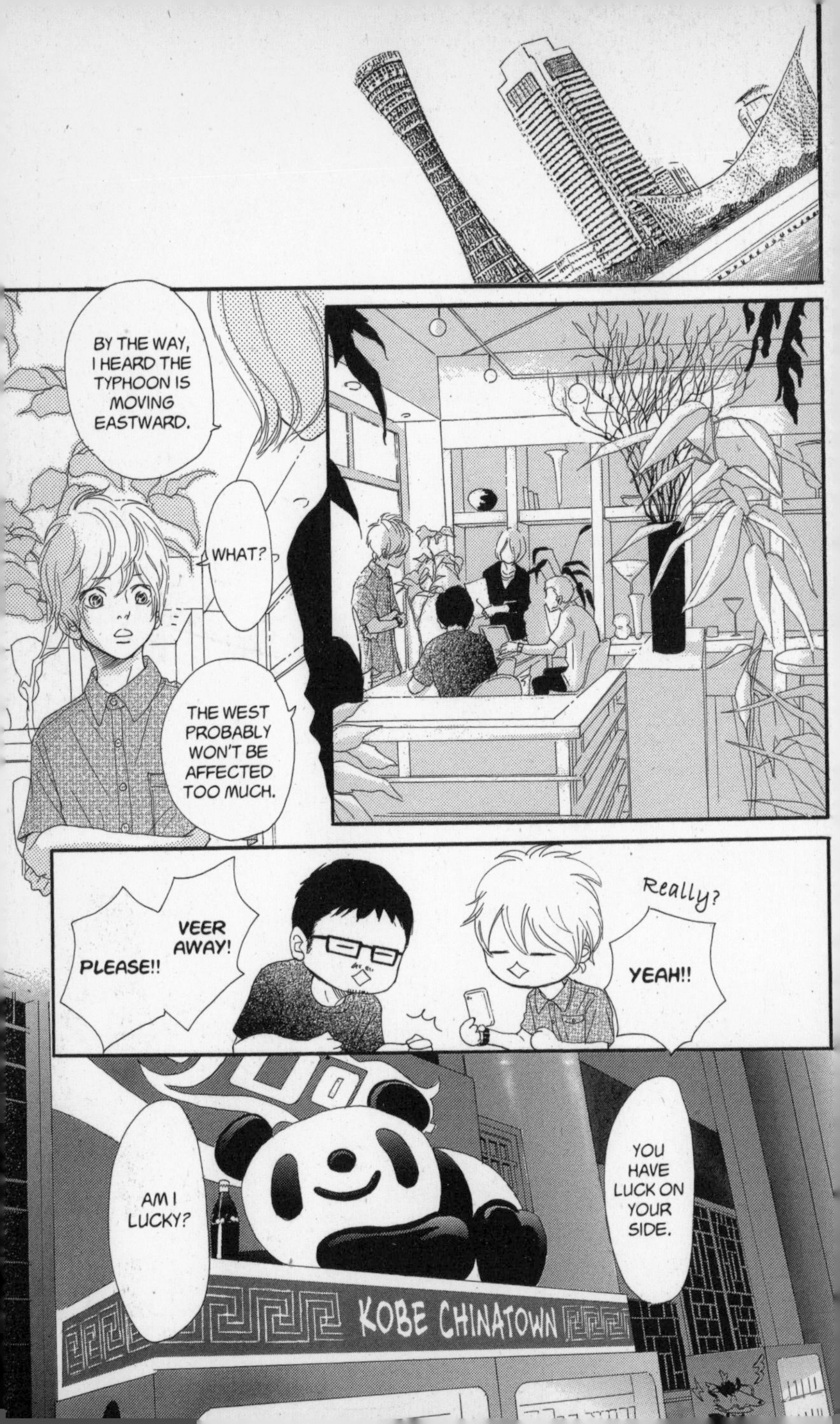
BY THE WAY, I HEARD THE TYPHOON IS MOVING EASTWARD.
WHAT?
THE WEST PROBABLY WON'T BE AFFECTED TOO MUCH.
Really?
YEAH!!
VEER AWAY!
PLEASE!!
YOU HAVE LUCK ON YOUR SIDE.
AM I LUCKY?
KOBE CHINATOWN

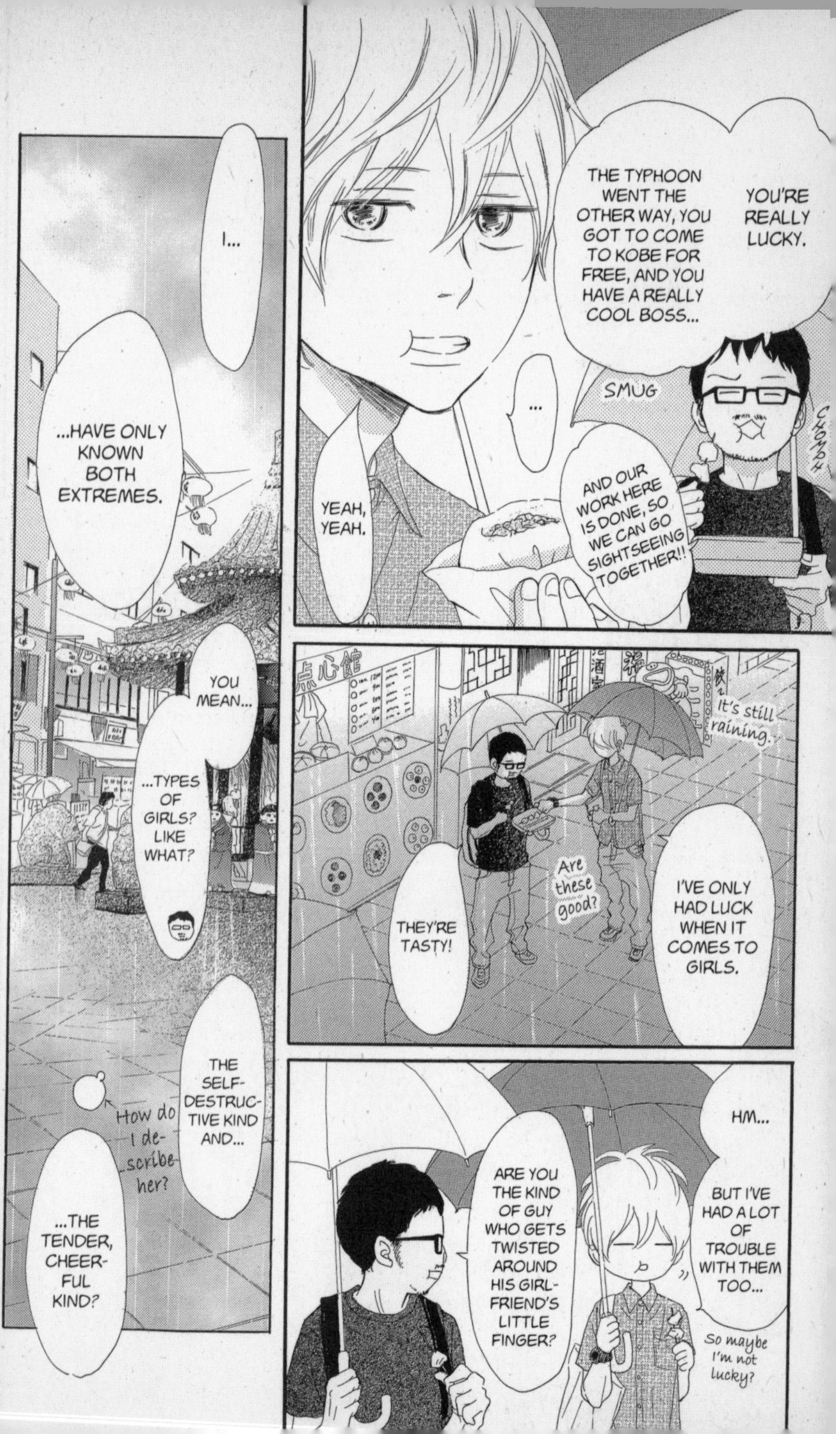
THE TYPHOON WENT THE OTHER WAY, YOU GOT TO COME TO KOBE FOR FREE, AND YOU HAVE A REALLY COOL BOSS...
YOU'RE REALLY LUCKY.
SMUG
CHOMP
AND OUR WORK HERE IS DONE, SO WE CAN GO SIGHTSEEING TOGETHER!!
...
YEAH, YEAH.
It's still raining.
I'VE ONLY HAD LUCK WHEN IT COMES TO GIRLS.
Are these good?
THEY'RE TASTY!
HM...
BUT I'VE HAD A LOT OF TROUBLE WITH THEM TOO...
So maybe I'm not lucky?
ARE YOU THE KIND OF GUY WHO GETS TWISTED AROUND HIS GIRLFRIEND'S LITTLE FINGER?
I...
...HAVE ONLY KNOWN BOTH EXTREMES.
YOU MEAN...
...TYPES OF GIRLS? LIKE WHAT?
THE SELF-DESTRUCTIVE KIND AND...
How do I describe her?
...THE TENDER, CHEERFUL KIND?

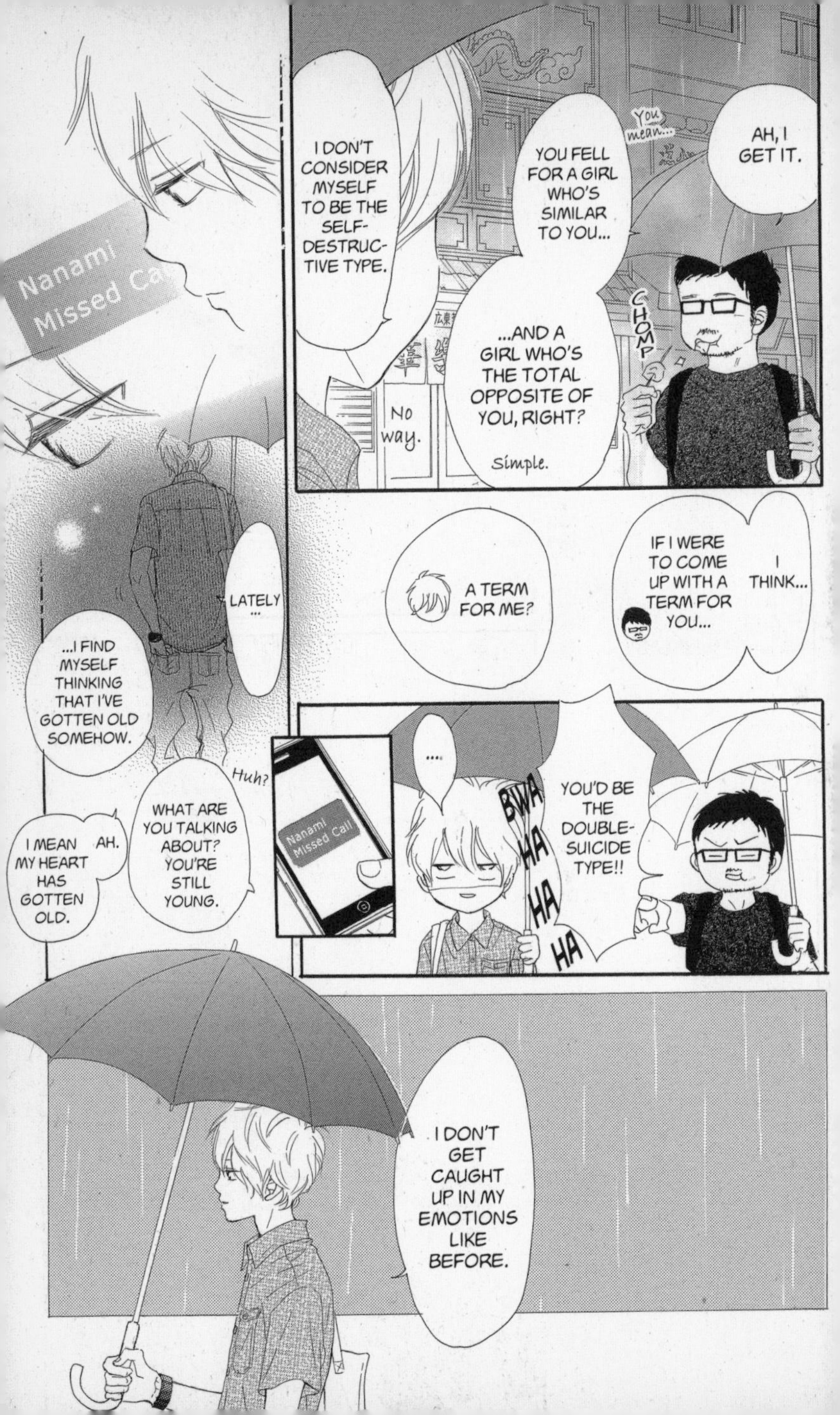
AH, I GET IT.
You mean...
YOU FELL FOR A GIRL WHO'S SIMILAR TO YOU...
CHOMP
...AND A GIRL WHO'S THE TOTAL OPPOSITE OF YOU, RIGHT?
Simple.
I DON'T CONSIDER MYSELF TO BE THE SELF-DESTRUCTIVE TYPE.
No way.
IF I WERE TO COME UP WITH A TERM FOR YOU... I THINK...
A TERM FOR ME?
YOU'D BE THE DOUBLE-SUICIDE TYPE!!
BWAHAHAHAHA
...
Nanami Missed Call
Nanami Missed Call
LATELY...
...I FIND MYSELF THINKING THAT I'VE GOTTEN OLD SOMEHOW.
Huh?
WHAT ARE YOU TALKING ABOUT? YOU'RE STILL YOUNG.
AH.
I MEAN MY HEART HAS GOTTEN OLD.
I DON'T GET CAUGHT UP IN MY EMOTIONS LIKE BEFORE.

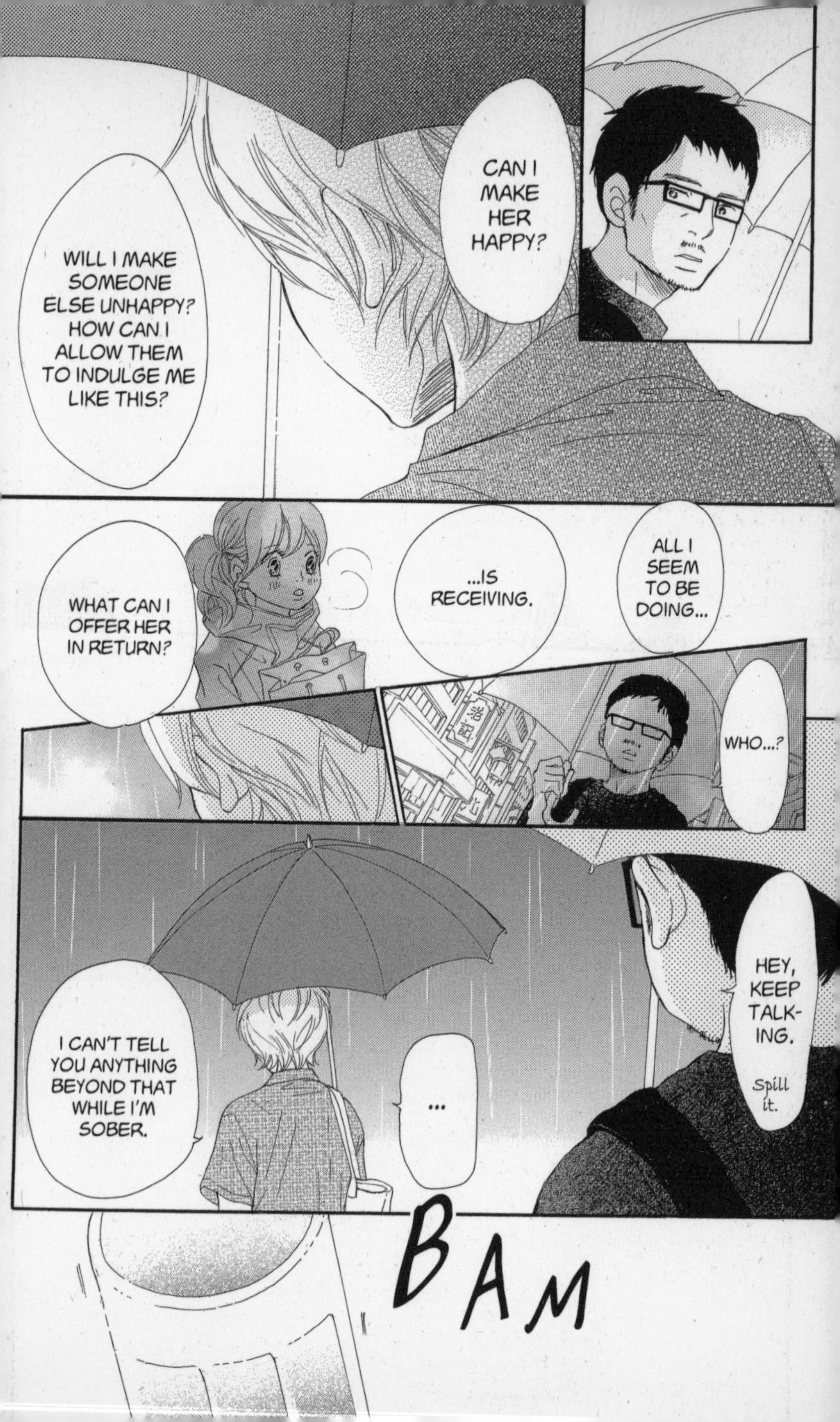
CAN I MAKE HER HAPPY?
WILL I MAKE SOMEONE ELSE UNHAPPY? HOW CAN I ALLOW THEM TO INDULGE ME LIKE THIS?
ALL I SEEM TO BE DOING...
...IS RECEIVING.
WHAT CAN I OFFER HER IN RETURN?
WHO...?
HEY, KEEP TALK-ING.
Spill it.
...
I CAN'T TELL YOU ANYTHING BEYOND THAT WHILE I'M SOBER.
BAM

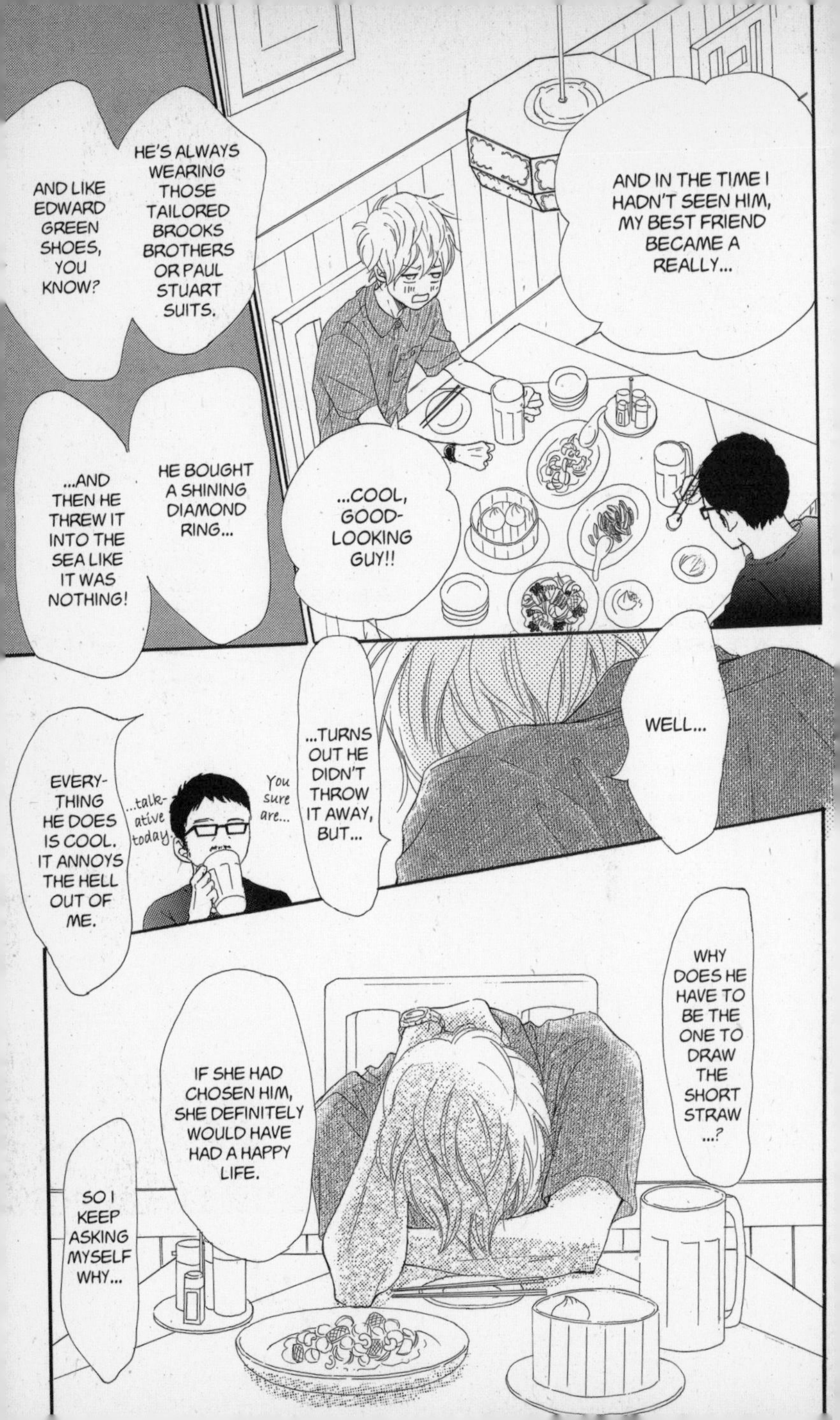
AND IN THE TIME I HADN'T SEEN HIM, MY BEST FRIEND BECAME A REALLY...
...COOL, GOOD-LOOKING GUY!!
HE'S ALWAYS WEARING THOSE TAILORED BROOKS BROTHERS OR PAUL STUART SUITS.
AND LIKE EDWARD GREEN SHOES, YOU KNOW?
HE BOUGHT A SHINING DIAMOND RING...
...AND THEN HE THREW IT INTO THE SEA LIKE IT WAS NOTHING!
WELL...
...TURNS OUT HE DIDN'T THROW IT AWAY, BUT...
You sure are...
...talkative today.
EVERYTHING HE DOES IS COOL. IT ANNOYS THE HELL OUT OF ME.
WHY DOES HE HAVE TO BE THE ONE TO DRAW THE SHORT STRAW...?
IF SHE HAD CHOSEN HIM, SHE DEFINITELY WOULD HAVE HAD A HAPPY LIFE.
SO I KEEP ASKING MYSELF WHY...

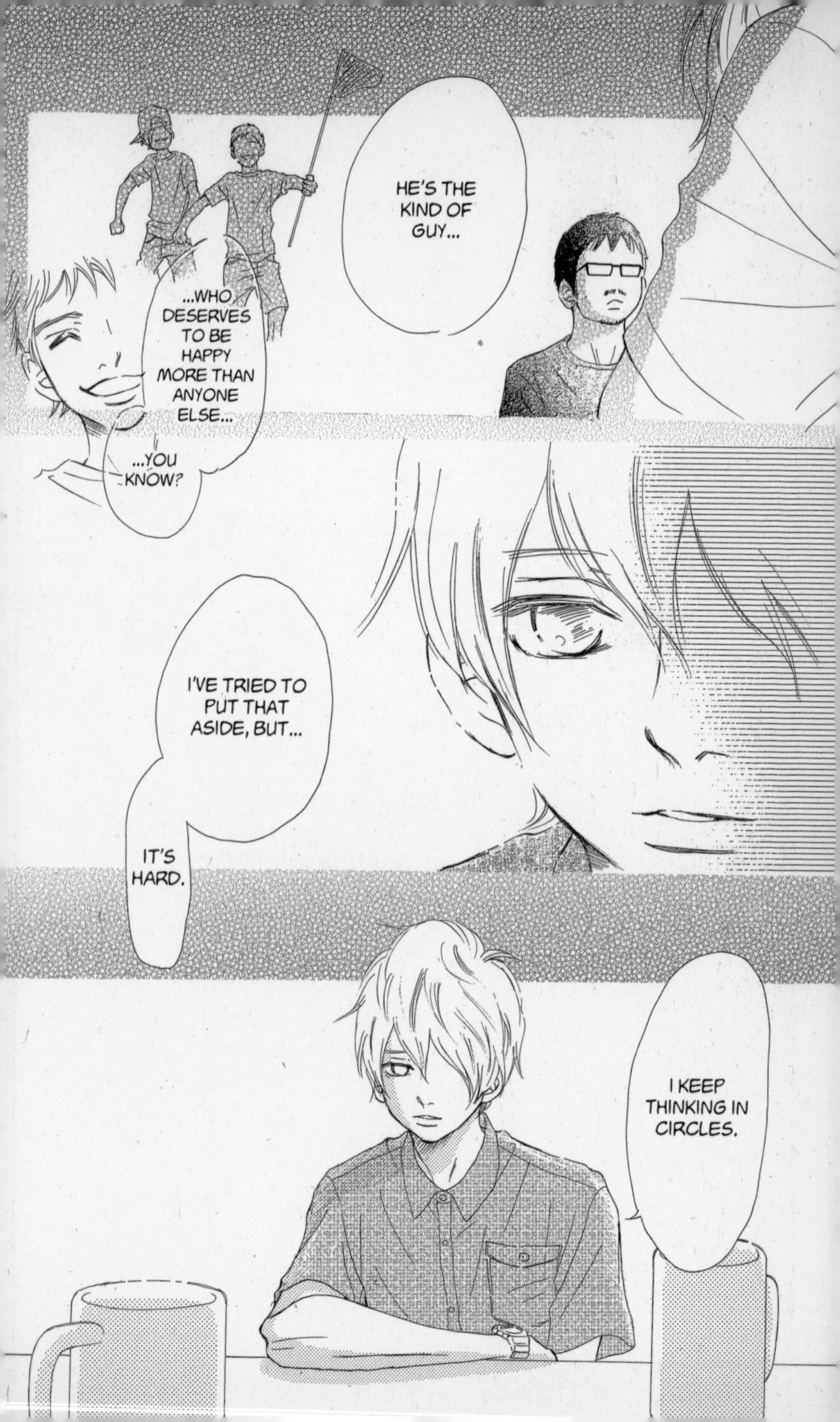
HE'S THE KIND OF GUY...
...WHO DESERVES TO BE HAPPY MORE THAN ANYONE ELSE...
...YOU KNOW?
I'VE TRIED TO PUT THAT ASIDE, BUT...
IT'S HARD.
I KEEP THINKING IN CIRCLES.

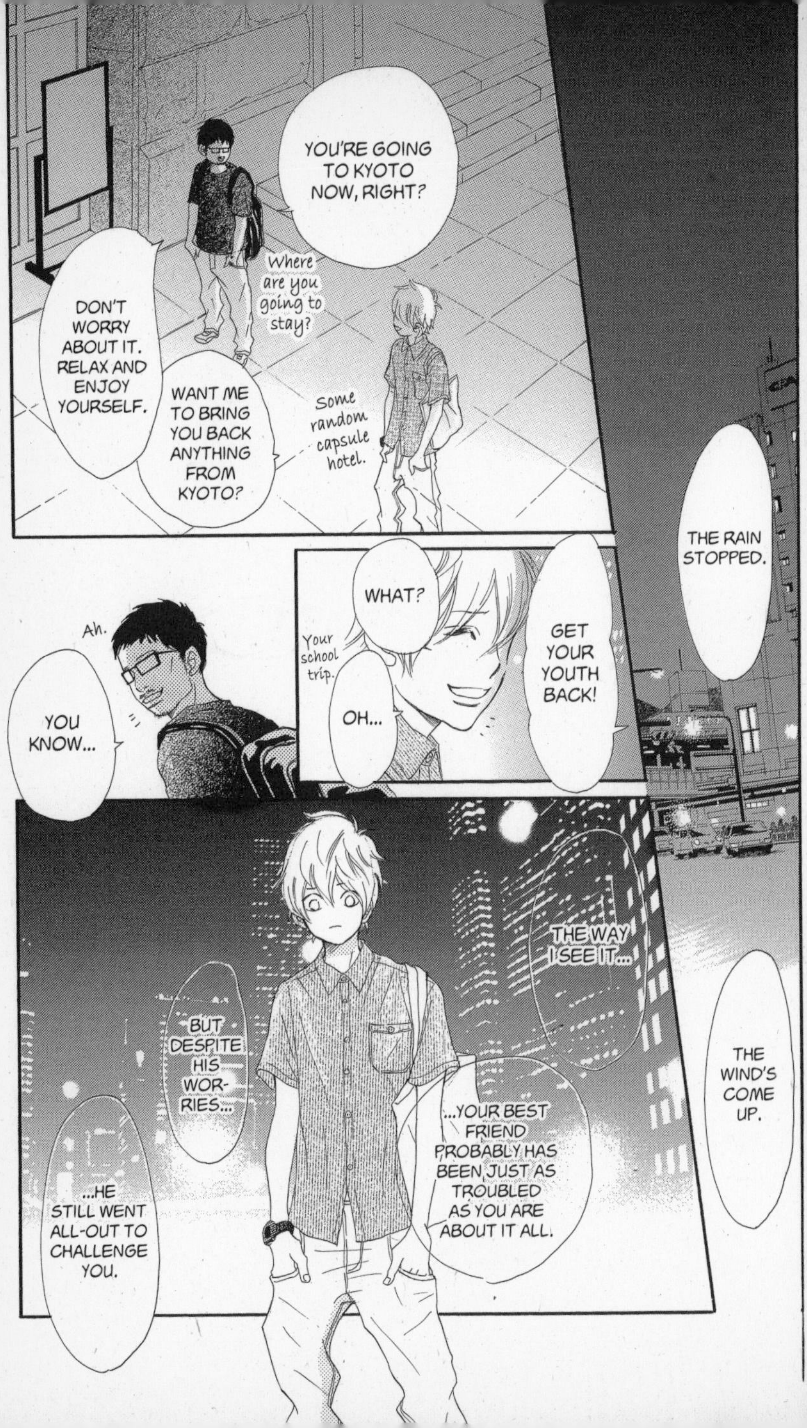
THE RAIN STOPPED.
THE WIND'S COME UP.
YOU'RE GOING TO KYOTO NOW, RIGHT?
Where are you going to stay?
Some random capsule hotel.
WANT ME TO BRING YOU BACK ANYTHING FROM KYOTO?
DON'T WORRY ABOUT IT. RELAX AND ENJOY YOURSELF.
GET YOUR YOUTH BACK!
WHAT?
Your school trip.
OH...
Ah.
YOU KNOW...
THE WAY I SEE IT...
...YOUR BEST FRIEND PROBABLY HAS BEEN JUST AS TROUBLED AS YOU ARE ABOUT IT ALL.
BUT DESPITE HIS WOR-RIES...
...HE STILL WENT ALL-OUT TO CHALLENGE YOU.

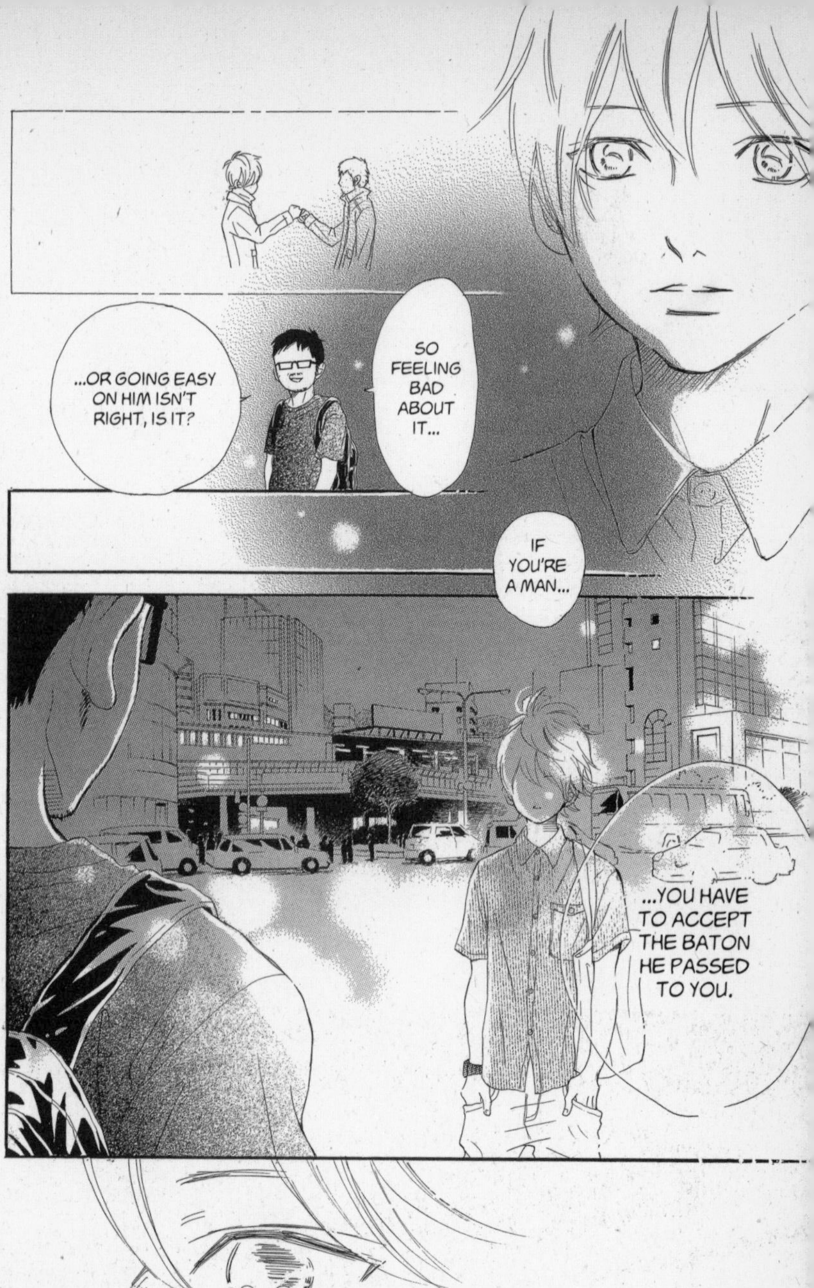
SO FEELING BAD ABOUT IT...
...OR GOING EASY ON HIM ISN'T RIGHT, IS IT?
IF YOU'RE A MAN...
...YOU HAVE TO ACCEPT THE BATON HE PASSED TO YOU.

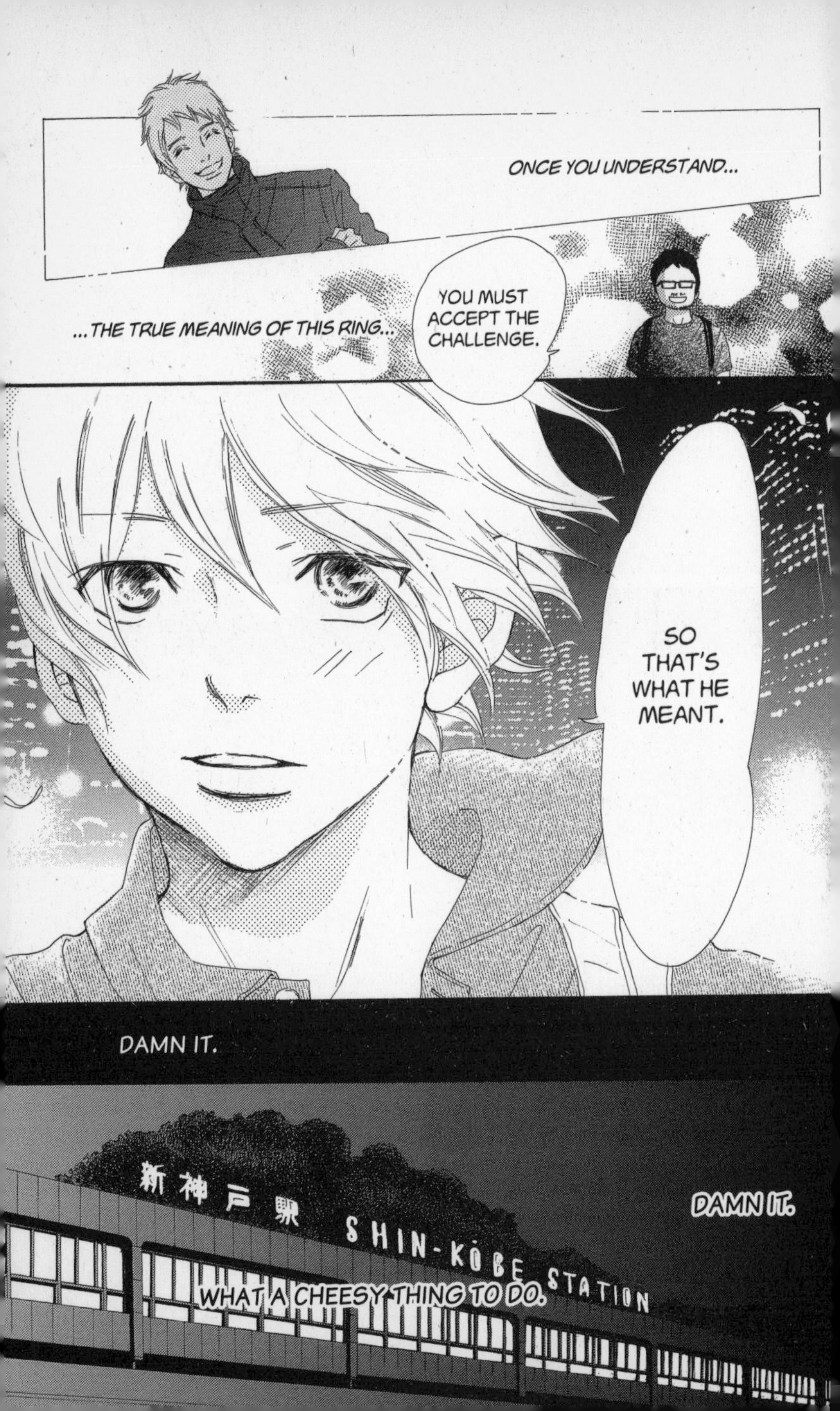

ONCE YOU UNDERSTAND...
...THE TRUE MEANING OF THIS RING...
YOU MUST ACCEPT THE CHALLENGE.
SO THAT'S WHAT HE MEANT.
DAMN IT.
新神戸駅 SHIN-KŌBE STATION
DAMN IT.
WHAT A CHEESY THING TO DO.

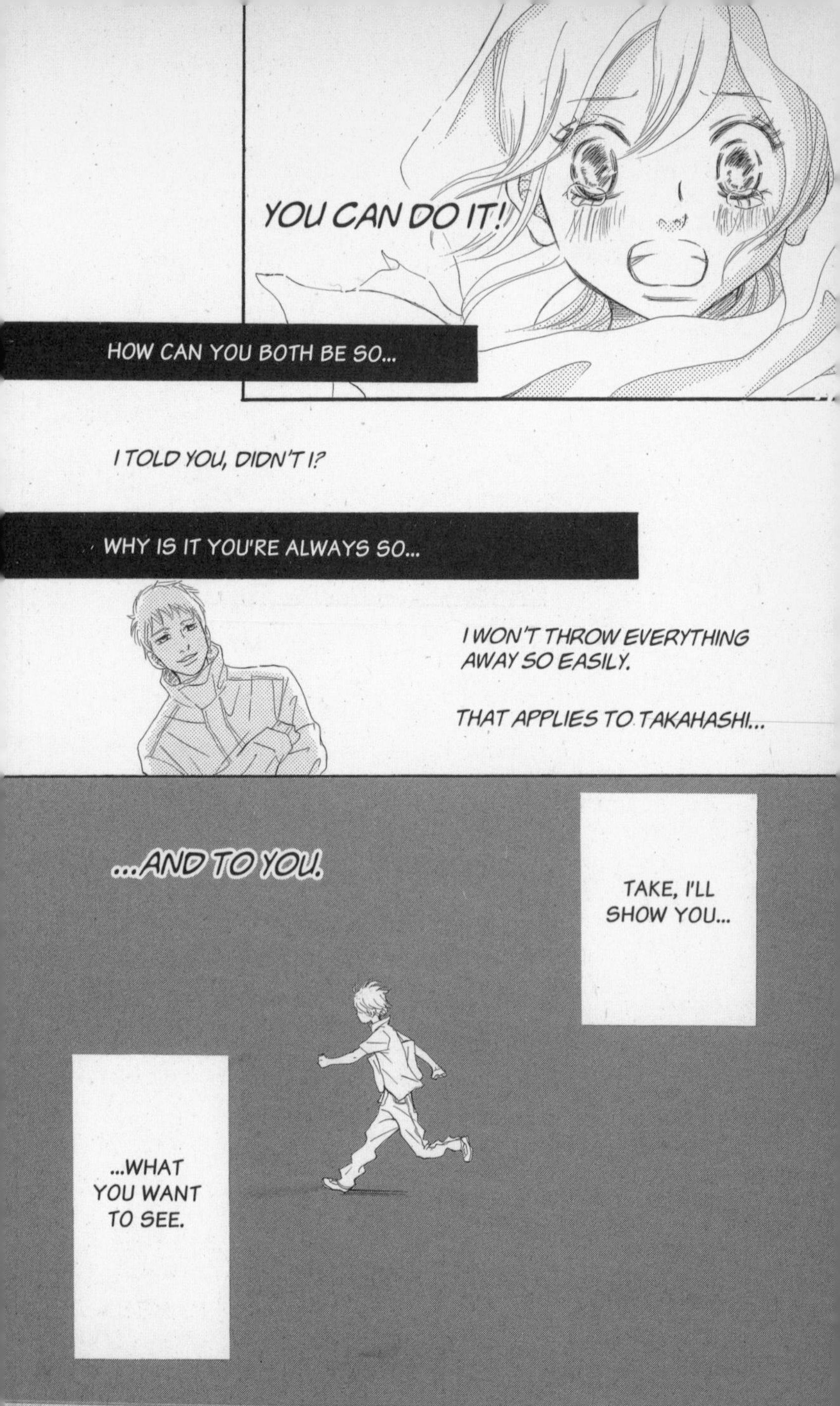
YOU CAN DO IT!
HOW CAN YOU BOTH BE SO...
I TOLD YOU, DIDN'T I?
WHY IS IT YOU'RE ALWAYS SO...
I WON'T THROW EVERYTHING AWAY SO EASILY.
THAT APPLIES TO TAKAHASHI...
...AND TO YOU.
TAKE, I'LL SHOW YOU...
...WHAT YOU WANT TO SEE.

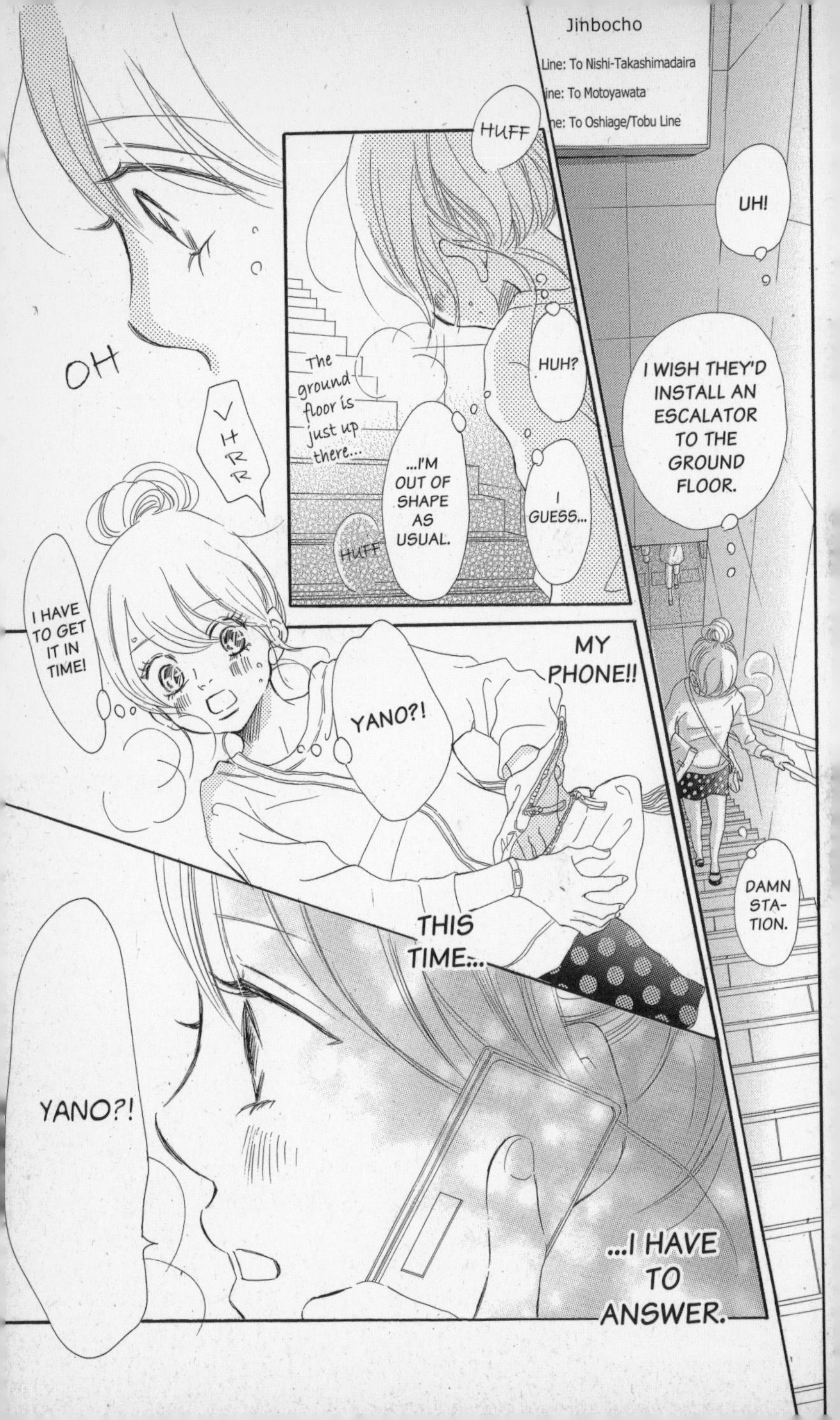
Jinbocho
Line: To Nishi-Takashimadaira
ine: To Motoyawata
ne: To Oshiage/Tobu Line
UH!
I WISH THEY'D INSTALL AN ESCALATOR TO THE GROUND FLOOR.
DAMN STA-TION.
HUFF
HUH?
I GUESS...
The ground floor is just up there...
...I'M OUT OF SHAPE AS USUAL.
HUFF
VHRR
OH
MY PHONE!!
YANO?!
I HAVE TO GET IT IN TIME!
THIS TIME...
...I HAVE TO ANSWER.
YANO?!

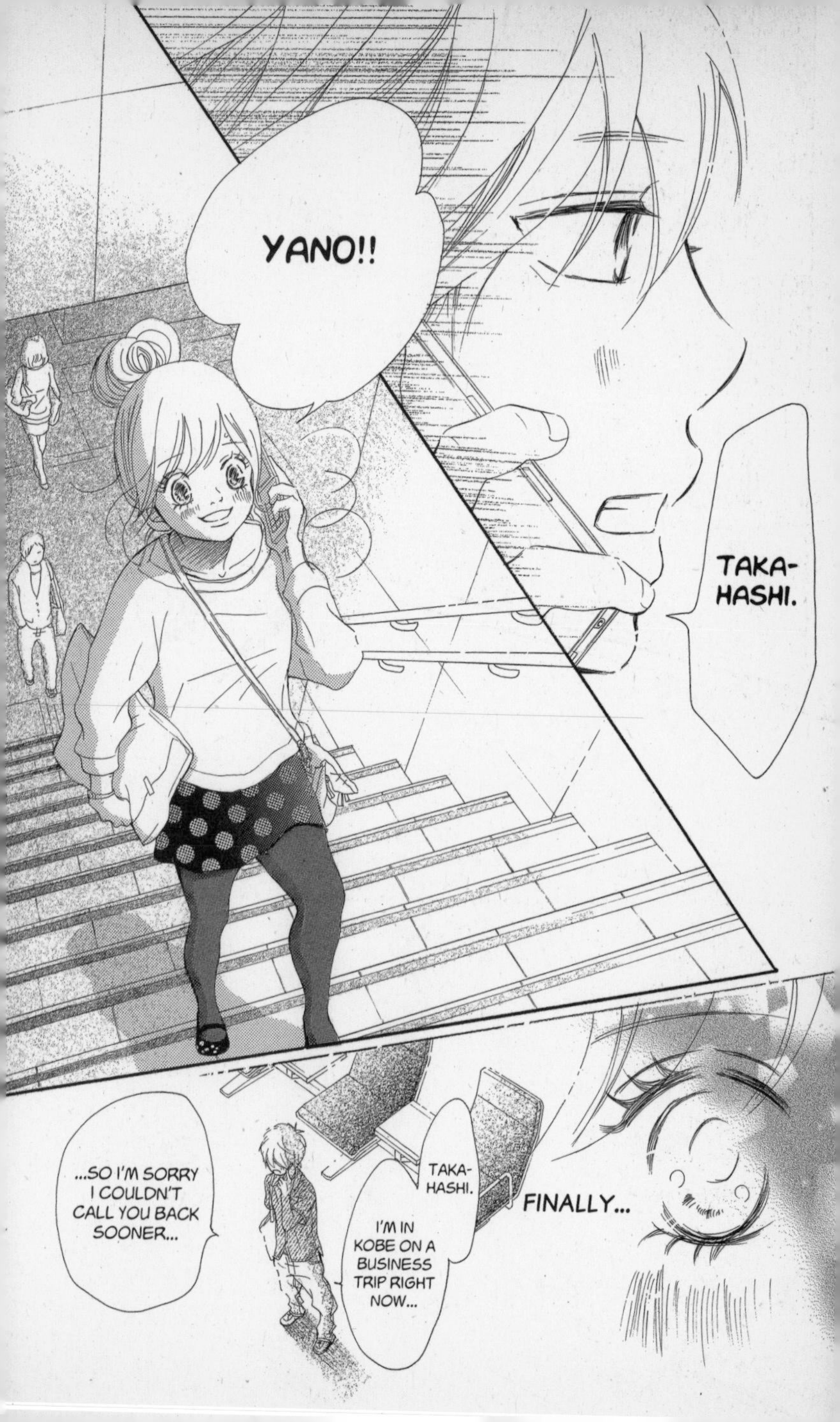
TAKA-HASHI.
YANO!!
FINALLY...
TAKA-HASHI.
I'M IN KOBE ON A BUSINESS TRIP RIGHT NOW...
...SO I'M SORRY I COULDN'T CALL YOU BACK SOONER...

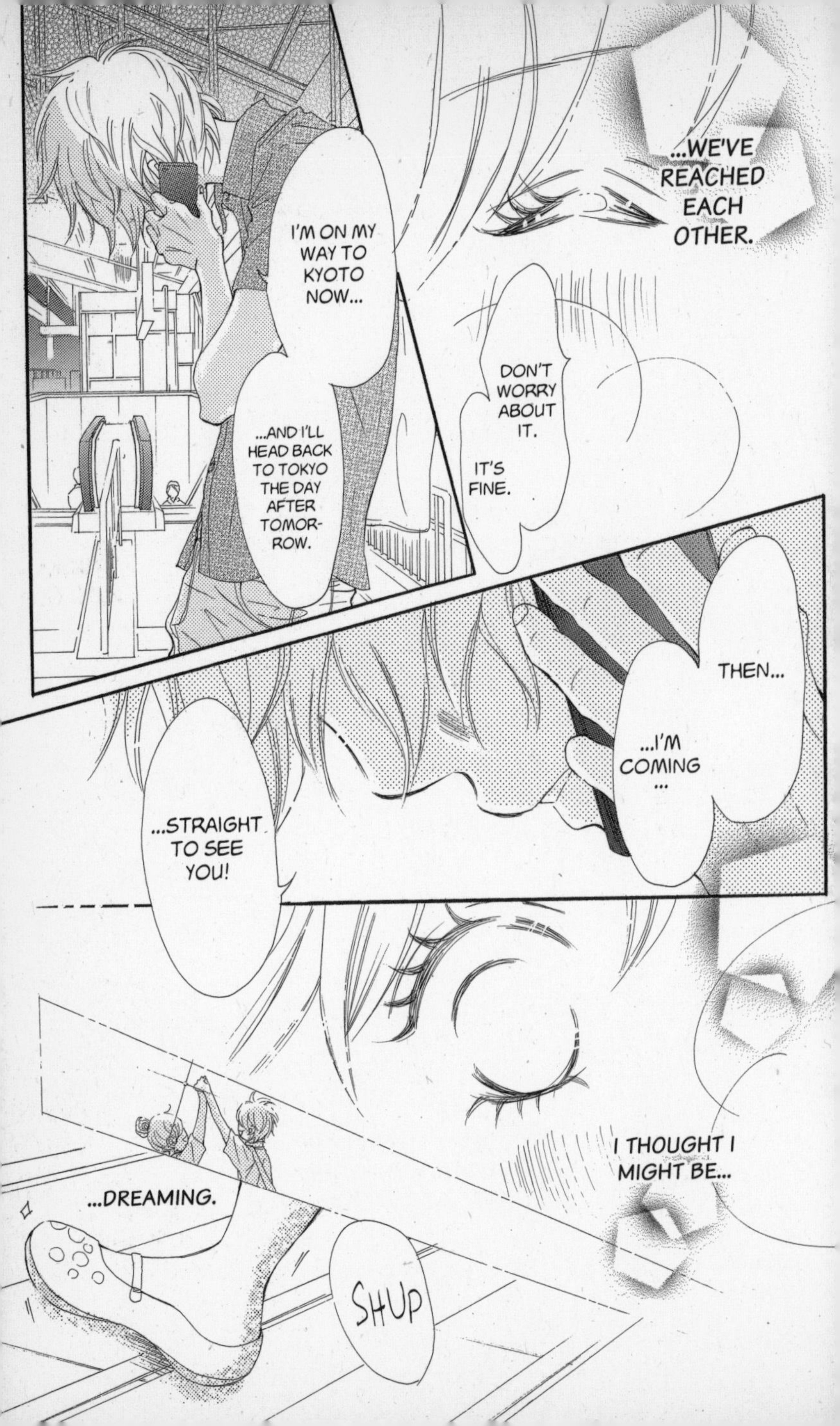
...WE'VE REACHED EACH OTHER.
DON'T WORRY ABOUT IT.
IT'S FINE.
I'M ON MY WAY TO KYOTO NOW...
...AND I'LL HEAD BACK TO TOKYO THE DAY AFTER TOMOR-ROW.
THEN...
...I'M COMING...
...STRAIGHT TO SEE YOU!
I THOUGHT I MIGHT BE...
...DREAMING.
SHUP

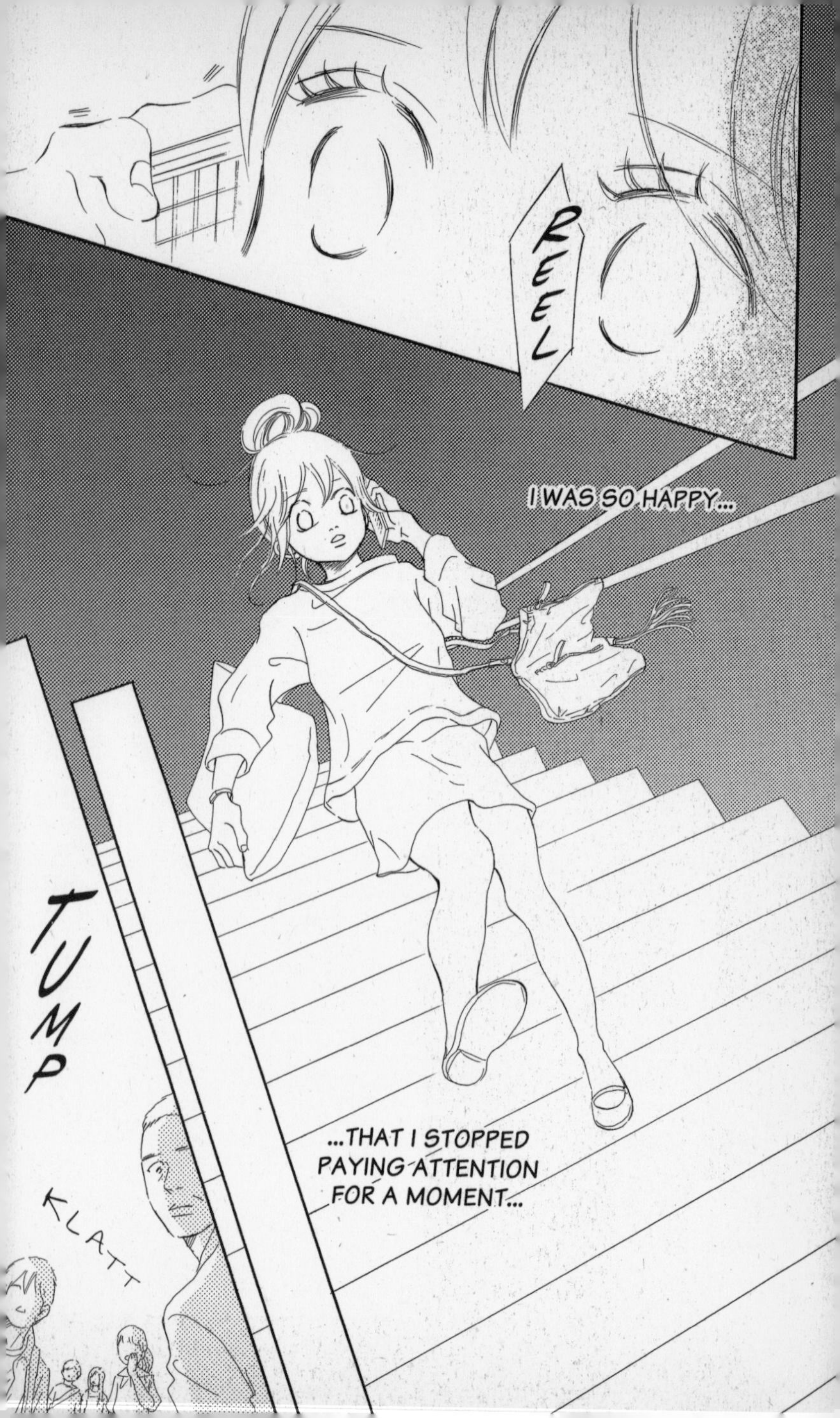
REEL
I WAS SO HAPPY...
...THAT I STOPPED PAYING ATTENTION FOR A MOMENT...
TUMP
KLATT

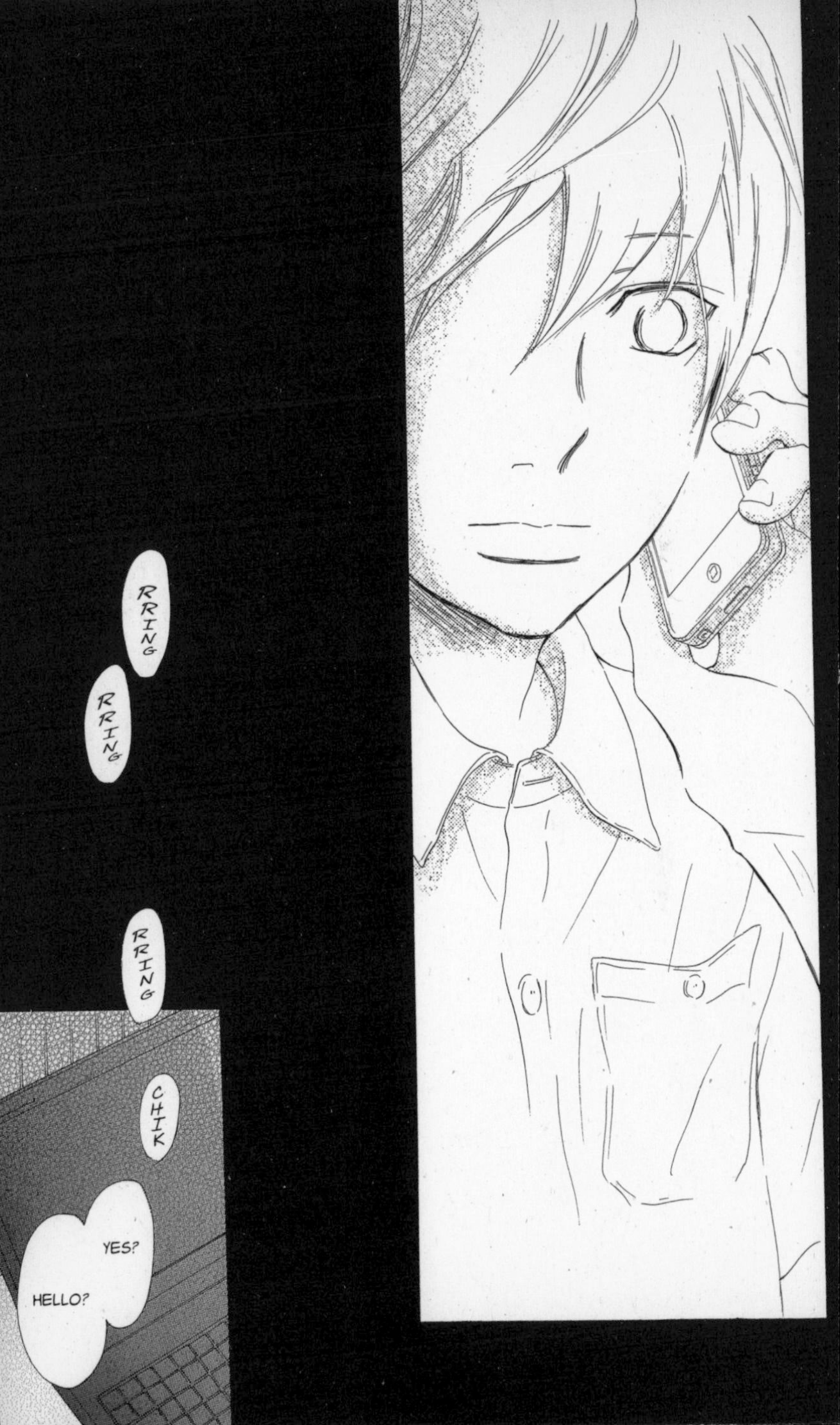
RRING
RRING
RRING
CHIK
YES?
HELLO?

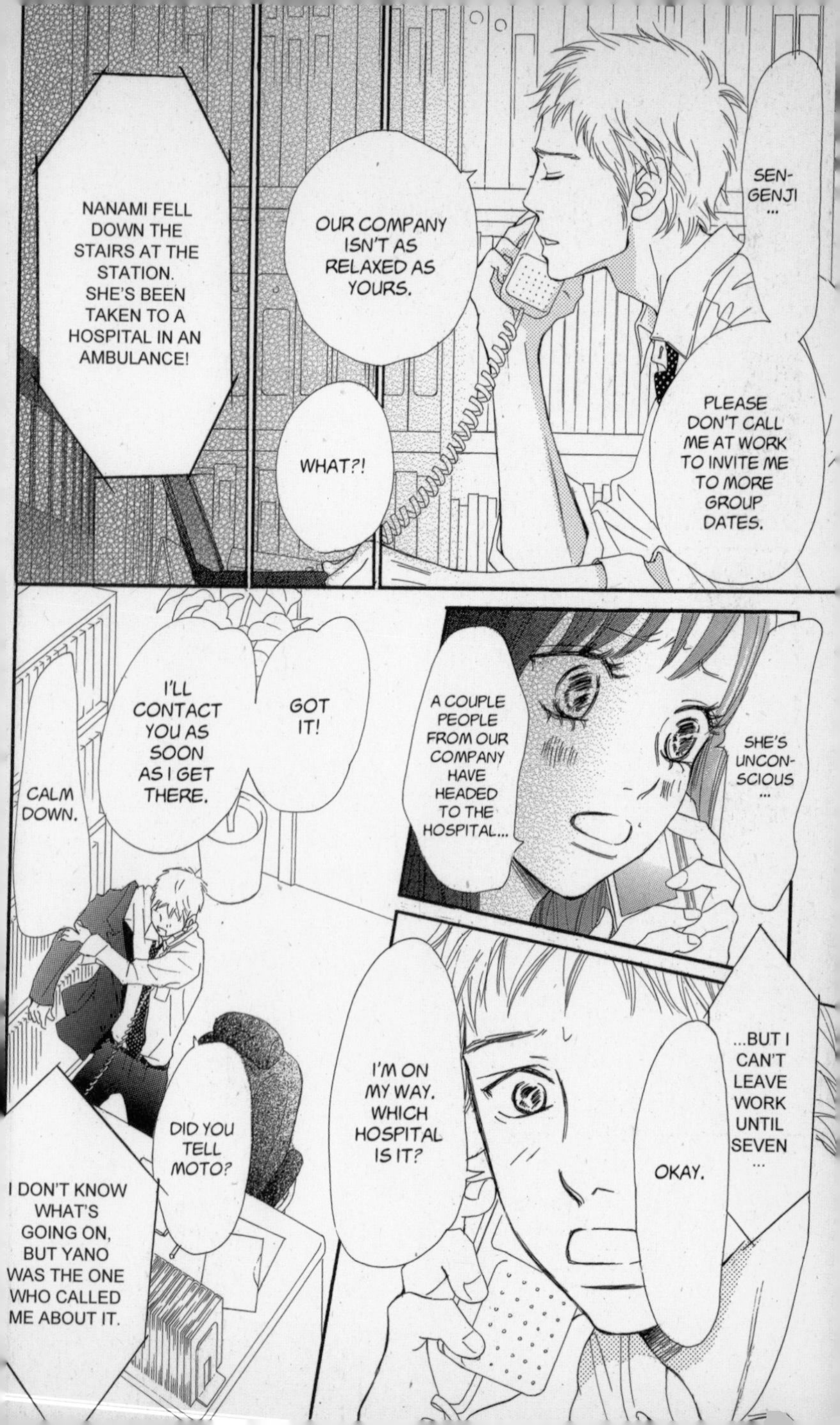
SEN-GENJI ...
PLEASE DON'T CALL ME AT WORK TO INVITE ME TO MORE GROUP DATES.
OUR COMPANY ISN'T AS RELAXED AS YOURS.
WHAT?!
NANAMI FELL DOWN THE STAIRS AT THE STATION. SHE'S BEEN TAKEN TO A HOSPITAL IN AN AMBULANCE!
SHE'S UNCON-SCIOUS ...
A COUPLE PEOPLE FROM OUR COMPANY HAVE HEADED TO THE HOSPITAL...
...BUT I CAN'T LEAVE WORK UNTIL SEVEN ...
OKAY.
I'M ON MY WAY. WHICH HOSPITAL IS IT?
GOT IT!
I'LL CONTACT YOU AS SOON AS I GET THERE.
CALM DOWN.
DID YOU TELL MOTO?
I DON'T KNOW WHAT'S GOING ON, BUT YANO WAS THE ONE WHO CALLED ME ABOUT IT.

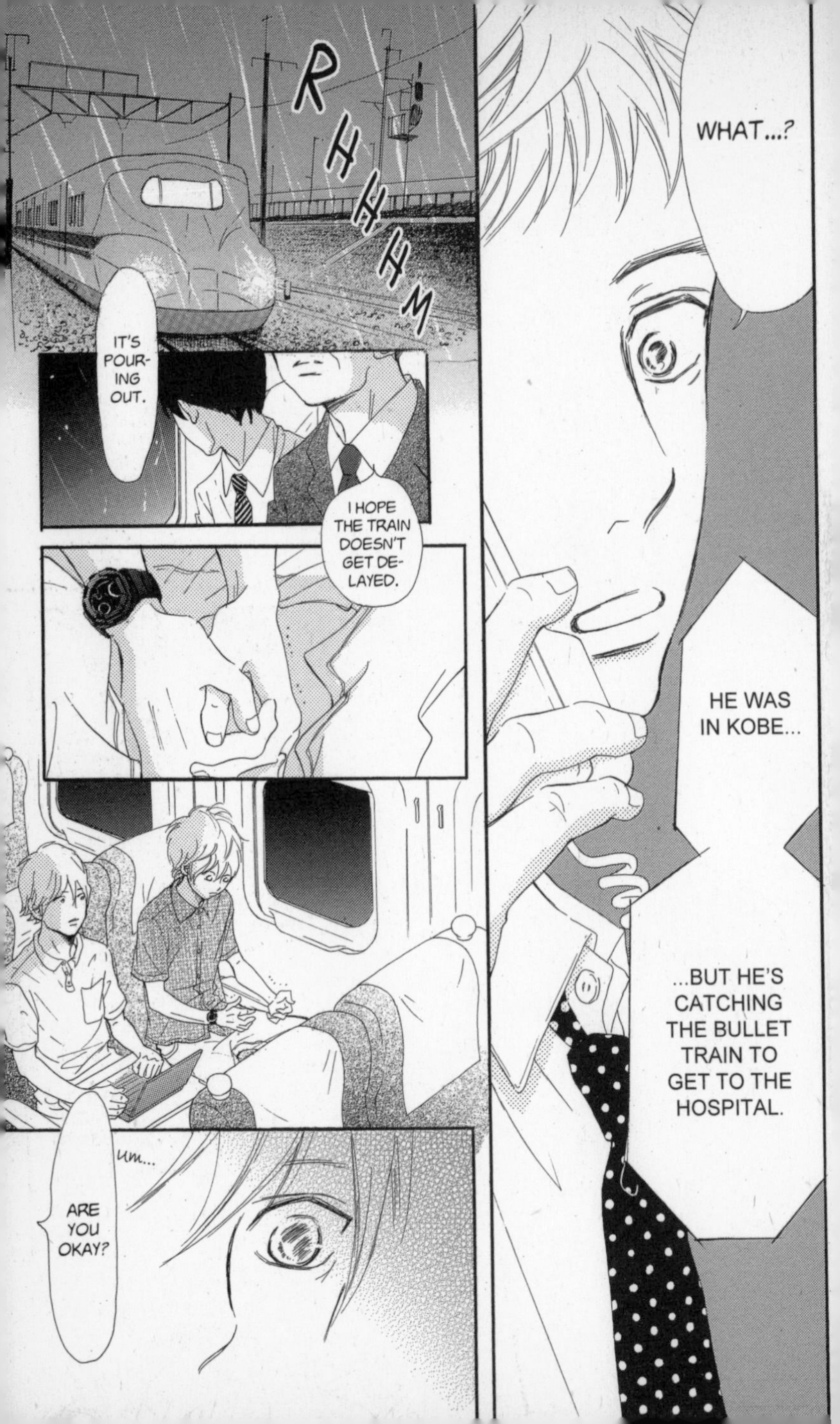
WHAT...?
HE WAS IN KOBE...
...BUT HE'S CATCHING THE BULLET TRAIN TO GET TO THE HOSPITAL.
RHHHHM
IT'S POURING OUT.
I HOPE THE TRAIN DOESN'T GET DELAYED.
UM...
ARE YOU OKAY?

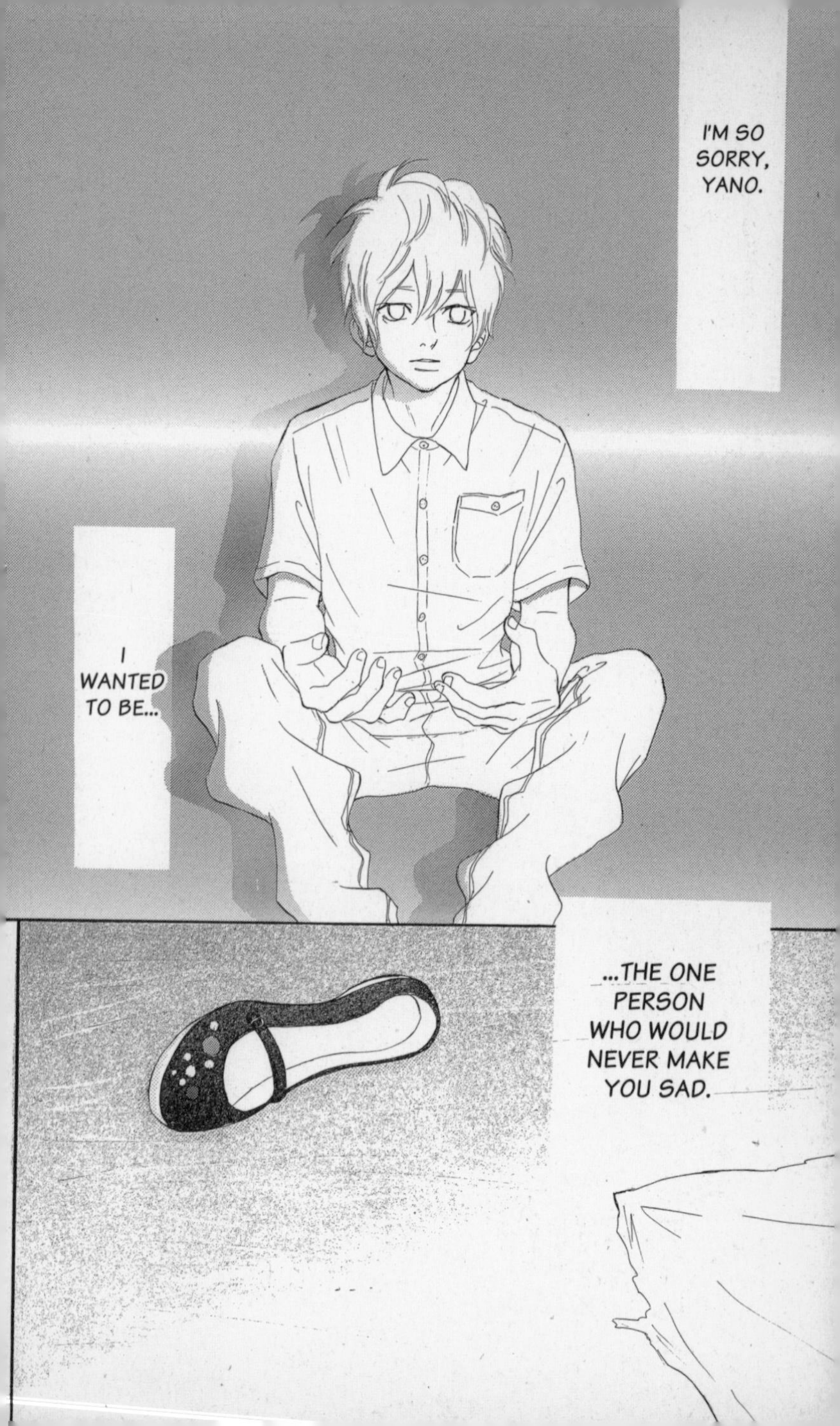
I'M SO SORRY, YANO.
I WANTED TO BE...
...THE ONE PERSON WHO WOULD NEVER MAKE YOU SAD.

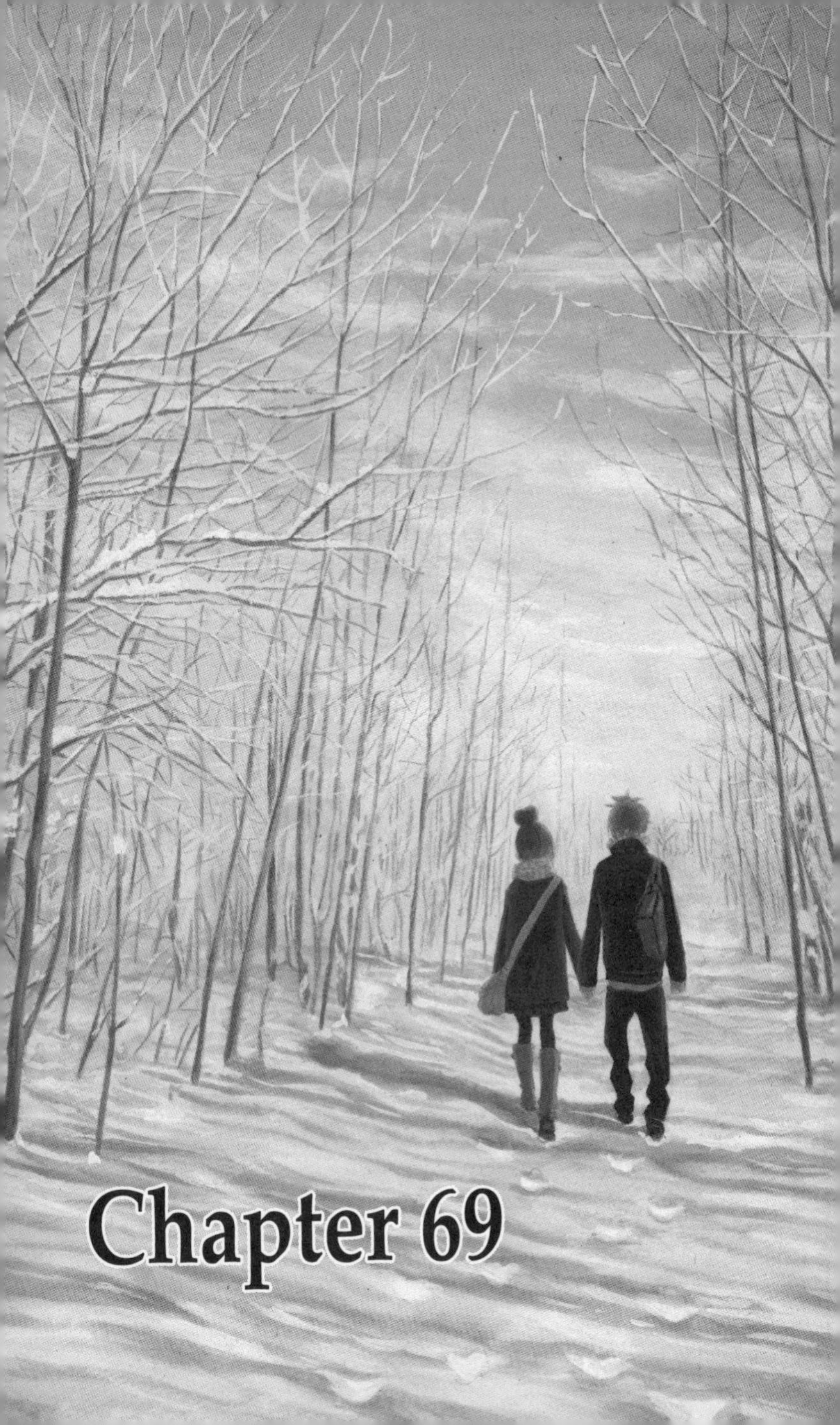
Chapter 69

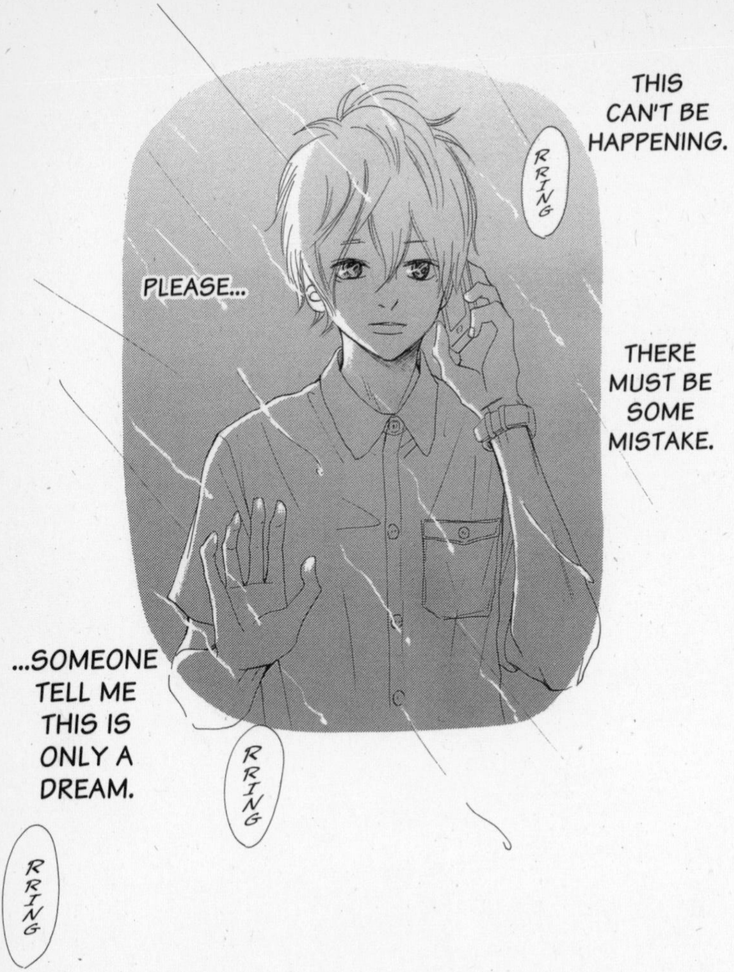
THIS CAN'T BE HAPPENING.
RRING
THERE MUST BE SOME MISTAKE.
PLEASE...
...SOMEONE TELL ME THIS IS ONLY A DREAM.
RRING
RRING

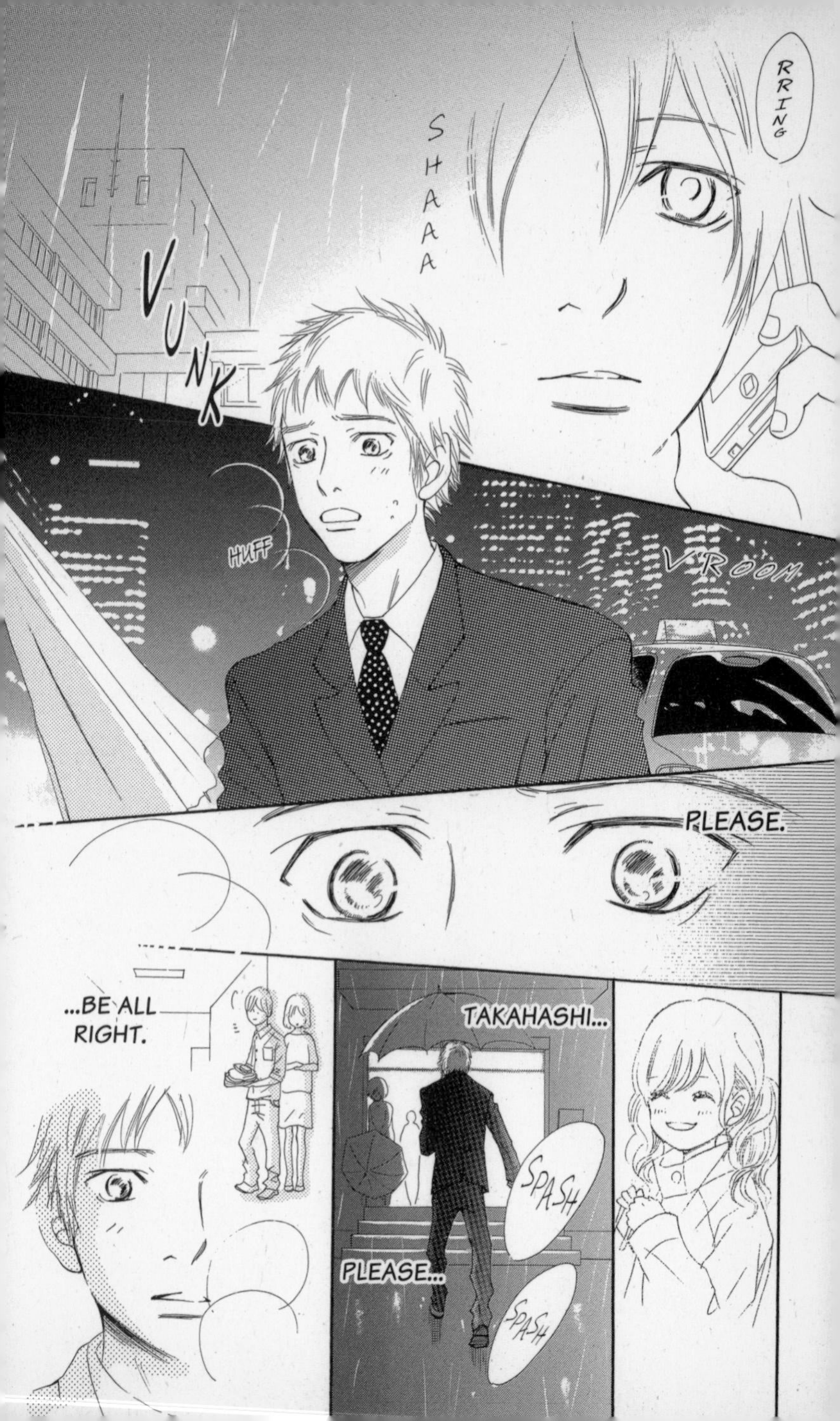
RRING
SHAAA
VUNK
V'ROOM
HUFF
PLEASE.
TAKAHASHI...
SPASH
PLEASE...
SPASH
...BE ALL RIGHT.

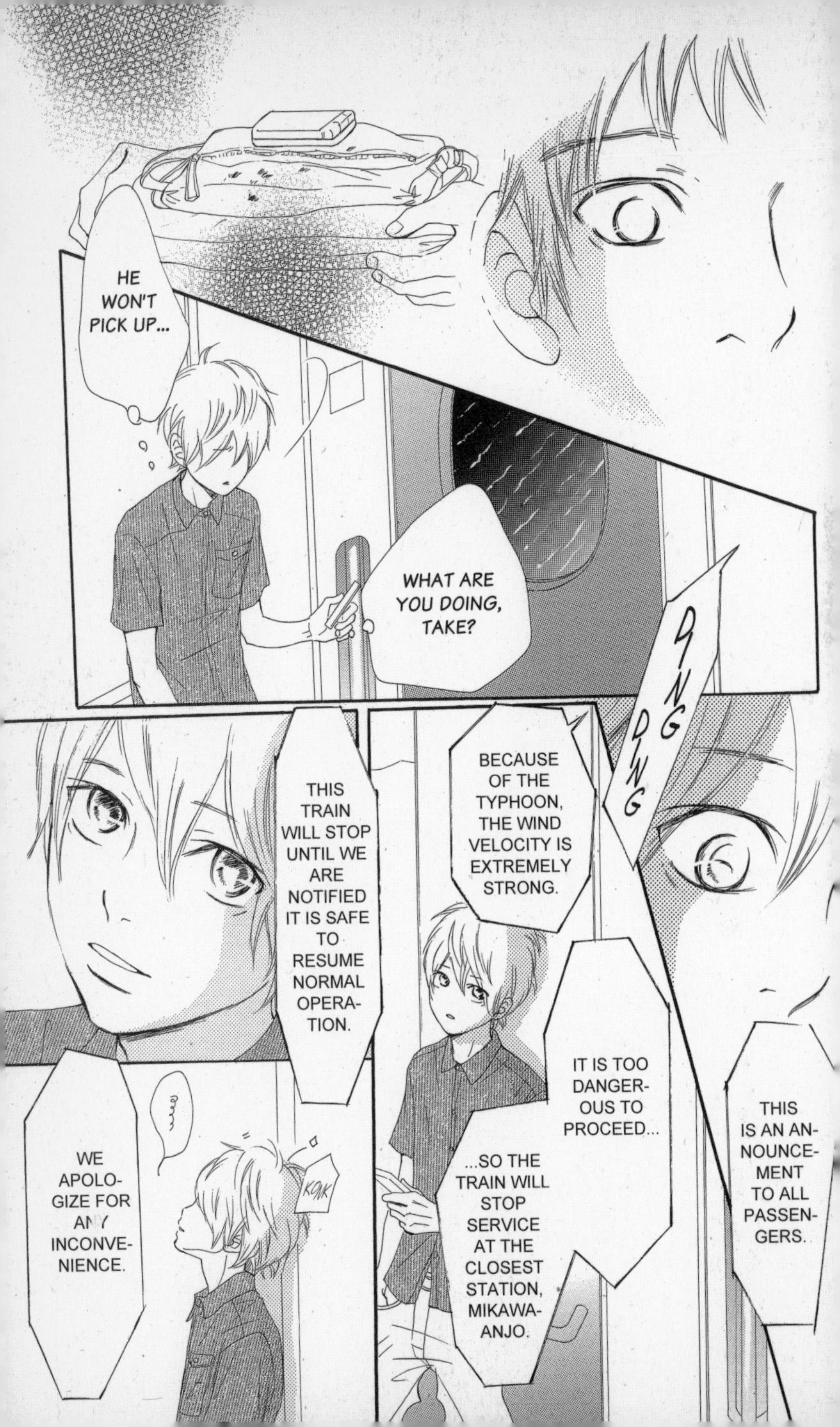
HE WON'T PICK UP...
WHAT ARE YOU DOING, TAKE?
DING DING
THIS IS AN ANNOUNCEMENT TO ALL PASSENGERS.
BECAUSE OF THE TYPHOON, THE WIND VELOCITY IS EXTREMELY STRONG.
IT IS TOO DANGEROUS TO PROCEED...
...SO THE TRAIN WILL STOP SERVICE AT THE CLOSEST STATION, MIKAWA-ANJO.
THIS TRAIN WILL STOP UNTIL WE ARE NOTIFIED IT IS SAFE TO RESUME NORMAL OPERATION.
WE APOLOGIZE FOR ANY INCONVENIENCE.
KONK

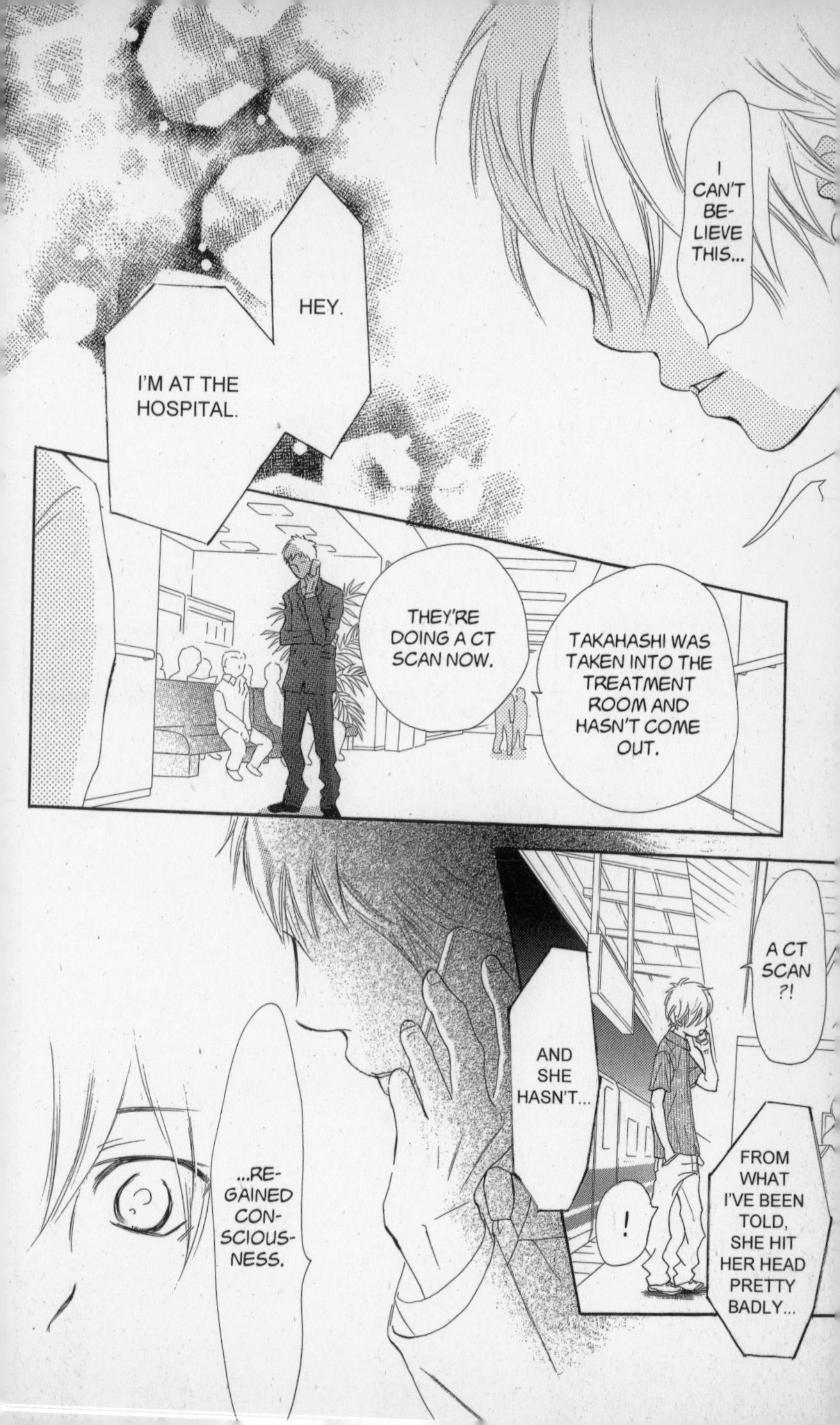
I CAN'T BE-LIEVE THIS...
HEY.
I'M AT THE HOSPITAL.
TAKAHASHI WAS TAKEN INTO THE TREATMENT ROOM AND HASN'T COME OUT.
THEY'RE DOING A CT SCAN NOW.
A CT SCAN ?!
FROM WHAT I'VE BEEN TOLD, SHE HIT HER HEAD PRETTY BADLY...
!
AND SHE HASN'T...
...RE-GAINED CON-SCIOUS-NESS.

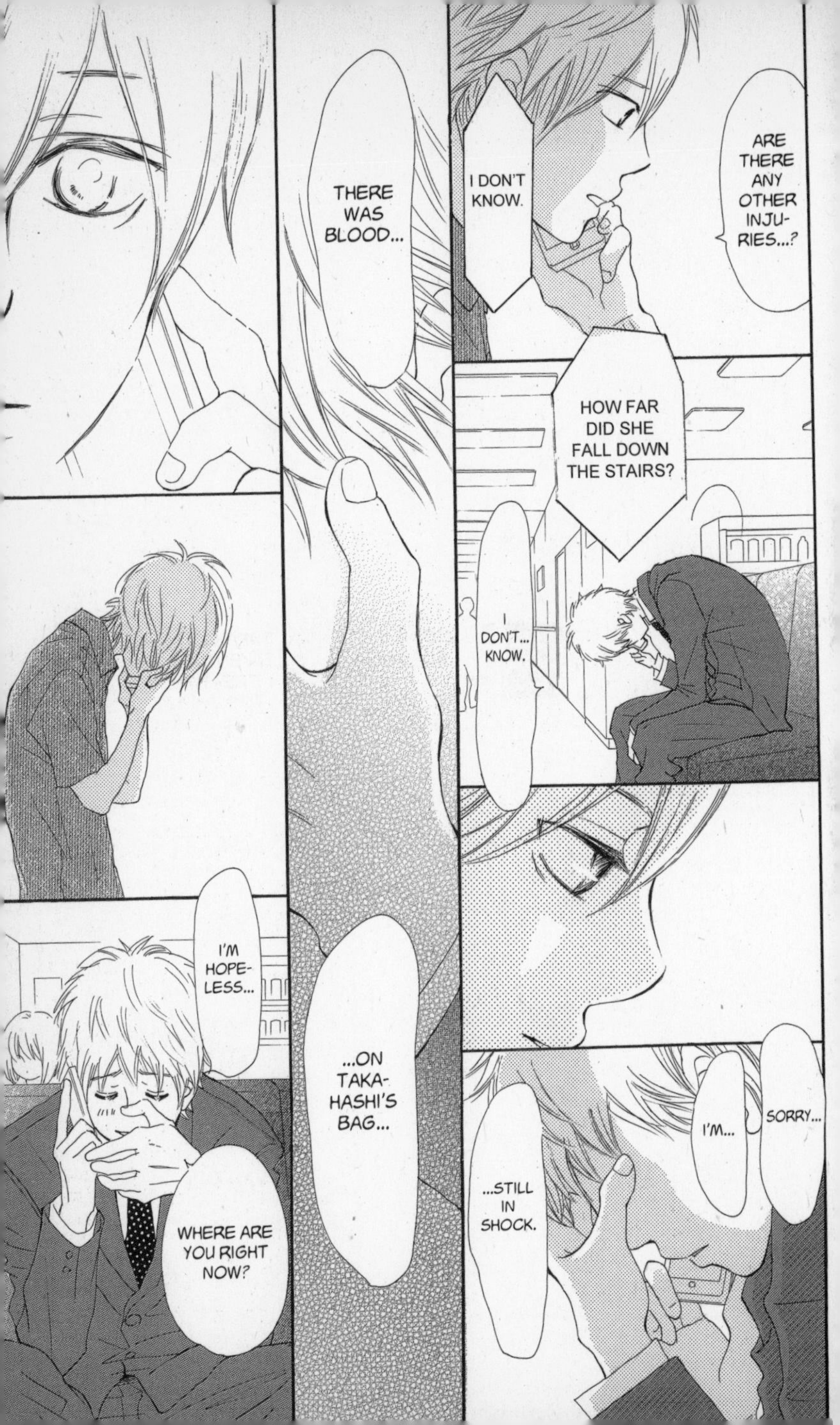
ARE THERE ANY OTHER INJURIES...?
I DON'T KNOW.
HOW FAR DID SHE FALL DOWN THE STAIRS?
I DON'T... KNOW.
SORRY...
I'M...
...STILL IN SHOCK.
THERE WAS BLOOD...
...ON TAKAHASHI'S BAG...
I'M HOPELESS...
WHERE ARE YOU RIGHT NOW?

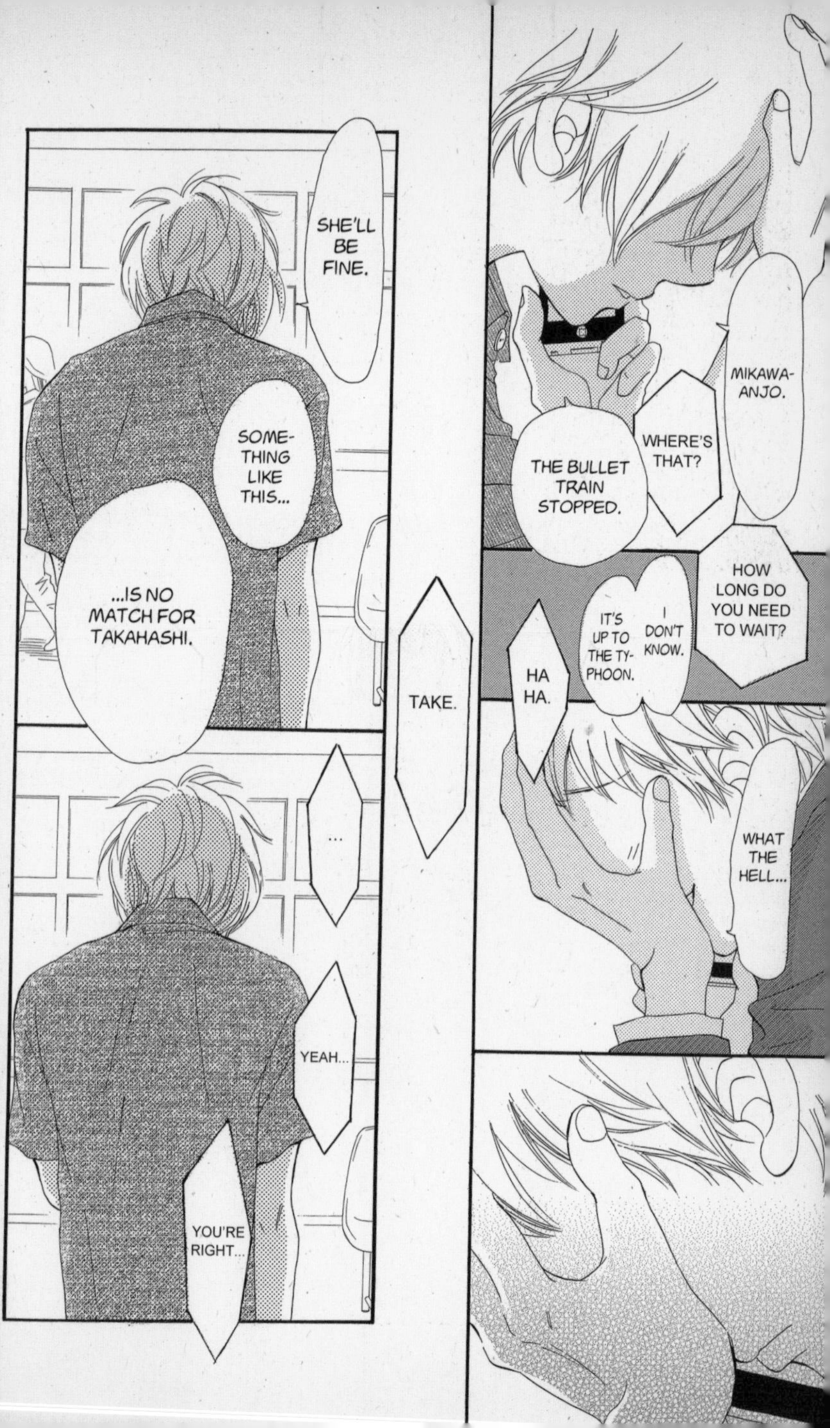
MIKAWA-ANJO.
WHERE'S THAT?
THE BULLET TRAIN STOPPED.
HOW LONG DO YOU NEED TO WAIT?
I DON'T KNOW.
IT'S UP TO THE TY-PHOON.
WHAT THE HELL...
HA HA.
TAKE.
SHE'LL BE FINE.
SOME-THING LIKE THIS...
...IS NO MATCH FOR TAKAHASHI.
...
YEAH...
YOU'RE RIGHT...

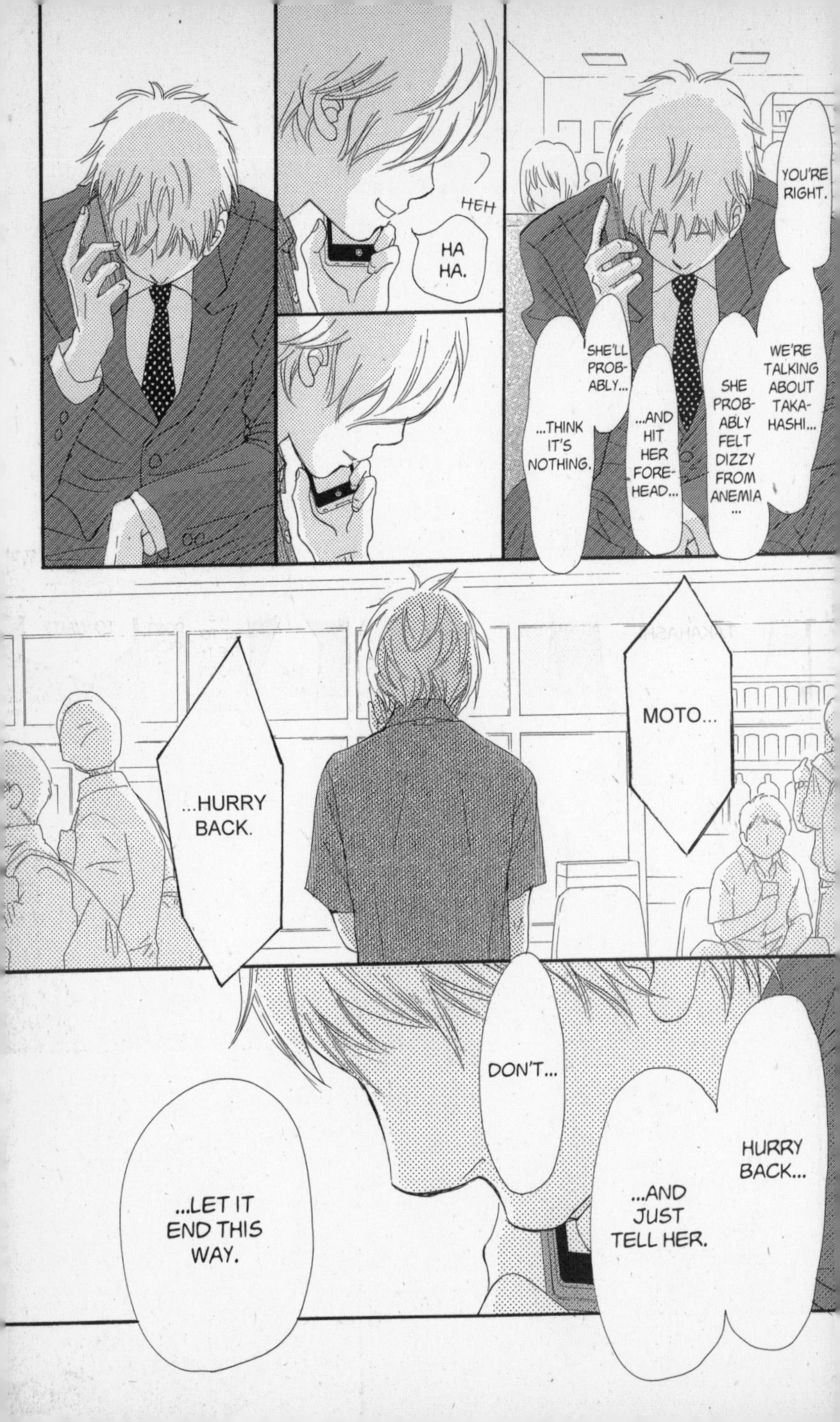
YOU'RE RIGHT.
WE'RE TALKING ABOUT TAKA-HASHI...
SHE PROB-ABLY FELT DIZZY FROM ANEMIA...
...AND HIT HER FORE-HEAD...
SHE'LL PROB-ABLY...
...THINK IT'S NOTHING.
HEH
HA HA.
MOTO...
...HURRY BACK.
HURRY BACK...
...AND JUST TELL HER.
DON'T...
...LET IT END THIS WAY.

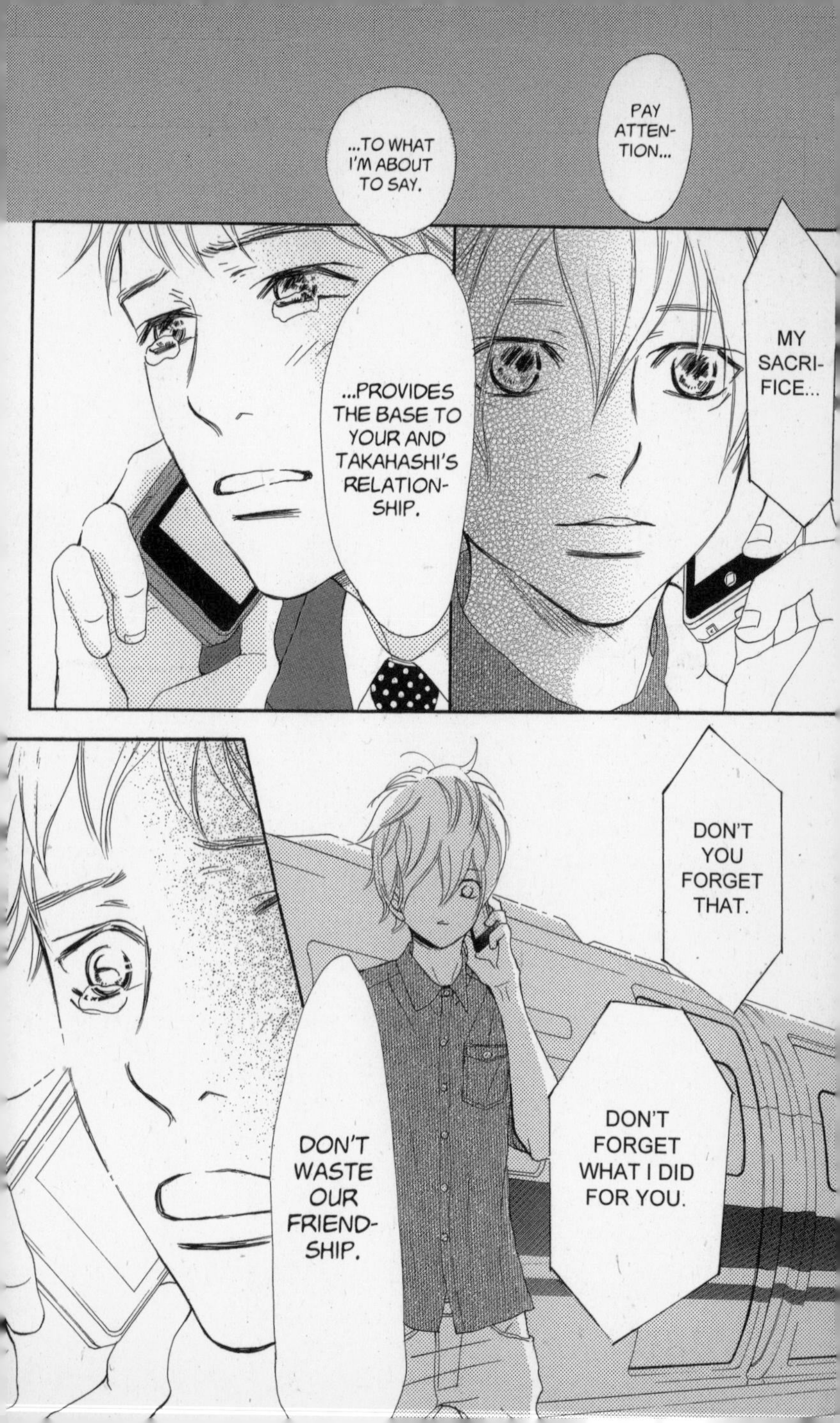
PAY ATTEN-TION...
...TO WHAT I'M ABOUT TO SAY.
MY SACRI-FICE...
...PROVIDES THE BASE TO YOUR AND TAKAHASHI'S RELATION-SHIP.
DON'T YOU FORGET THAT.
DON'T FORGET WHAT I DID FOR YOU.
DON'T WASTE OUR FRIEND-SHIP.

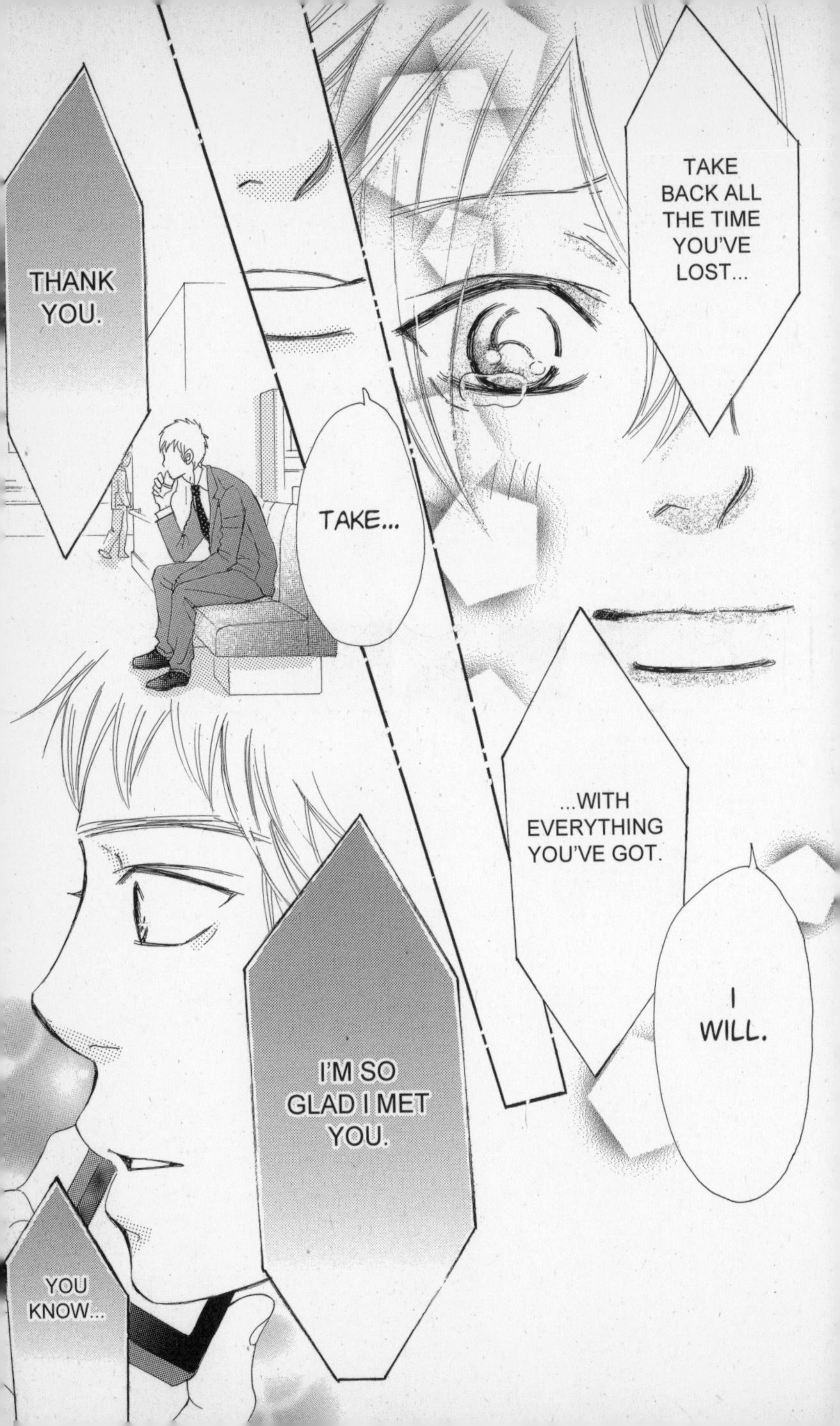
TAKE BACK ALL THE TIME YOU'VE LOST...
...WITH EVERYTHING YOU'VE GOT.
I WILL.
TAKE...
THANK YOU.
I'M SO GLAD I MET YOU.
YOU KNOW...

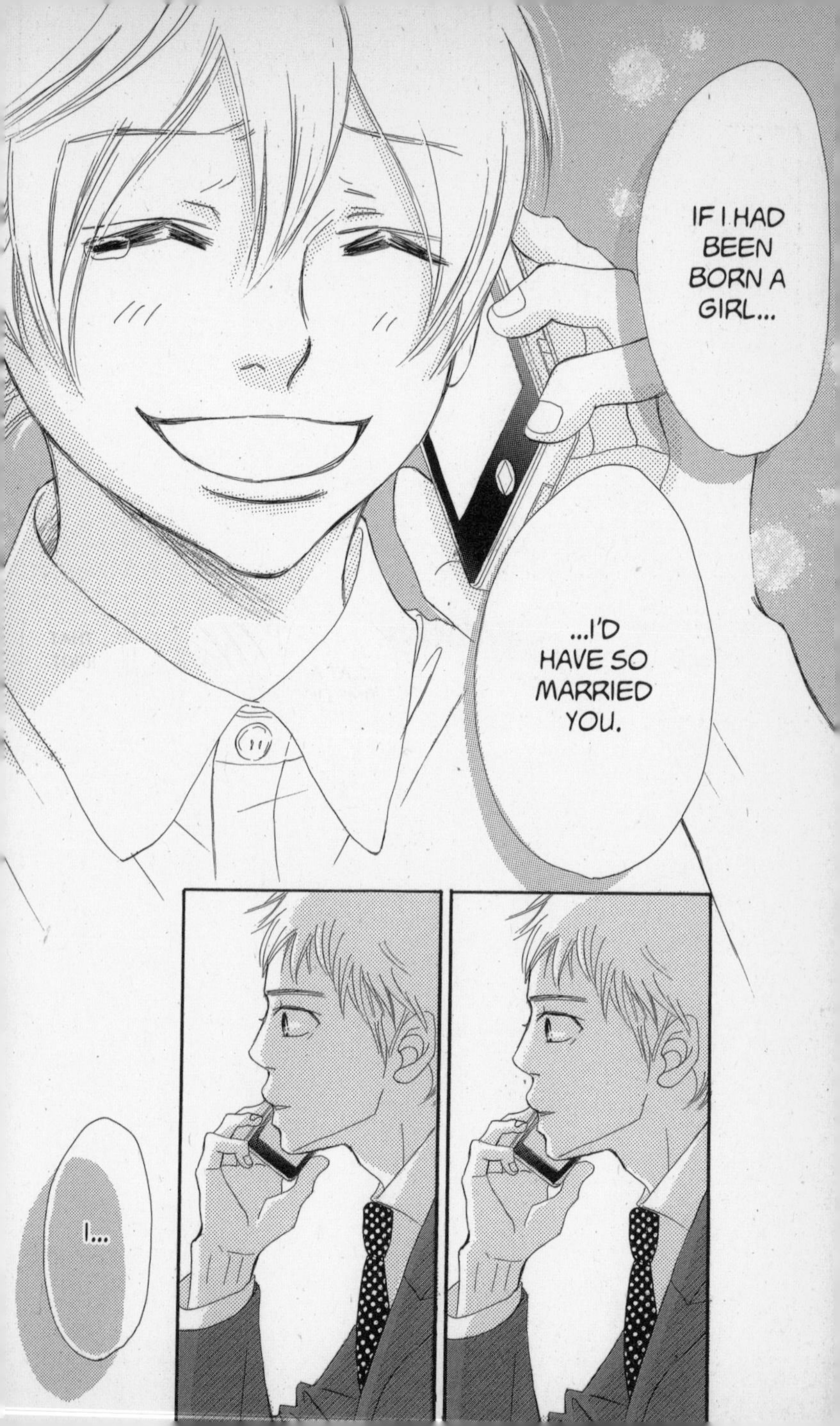
IF I HAD BEEN BORN A GIRL...
...I'D HAVE SO MARRIED YOU.
I...

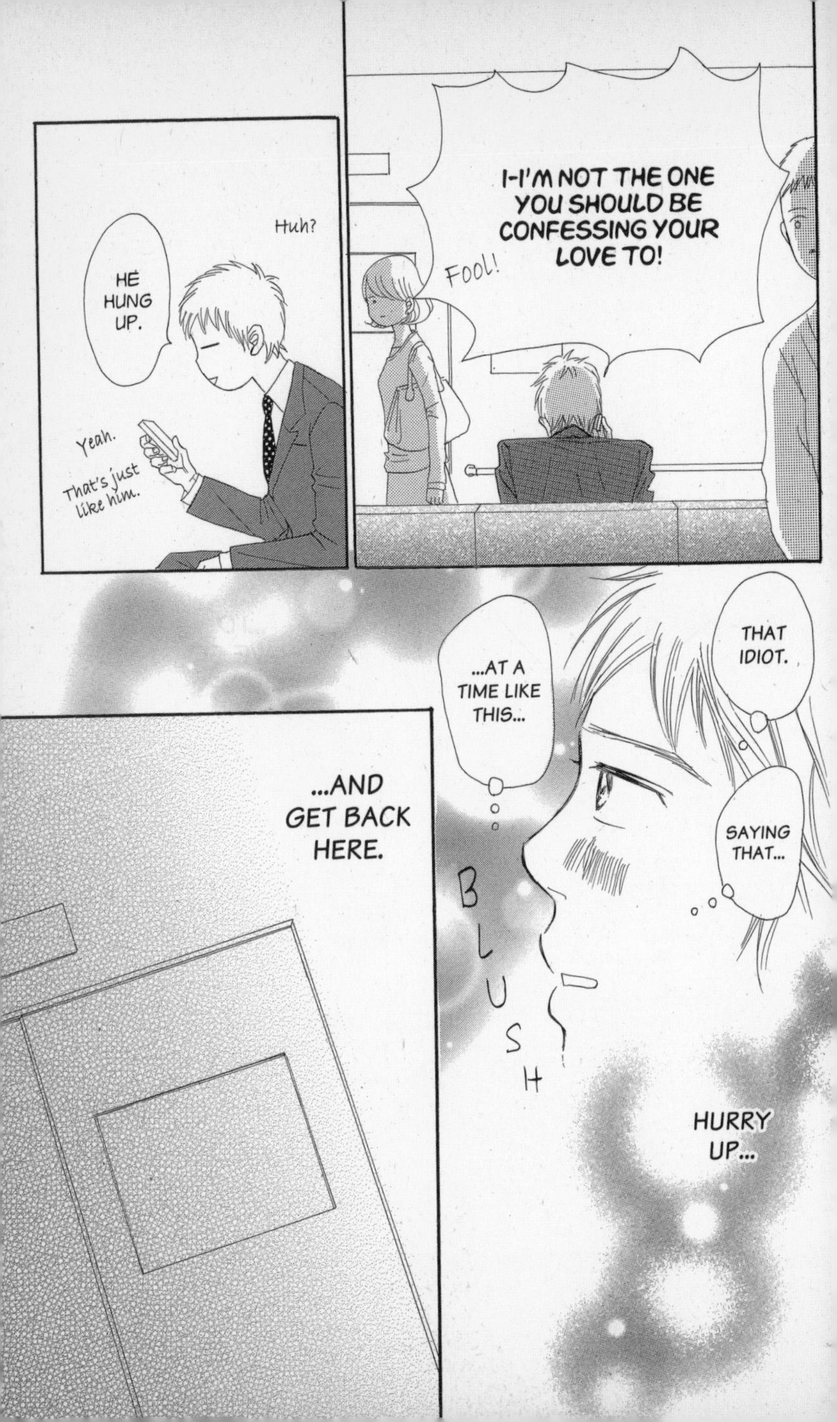
I-I'M NOT THE ONE YOU SHOULD BE CONFESSING YOUR LOVE TO!
FOOL!
Huh?
HE HUNG UP.
Yeah.
That's just like him.
THAT IDIOT.
SAYING THAT...
...AT A TIME LIKE THIS...
BLUSH
HURRY UP...
...AND GET BACK HERE.

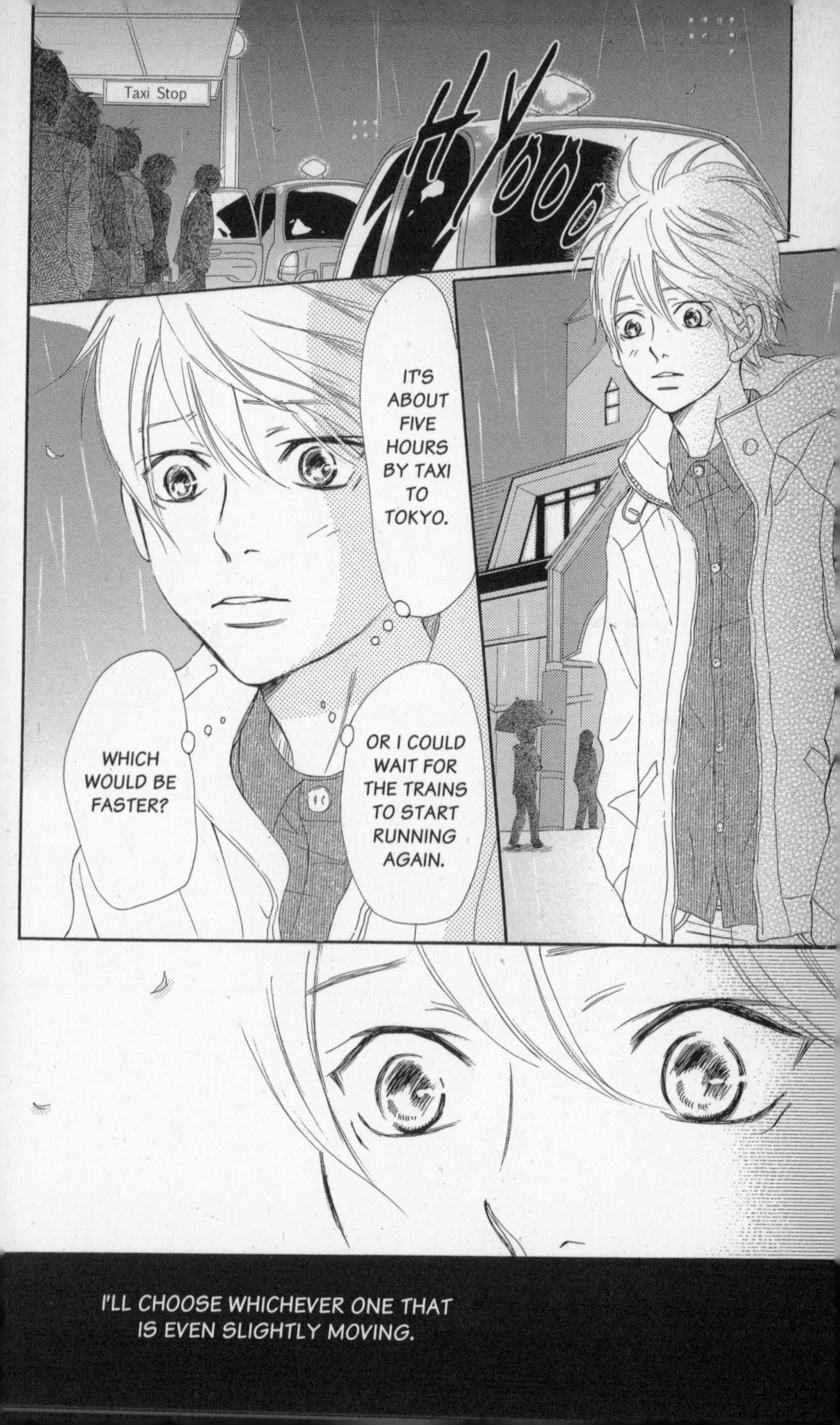
Taxi Stop
IT'S ABOUT FIVE HOURS BY TAXI TO TOKYO.
OR I COULD WAIT FOR THE TRAINS TO START RUNNING AGAIN.
WHICH WOULD BE FASTER?
I'LL CHOOSE WHICHEVER ONE THAT IS EVEN SLIGHTLY MOVING.

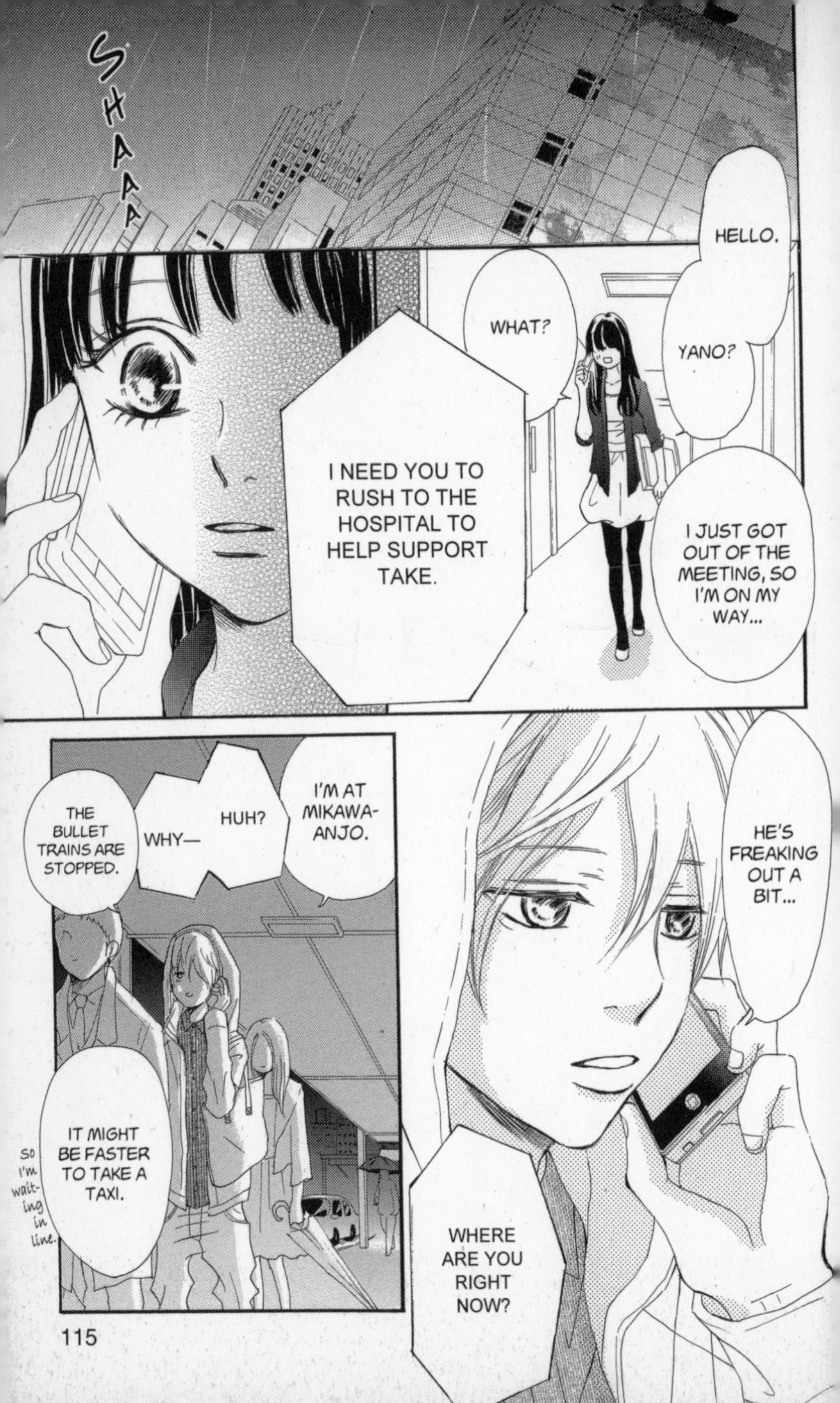
SHAAA
HELLO.
YANO?
WHAT?
I JUST GOT OUT OF THE MEETING, SO I'M ON MY WAY...
I NEED YOU TO RUSH TO THE HOSPITAL TO HELP SUPPORT TAKE.
HE'S FREAKING OUT A BIT...
WHERE ARE YOU RIGHT NOW?
I'M AT MIKAWA-ANJO.
HUH?
WHY—
THE BULLET TRAINS ARE STOPPED.
IT MIGHT BE FASTER TO TAKE A TAXI.
So I'm wait-ing in line.

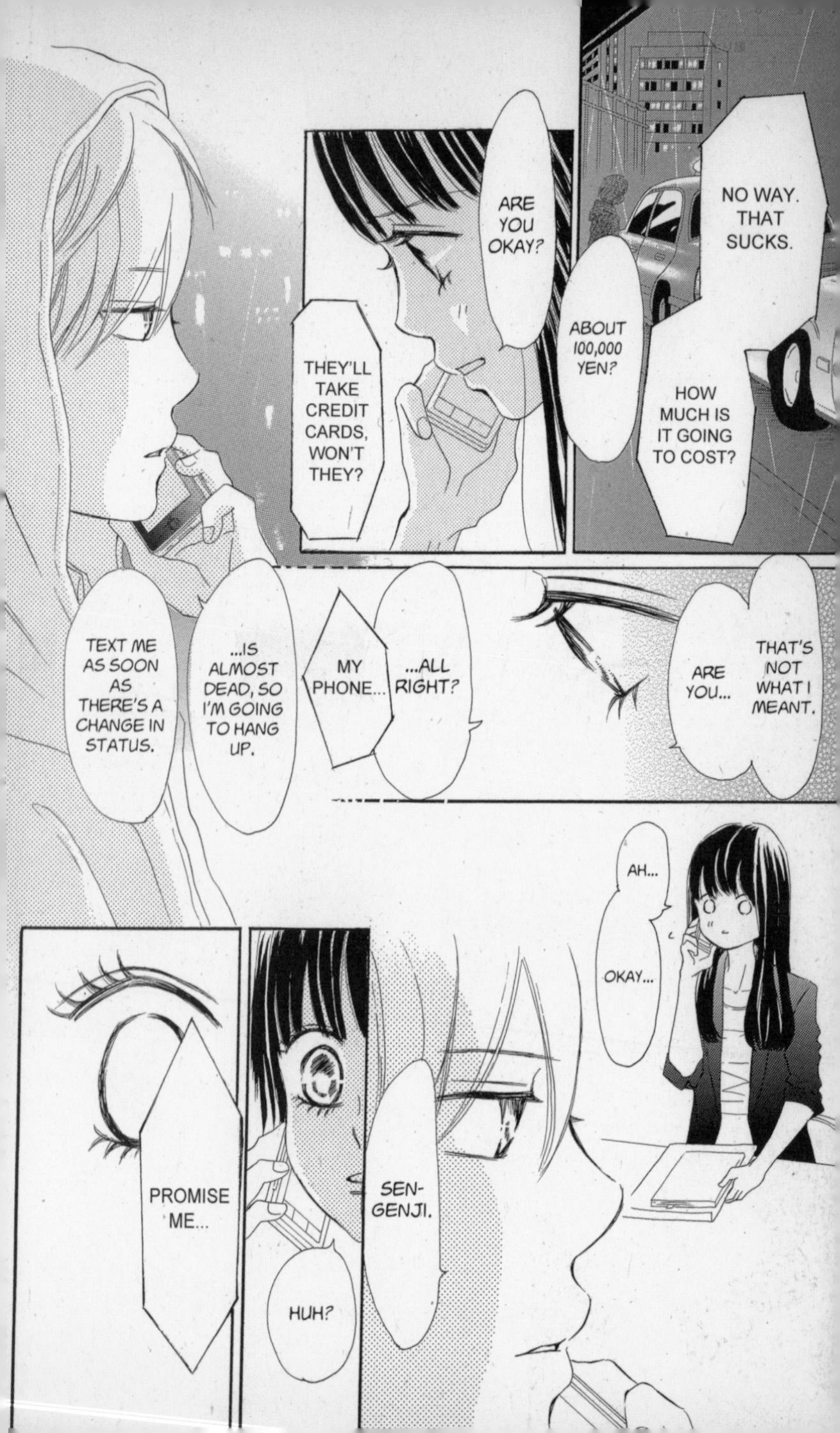
NO WAY. THAT SUCKS.
HOW MUCH IS IT GOING TO COST?
ABOUT 100,000 YEN?
ARE YOU OKAY?
THEY'LL TAKE CREDIT CARDS, WON'T THEY?
THAT'S NOT WHAT I MEANT.
ARE YOU...
...ALL RIGHT?
MY PHONE...
...IS ALMOST DEAD, SO I'M GOING TO HANG UP.
TEXT ME AS SOON AS THERE'S A CHANGE IN STATUS.
AH...
OKAY...
SEN-GENJI.
HUH?
PROMISE ME...

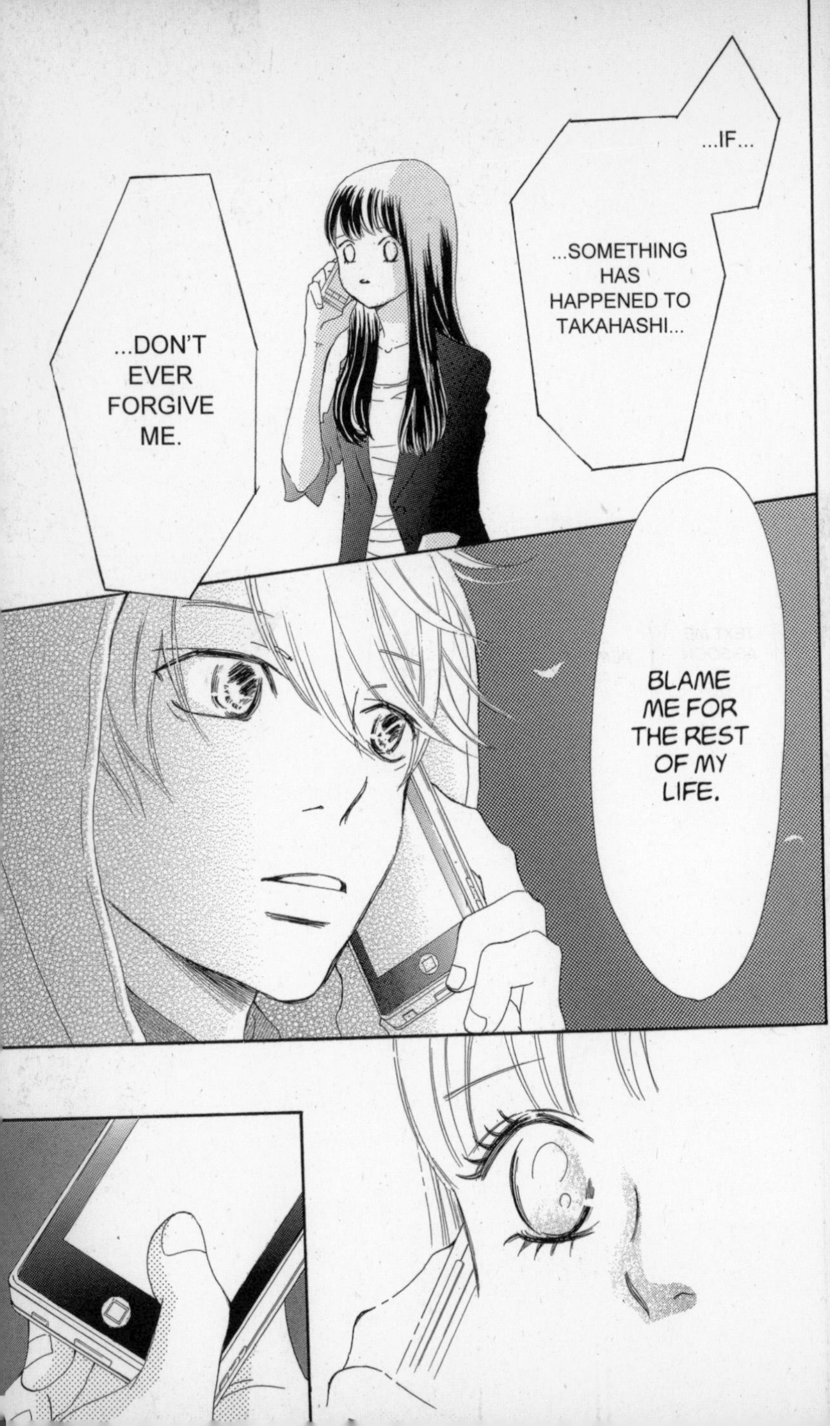
...IF...
...SOMETHING HAS HAPPENED TO TAKAHASHI...
...DON'T EVER FORGIVE ME.
BLAME ME FOR THE REST OF MY LIFE.

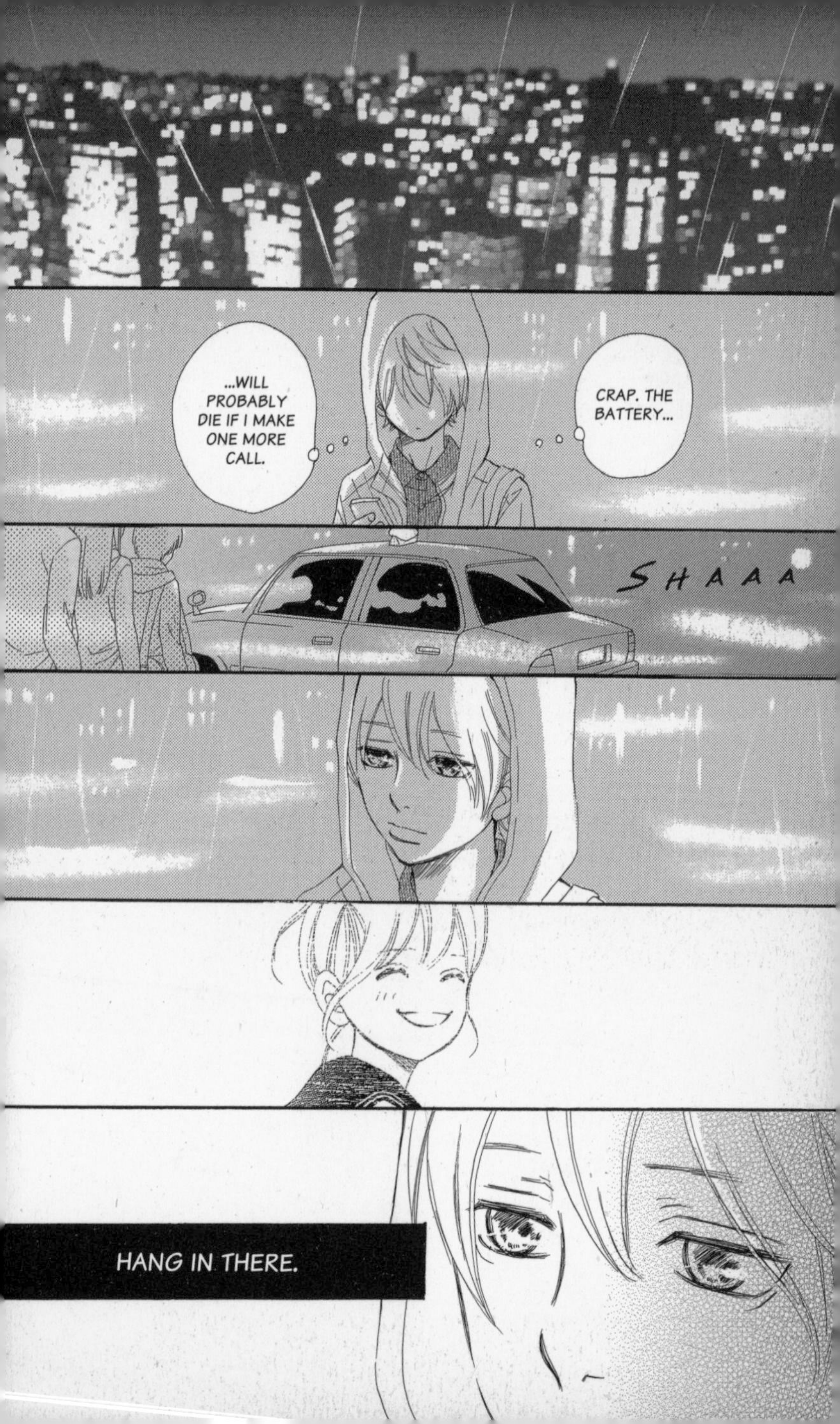
CRAP. THE BATTERY...
...WILL PROBABLY DIE IF I MAKE ONE MORE CALL.
SHAAA
HANG IN THERE.

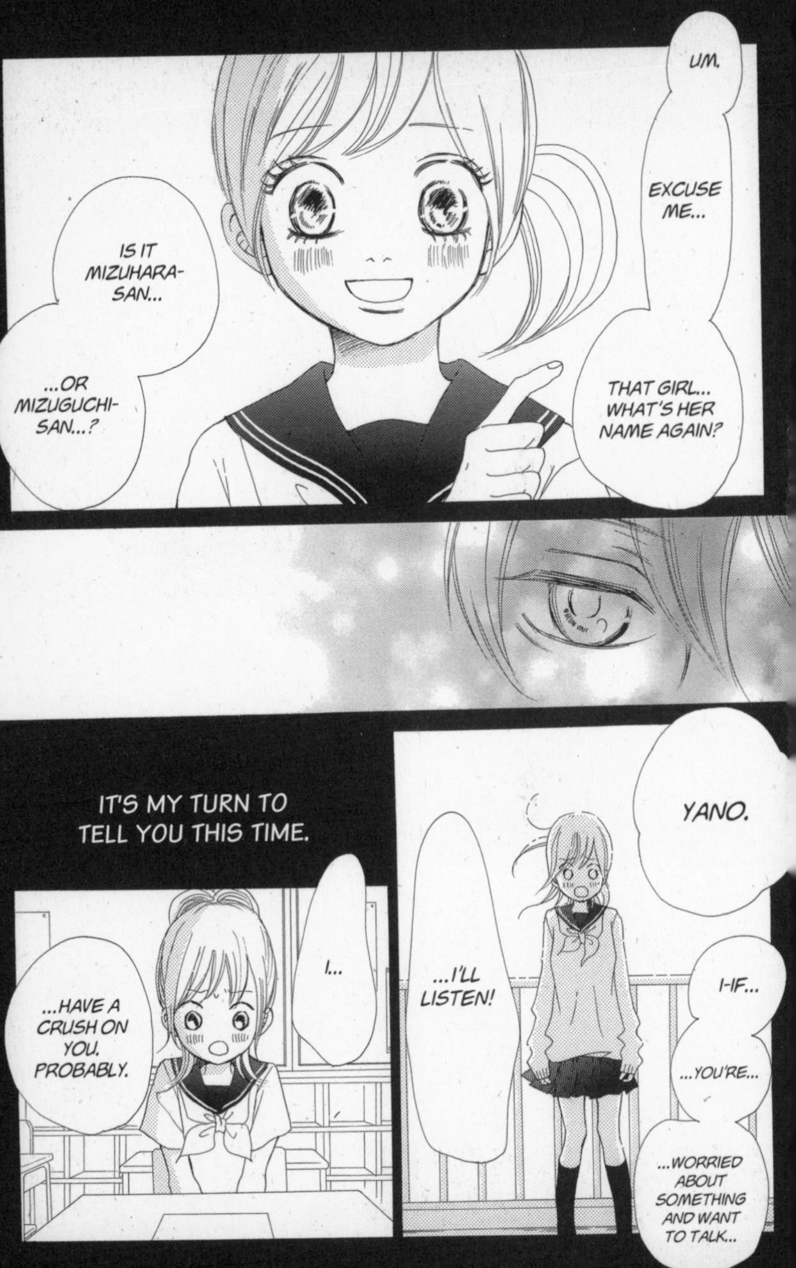
UM.
EXCUSE ME...
THAT GIRL... WHAT'S HER NAME AGAIN?
IS IT MIZUHARA-SAN...
...OR MIZUGUCHI-SAN...?
YANO.
I-IF...
...YOU'RE...
...WORRIED ABOUT SOMETHING AND WANT TO TALK...
...I'LL LISTEN!
IT'S MY TURN TO TELL YOU THIS TIME.
I...
...HAVE A CRUSH ON YOU. PROBABLY.

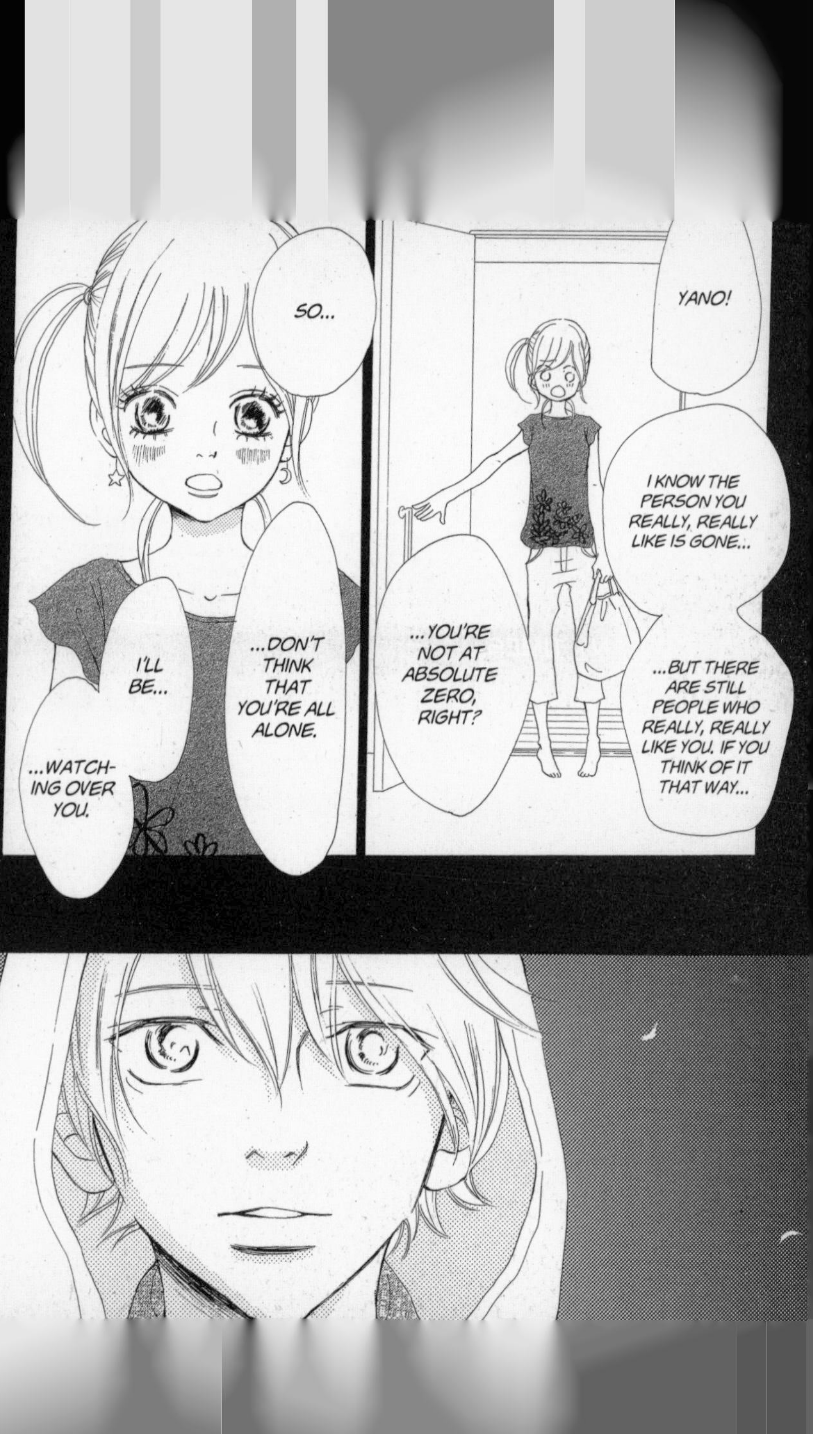
YANO!
I KNOW THE PERSON YOU REALLY, REALLY LIKE IS GONE...
...BUT THERE ARE STILL PEOPLE WHO REALLY, REALLY LIKE YOU. IF YOU THINK OF IT THAT WAY...
...YOU'RE NOT AT ABSOLUTE ZERO, RIGHT?
SO...
...DON'T THINK THAT YOU'RE ALL ALONE.
I'LL BE...
...WATCH-ING OVER YOU.

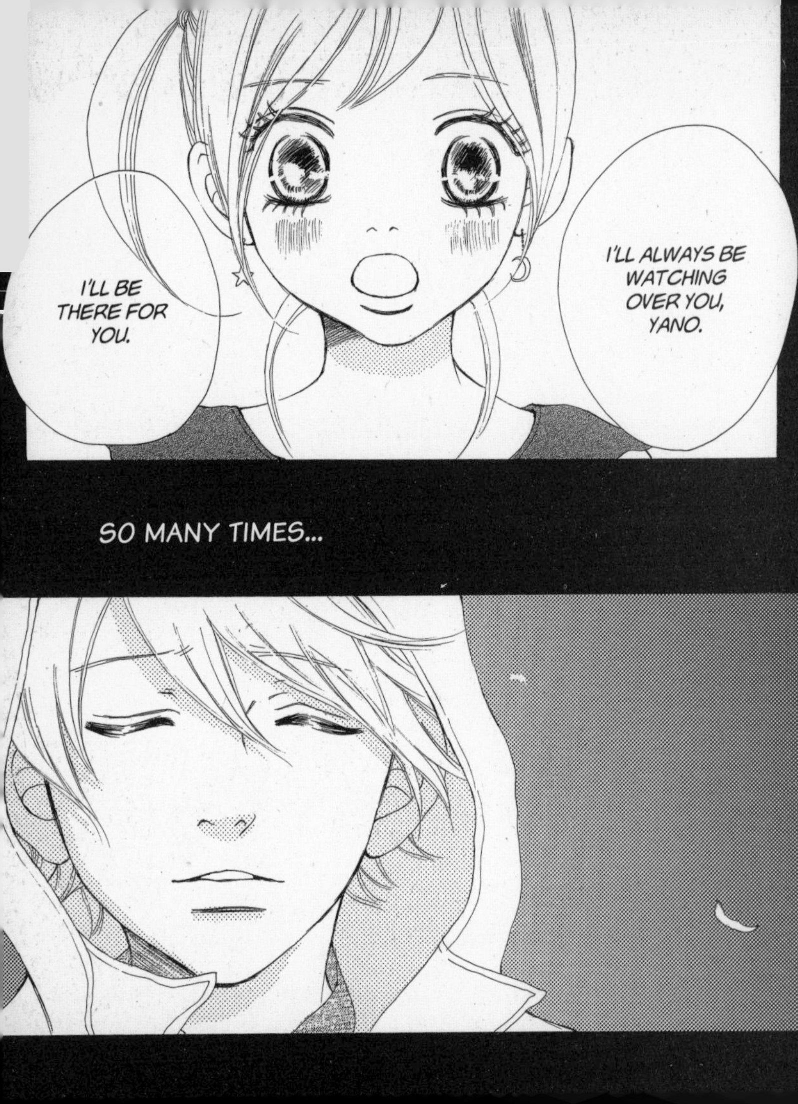
I'LL ALWAYS BE WATCHING OVER YOU, YANO.
I'LL BE THERE FOR YOU.
SO MANY TIMES...

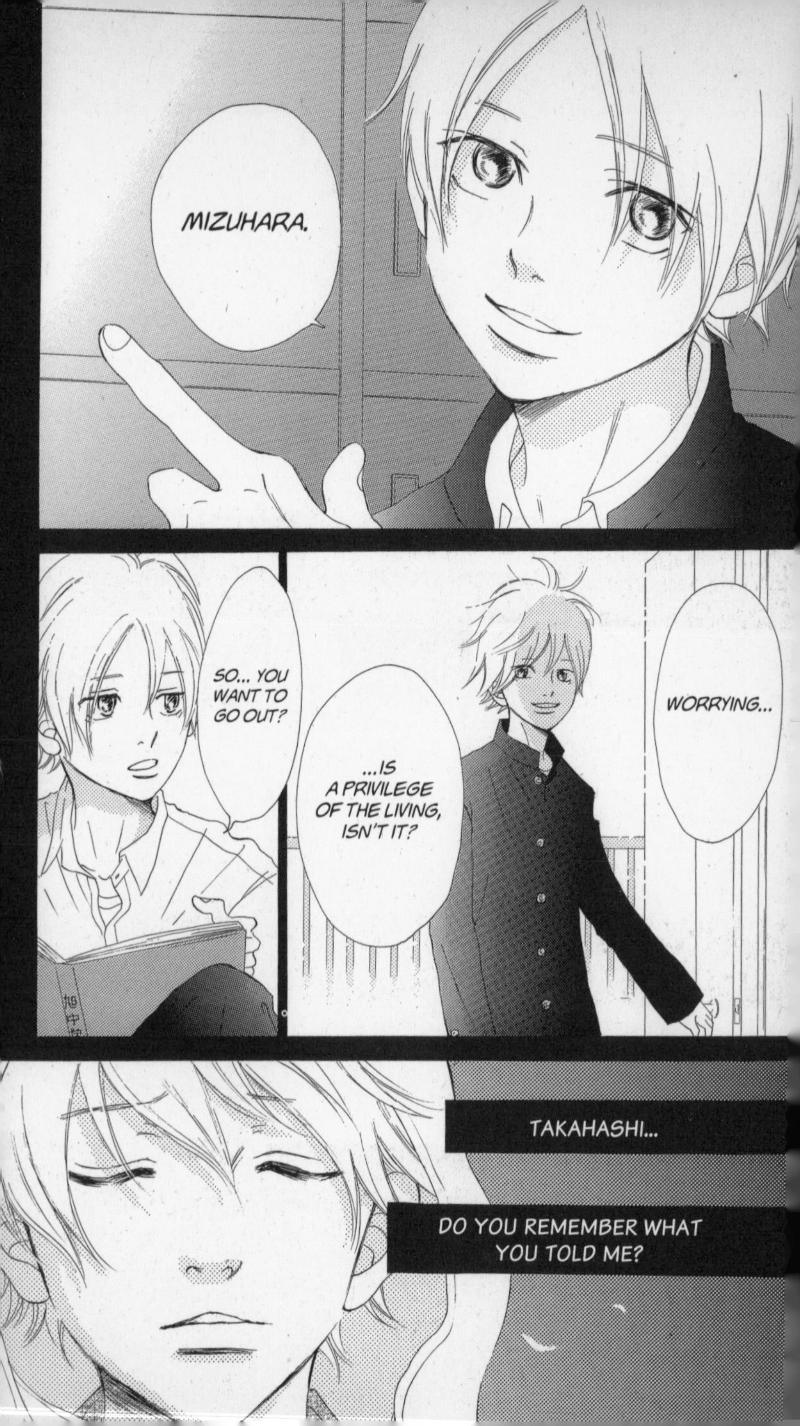
MIZUHARA.
WORRYING...
...IS A PRIVILEGE OF THE LIVING, ISN'T IT?
SO... YOU WANT TO GO OUT?
TAKAHASHI...
DO YOU REMEMBER WHAT YOU TOLD ME?

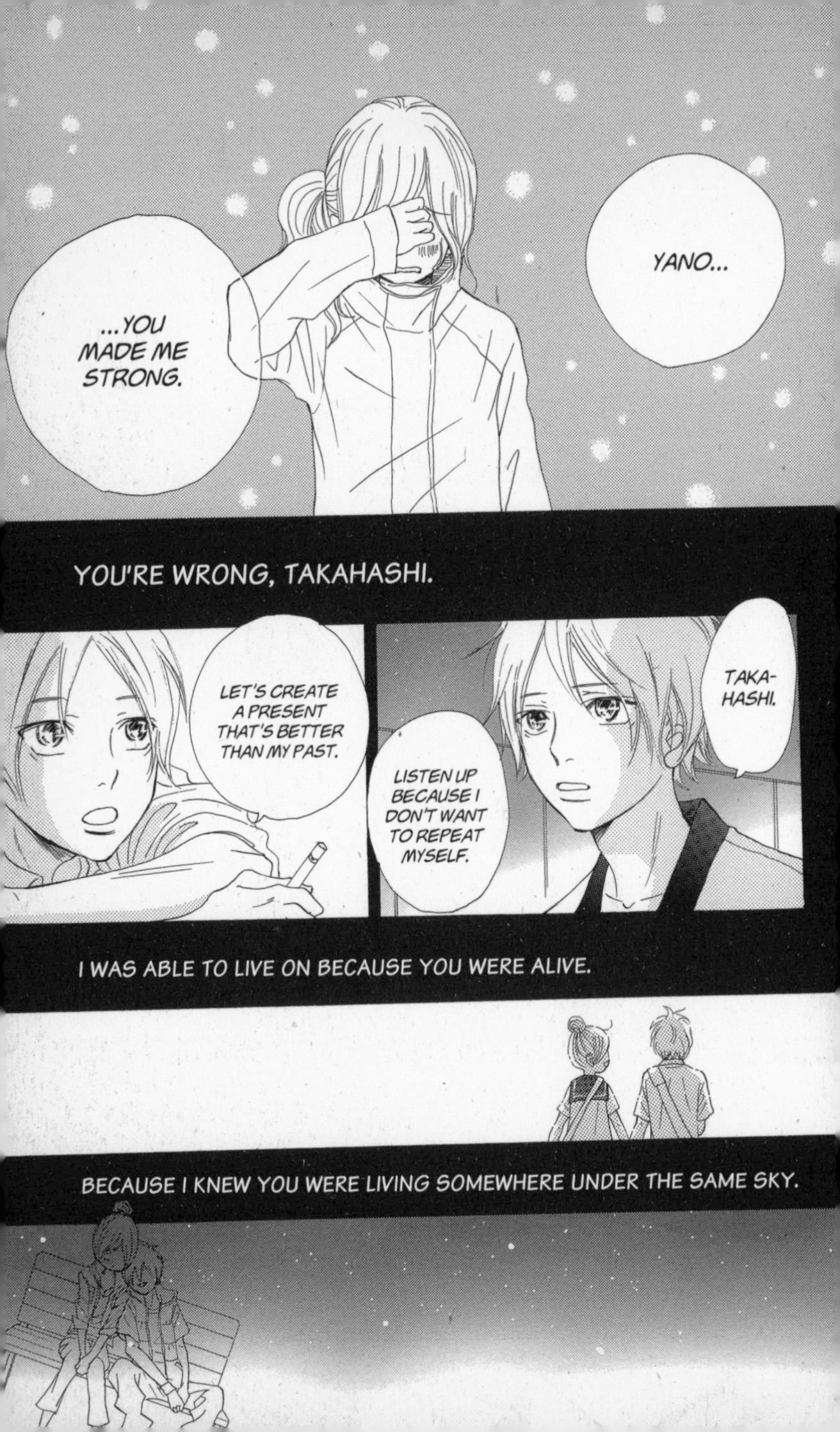
YANO...
...YOU MADE ME STRONG.
YOU'RE WRONG, TAKAHASHI.
TAKA-HASHI.
LISTEN UP BECAUSE I DON'T WANT TO REPEAT MYSELF.
LET'S CREATE A PRESENT THAT'S BETTER THAN MY PAST.
I WAS ABLE TO LIVE ON BECAUSE YOU WERE ALIVE.
BECAUSE I KNEW YOU WERE LIVING SOMEWHERE UNDER THE SAME SKY.

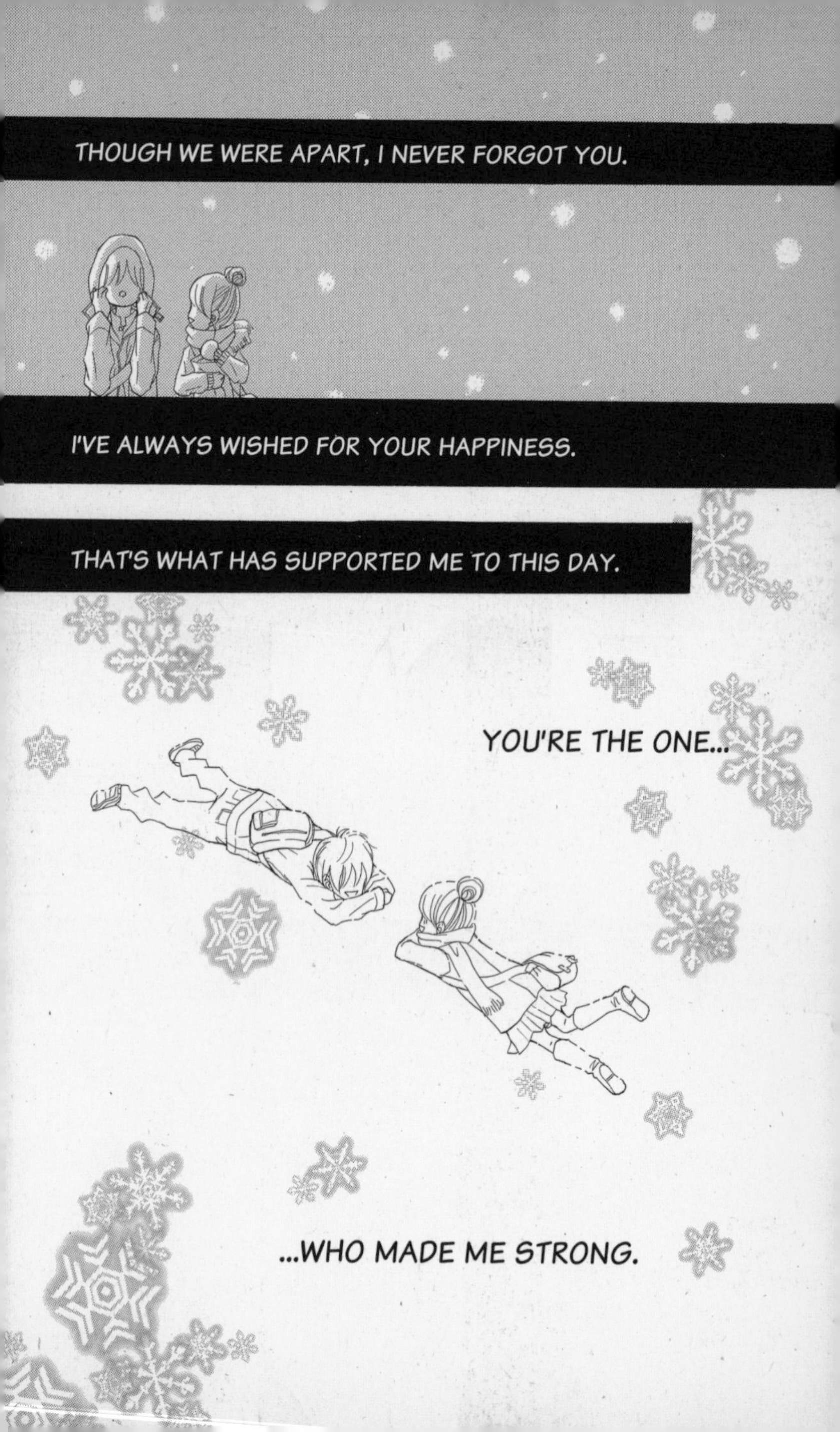
THOUGH WE WERE APART, I NEVER FORGOT YOU.
I'VE ALWAYS WISHED FOR YOUR HAPPINESS.
THAT'S WHAT HAS SUPPORTED ME TO THIS DAY.
YOU'RE THE ONE...
...WHO MADE ME STRONG.

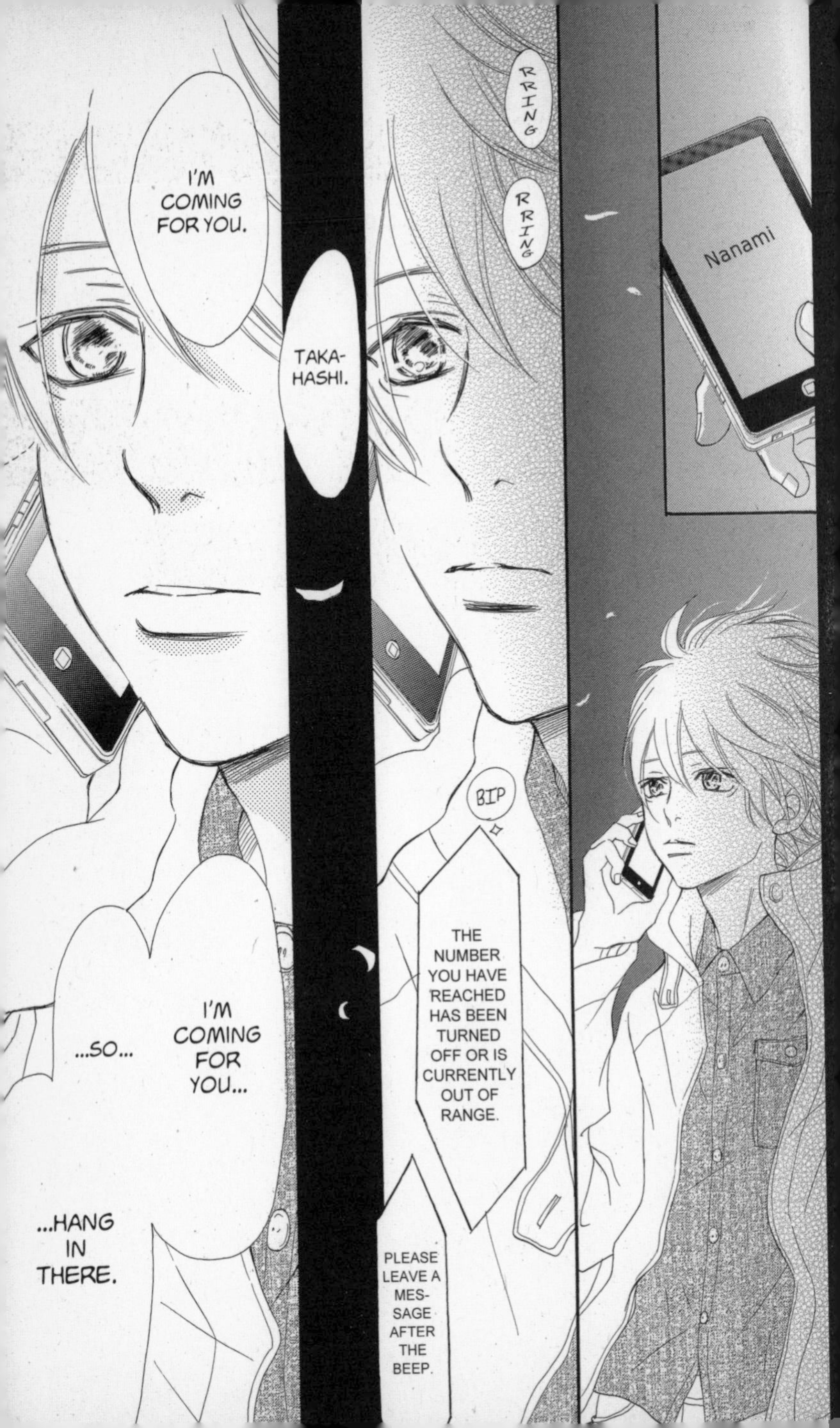

Nanami
RRING
RRING
TAKA-HASHI.
BIP
THE NUMBER YOU HAVE REACHED HAS BEEN TURNED OFF OR IS CURRENTLY OUT OF RANGE.
PLEASE LEAVE A MES-SAGE AFTER THE BEEP.
I'M COMING FOR YOU.
I'M COMING FOR YOU...
...SO...
...HANG IN THERE.

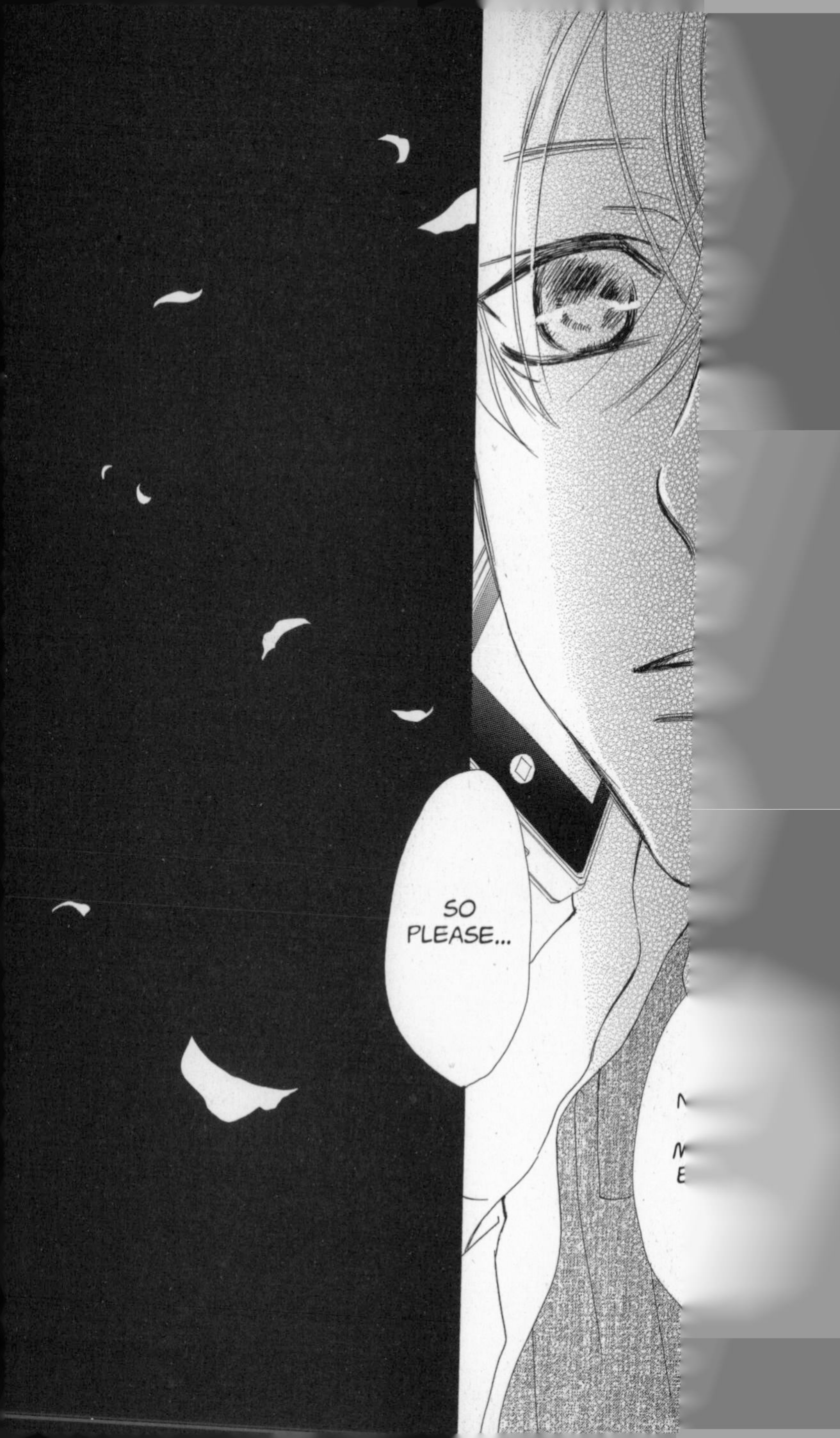
SO PLEASE...

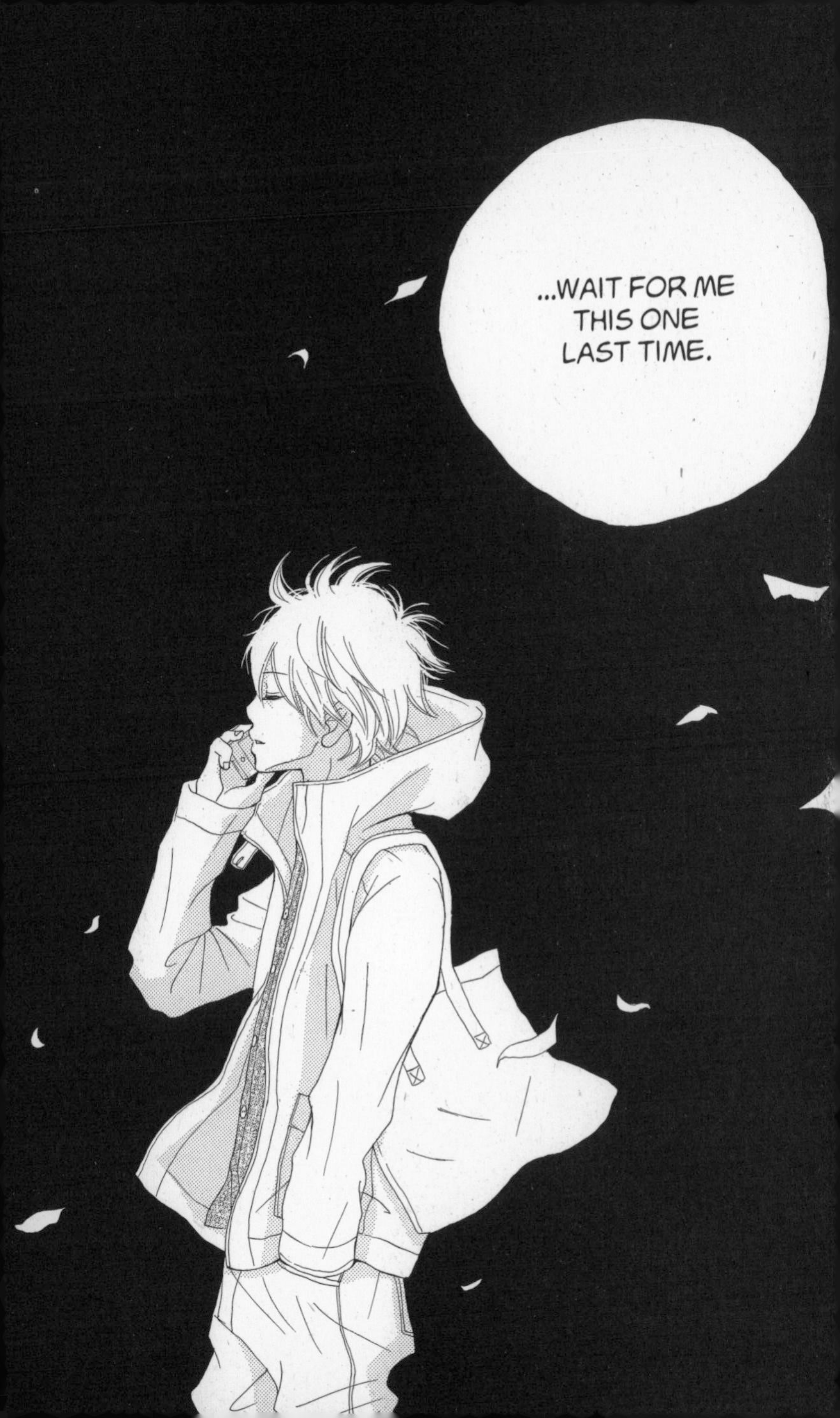
...WAIT FOR ME THIS ONE LAST TIME.

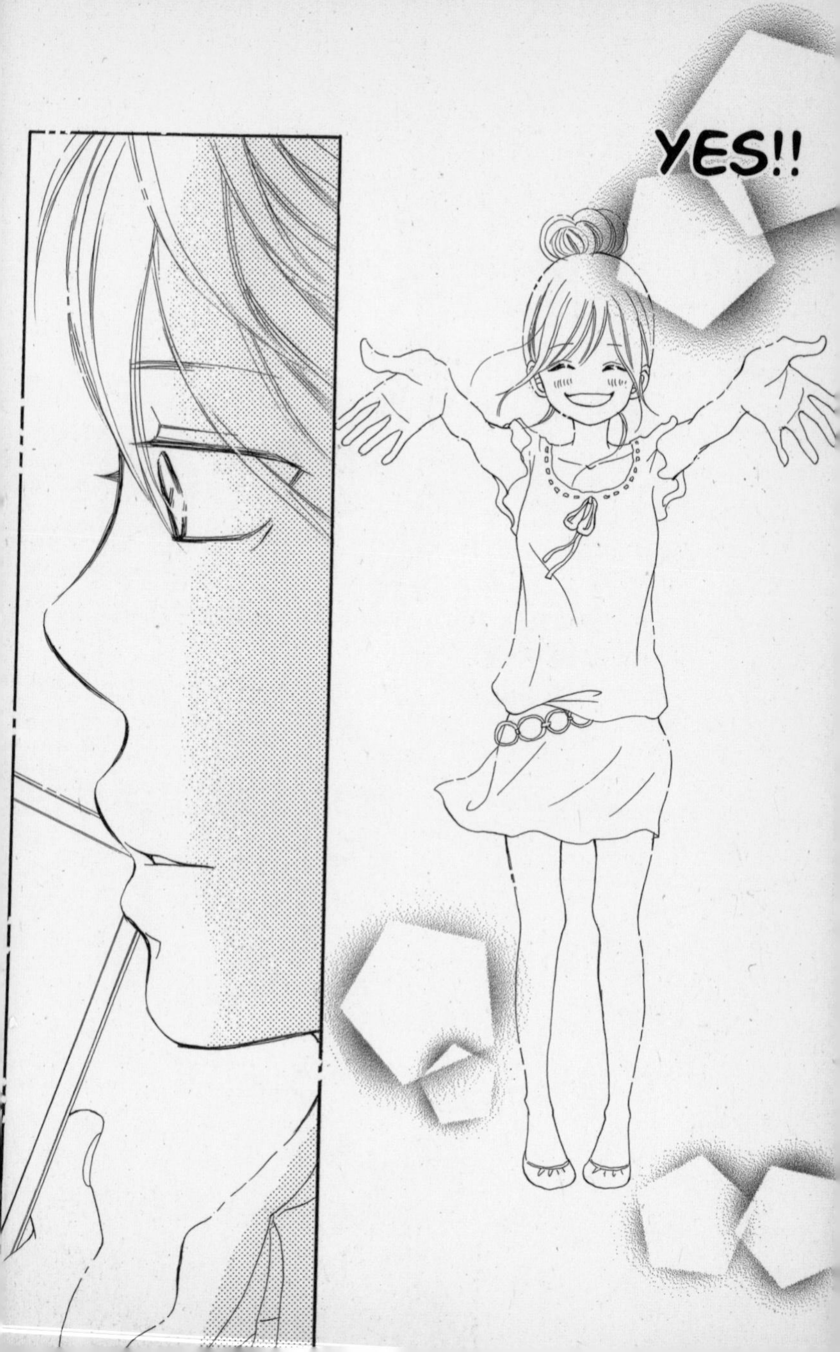
YES!!

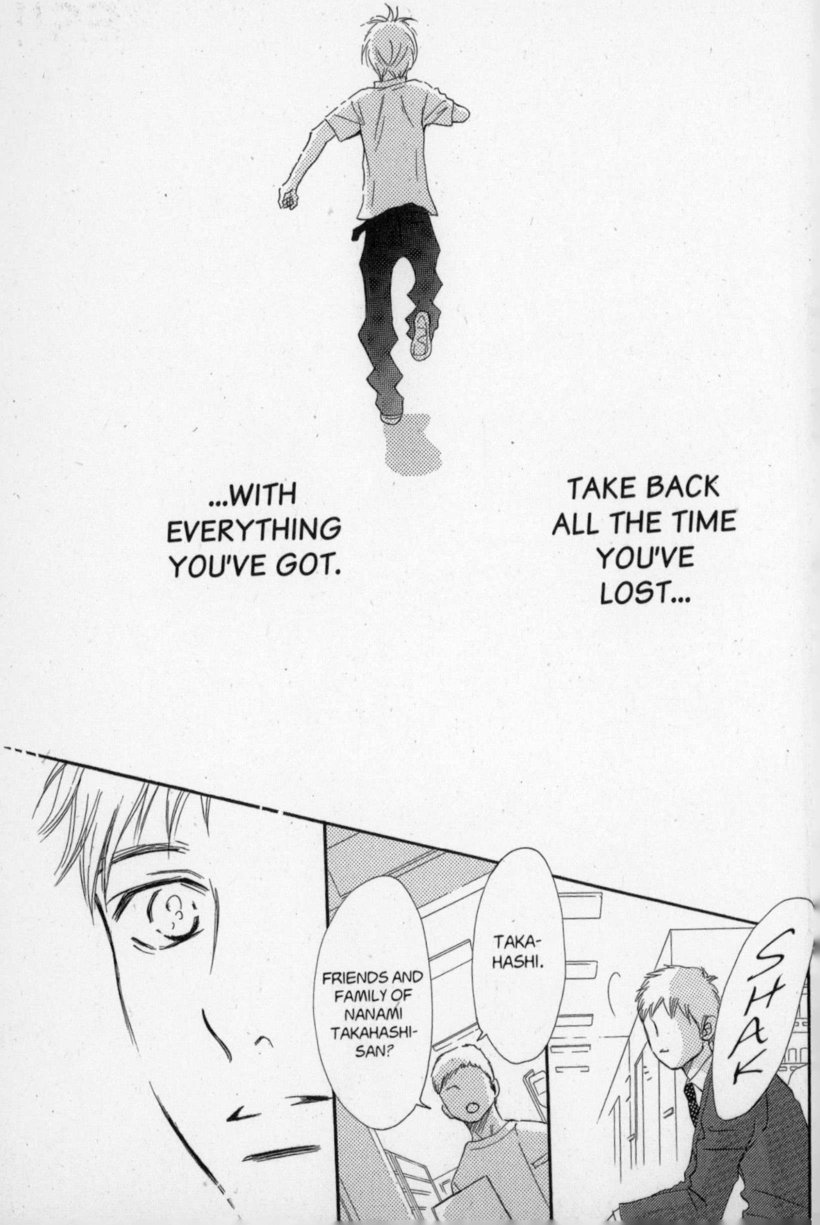
TAKE BACK ALL THE TIME YOU'VE LOST...
...WITH EVERYTHING YOU'VE GOT.
SHAK
TAKA-HASHI.
FRIENDS AND FAMILY OF NANAMI TAKAHASHI-SAN?

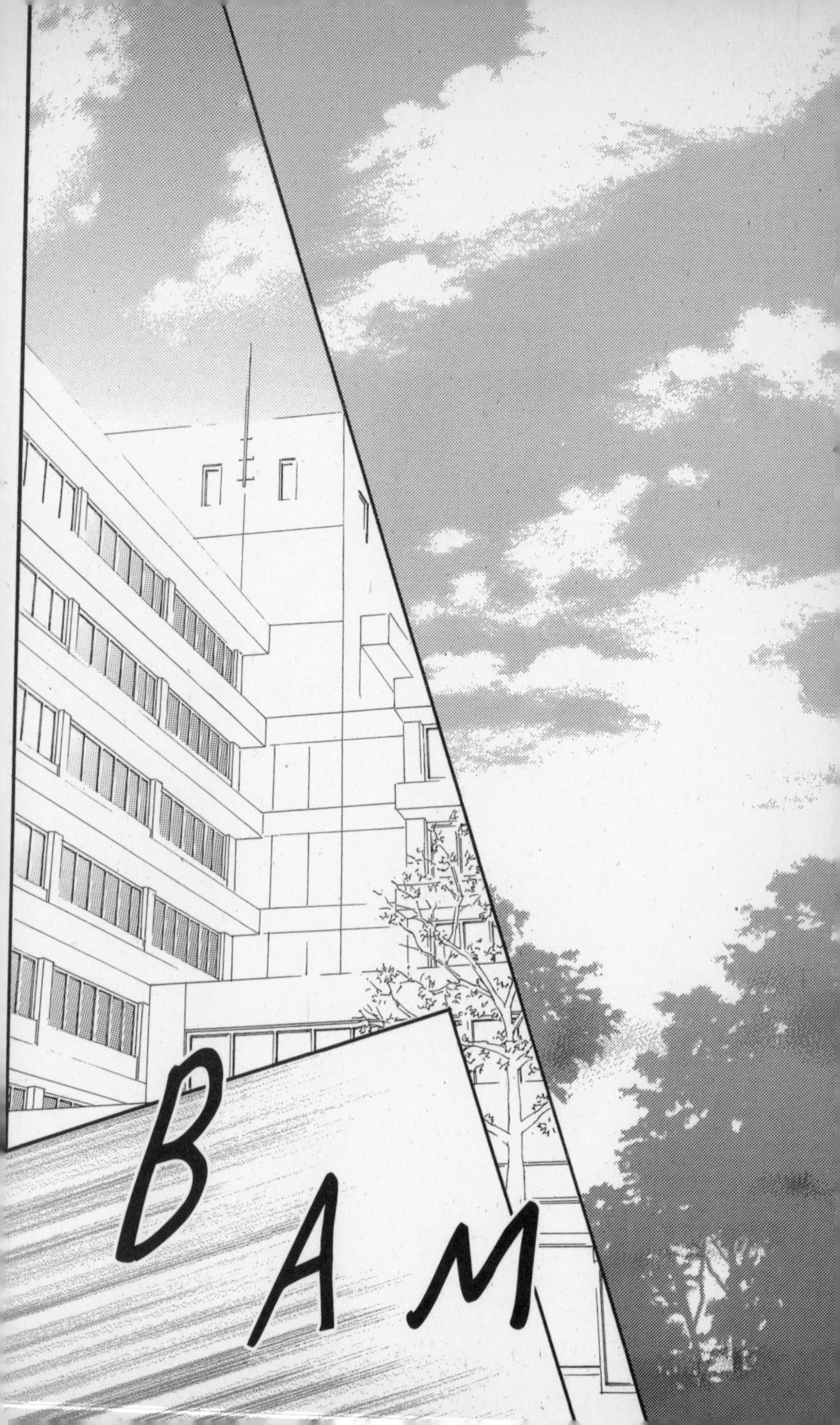
BAM

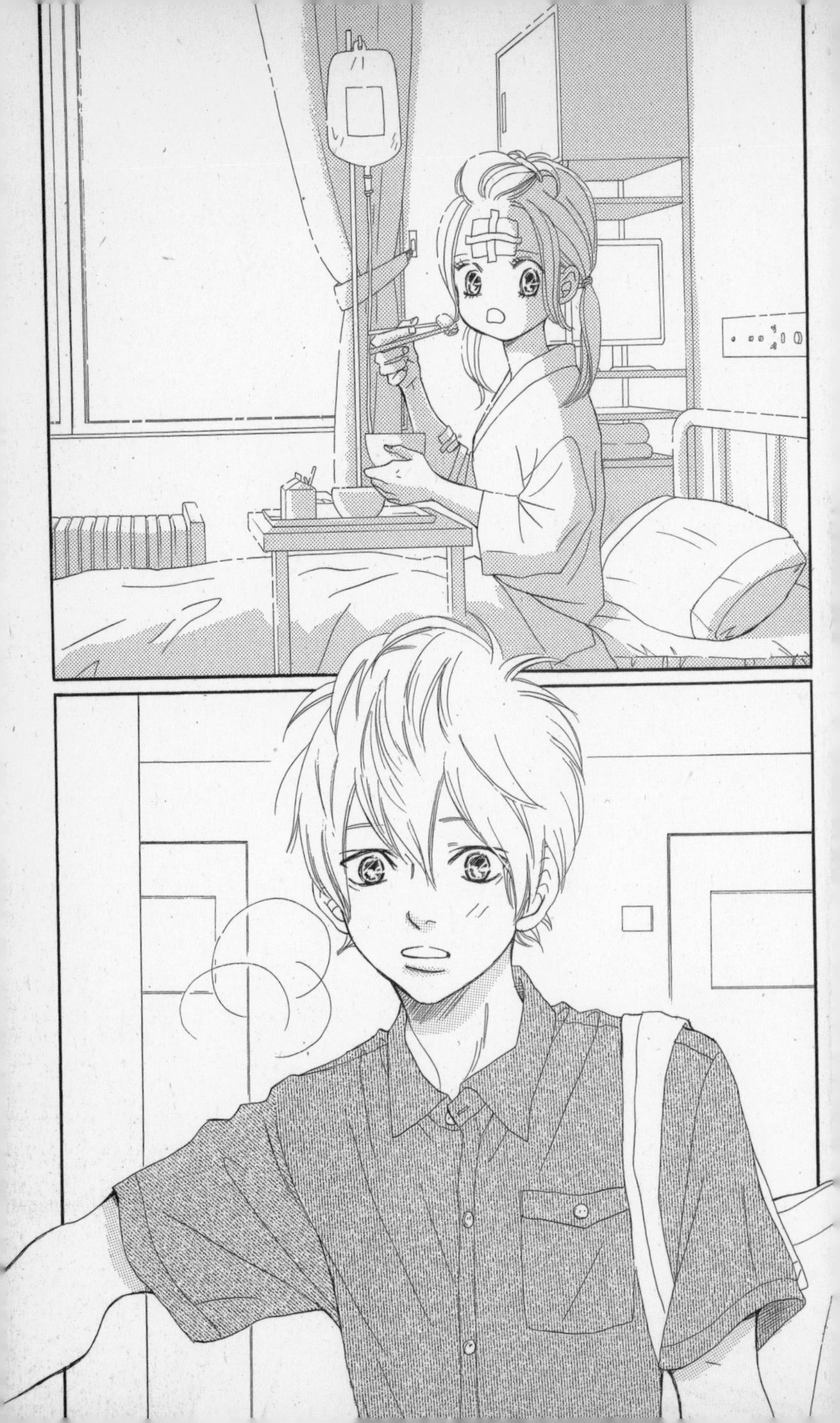

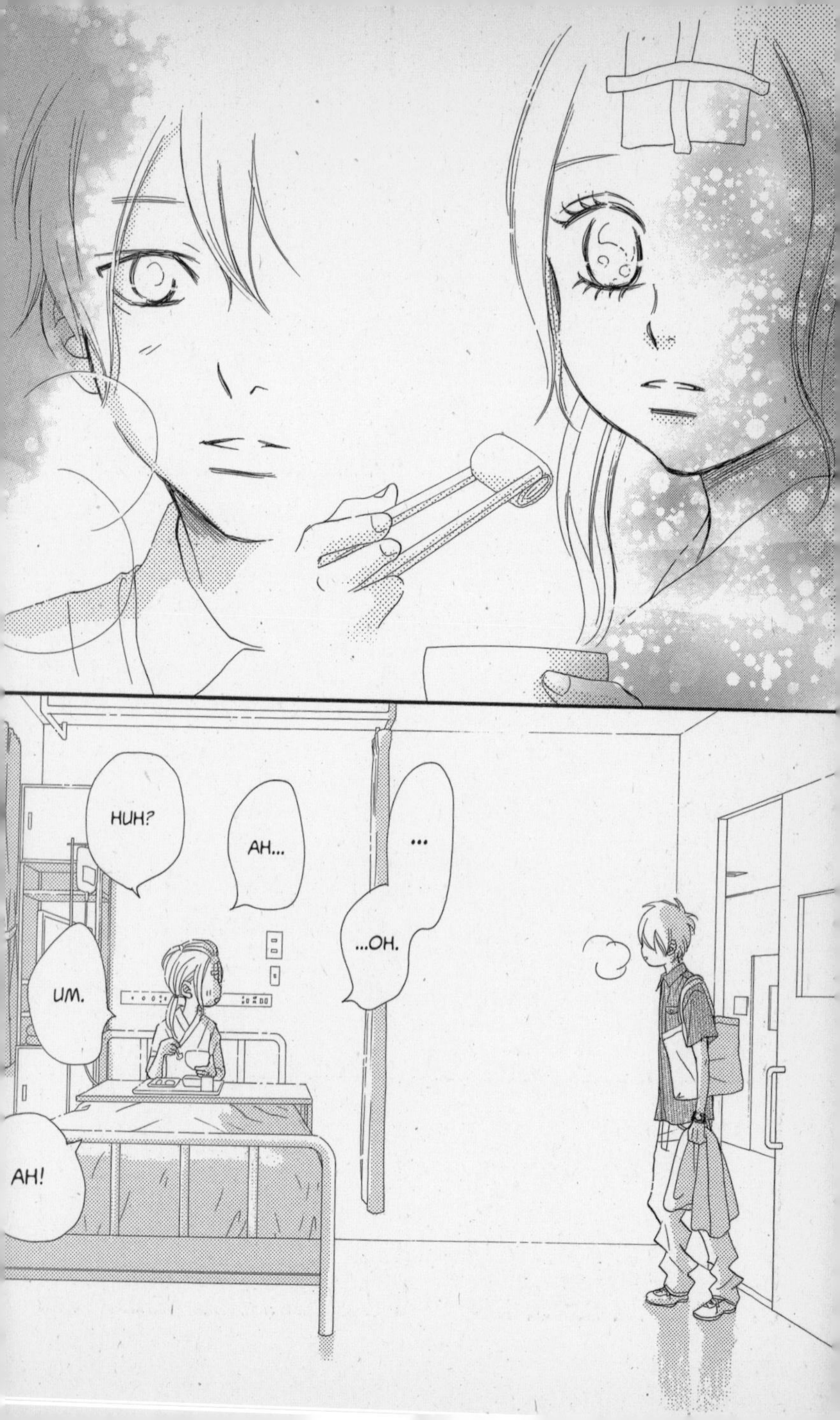
...
...OH.
AH...
HUH?
UM.
AH!

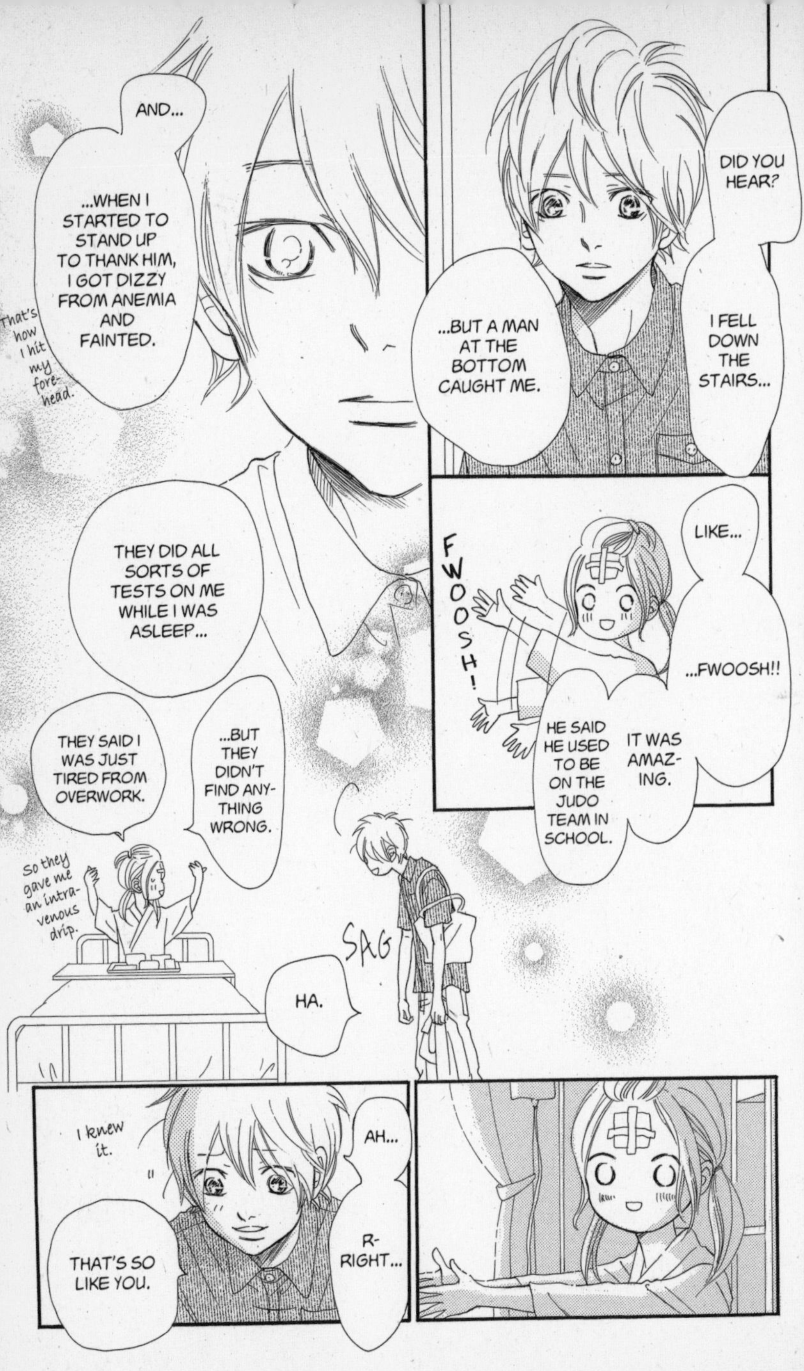
DID YOU HEAR?
I FELL DOWN THE STAIRS...
...BUT A MAN AT THE BOTTOM CAUGHT ME.
LIKE...
...FWOOSH!!
FWOOSH!
IT WAS AMAZ-ING.
HE SAID HE USED TO BE ON THE JUDO TEAM IN SCHOOL.
AND...
...WHEN I STARTED TO STAND UP TO THANK HIM, I GOT DIZZY FROM ANEMIA AND FAINTED.
That's how I hit my fore-head.
THEY DID ALL SORTS OF TESTS ON ME WHILE I WAS ASLEEP...
...BUT THEY DIDN'T FIND ANY-THING WRONG.
THEY SAID I WAS JUST TIRED FROM OVERWORK.
So they gave me an intra-venous drip.
SAG
HA.
AH...
R-RIGHT...
I knew it.
THAT'S SO LIKE YOU.

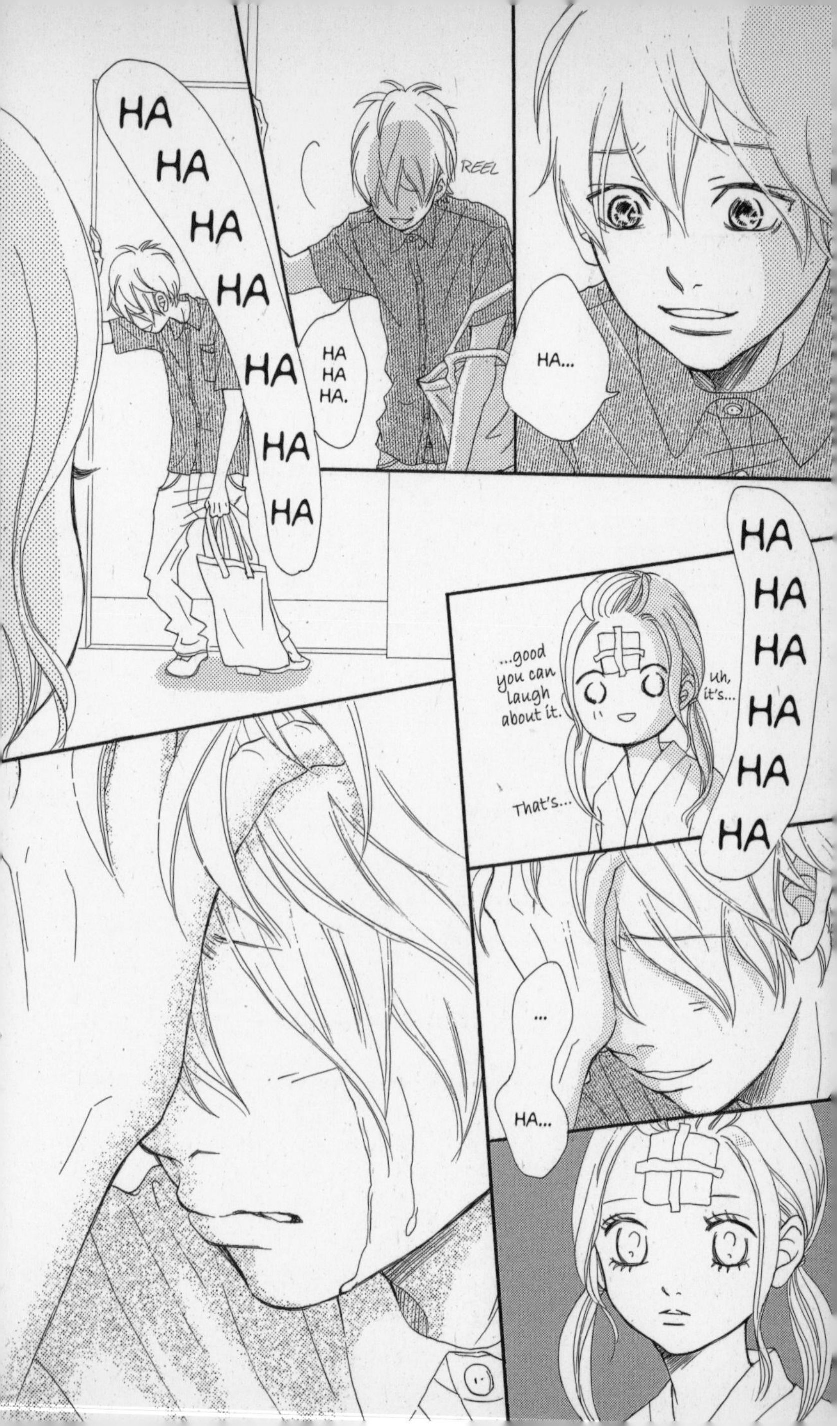
HA...
REEL
HA HA HA.
HA HA HA HA HA HA HA
HA HA HA HA HA HA
Uh, it's...
...good you can laugh about it.
That's...
...
HA...

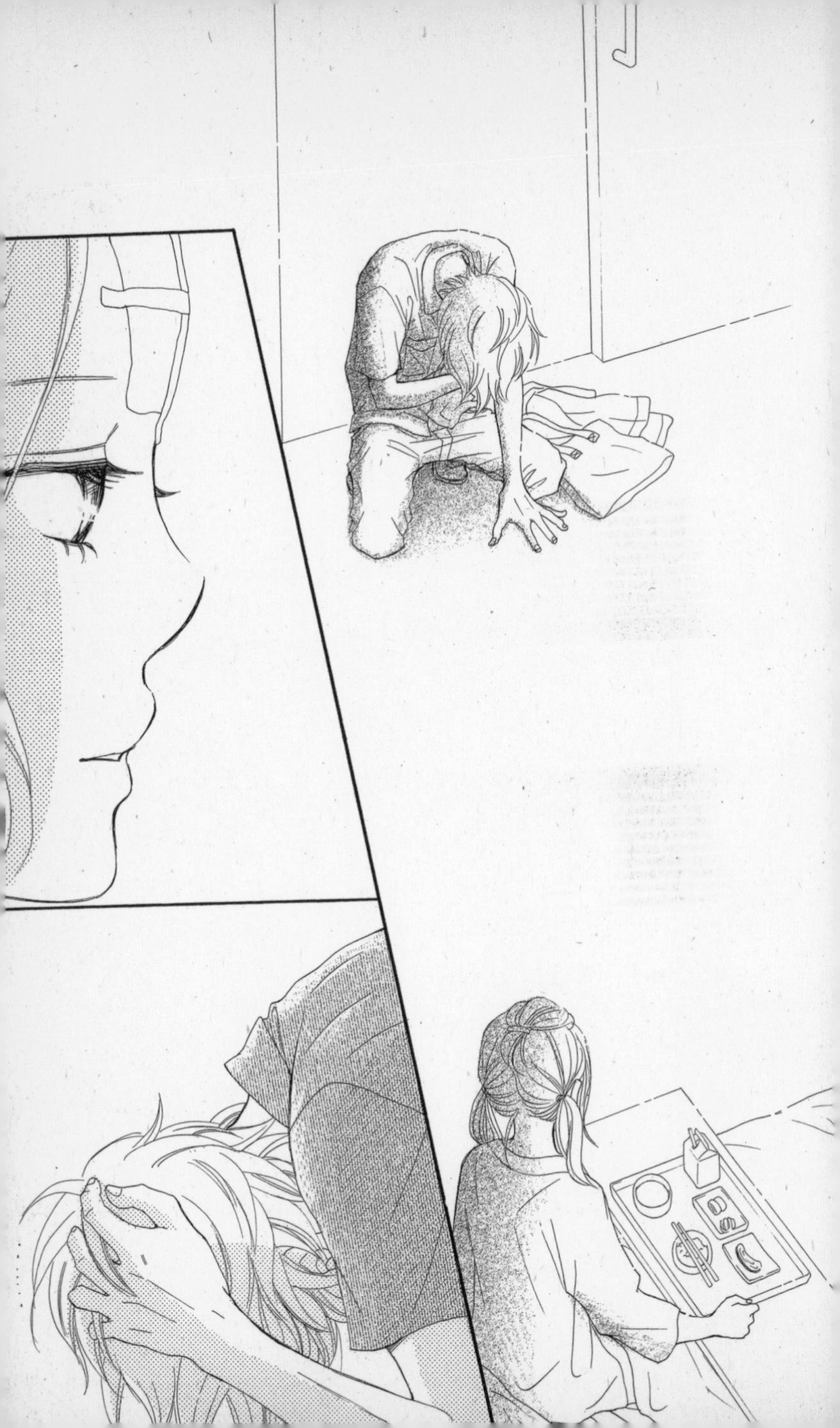

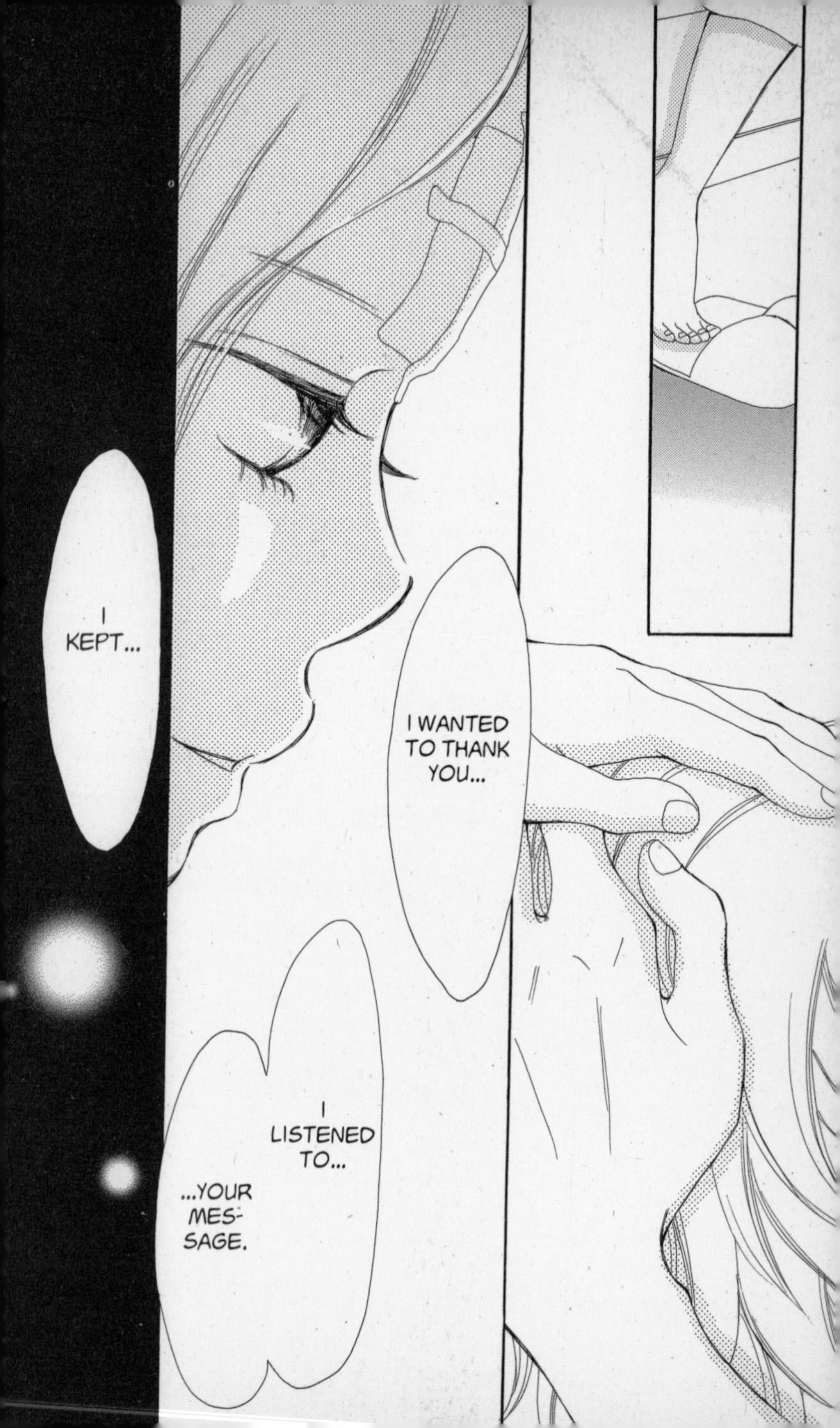
I WANTED TO THANK YOU...
I KEPT...
I LISTENED TO...
...YOUR MES-SAGE.

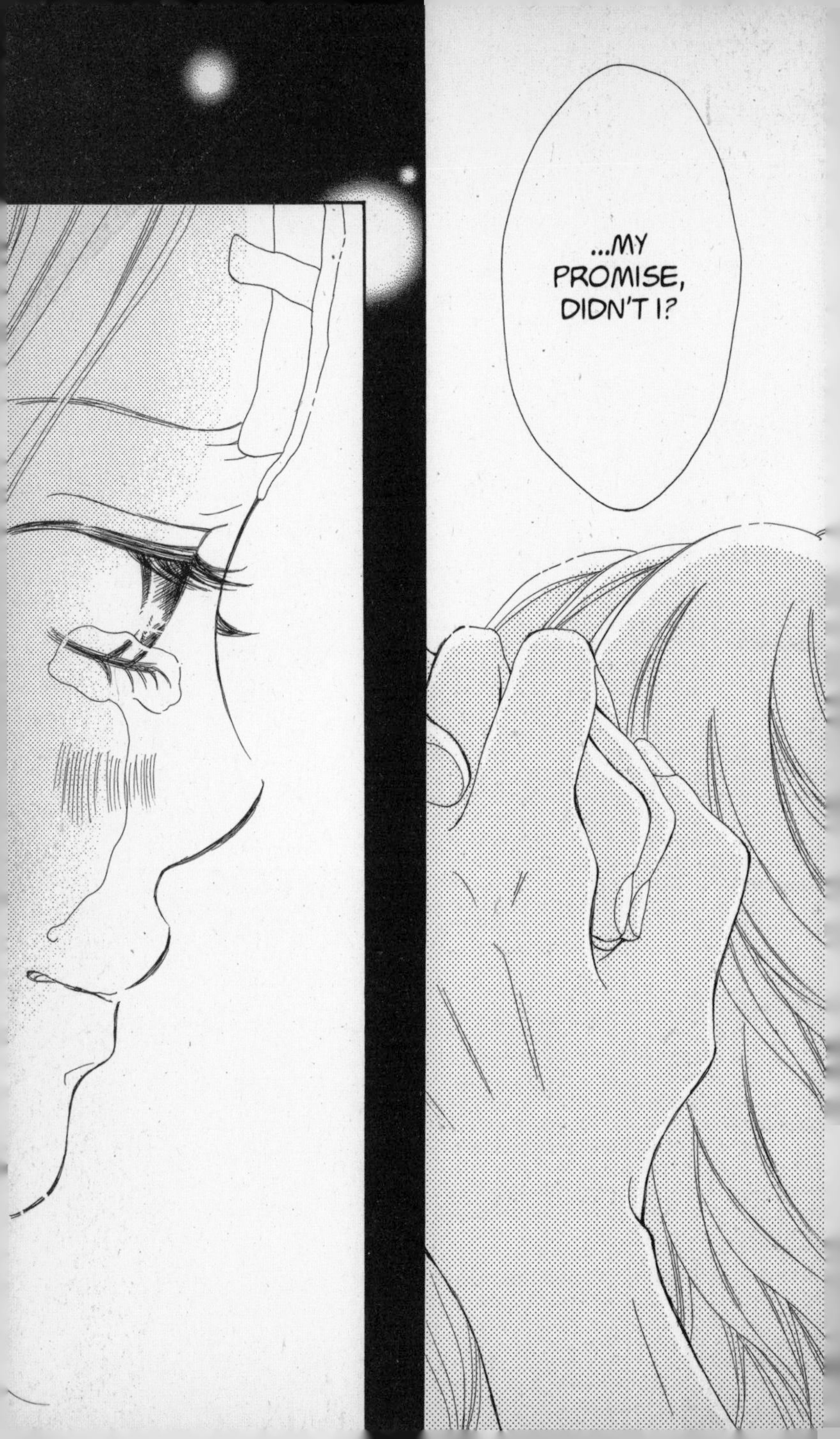
...MY PROMISE, DIDN'T I?

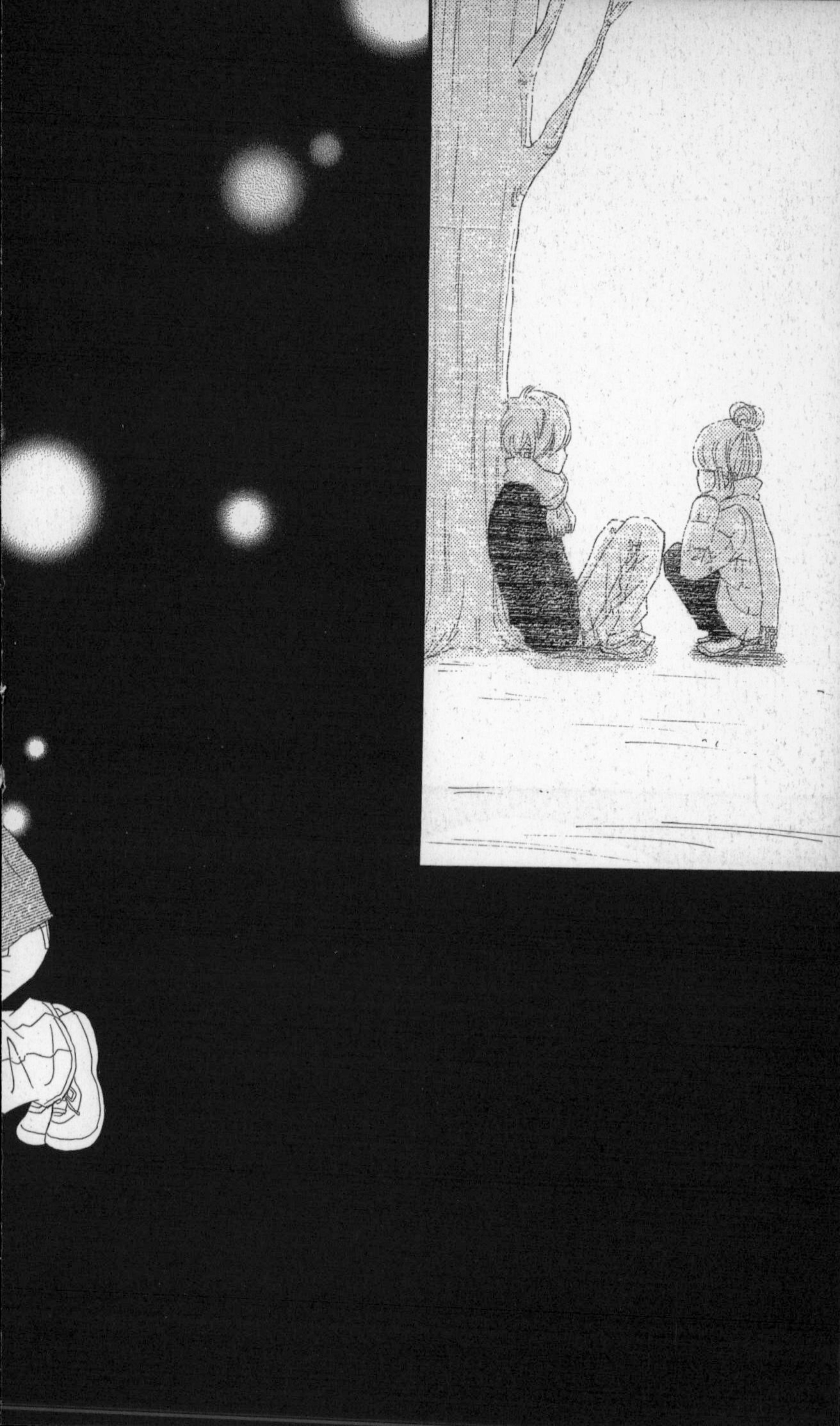

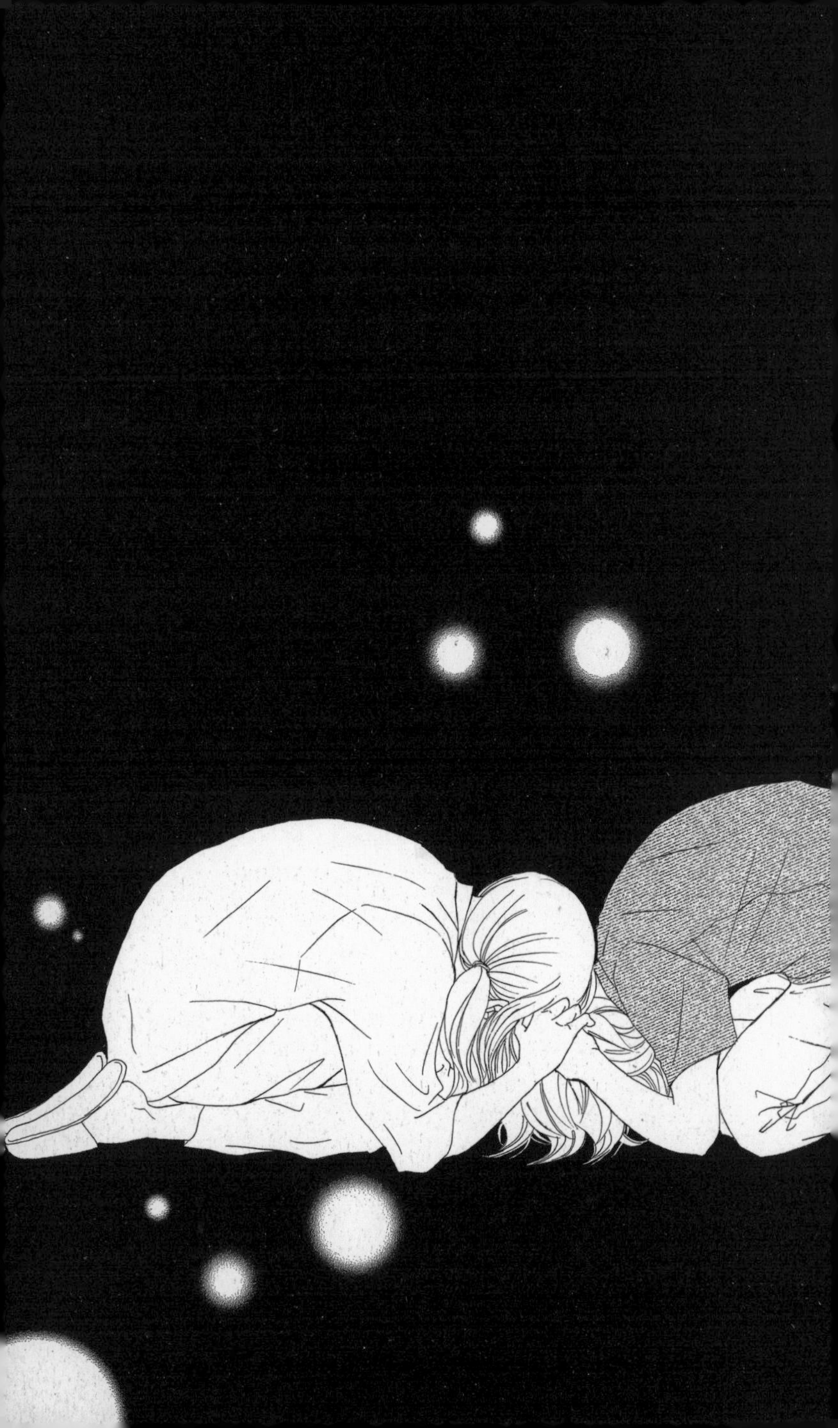

I'M SORRY. I PROMISED TO ALWAYS WATCH OVER YOU.

BUT I LOST SIGHT OF YOU ON THE WAY.

I RAN AWAY.

YOU DIDN'T RUN AWAY.

YOU JUST TOOK A DETOUR.

YOU LOST YOUR WAY FOR A LITTLE WHILE.

YOUR COMPASS WAS BROKEN.

BUT YOU'VE COME BACK.

I'VE COME BACK.

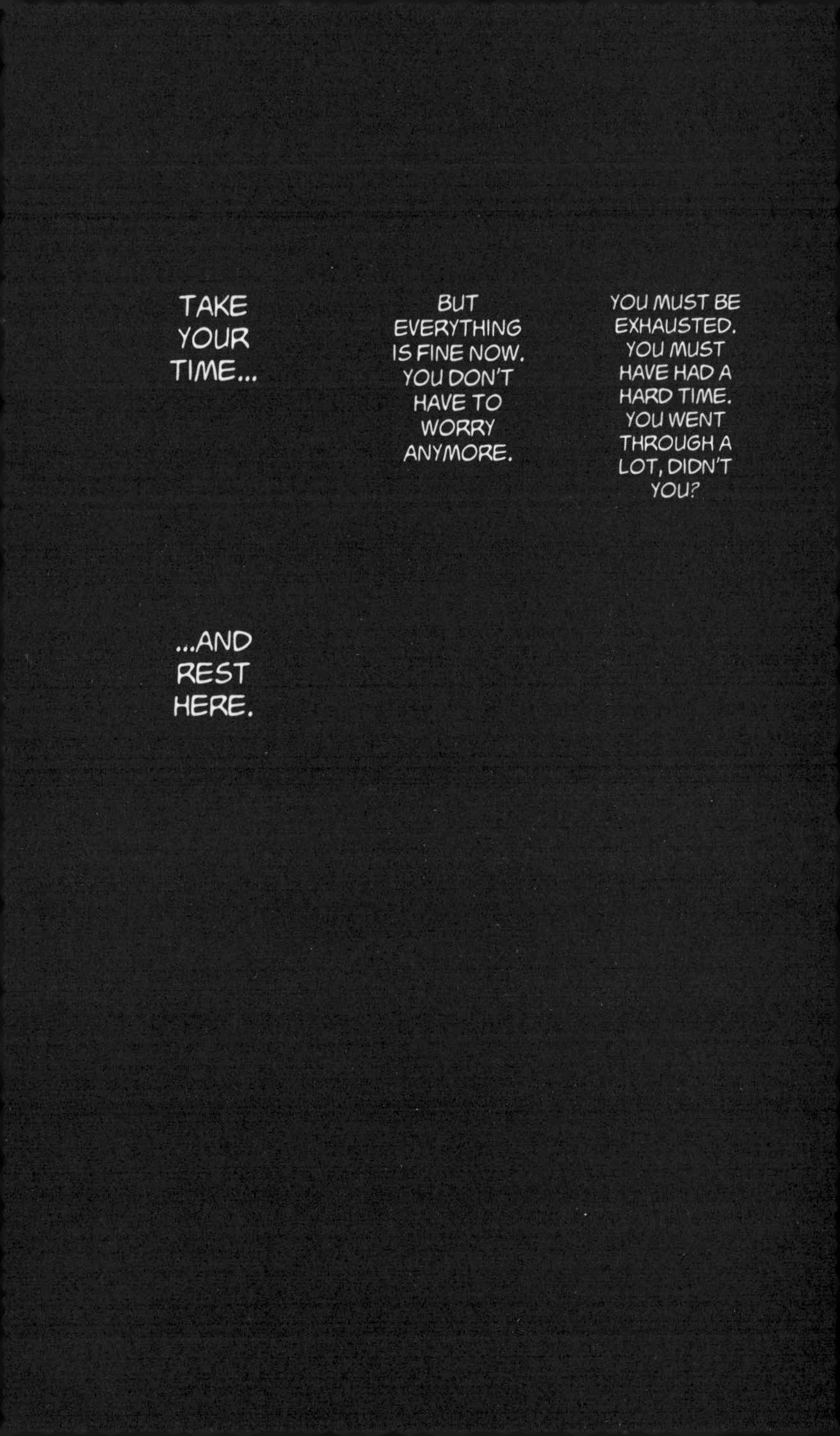
YOU MUST BE EXHAUSTED. YOU MUST HAVE HAD A HARD TIME. YOU WENT THROUGH A LOT, DIDN'T YOU?
BUT EVERYTHING IS FINE NOW. YOU DON'T HAVE TO WORRY ANYMORE.
TAKE YOUR TIME...
...AND REST HERE.

THANK
YOU FOR
WAITING
FOR ME.

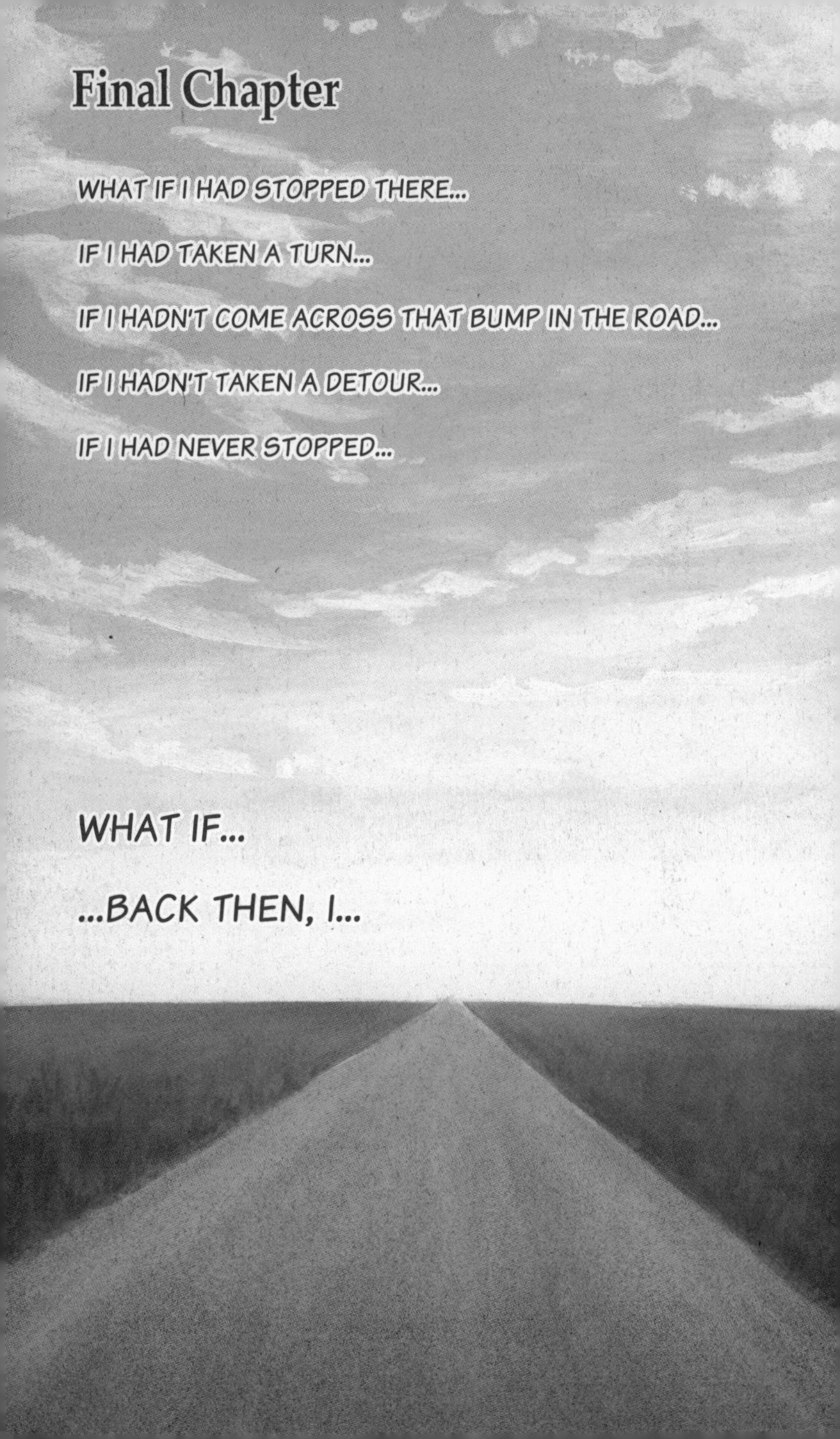
Final Chapter
WHAT IF I HAD STOPPED THERE...
IF I HAD TAKEN A TURN...
IF I HADN'T COME ACROSS THAT BUMP IN THE ROAD...
IF I HADN'T TAKEN A DETOUR...
IF I HAD NEVER STOPPED...
WHAT IF...
...BACK THEN, I...

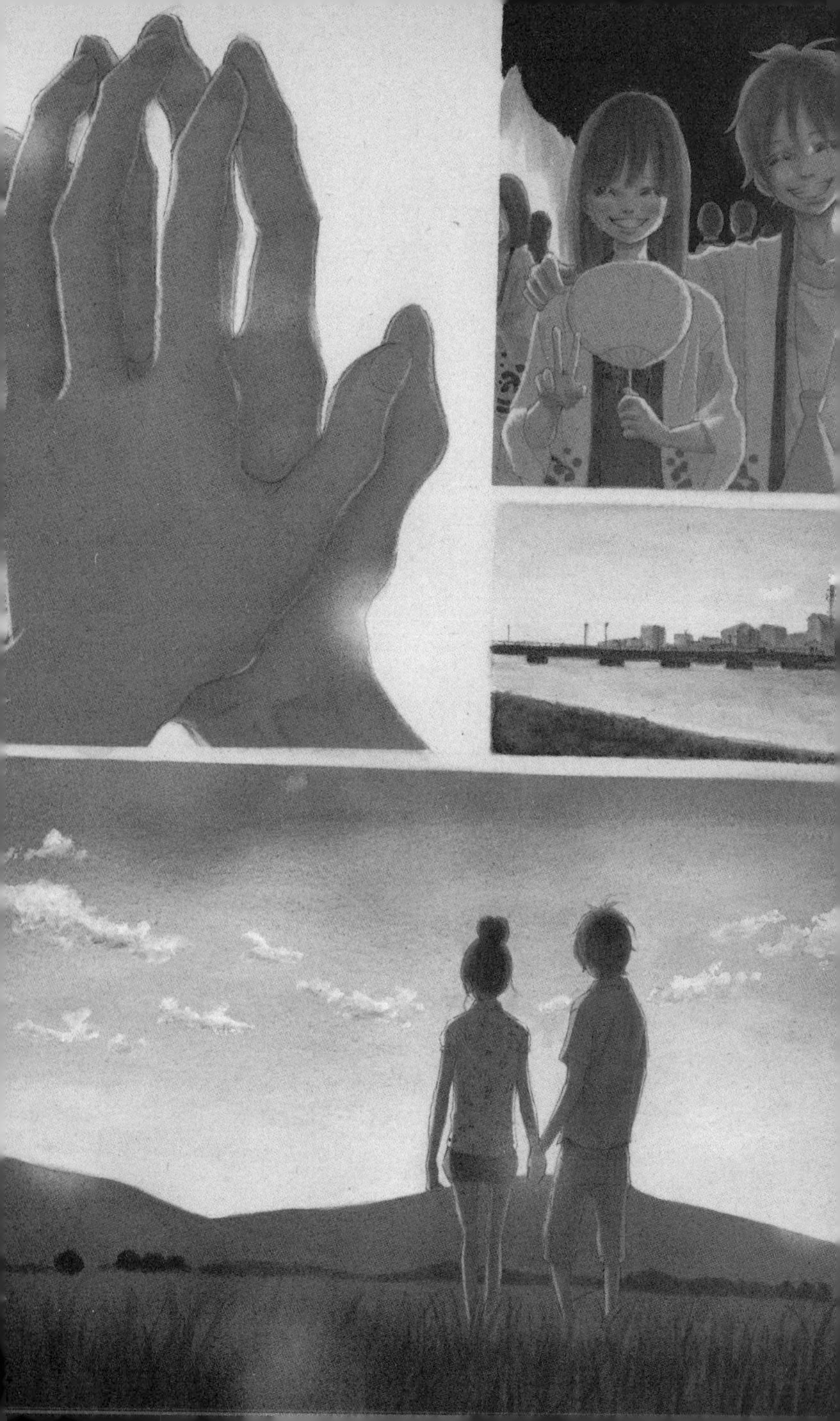

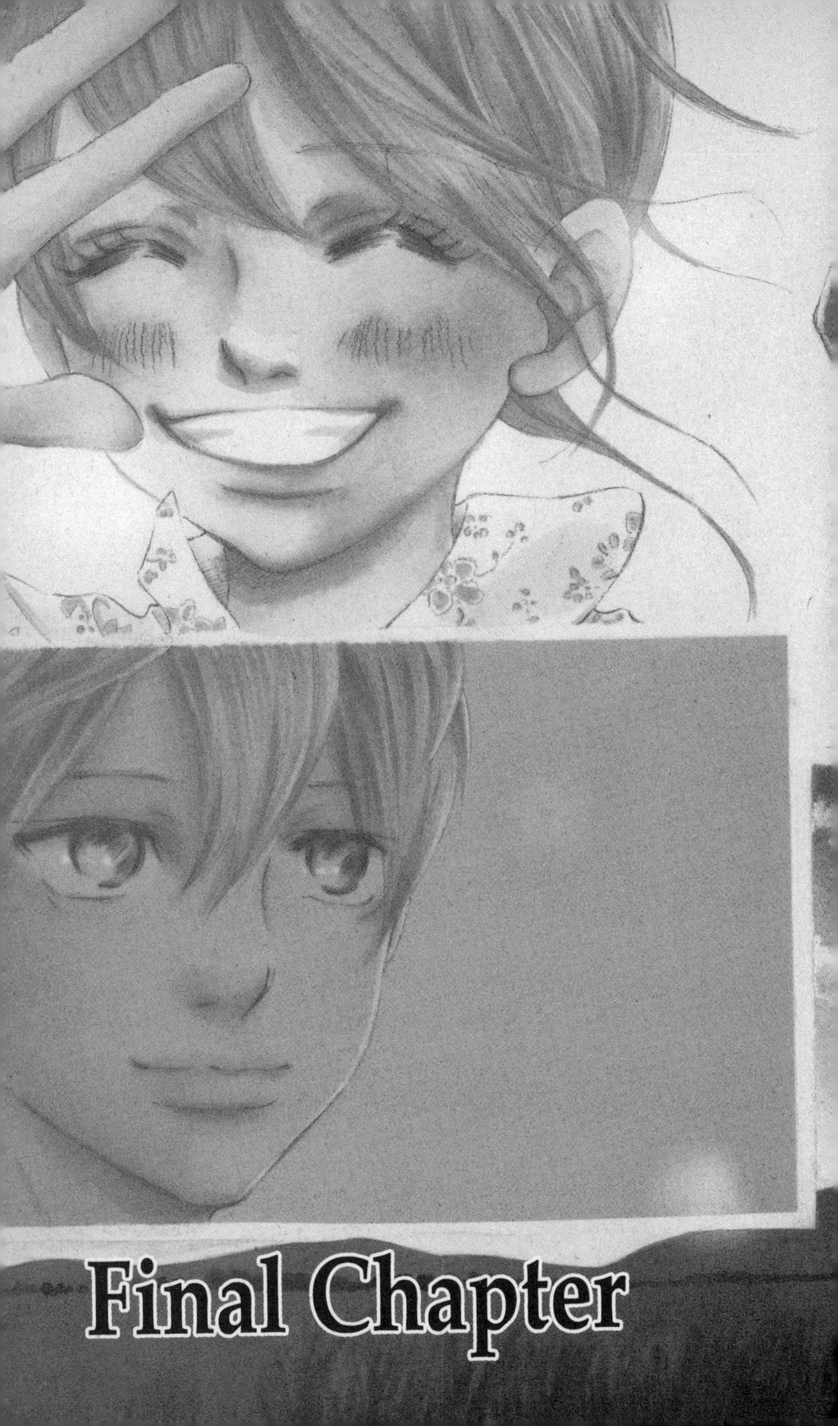

Final Chapter

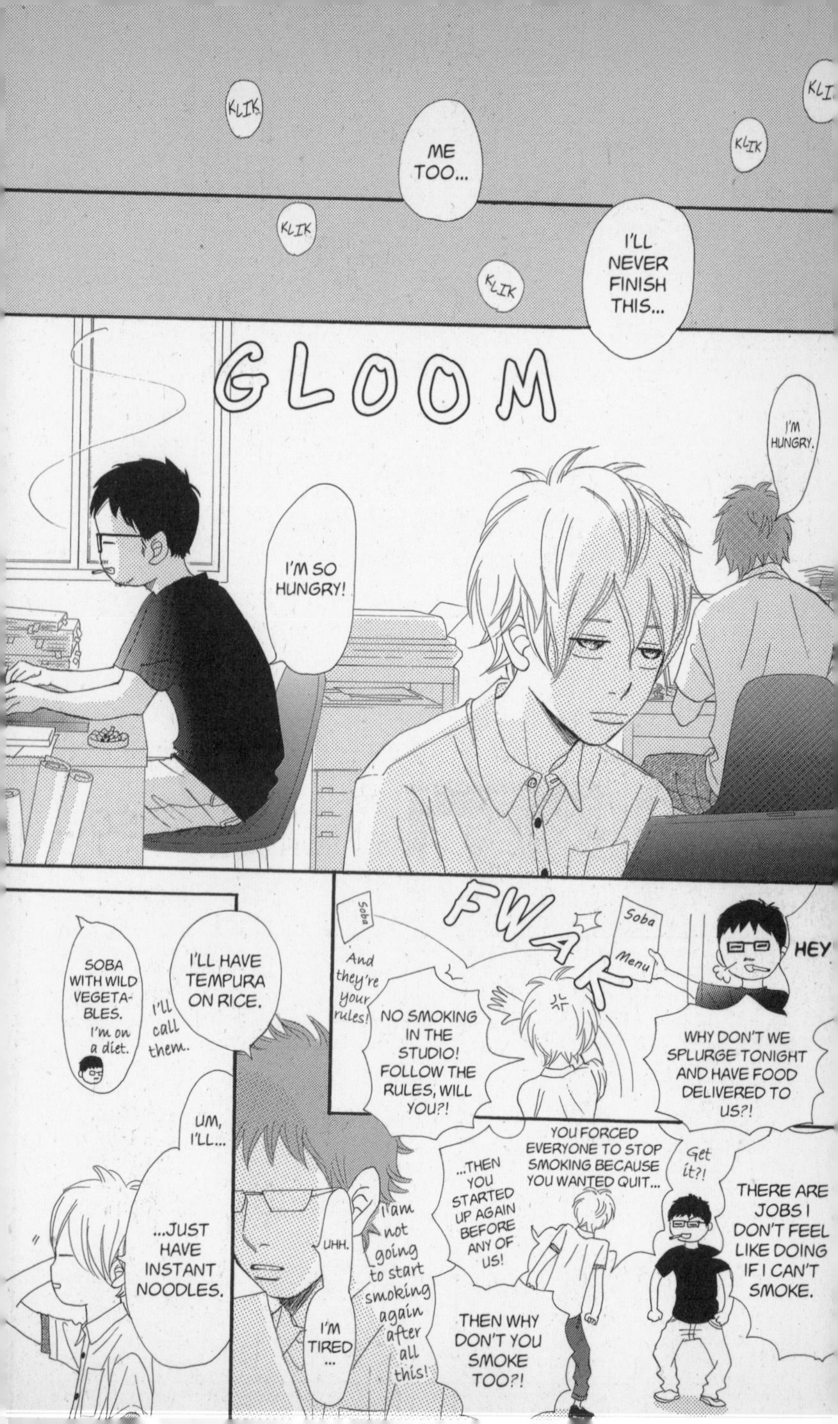
KLI
KLIK
ME TOO...
KLIK
I'LL NEVER FINISH THIS...
KLIK
KLIK
GLOOM
I'M HUNGRY.
I'M SO HUNGRY!
HEY
FWAK
Soba Menu
Soba
WHY DON'T WE SPLURGE TONIGHT AND HAVE FOOD DELIVERED TO US?!
NO SMOKING IN THE STUDIO! FOLLOW THE RULES, WILL YOU?!
And they're your rules!
THERE ARE JOBS I DON'T FEEL LIKE DOING IF I CAN'T SMOKE.
Get it?!
YOU FORCED EVERYONE TO STOP SMOKING BECAUSE YOU WANTED QUIT...
...THEN YOU STARTED UP AGAIN BEFORE ANY OF US!
THEN WHY DON'T YOU SMOKE TOO?!
I'm not going to start smoking again after all this!
UHH.
I'M TIRED...
I'LL HAVE TEMPURA ON RICE.
SOBA WITH WILD VEGETA-BLES.
I'm on a diet.
I'll call them.
UM, I'LL...
...JUST HAVE INSTANT NOODLES.

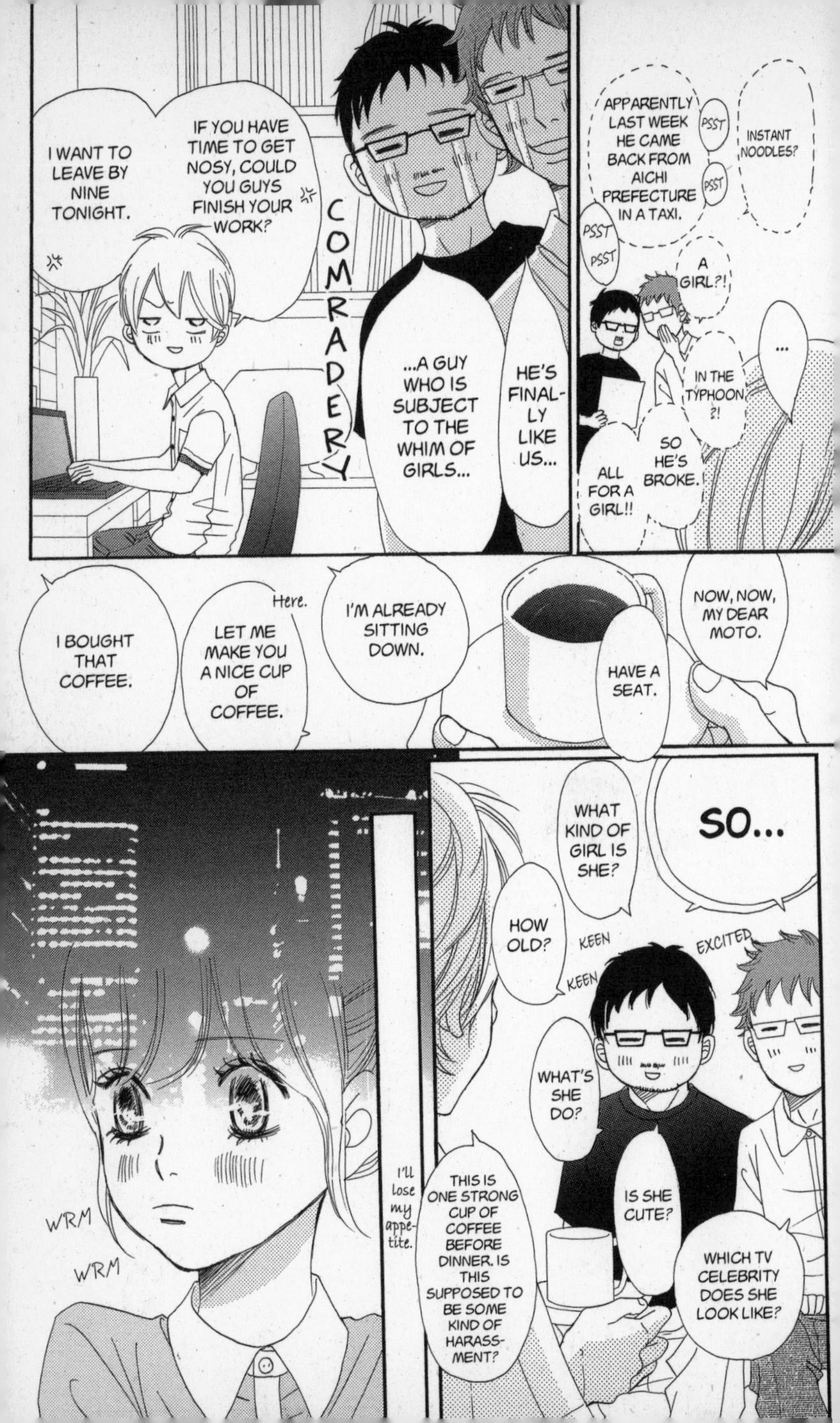
INSTANT NOODLES?
APPARENTLY LAST WEEK HE CAME BACK FROM AICHI PREFECTURE IN A TAXI.
PSST
PSST
PSST
PSST
A GIRL?!
...
IN THE TYPHOON?!
SO HE'S BROKE.
ALL FOR A GIRL!!
HE'S FINAL-LY LIKE US...
...A GUY WHO IS SUBJECT TO THE WHIM OF GIRLS...
COMRADERY
IF YOU HAVE TIME TO GET NOSY, COULD YOU GUYS FINISH YOUR WORK?
I WANT TO LEAVE BY NINE TONIGHT.
NOW, NOW, MY DEAR MOTO.
HAVE A SEAT.
I'M ALREADY SITTING DOWN.
Here.
LET ME MAKE YOU A NICE CUP OF COFFEE.
I BOUGHT THAT COFFEE.
SO...
WHAT KIND OF GIRL IS SHE?
EXCITED
KEEN
KEEN
HOW OLD?
WHAT'S SHE DO?
IS SHE CUTE?
WHICH TV CELEBRITY DOES SHE LOOK LIKE?
THIS IS ONE STRONG CUP OF COFFEE BEFORE DINNER. IS THIS SUPPOSED TO BE SOME KIND OF HARASS-MENT?
I'll lose my appe-tite.
WRM
WRM

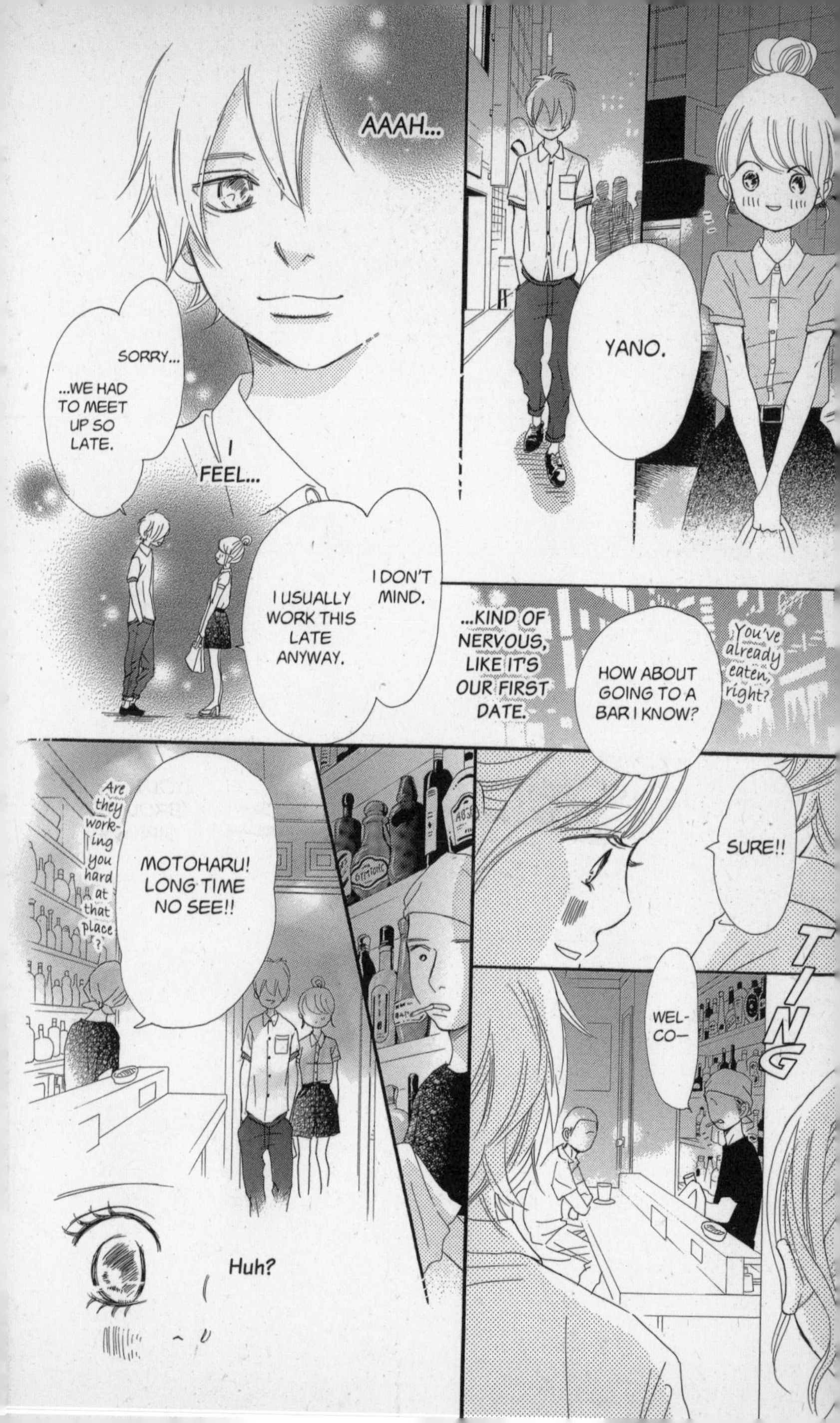
YANO.
AAAH...
I FEEL...
SORRY... ...WE HAD TO MEET UP SO LATE.
I DON'T MIND.
I USUALLY WORK THIS LATE ANYWAY.
...KIND OF NERVOUS, LIKE IT'S OUR FIRST DATE.
You've already eaten, right?
HOW ABOUT GOING TO A BAR I KNOW?
SURE!!
TING
WEL- CO—
Are they working you hard at that place?
MOTOHARU! LONG TIME NO SEE!!
Huh?

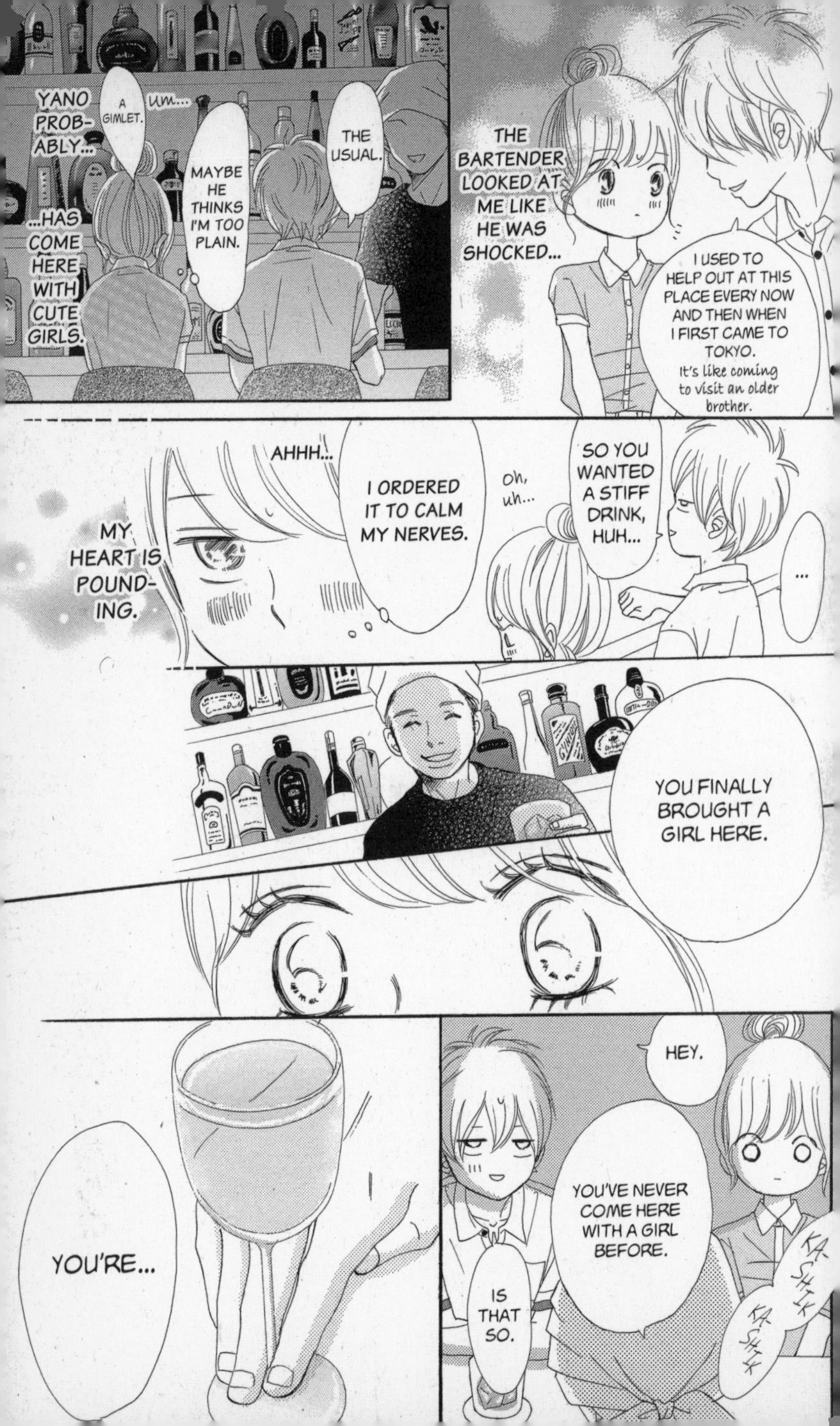
THE BARTENDER LOOKED AT ME LIKE HE WAS SHOCKED...
I USED TO HELP OUT AT THIS PLACE EVERY NOW AND THEN WHEN I FIRST CAME TO TOKYO. It's like coming to visit an older brother.
THE USUAL.
um...
A GIMLET.
MAYBE HE THINKS I'M TOO PLAIN.
YANO PROBABLY...
...HAS COME HERE WITH CUTE GIRLS.
...
SO YOU WANTED A STIFF DRINK, HUH...
oh, uh...
I ORDERED IT TO CALM MY NERVES.
AHHH...
MY HEART IS POUNDING.
YOU FINALLY BROUGHT A GIRL HERE.
HEY.
KA-SHIK KA-SHIK
YOU'VE NEVER COME HERE WITH A GIRL BEFORE.
IS THAT SO.
YOU'RE...

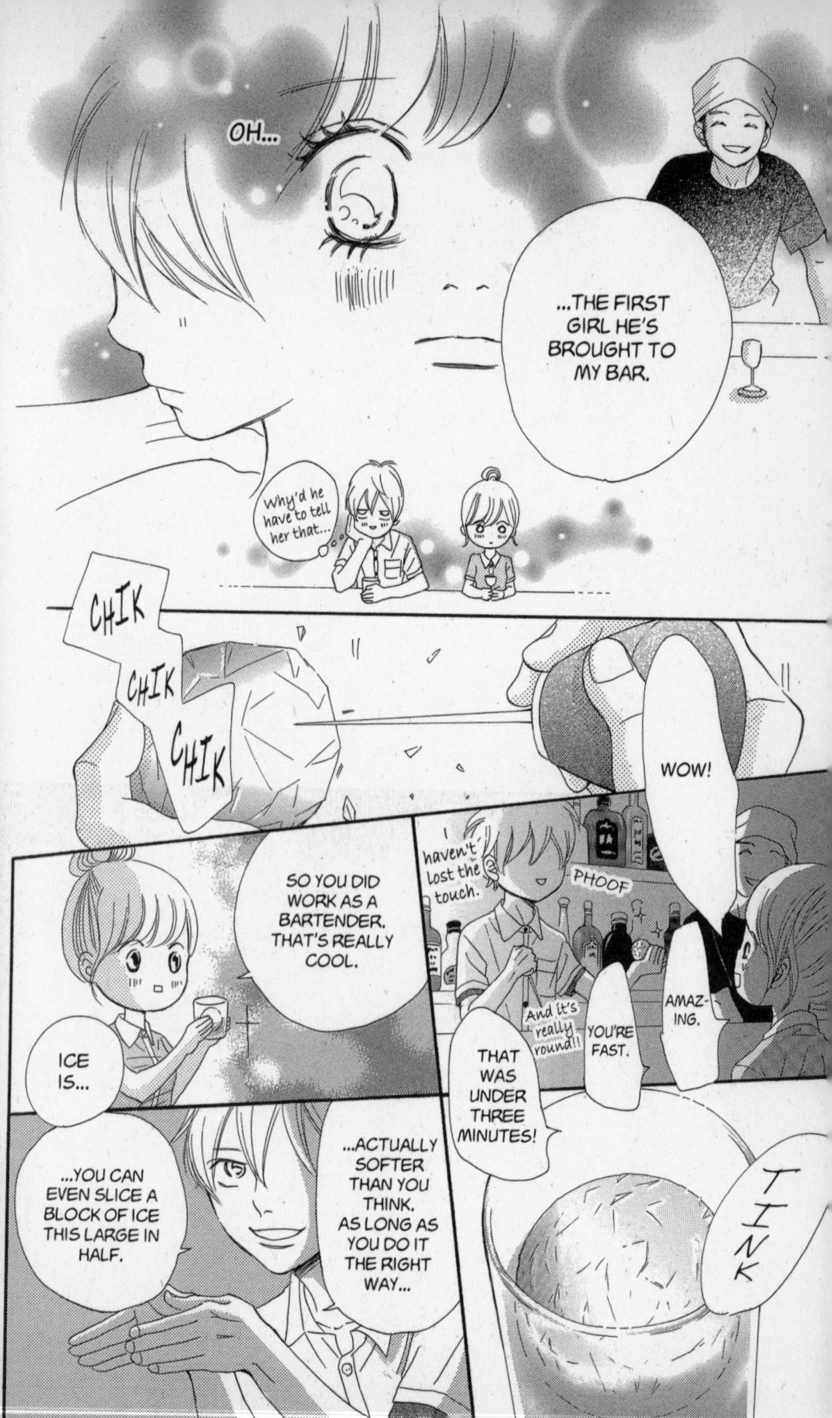

...THE FIRST GIRL HE'S BROUGHT TO MY BAR.
OH...
Why'd he have to tell her that...
CHIK
CHIK
CHIK
WOW!
I haven't lost the touch.
PHOOF
AMAZ-ING.
YOU'RE FAST.
And it's really round!!
THAT WAS UNDER THREE MINUTES!
SO YOU DID WORK AS A BARTENDER. THAT'S REALLY COOL.
ICE IS...
TINK
...ACTUALLY SOFTER THAN YOU THINK. AS LONG AS YOU DO IT THE RIGHT WAY...
...YOU CAN EVEN SLICE A BLOCK OF ICE THIS LARGE IN HALF.

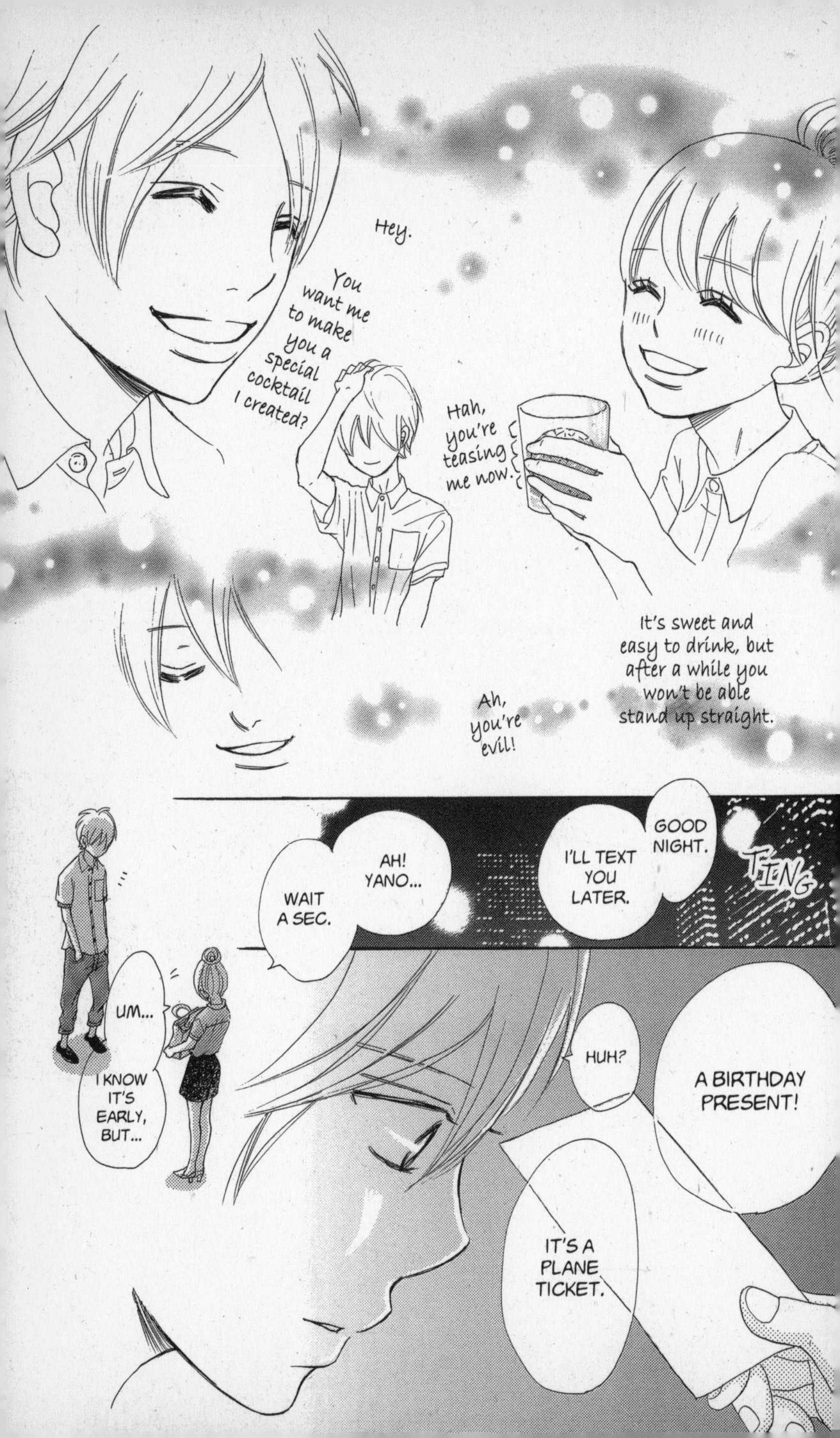
Hey.
You want me to make you a special cocktail I created?
Hah, you're teasing me now.
It's sweet and easy to drink, but after a while you won't be able stand up straight.
Ah, you're evil!
FING
GOOD NIGHT.
I'LL TEXT YOU LATER.
AH! YANO...
WAIT A SEC.
UM...
I KNOW IT'S EARLY, BUT...
HUH?
A BIRTHDAY PRESENT!
IT'S A PLANE TICKET.

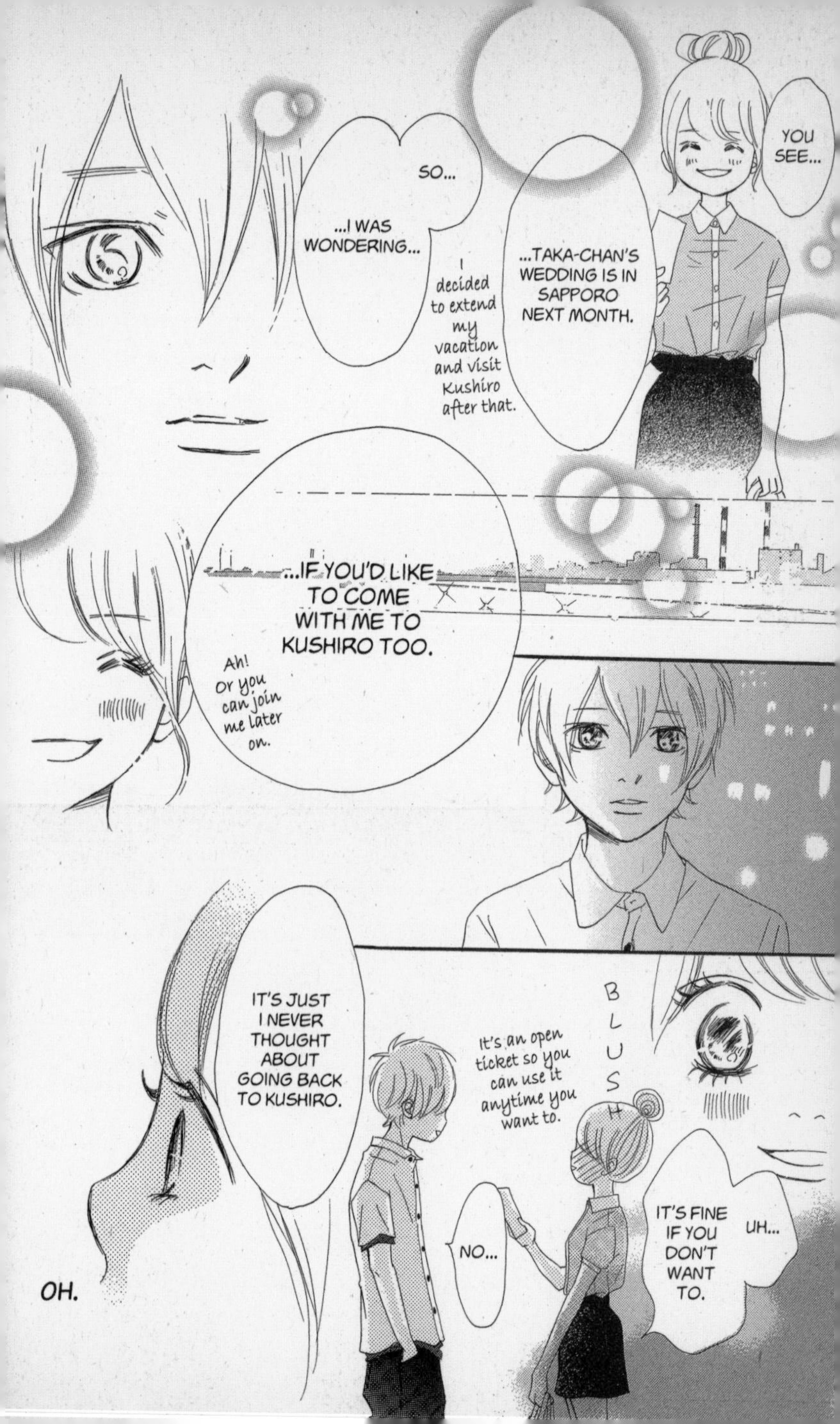
YOU SEE...
...TAKA-CHAN'S WEDDING IS IN SAPPORO NEXT MONTH.
I decided to extend my vacation and visit Kushiro after that.
SO...
...I WAS WONDERING...
...IF YOU'D LIKE TO COME WITH ME TO KUSHIRO TOO.
Ah! Or you can join me later on.
UH...
IT'S FINE IF YOU DON'T WANT TO.
BLUSH
It's an open ticket so you can use it anytime you want to.
NO...
IT'S JUST I NEVER THOUGHT ABOUT GOING BACK TO KUSHIRO.
OH.

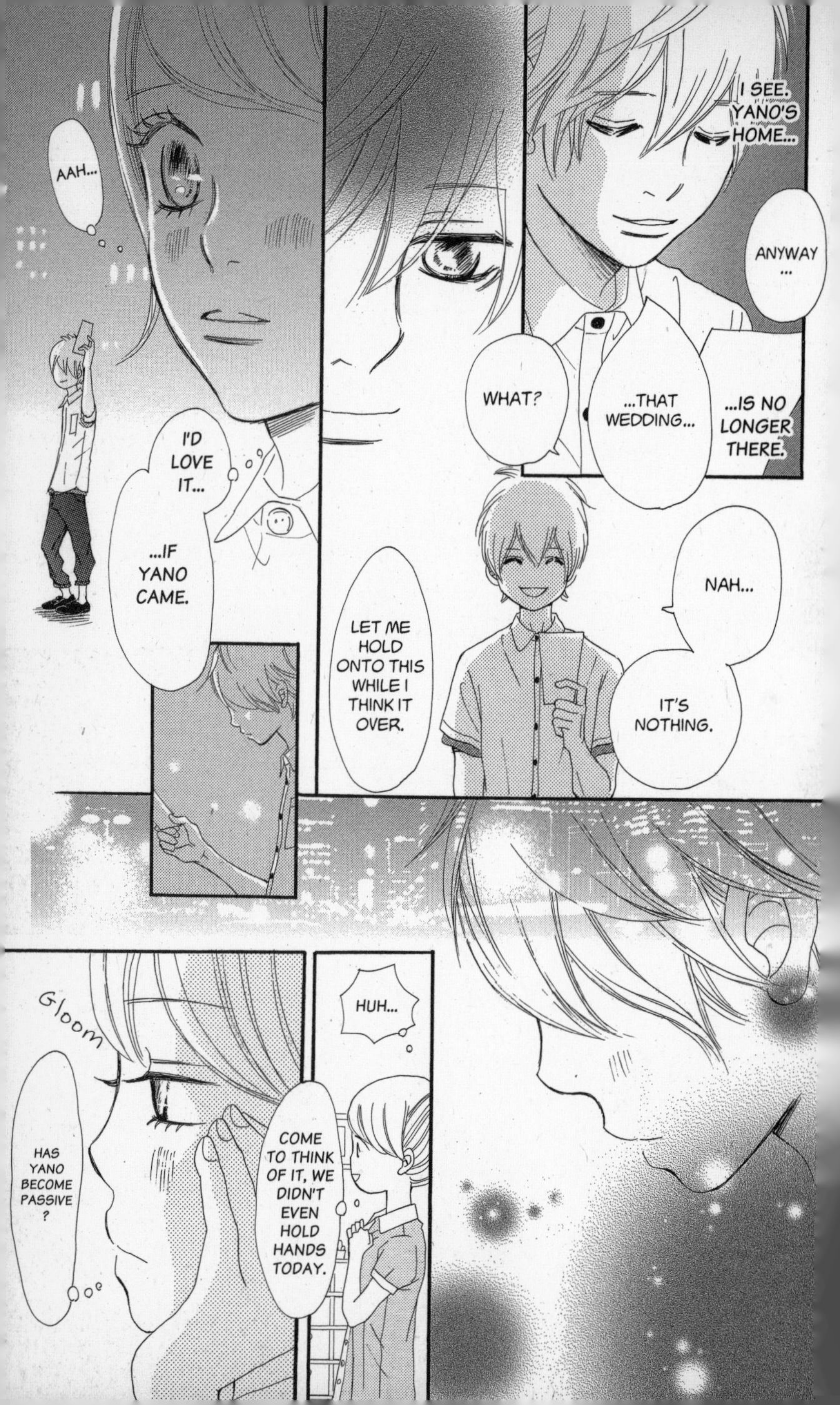
I SEE. YANO'S HOME...
ANYWAY ...
...IS NO LONGER THERE.
...THAT WEDDING...
WHAT?
NAH...
IT'S NOTHING.
LET ME HOLD ONTO THIS WHILE I THINK IT OVER.
AAH...
I'D LOVE IT...
...IF YANO CAME.
HUH...
COME TO THINK OF IT, WE DIDN'T EVEN HOLD HANDS TODAY.
Gloom
HAS YANO BECOME PASSIVE ?

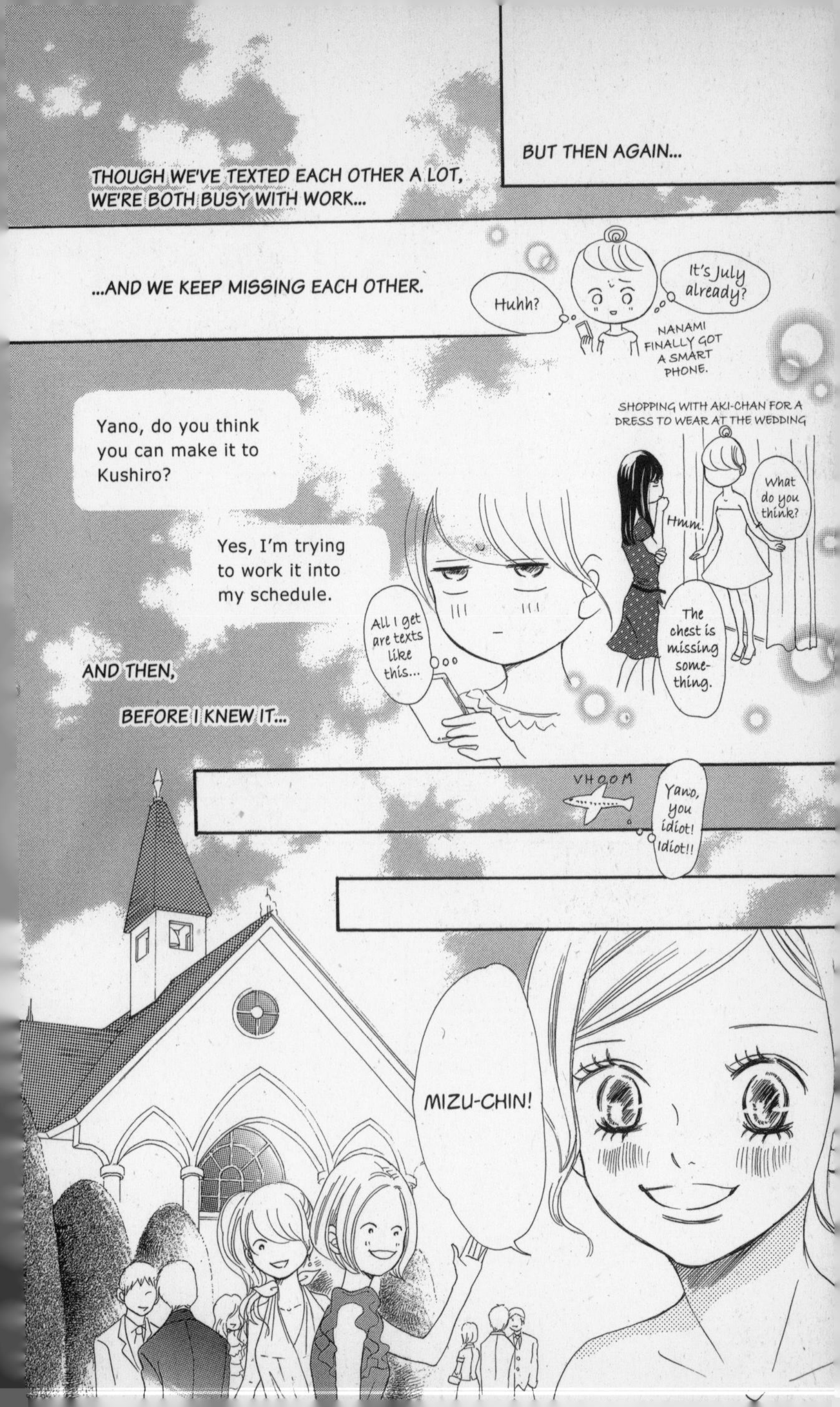

BUT THEN AGAIN...
THOUGH WE'VE TEXTED EACH OTHER A LOT, WE'RE BOTH BUSY WITH WORK...
It's July already?
Huhh?
NANAMI FINALLY GOT A SMART PHONE.
...AND WE KEEP MISSING EACH OTHER.
SHOPPING WITH AKI-CHAN FOR A DRESS TO WEAR AT THE WEDDING
What do you think?
Hmm.
The chest is missing something.
Yano, do you think you can make it to Kushiro?
Yes, I'm trying to work it into my schedule.
All I get are texts like this...
AND THEN,
BEFORE I KNEW IT...
Yano, you idiot! Idiot!!
VHOOM
MIZU-CHIN!

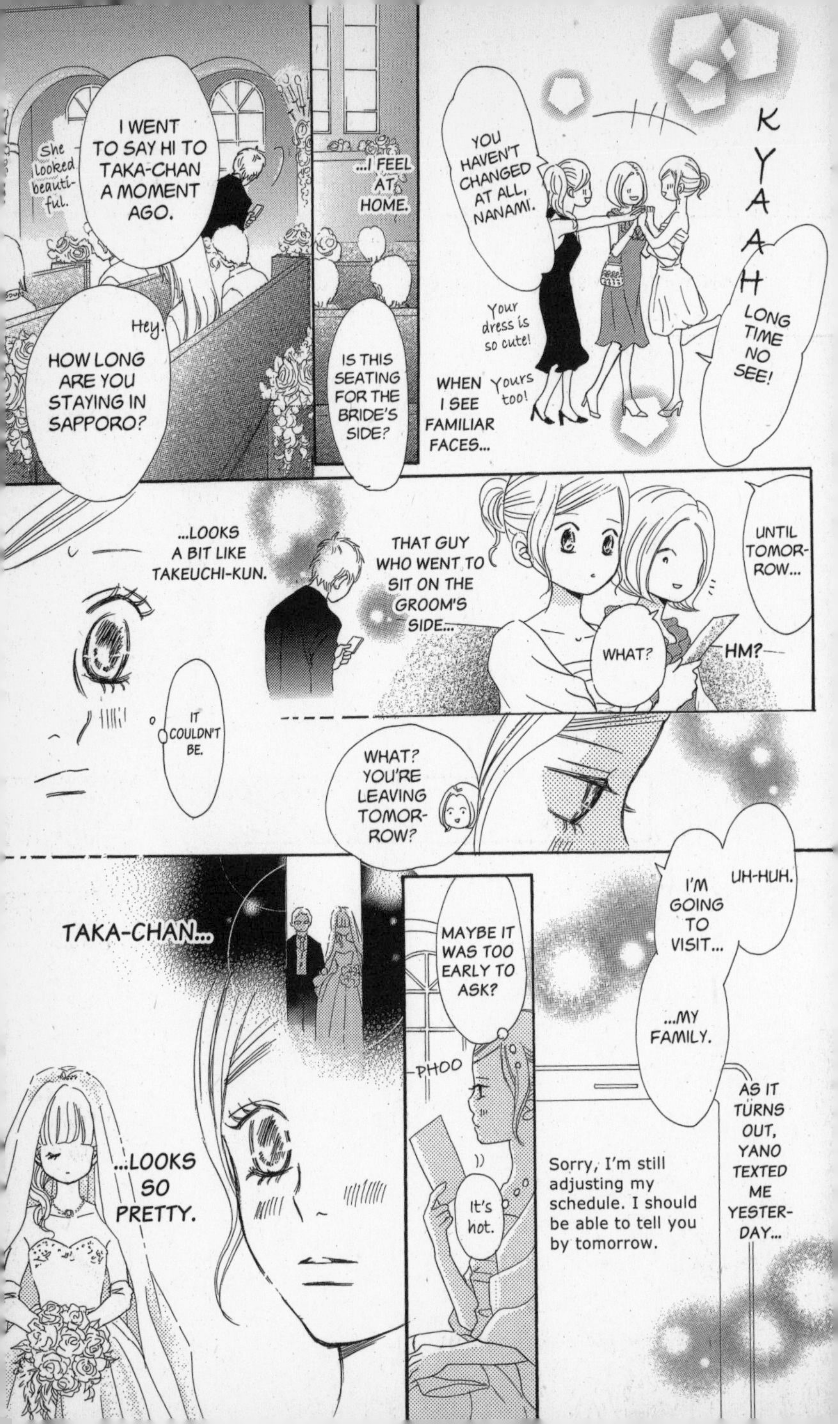
KYAAH
LONG TIME NO SEE!
YOU HAVEN'T CHANGED AT ALL, NANAMI.
Your dress is so cute!
Yours too!
WHEN I SEE FAMILIAR FACES...
...I FEEL AT HOME.
IS THIS SEATING FOR THE BRIDE'S SIDE?
She looked beautiful.
I WENT TO SAY HI TO TAKA-CHAN A MOMENT AGO.
Hey.
HOW LONG ARE YOU STAYING IN SAPPORO?
UNTIL TOMORROW...
HM?
WHAT?
THAT GUY WHO WENT TO SIT ON THE GROOM'S SIDE...
...LOOKS A BIT LIKE TAKEUCHI-KUN.
WHAT? YOU'RE LEAVING TOMORROW?
IT COULDN'T BE.
UH-HUH.
I'M GOING TO VISIT...
...MY FAMILY.
AS IT TURNS OUT, YANO TEXTED ME YESTERDAY...
Sorry, I'm still adjusting my schedule. I should be able to tell you by tomorrow.
MAYBE IT WAS TOO EARLY TO ASK?
PHOO
It's hot.
TAKA-CHAN...
...LOOKS SO PRETTY.

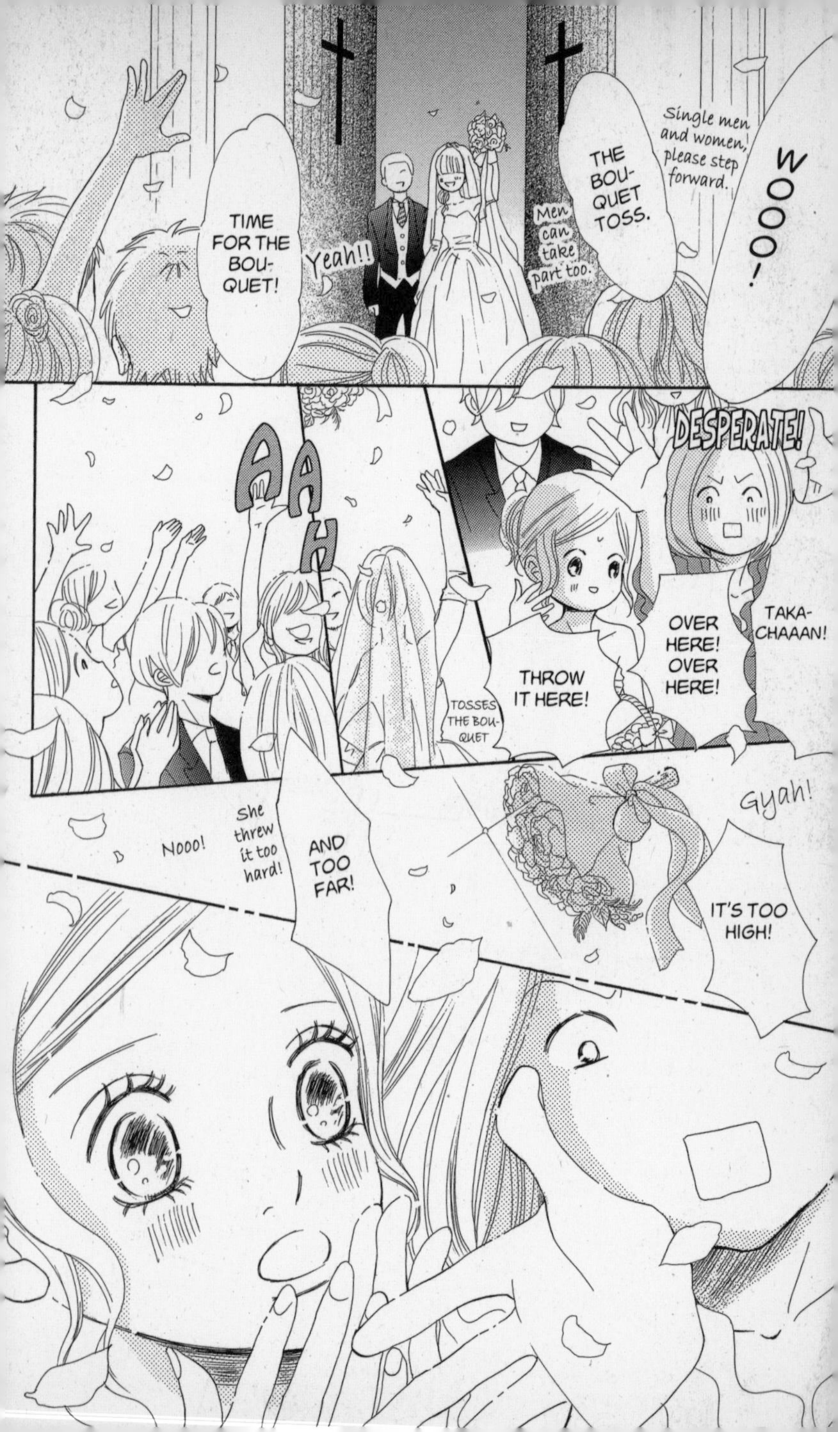
WOOOO!
Single men and women, please step forward.
THE BOUQUET TOSS.
Men can take part too.
Yeah!!
TIME FOR THE BOUQUET!
DESPERATE!
TAKA-CHAAAN!
OVER HERE! OVER HERE!
THROW IT HERE!
TOSSES THE BOUQUET
AAH
Gyah!
IT'S TOO HIGH!
AND TOO FAR!
She threw it too hard!
Nooo!

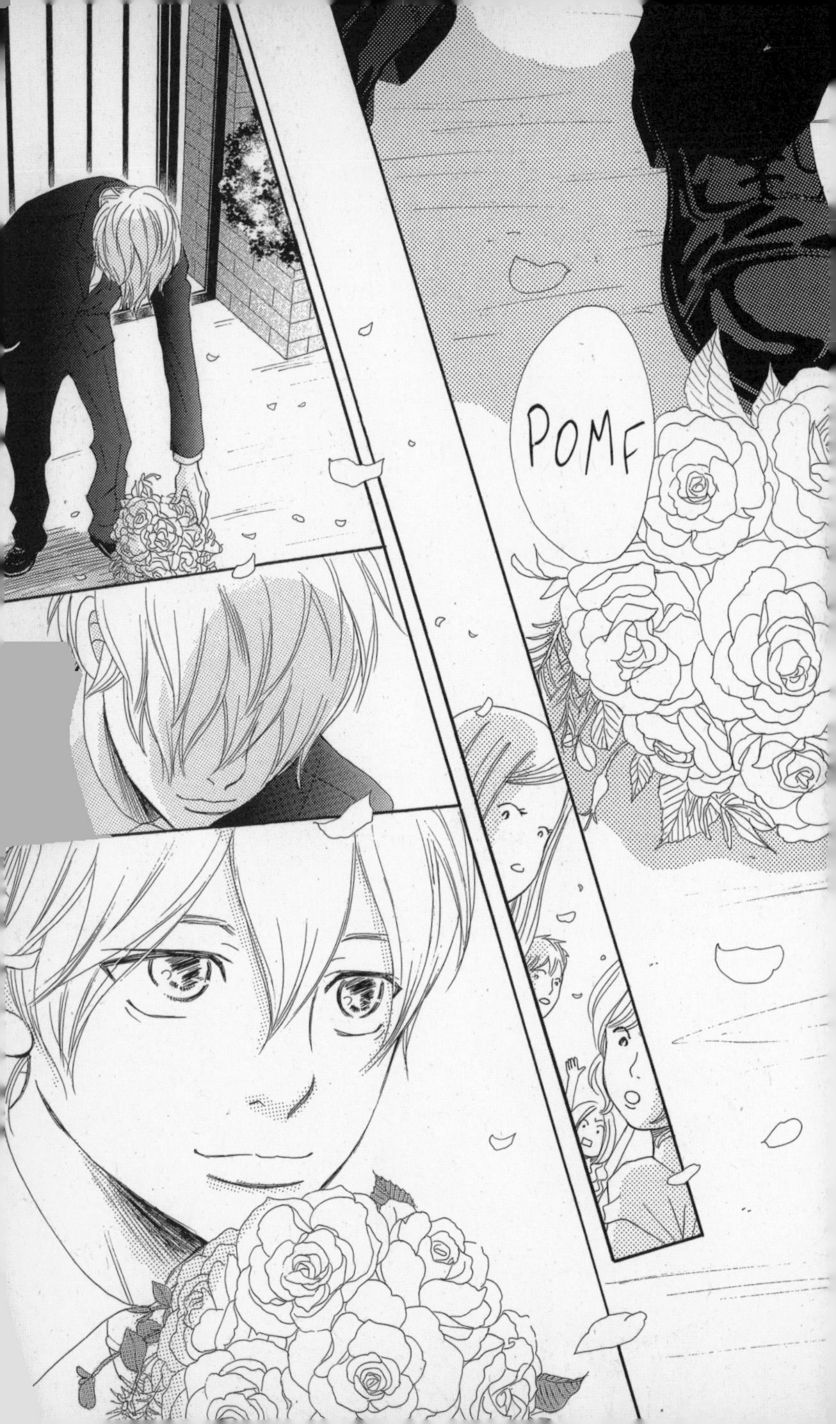
POMF

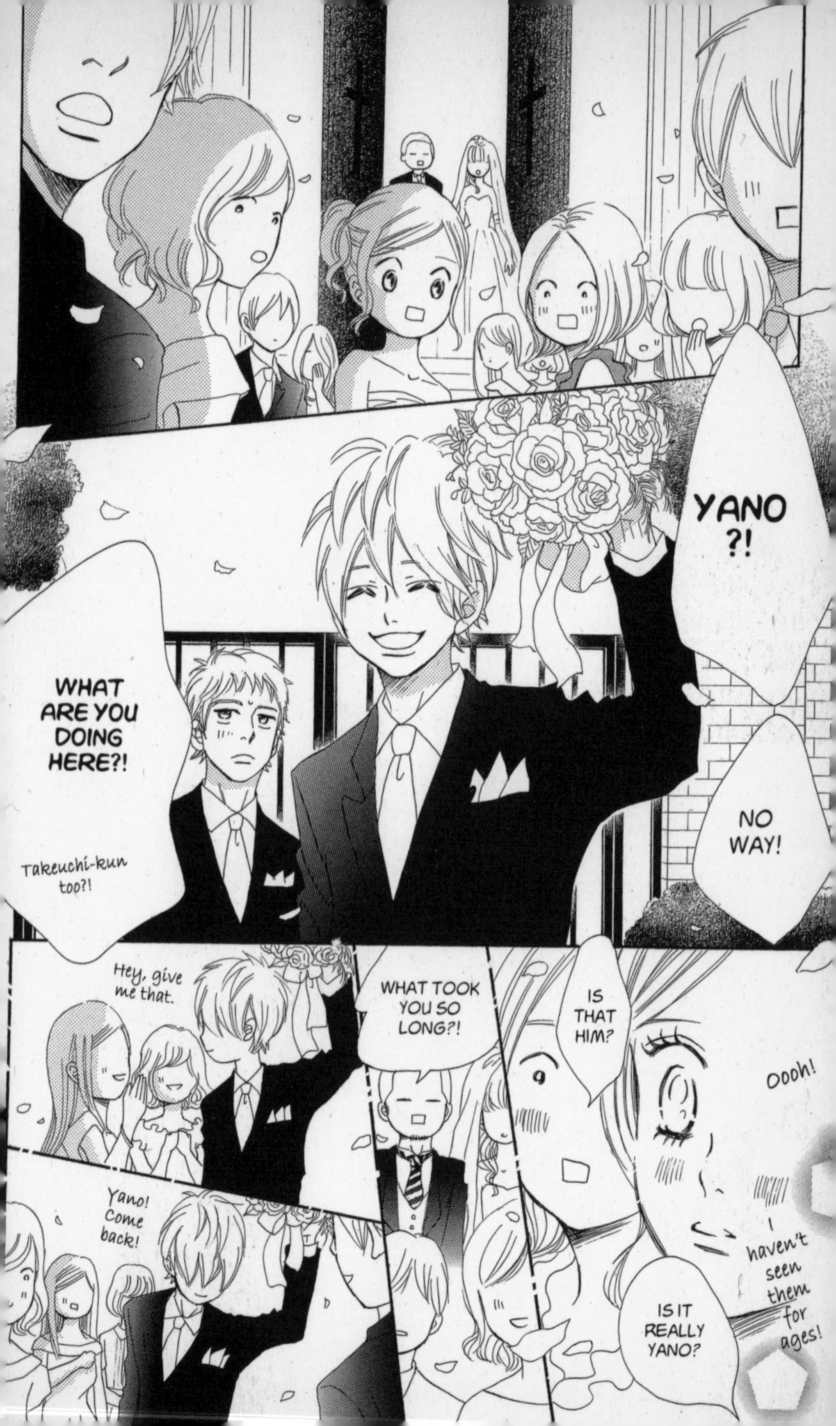
YANO ?!
WHAT ARE YOU DOING HERE?!
NO WAY!
Takeuchi-kun too?!
IS THAT HIM?
Oooh!
I haven't seen them for ages!
IS IT REALLY YANO?
WHAT TOOK YOU SO LONG?!
Hey, give me that.
Yano! Come back!

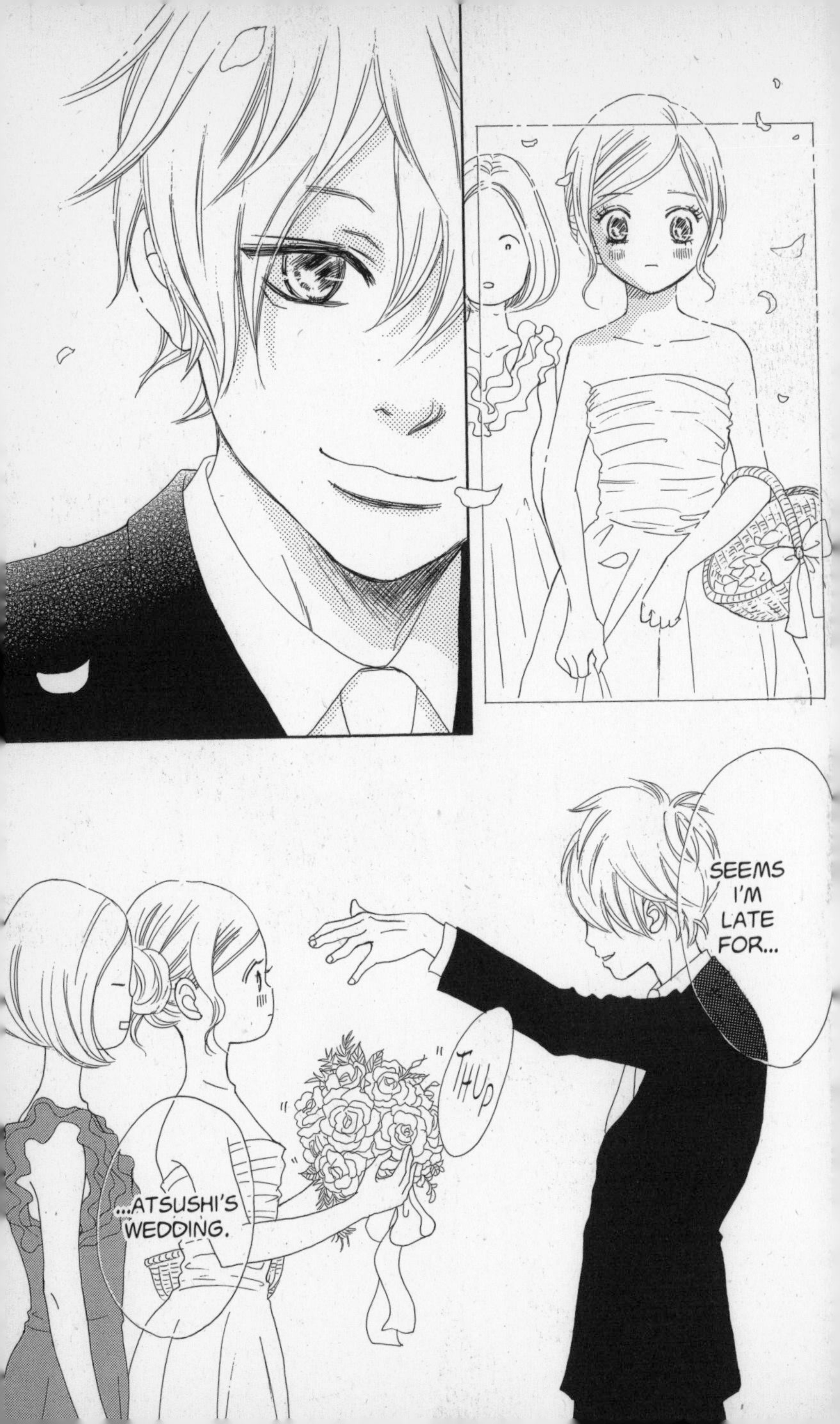
SEEMS I'M LATE FOR...
THUP
...ATSUSHI'S WEDDING.

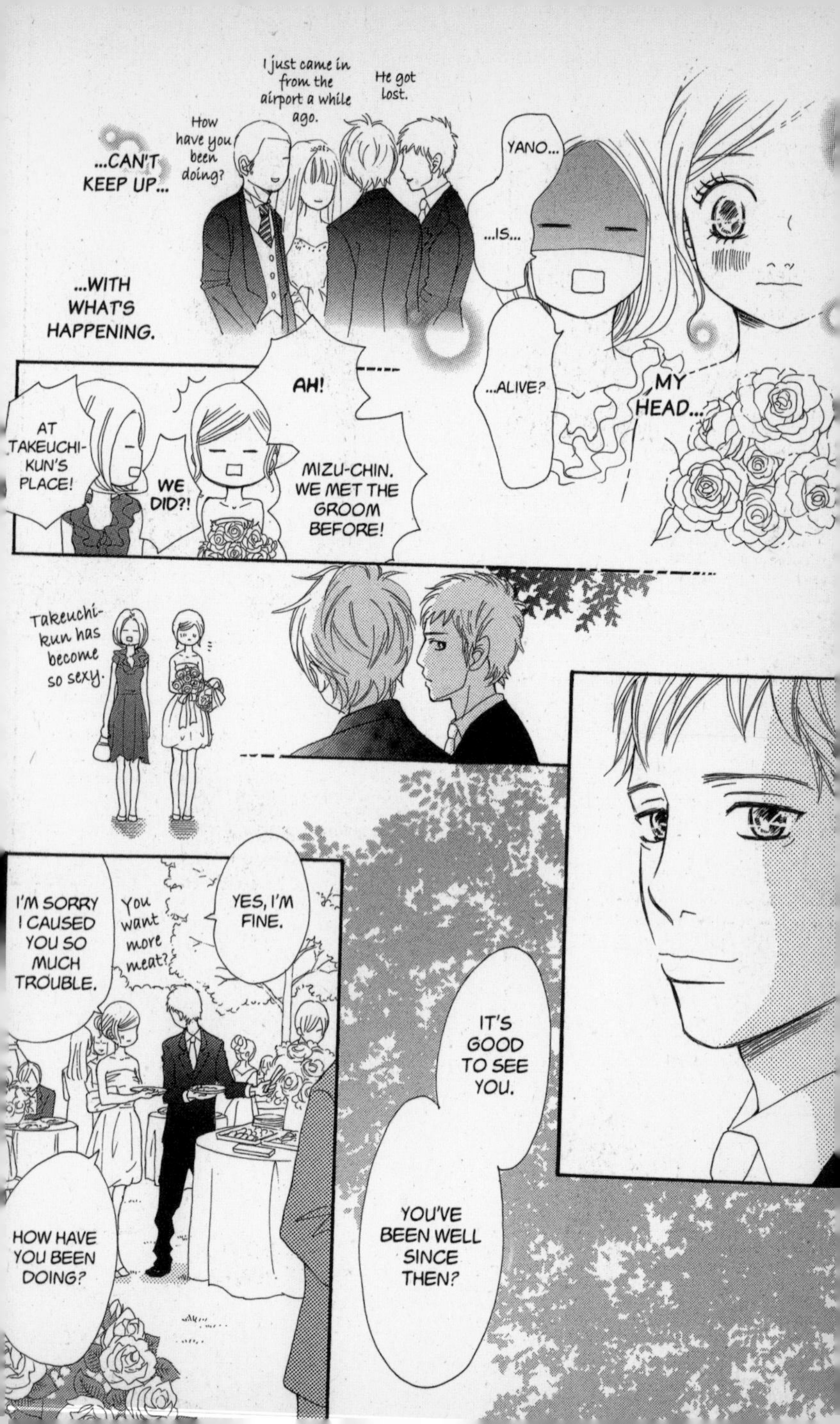
YANO...
...IS...
...ALIVE?
MY HEAD...
He got lost.
I just came in from the airport a while ago.
How have you been doing?
...CAN'T KEEP UP...
...WITH WHAT'S HAPPENING.
AH!
MIZU-CHIN. WE MET THE GROOM BEFORE!
WE DID?!
AT TAKEUCHI-KUN'S PLACE!
Takeuchi-kun has become so sexy.
IT'S GOOD TO SEE YOU.
YOU'VE BEEN WELL SINCE THEN?
YES, I'M FINE.
You want more meat?
I'M SORRY I CAUSED YOU SO MUCH TROUBLE.
HOW HAVE YOU BEEN DOING?

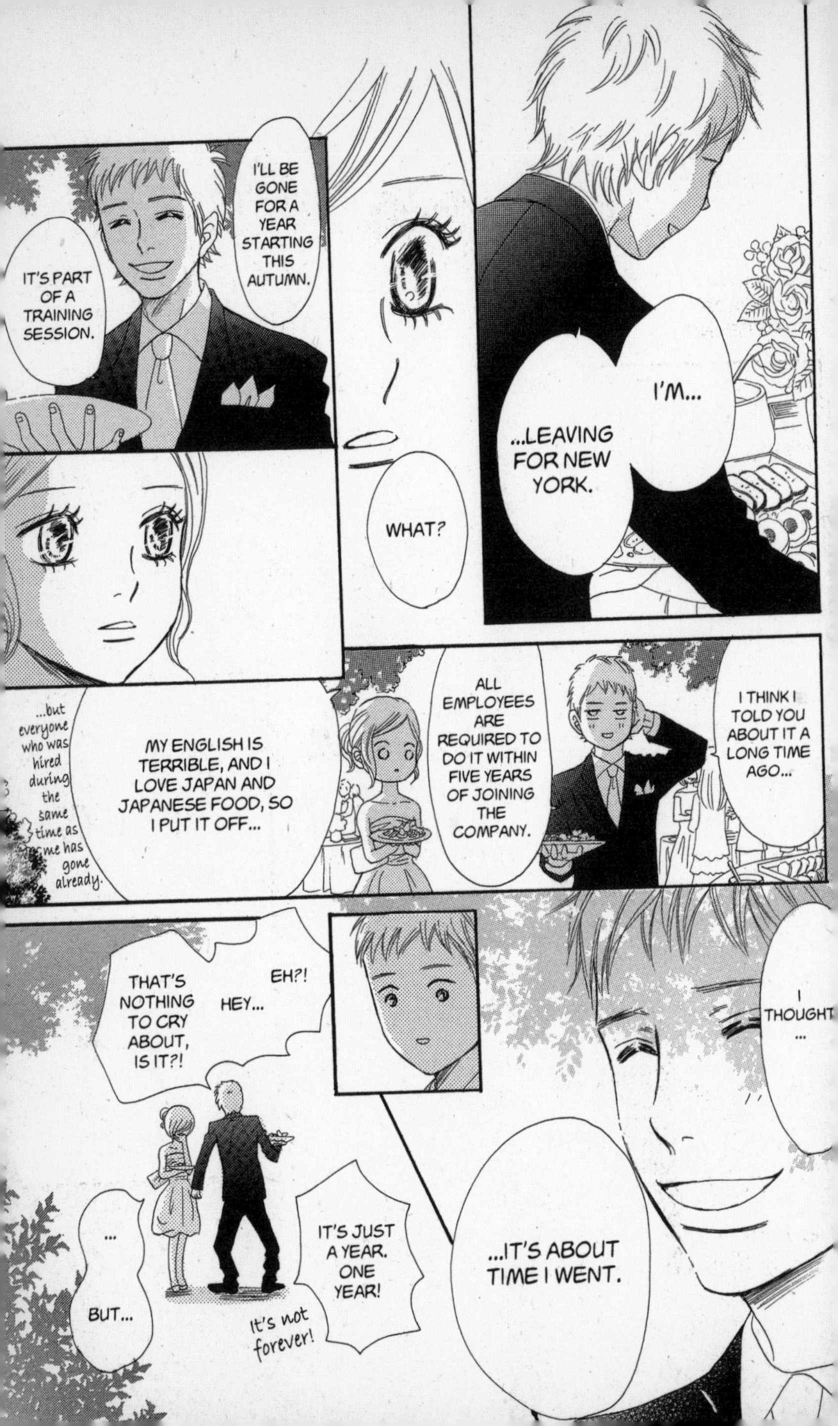
I'M...
...LEAVING FOR NEW YORK.
WHAT?
I'LL BE GONE FOR A YEAR STARTING THIS AUTUMN.
IT'S PART OF A TRAINING SESSION.
I THINK I TOLD YOU ABOUT IT A LONG TIME AGO...
ALL EMPLOYEES ARE REQUIRED TO DO IT WITHIN FIVE YEARS OF JOINING THE COMPANY.
MY ENGLISH IS TERRIBLE, AND I LOVE JAPAN AND JAPANESE FOOD, SO I PUT IT OFF...
...but everyone who was hired during the same time as me has gone already.
I THOUGHT...
...IT'S ABOUT TIME I WENT.
EH?!
HEY...
THAT'S NOTHING TO CRY ABOUT, IS IT?!
IT'S JUST A YEAR. ONE YEAR!
It's not forever!
...
BUT...

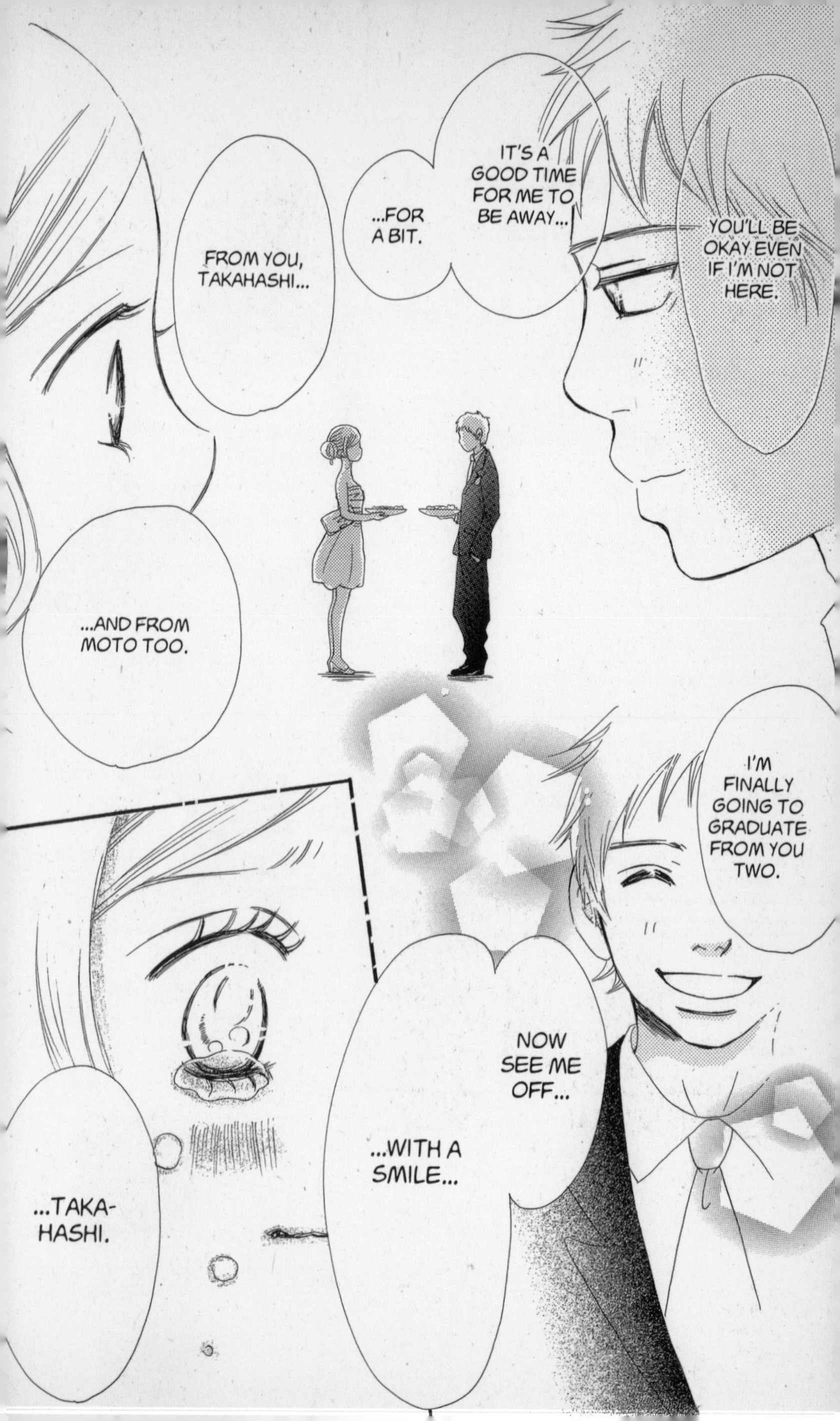
YOU'LL BE OKAY EVEN IF I'M NOT HERE.
IT'S A GOOD TIME FOR ME TO BE AWAY...
...FOR A BIT.
FROM YOU, TAKAHASHI...
...AND FROM MOTO TOO.
I'M FINALLY GOING TO GRADUATE FROM YOU TWO.
NOW SEE ME OFF...
...WITH A SMILE...
...TAKA-HASHI.

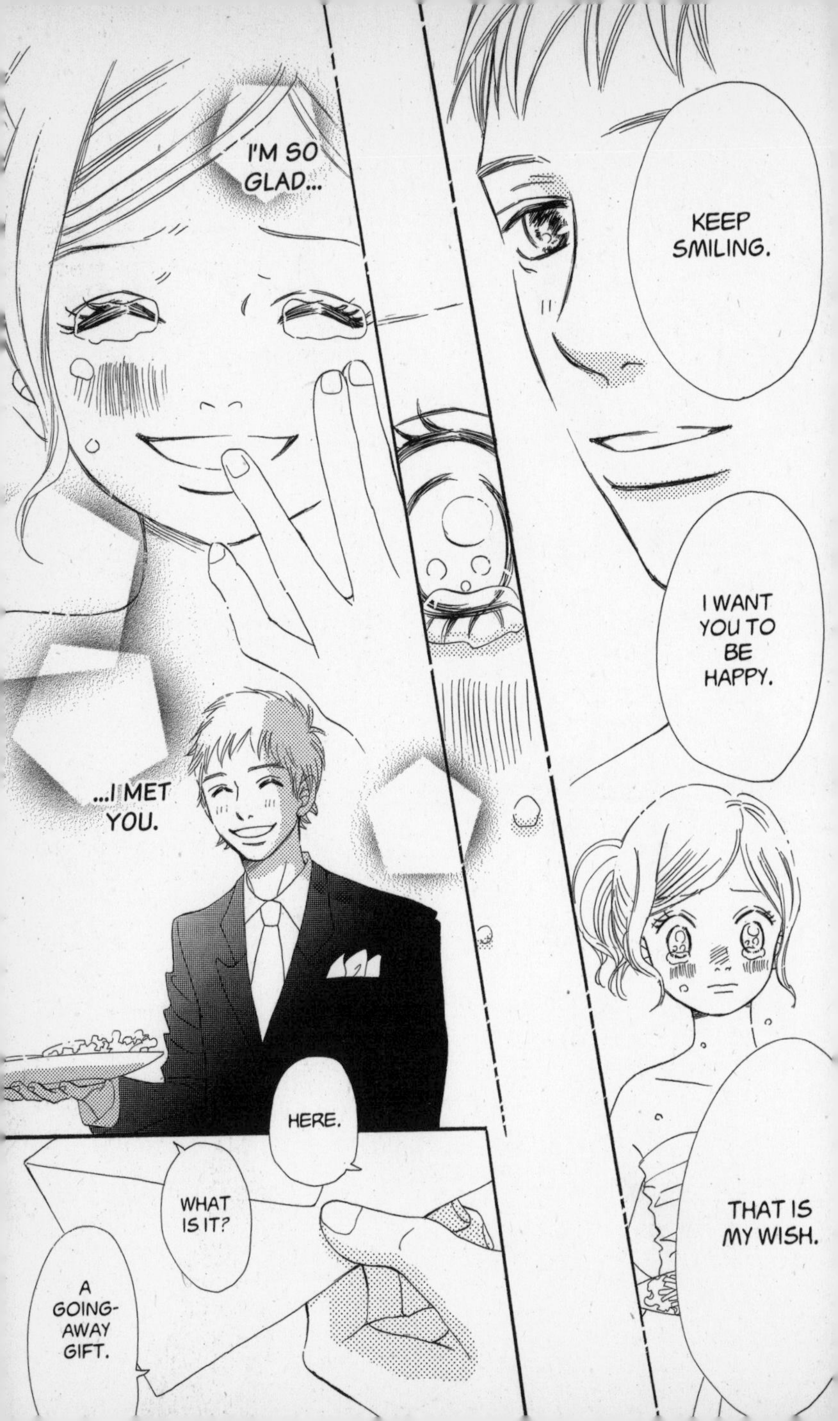
KEEP SMILING.
I WANT YOU TO BE HAPPY.
THAT IS MY WISH.
I'M SO GLAD...
...I MET YOU.
HERE.
WHAT IS IT?
A GOING-AWAY GIFT.

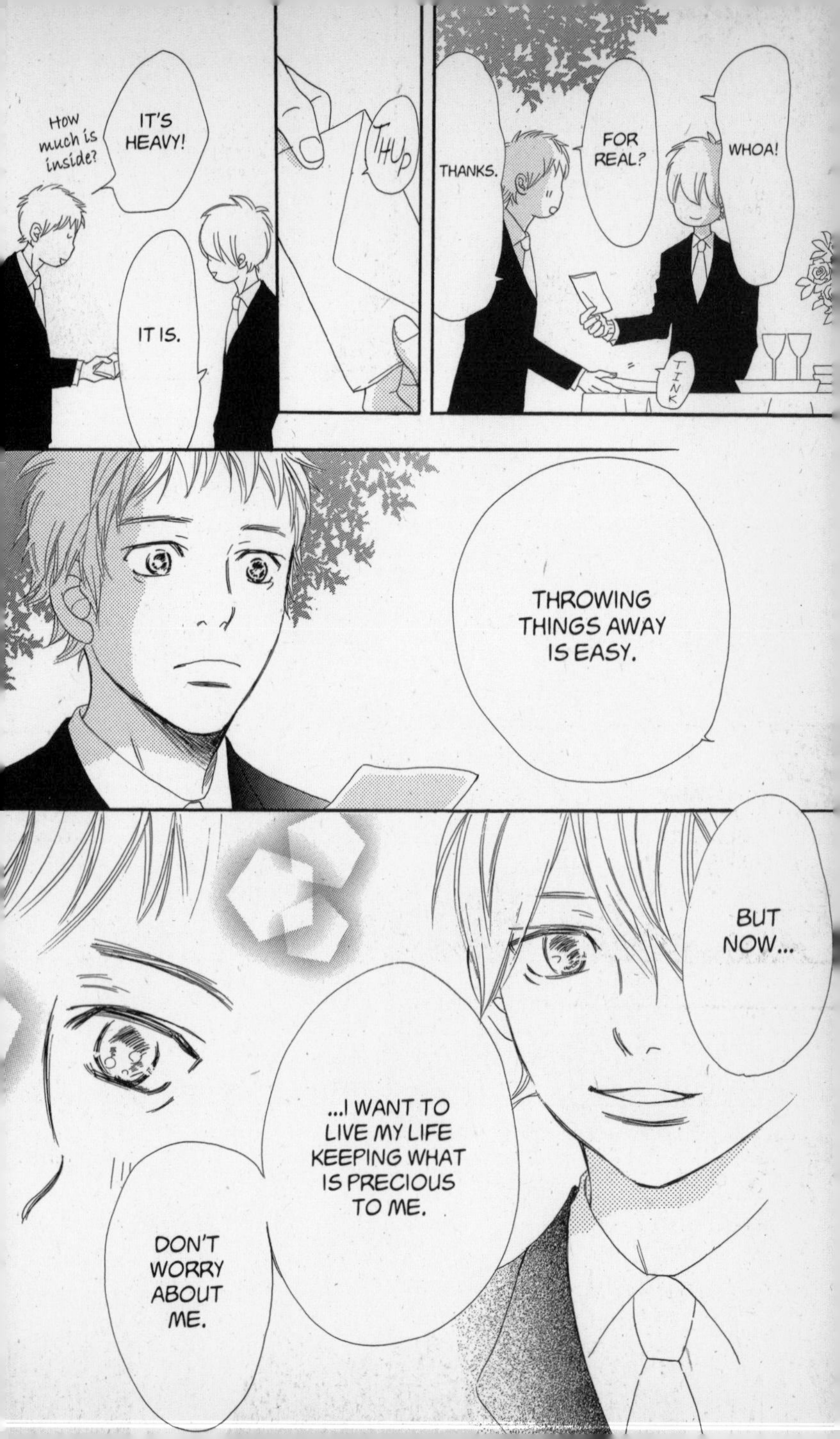
WHOA!
FOR REAL?
THANKS.
TINK
THUP
IT'S HEAVY!
How much is inside?
IT IS.
THROWING THINGS AWAY IS EASY.
BUT NOW...
...I WANT TO LIVE MY LIFE KEEPING WHAT IS PRECIOUS TO ME.
DON'T WORRY ABOUT ME.

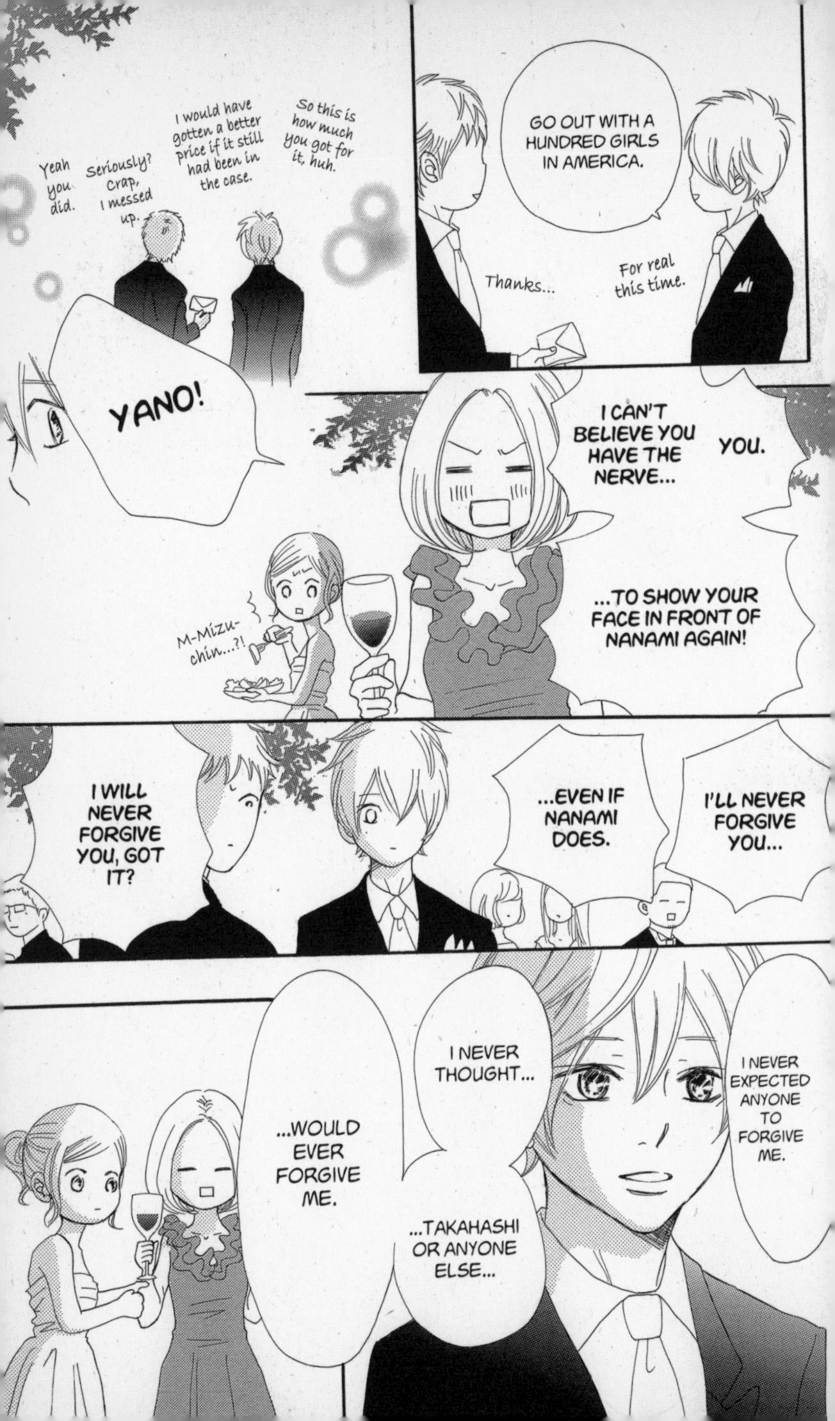
GO OUT WITH A HUNDRED GIRLS IN AMERICA.
For real this time.
Thanks...
So this is how much you got for it, huh.
I would have gotten a better price if it still had been in the case.
Seriously? Crap, I messed up.
Yeah you did.
YANO!
YOU.
I CAN'T BELIEVE YOU HAVE THE NERVE...
...TO SHOW YOUR FACE IN FRONT OF NANAMI AGAIN!
M-Mizu-chin...?!
I'LL NEVER FORGIVE YOU...
...EVEN IF NANAMI DOES.
I WILL NEVER FORGIVE YOU, GOT IT?
I NEVER EXPECTED ANYONE TO FORGIVE ME.
I NEVER THOUGHT...
...TAKAHASHI OR ANYONE ELSE...
...WOULD EVER FORGIVE ME.

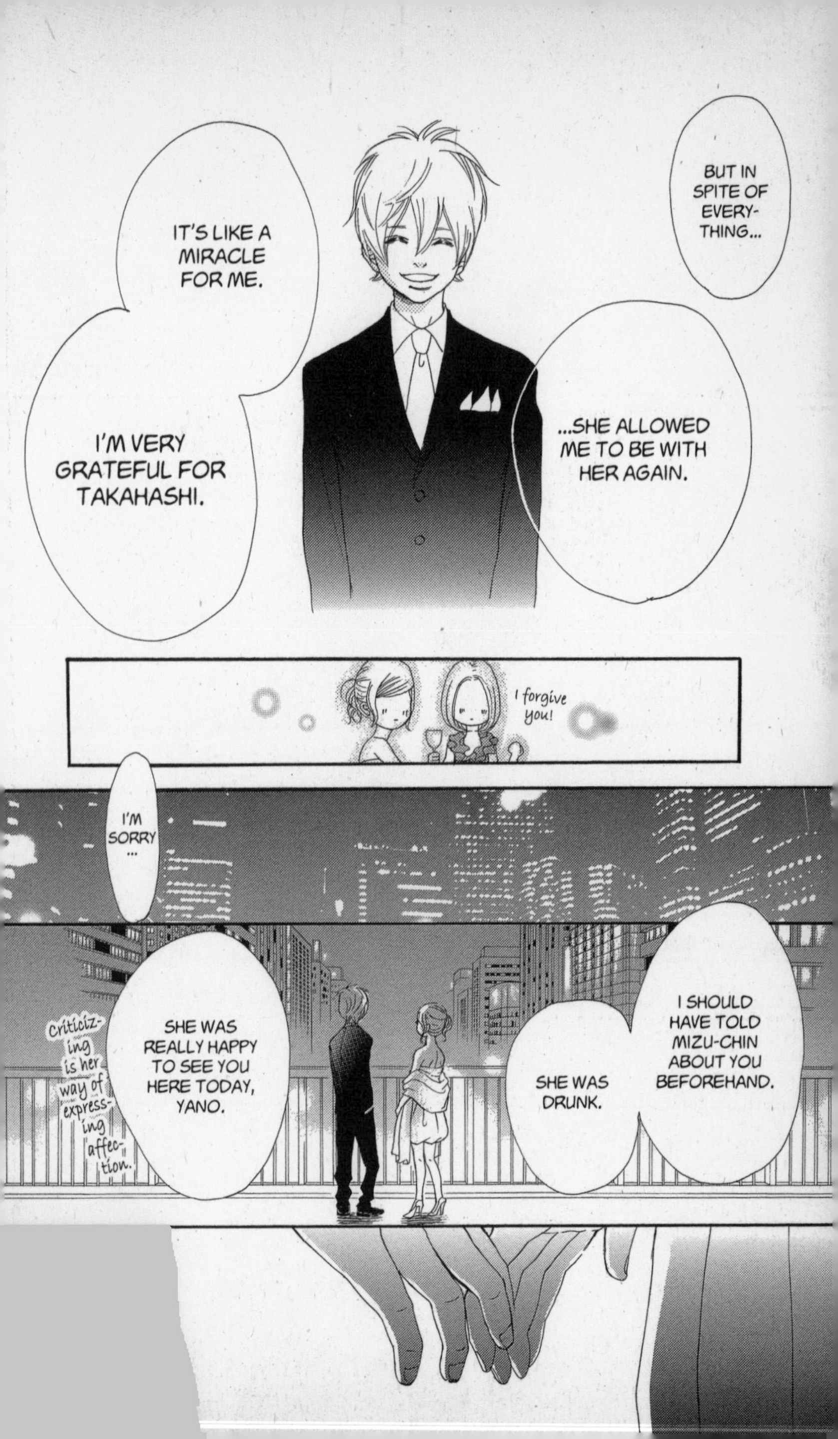
BUT IN SPITE OF EVERY-THING...
...SHE ALLOWED ME TO BE WITH HER AGAIN.
IT'S LIKE A MIRACLE FOR ME.
I'M VERY GRATEFUL FOR TAKAHASHI.
I forgive you!
I'M SORRY...
I SHOULD HAVE TOLD MIZU-CHIN ABOUT YOU BEFOREHAND.
SHE WAS DRUNK.
SHE WAS REALLY HAPPY TO SEE YOU HERE TODAY, YANO.
Criticiz-ing is her way of express-ing affec-tion.

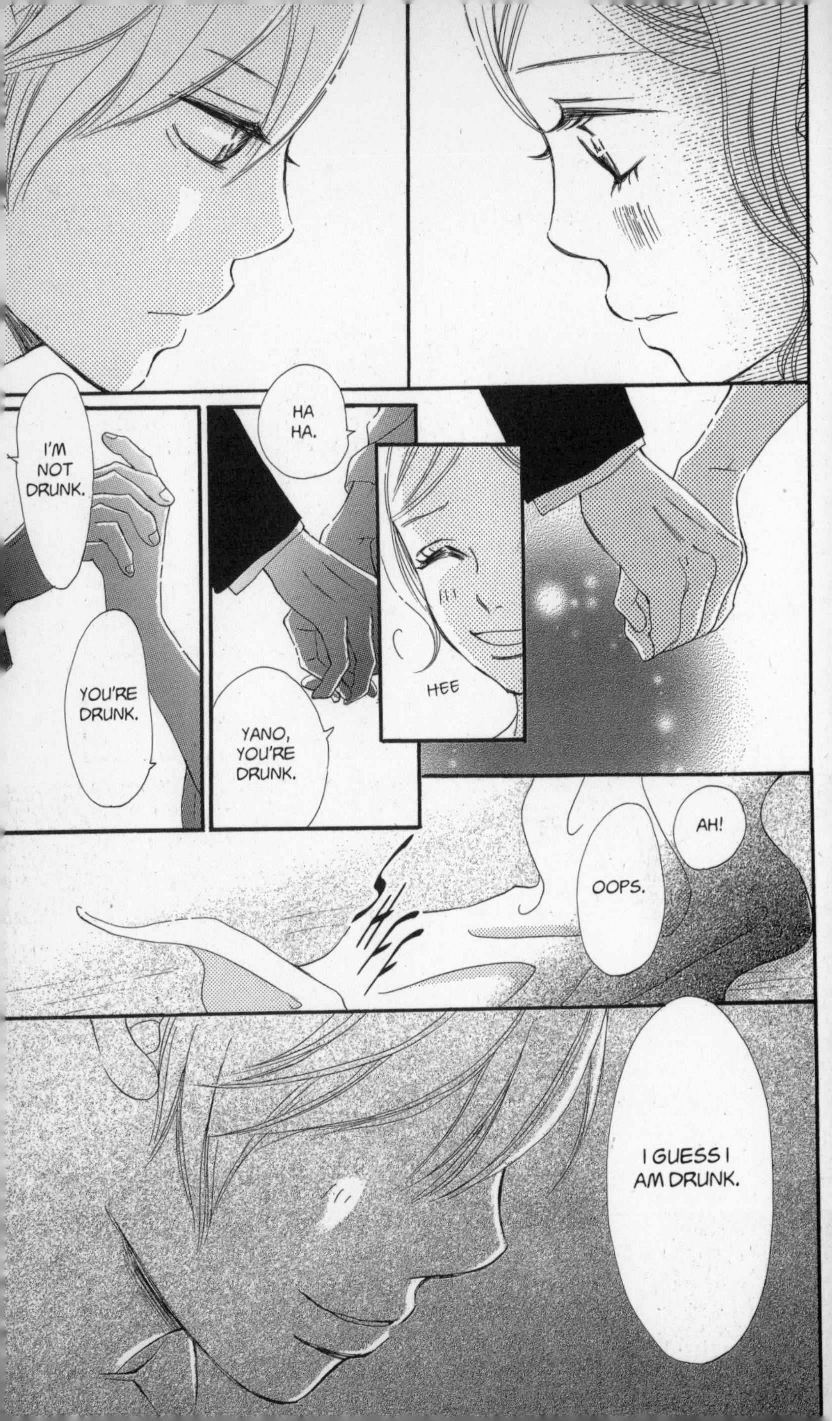
HEE
HA HA.
YANO, YOU'RE DRUNK.
I'M NOT DRUNK.
YOU'RE DRUNK.
AH!
OOPS.
I GUESS I AM DRUNK.

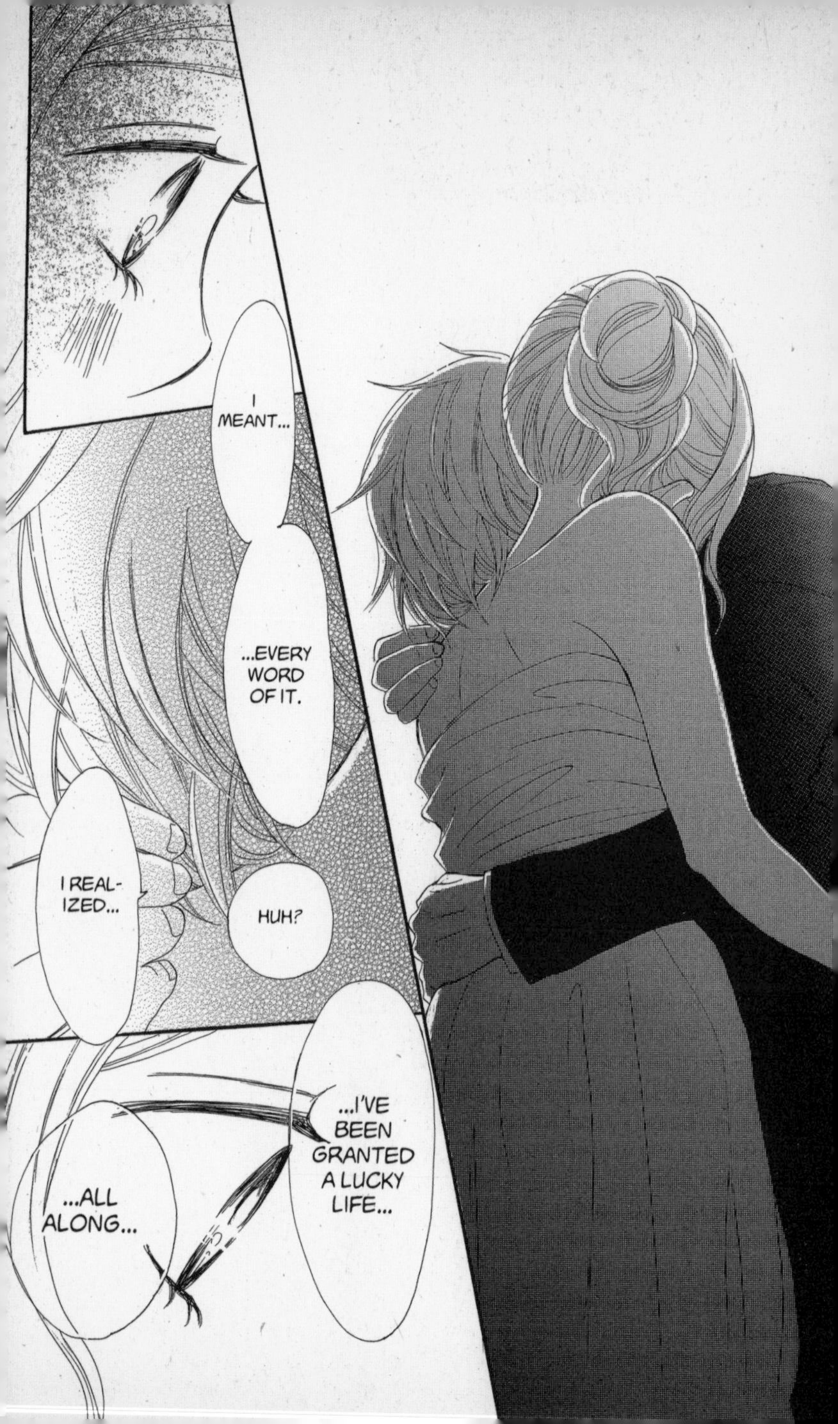
I MEANT...
...EVERY WORD OF IT.
HUH?
I REAL-IZED...
...I'VE BEEN GRANTED A LUCKY LIFE...
...ALL ALONG...

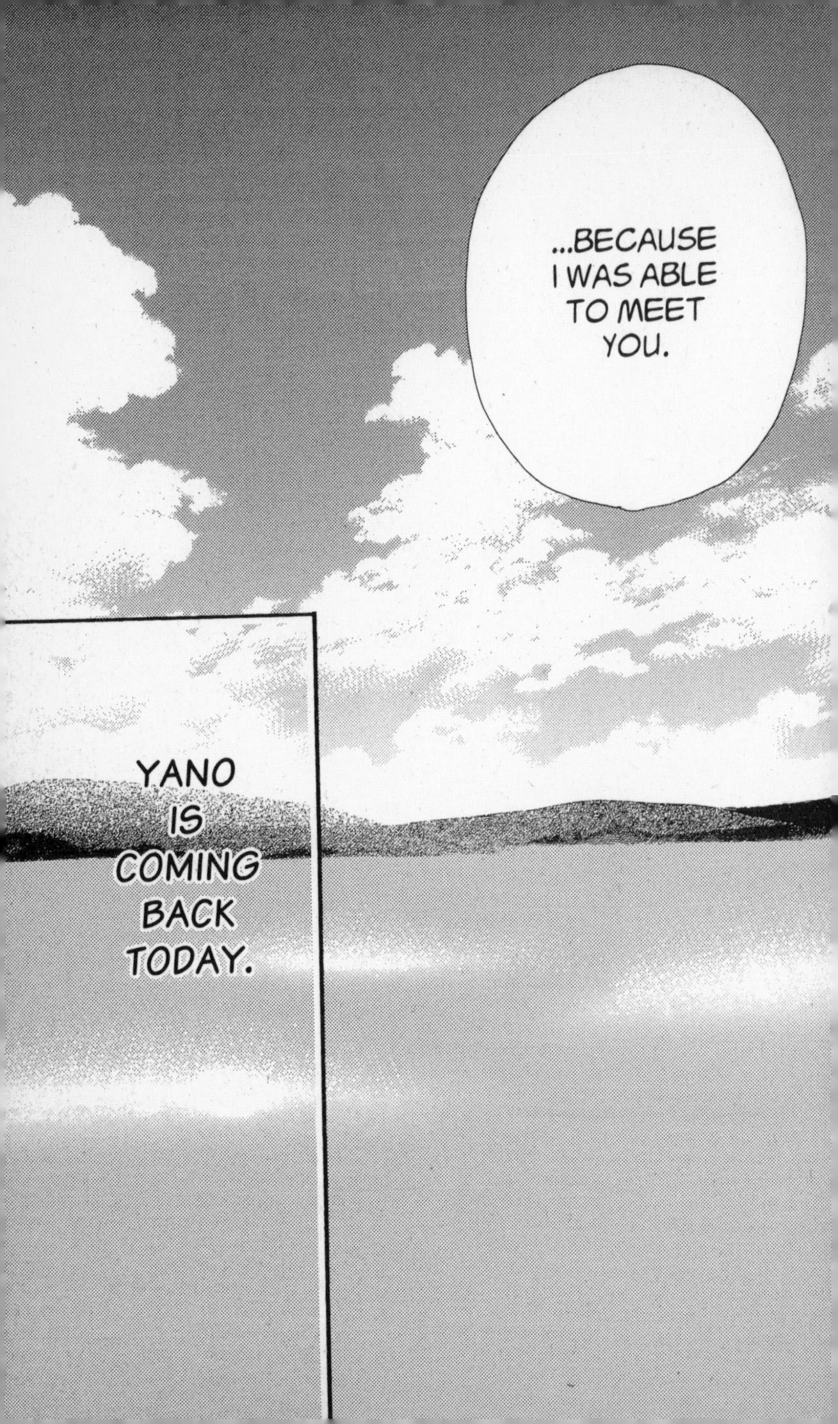
...BECAUSE I WAS ABLE TO MEET YOU.
YANO IS COMING BACK TODAY.

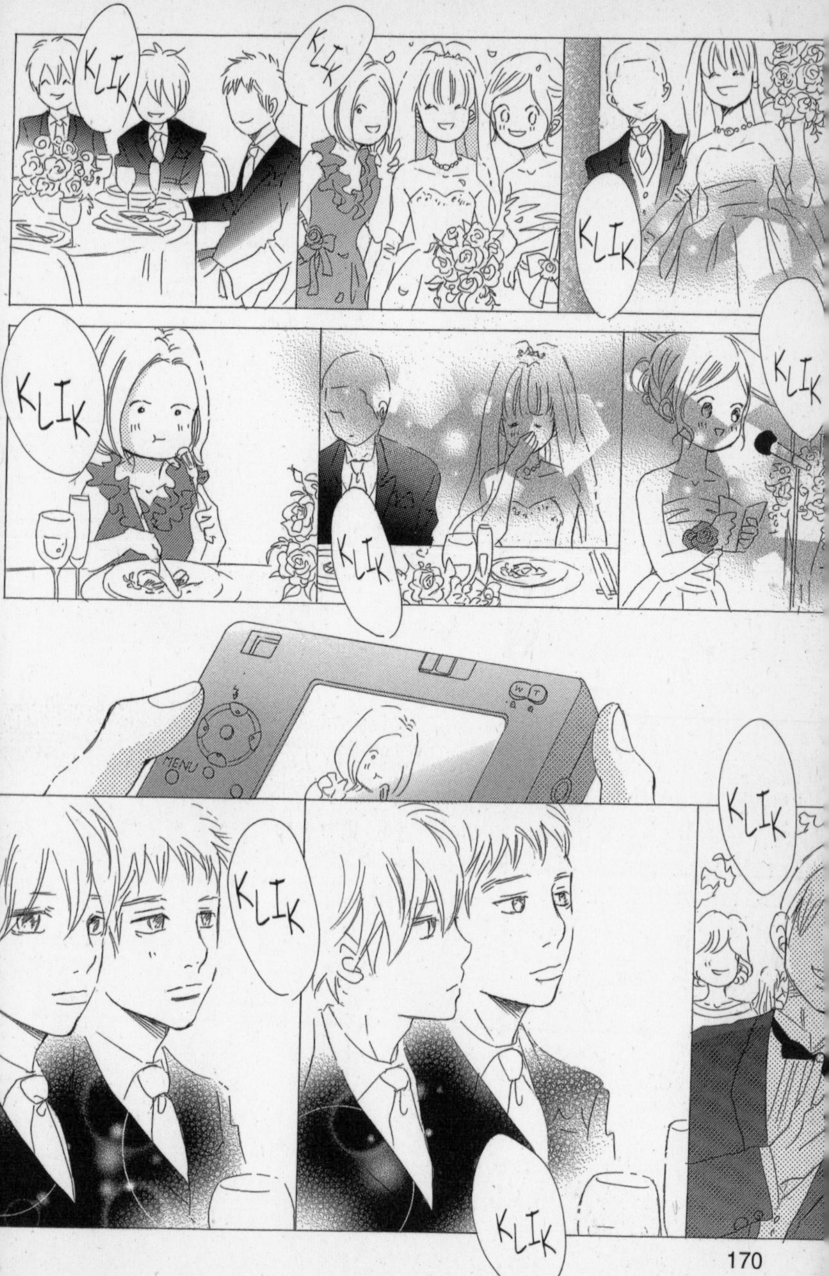
KLIK
KLIK
KLIK
KLIK
KLIK
KLIK
KLIK
KLIK
KLIK

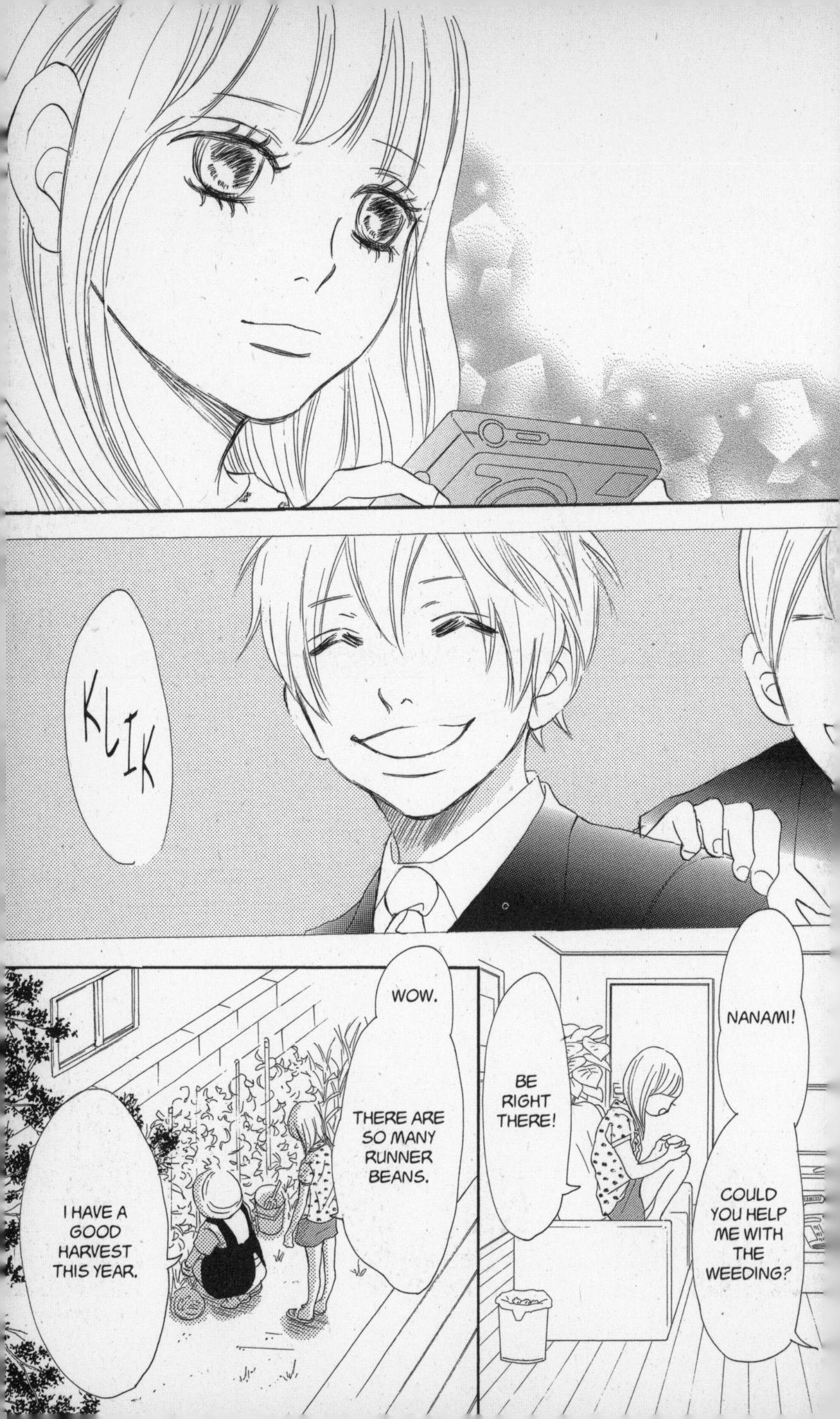
KLIK
NANAMI!
COULD YOU HELP ME WITH THE WEEDING?
BE RIGHT THERE!
WOW.
THERE ARE SO MANY RUNNER BEANS.
I HAVE A GOOD HARVEST THIS YEAR.

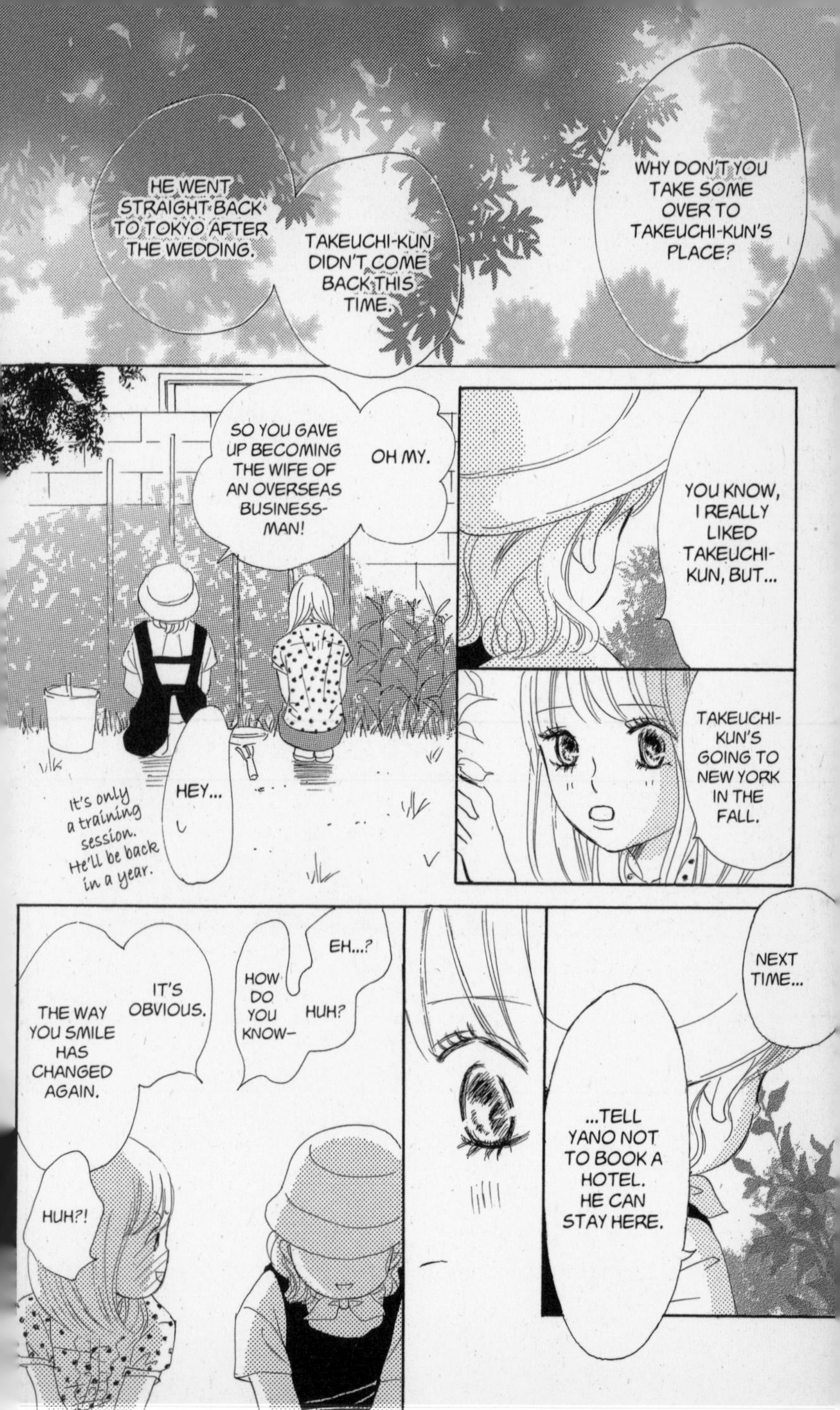
WHY DON'T YOU TAKE SOME OVER TO TAKEUCHI-KUN'S PLACE?
TAKEUCHI-KUN DIDN'T COME BACK THIS TIME.
HE WENT STRAIGHT BACK TO TOKYO AFTER THE WEDDING.
YOU KNOW, I REALLY LIKED TAKEUCHI-KUN, BUT...
TAKEUCHI-KUN'S GOING TO NEW YORK IN THE FALL.
OH MY.
SO YOU GAVE UP BECOMING THE WIFE OF AN OVERSEAS BUSINESS-MAN!
HEY...
It's only a training session. He'll be back in a year.
NEXT TIME...
...TELL YANO NOT TO BOOK A HOTEL. HE CAN STAY HERE.
EH...?
HUH?
HOW DO YOU KNOW-
IT'S OBVIOUS.
THE WAY YOU SMILE HAS CHANGED AGAIN.
HUH?!

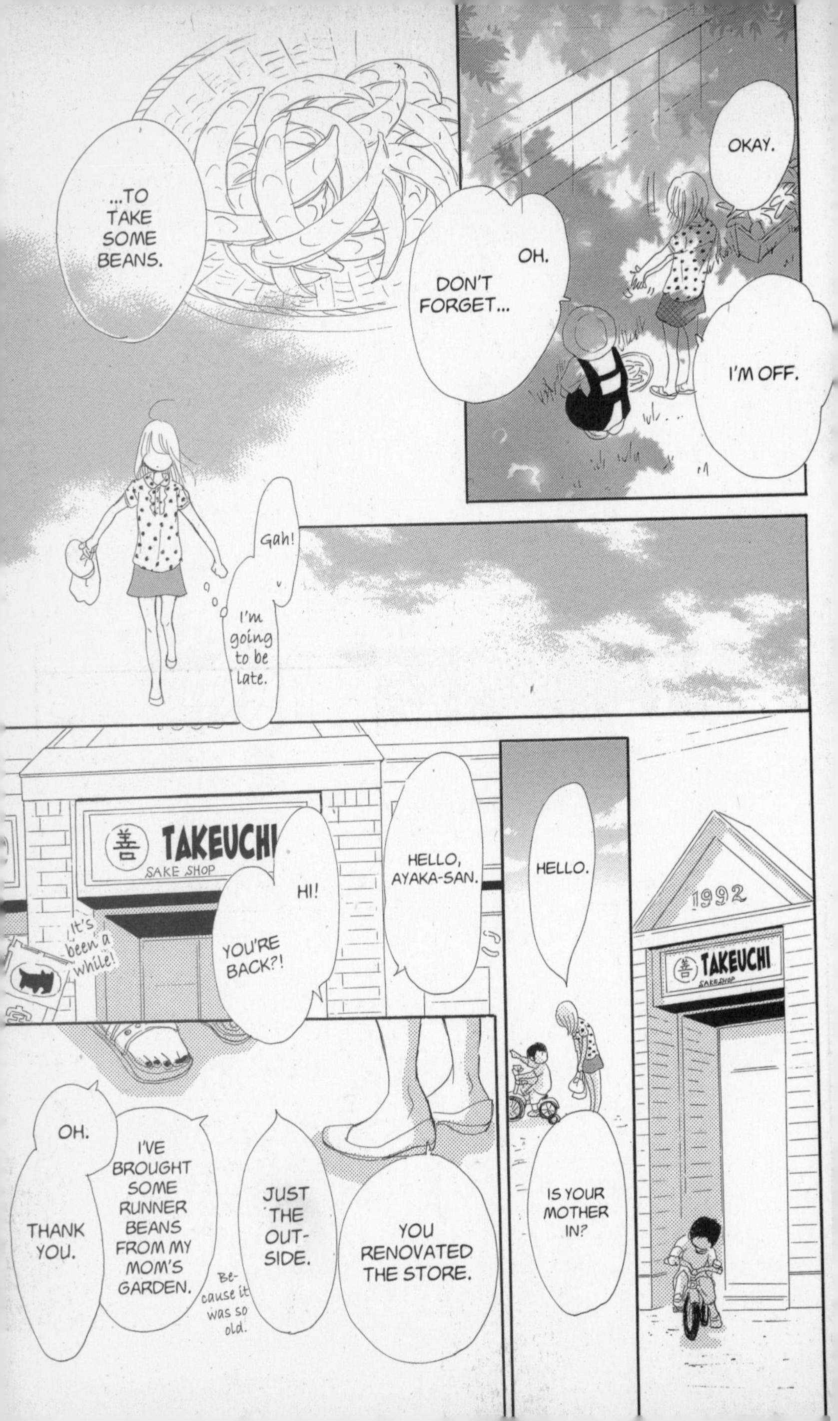
OKAY.
OH. DON'T FORGET...
I'M OFF.
...TO TAKE SOME BEANS.
Gah!
I'm going to be late.
HELLO.
1992
TAKEUCHI SAKE SHOP
IS YOUR MOTHER IN?
HELLO, AYAKA-SAN.
TAKEUCHI SAKE SHOP
HI!
YOU'RE BACK?!
It's been a while!
YOU RENOVATED THE STORE.
JUST THE OUT-SIDE.
Be-cause it was so old.
I'VE BROUGHT SOME RUNNER BEANS FROM MY MOM'S GARDEN.
OH.
THANK YOU.

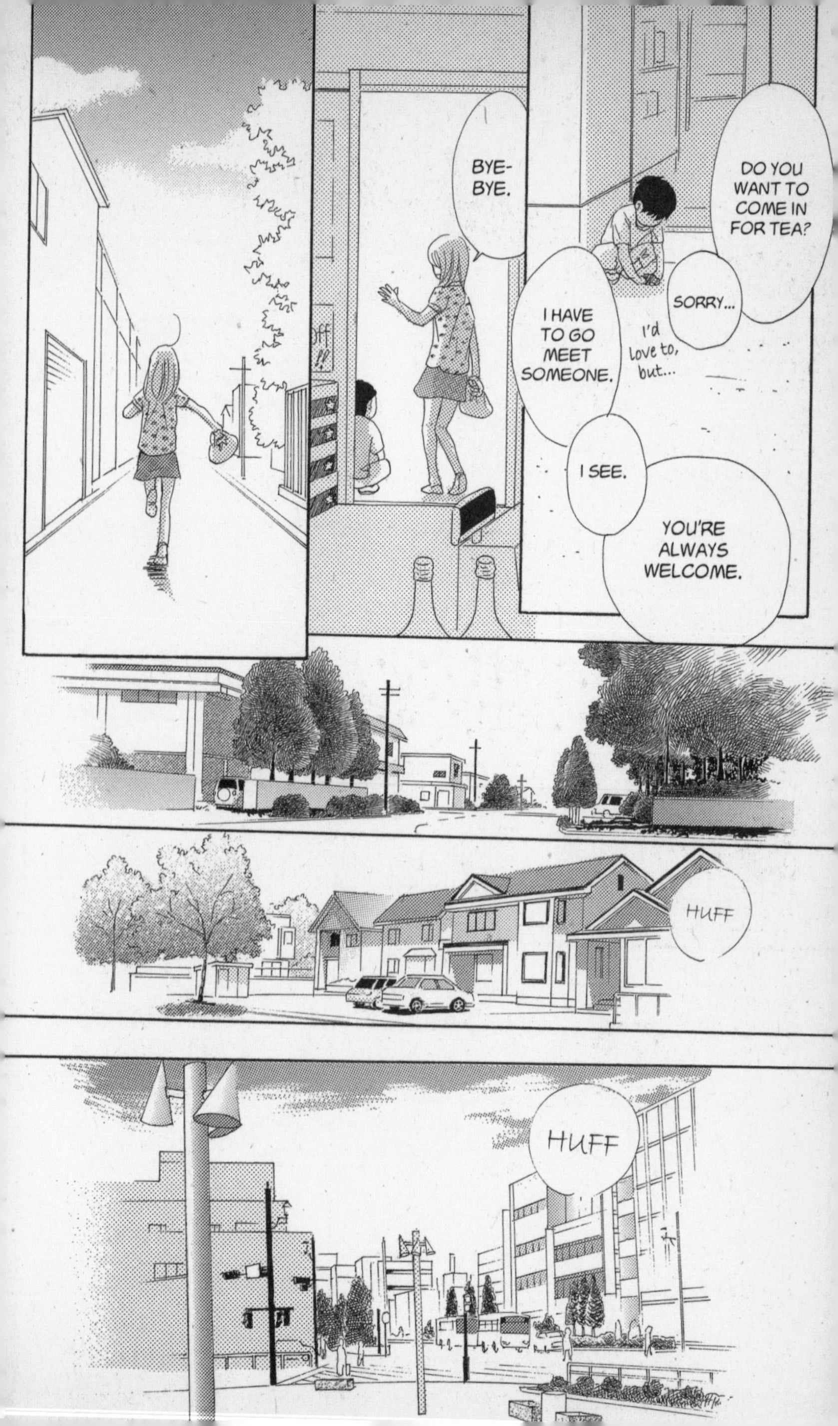
DO YOU WANT TO COME IN FOR TEA?
SORRY...
I'd love to, but...
I HAVE TO GO MEET SOMEONE.
I SEE.
YOU'RE ALWAYS WELCOME.
BYE-BYE.
HUFF
HUFF

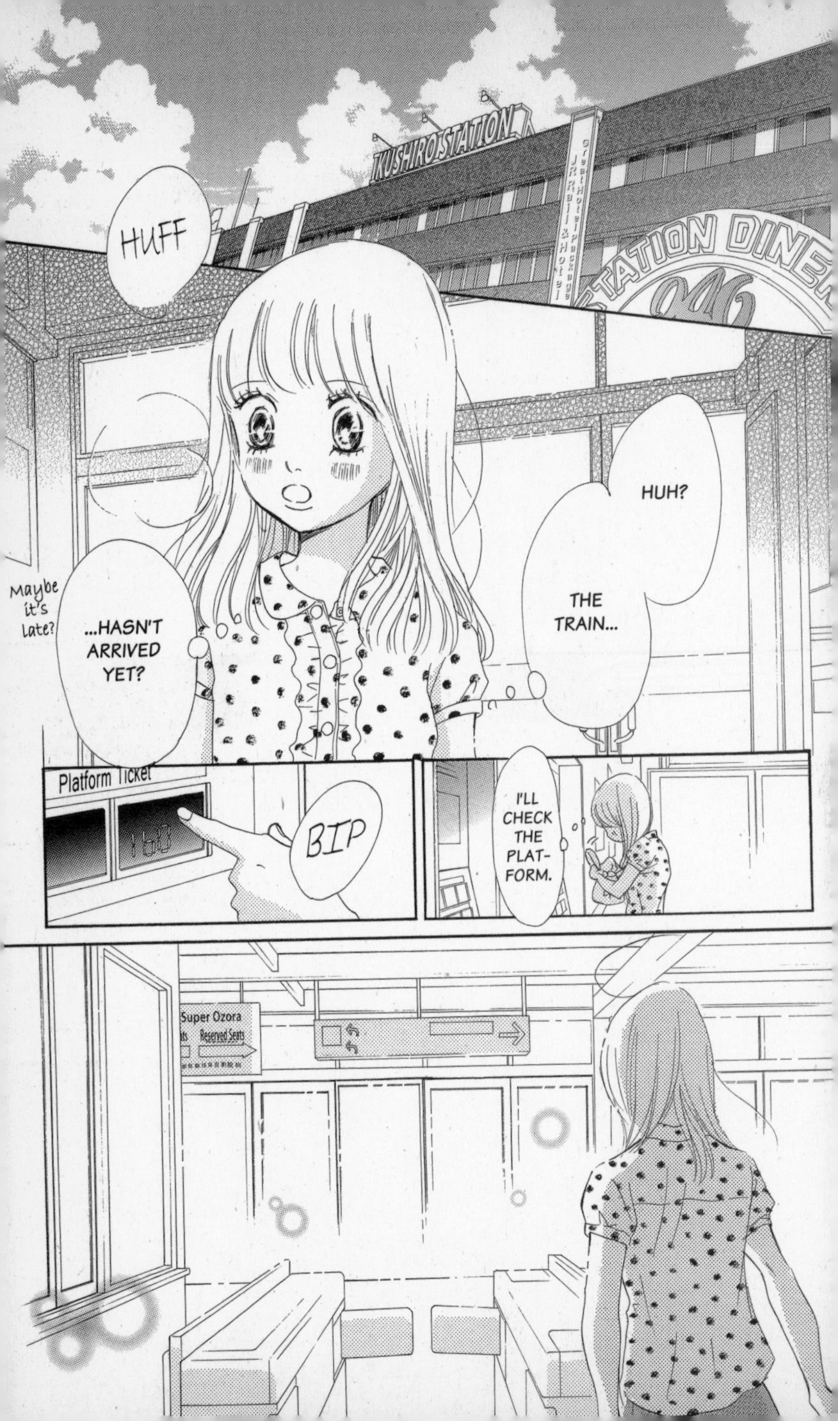
IKUSHIRO STATION
Great Hotel Package
JR Rail & Hotel
STATION DINER
HUFF
HUH?
THE TRAIN...
...HASN'T ARRIVED YET?
Maybe it's late?
I'LL CHECK THE PLAT-FORM.
Platform Ticket
BIP
Super Ozora
Reserved Seats

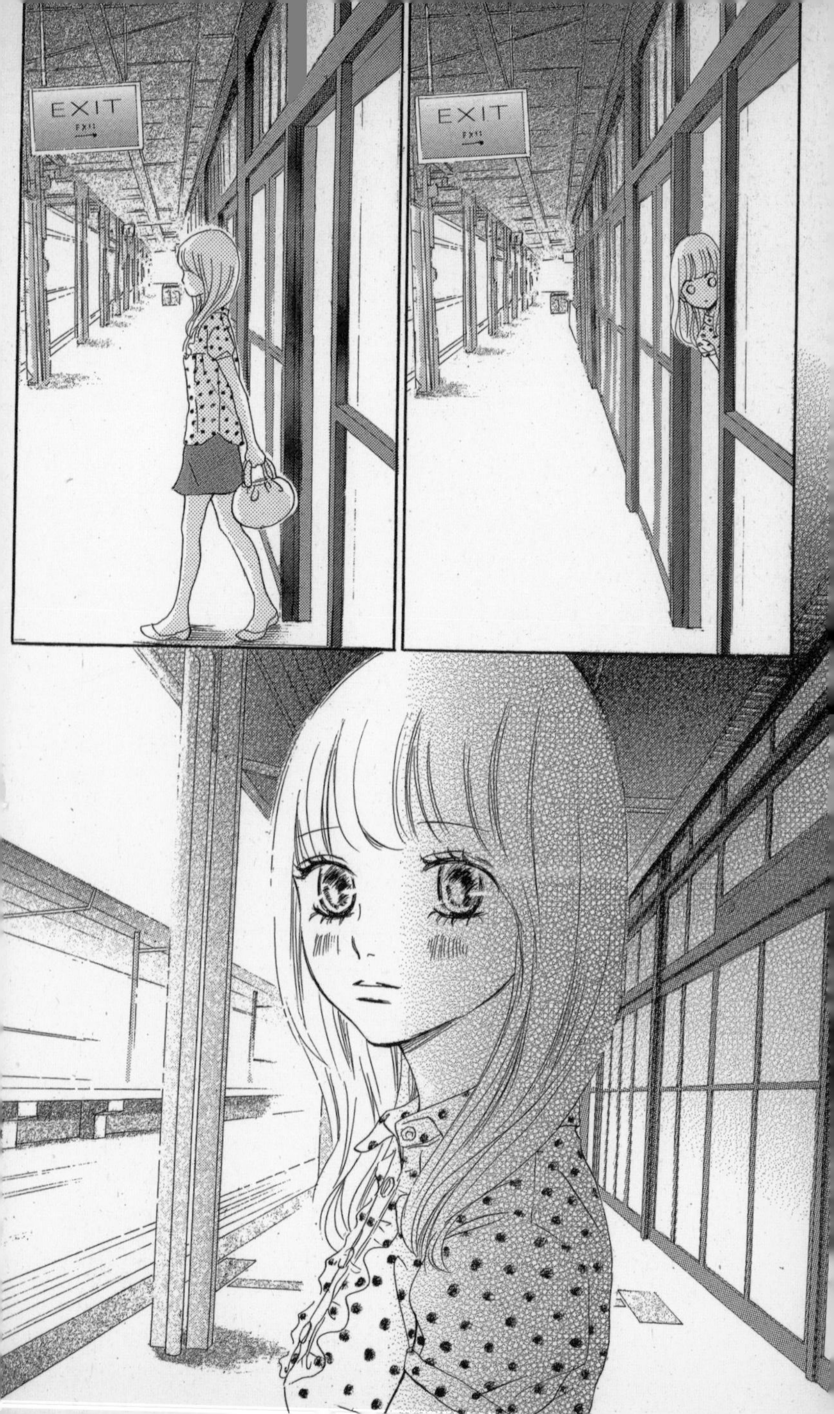
EXIT
EXIT

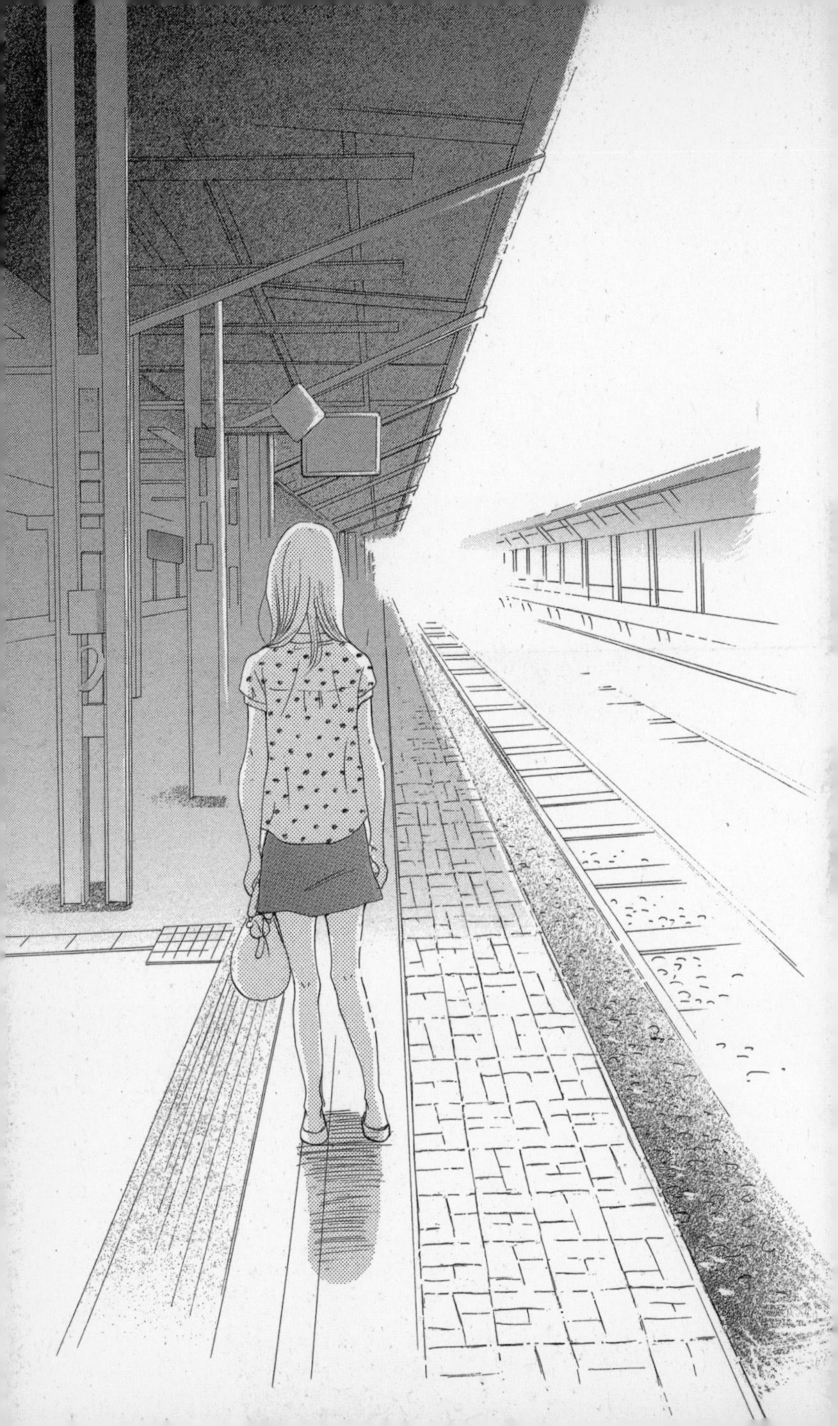

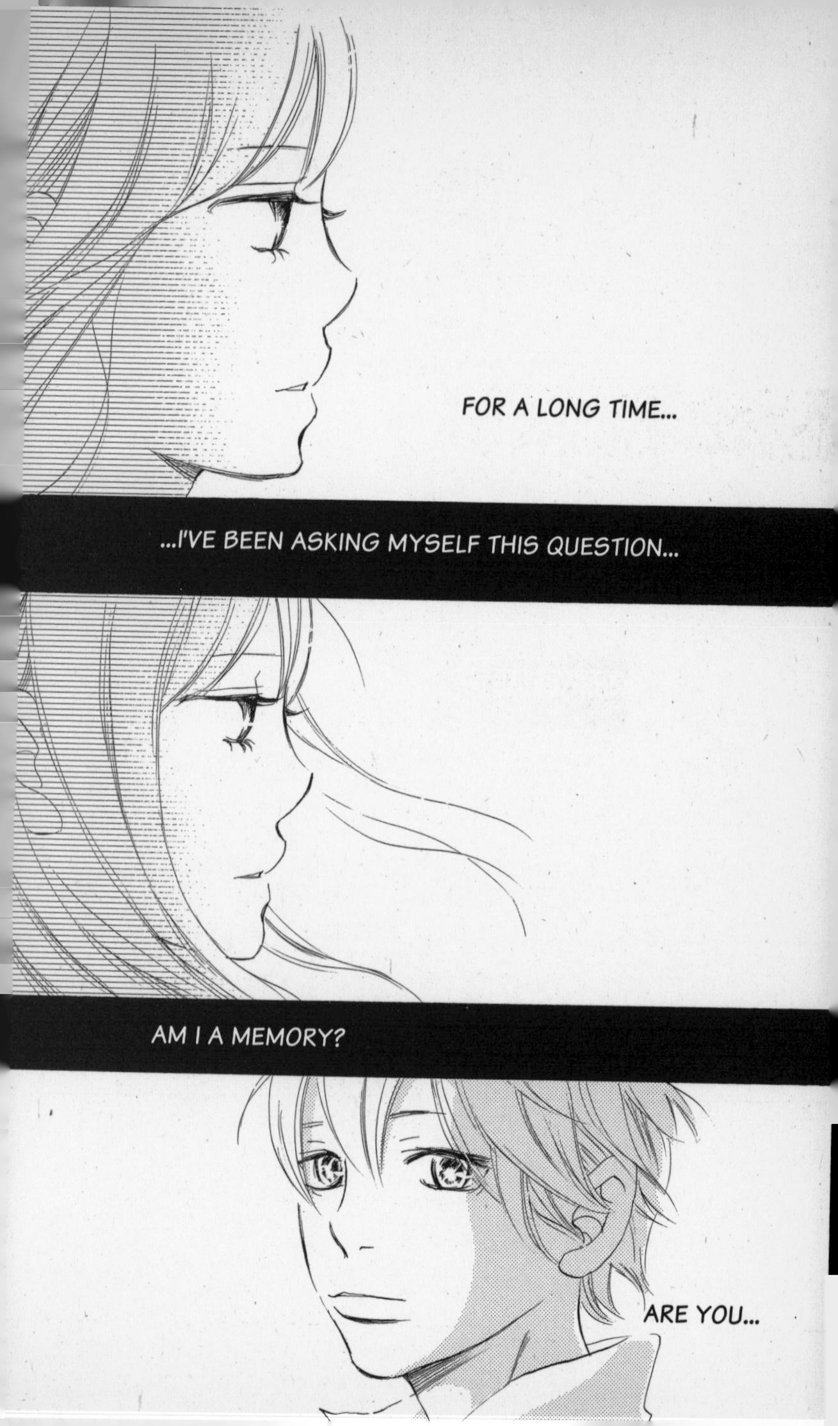
FOR A LONG TIME...
...I'VE BEEN ASKING MYSELF THIS QUESTION...
AM I A MEMORY?
ARE YOU...

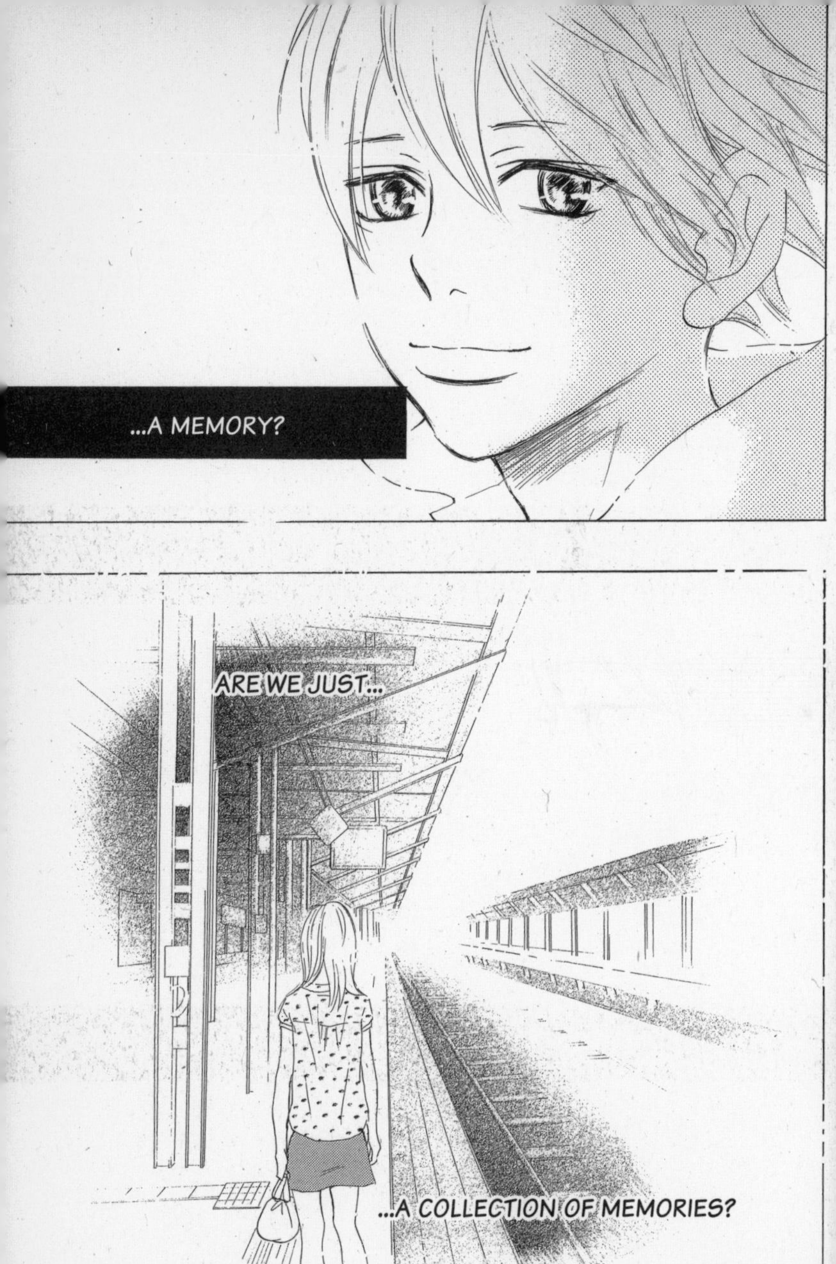
...A MEMORY?
ARE WE JUST...
...A COLLECTION OF MEMORIES?

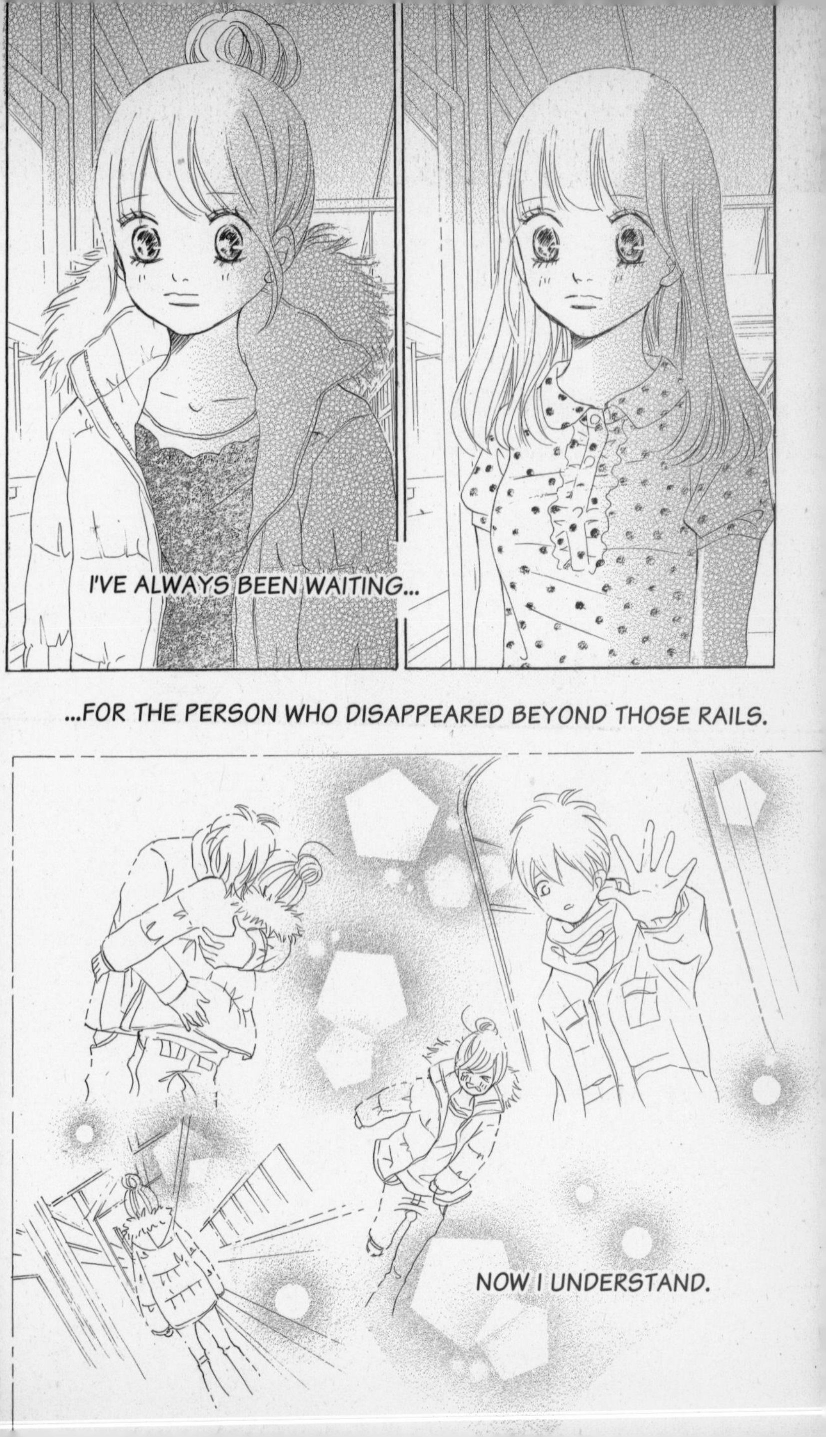
I'VE ALWAYS BEEN WAITING...
...FOR THE PERSON WHO DISAPPEARED BEYOND THOSE RAILS.
NOW I UNDERSTAND.

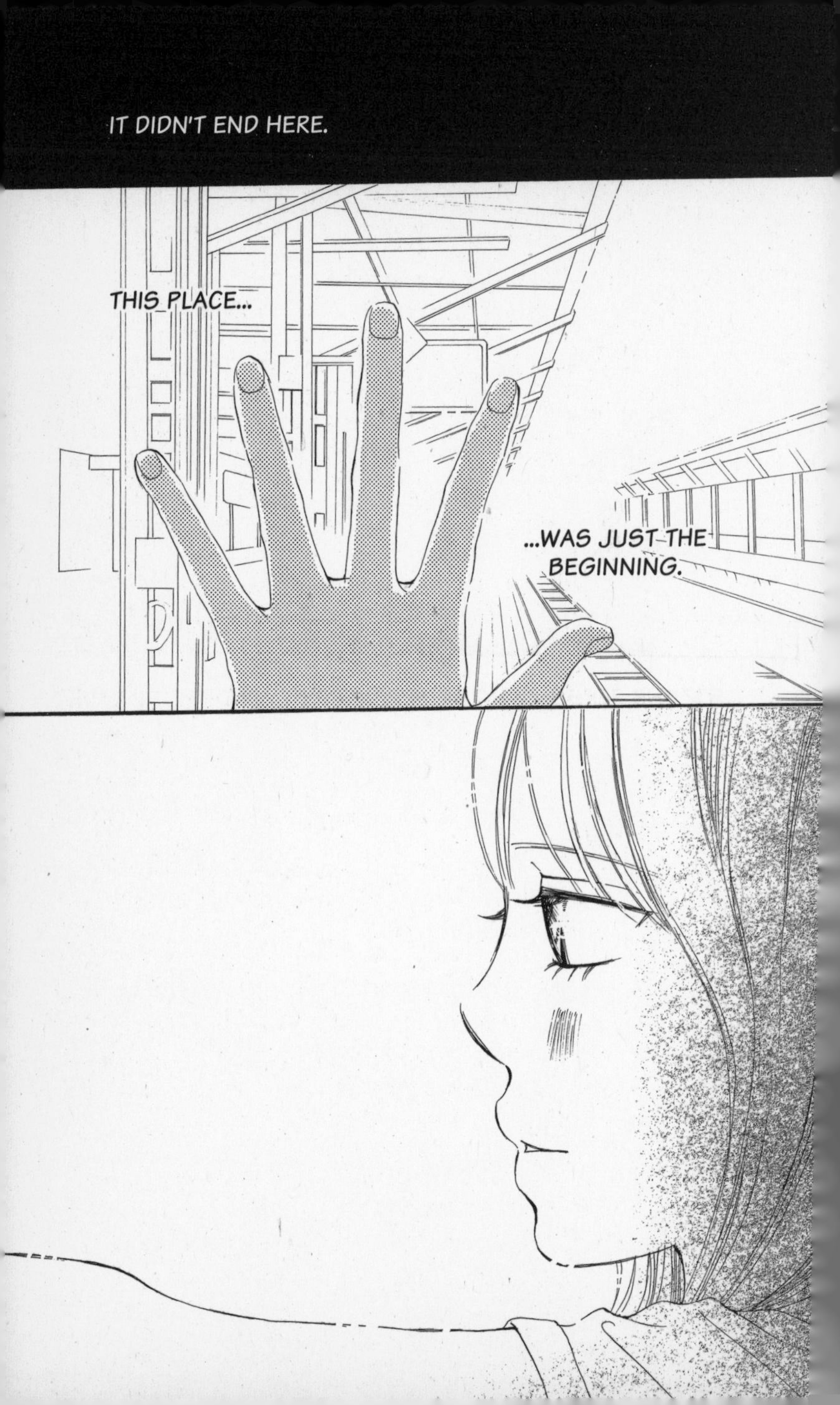
IT DIDN'T END HERE.
THIS PLACE...
...WAS JUST THE BEGINNING.

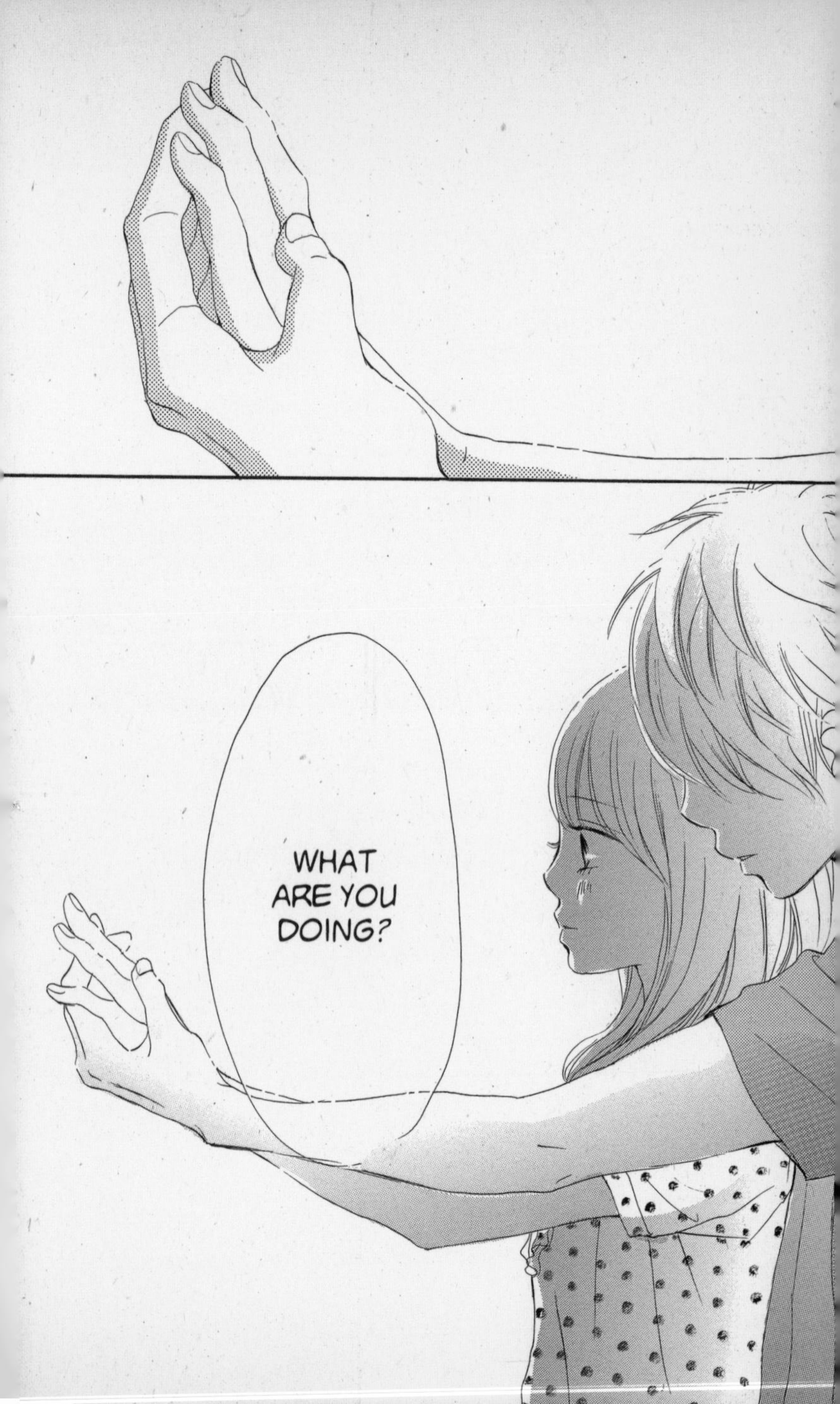
WHAT ARE YOU DOING?

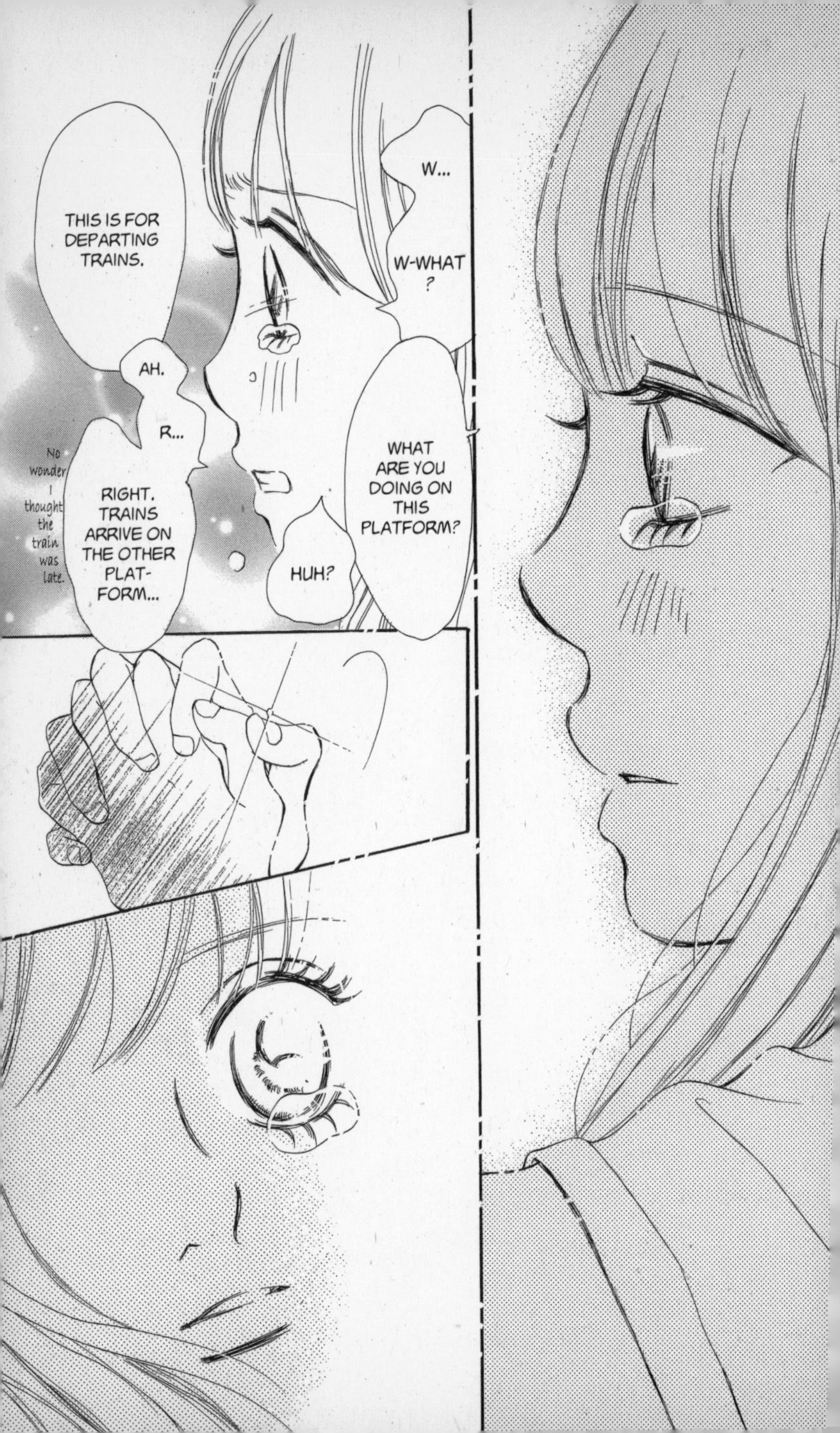
W...
W-WHAT?
WHAT ARE YOU DOING ON THIS PLATFORM?
HUH?
THIS IS FOR DEPARTING TRAINS.
AH.
R...
RIGHT. TRAINS ARRIVE ON THE OTHER PLAT-FORM...
No wonder I thought the train was late.

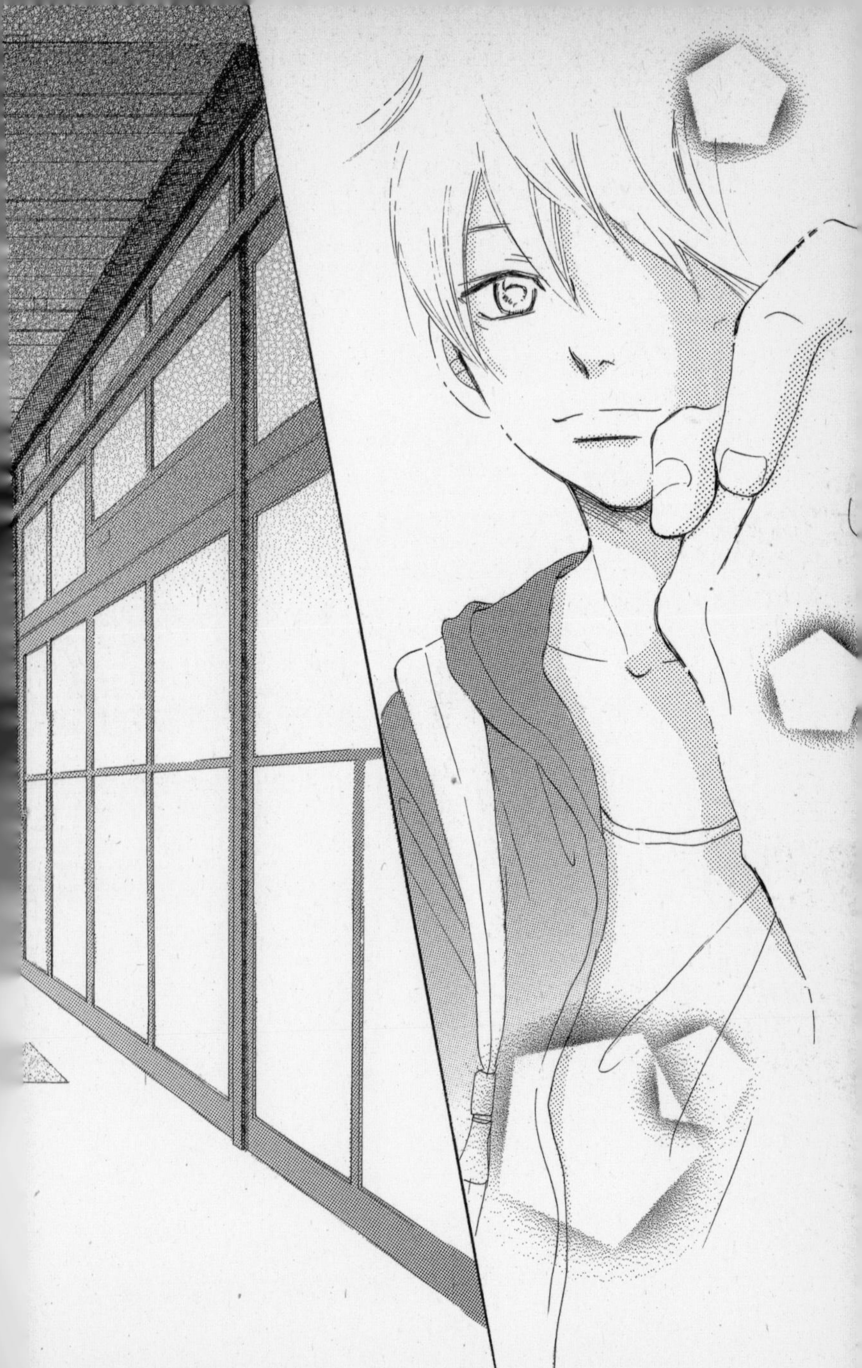

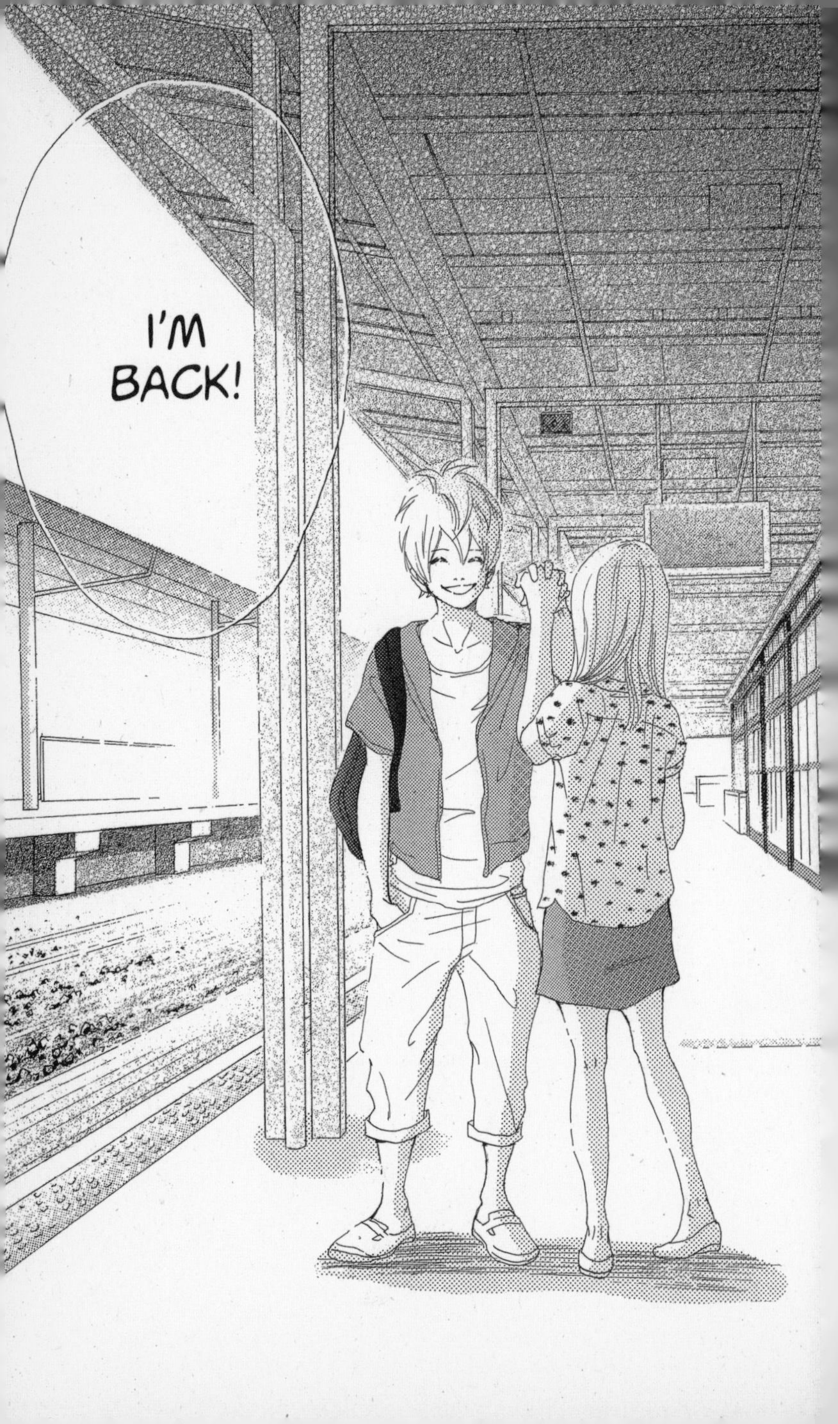
I'M BACK!

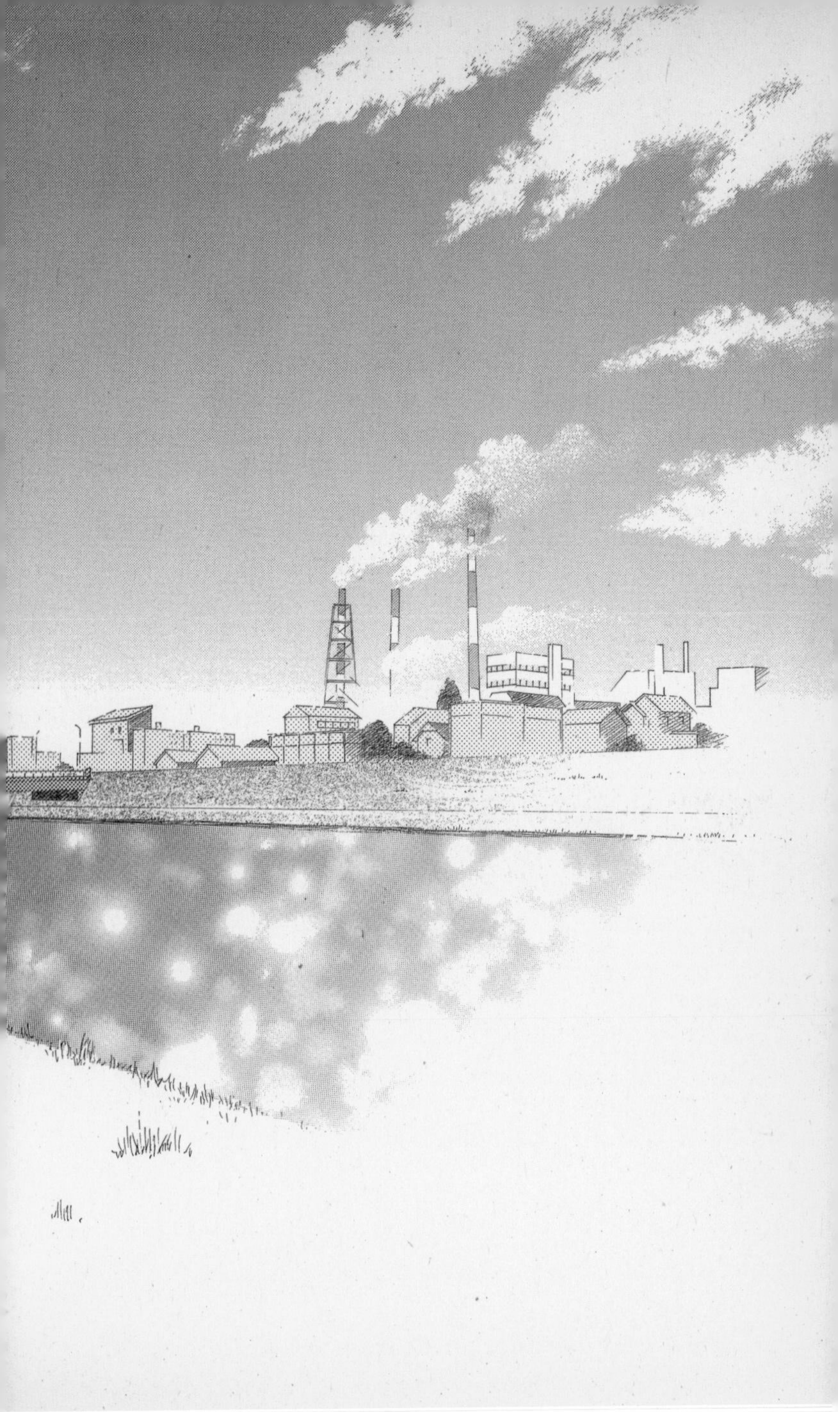

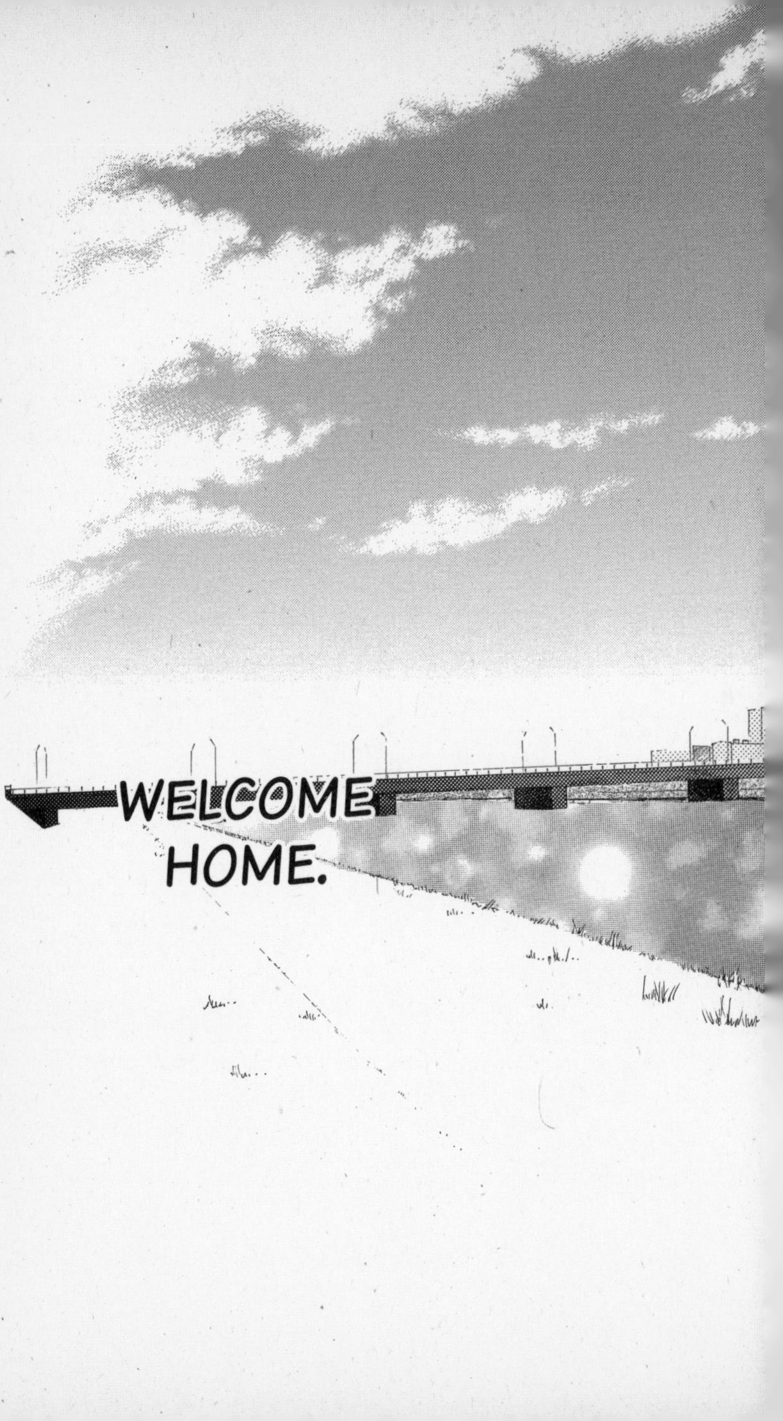
WELCOME HOME.

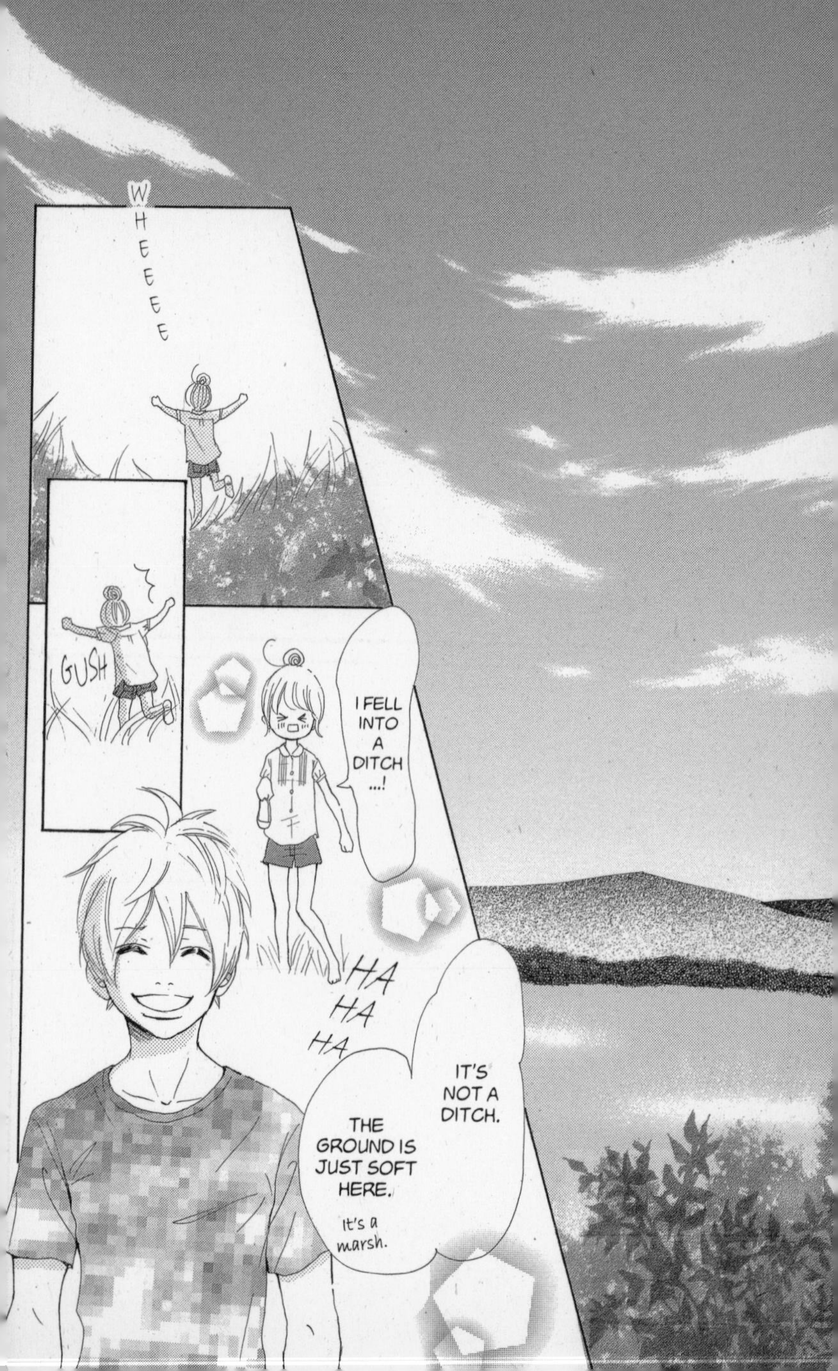
WHEEEEE
GUSH
I FELL INTO A DITCH ...!
HA HA HA
IT'S NOT A DITCH.
THE GROUND IS JUST SOFT HERE.
It's a marsh.

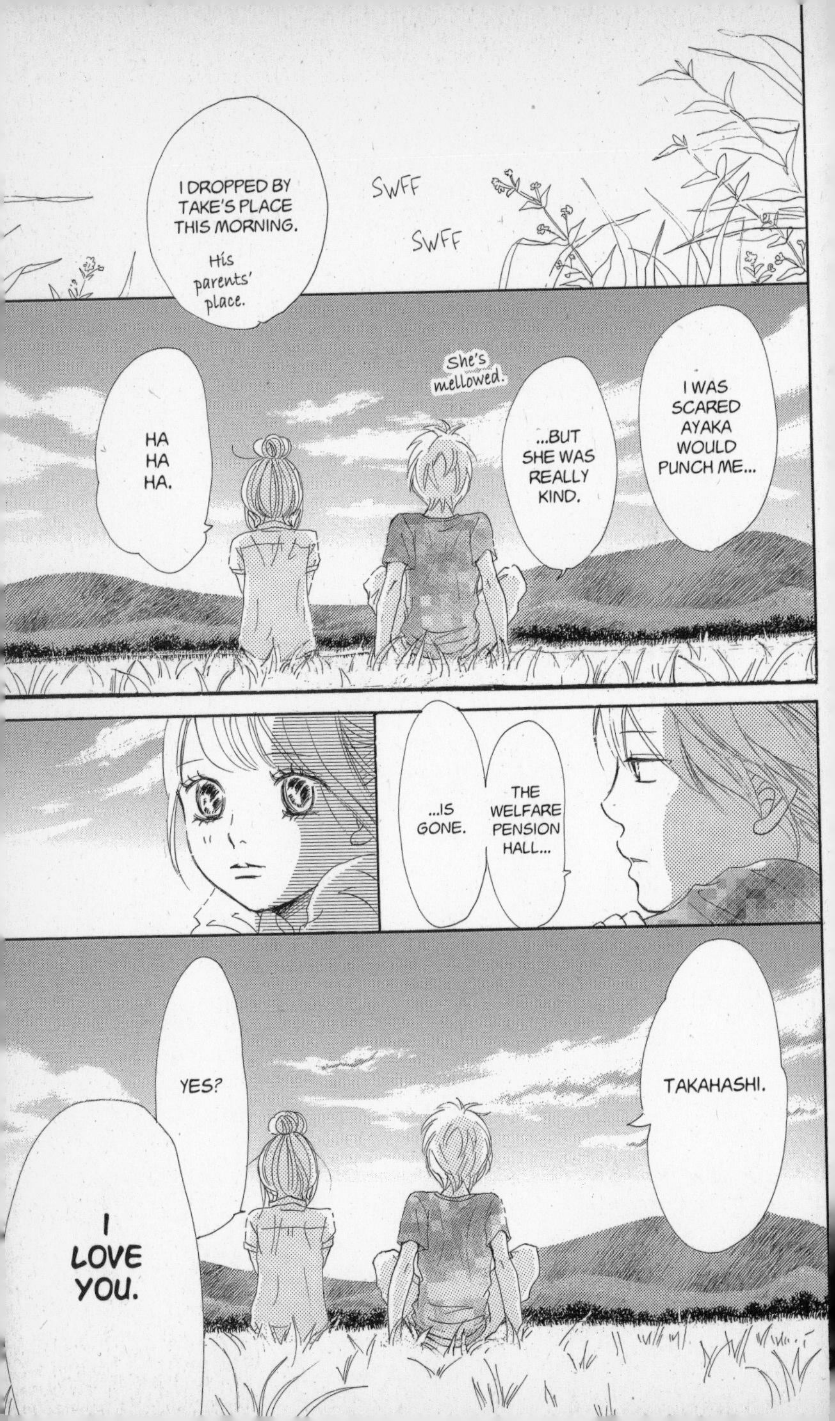
SWFF
SWFF
I DROPPED BY TAKE'S PLACE THIS MORNING.
His parents' place.
I WAS SCARED AYAKA WOULD PUNCH ME...
...BUT SHE WAS REALLY KIND.
She's mellowed.
HA HA HA.
THE WELFARE PENSION HALL...
...IS GONE.
TAKAHASHI.
YES?
I LOVE YOU.

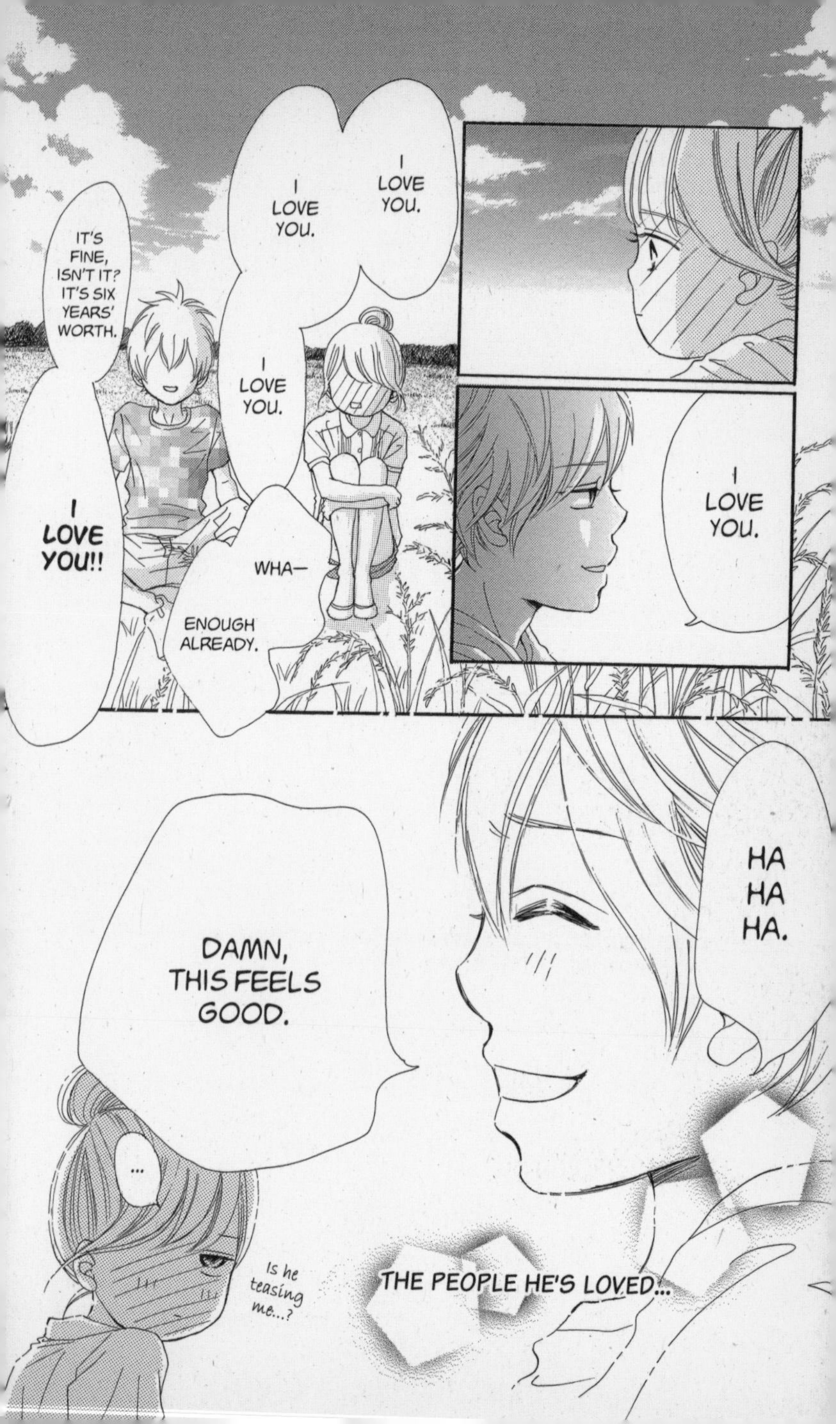
I LOVE YOU.
I LOVE YOU.
I LOVE YOU.
IT'S FINE, ISN'T IT? IT'S SIX YEARS' WORTH.
I LOVE YOU.
WHA—
ENOUGH ALREADY.
I LOVE YOU!!
HA HA HA.
DAMN, THIS FEELS GOOD.
THE PEOPLE HE'S LOVED...
...
Is he teasing me...?

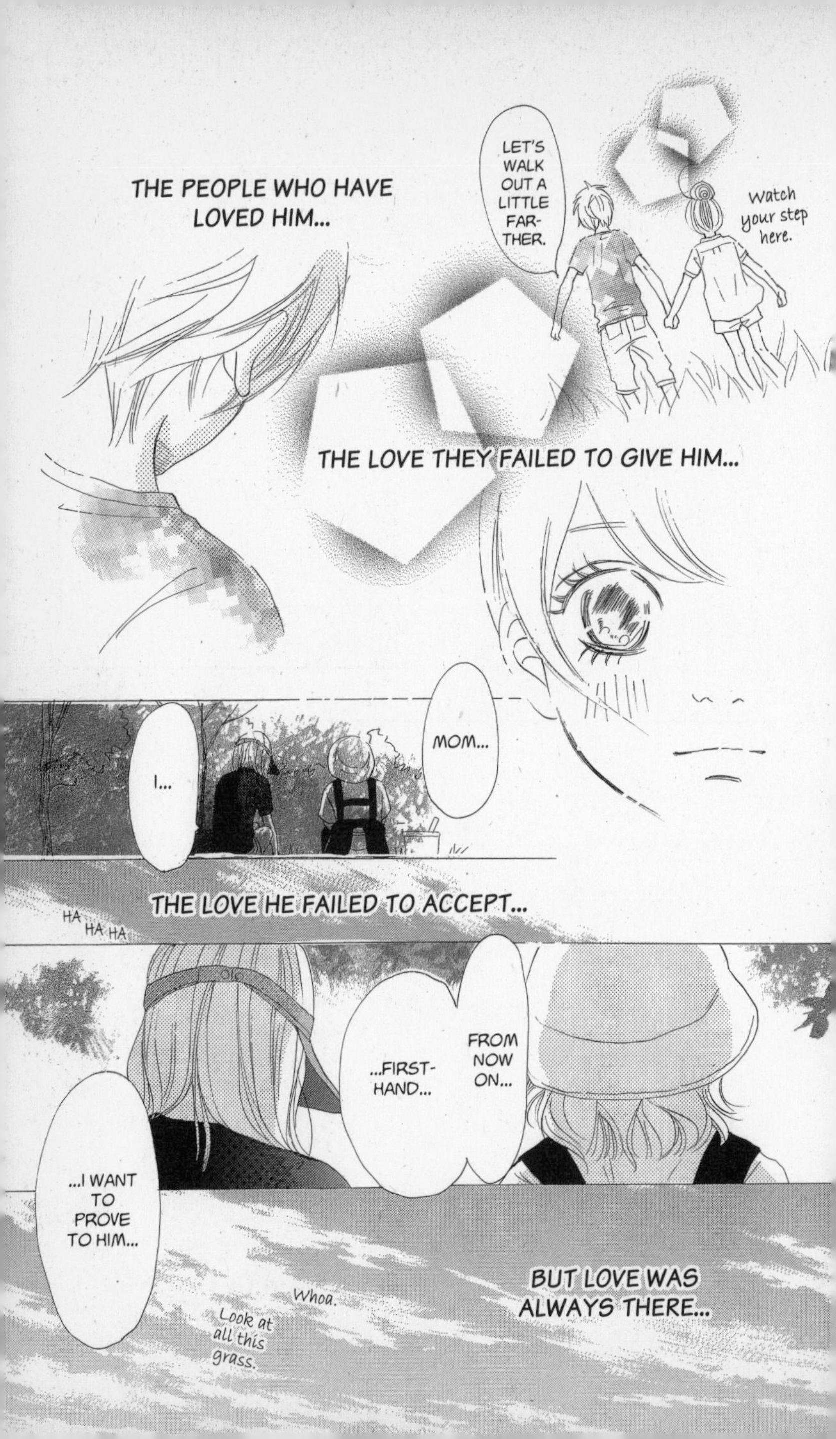
Watch your step here.
LET'S WALK OUT A LITTLE FAR-THER.
THE PEOPLE WHO HAVE LOVED HIM...
THE LOVE THEY FAILED TO GIVE HIM...
MOM...
I...
THE LOVE HE FAILED TO ACCEPT...
HA HA HA
FROM NOW ON...
...FIRST-HAND...
...I WANT TO PROVE TO HIM...
BUT LOVE WAS ALWAYS THERE...
Whoa.
Look at all this grass.

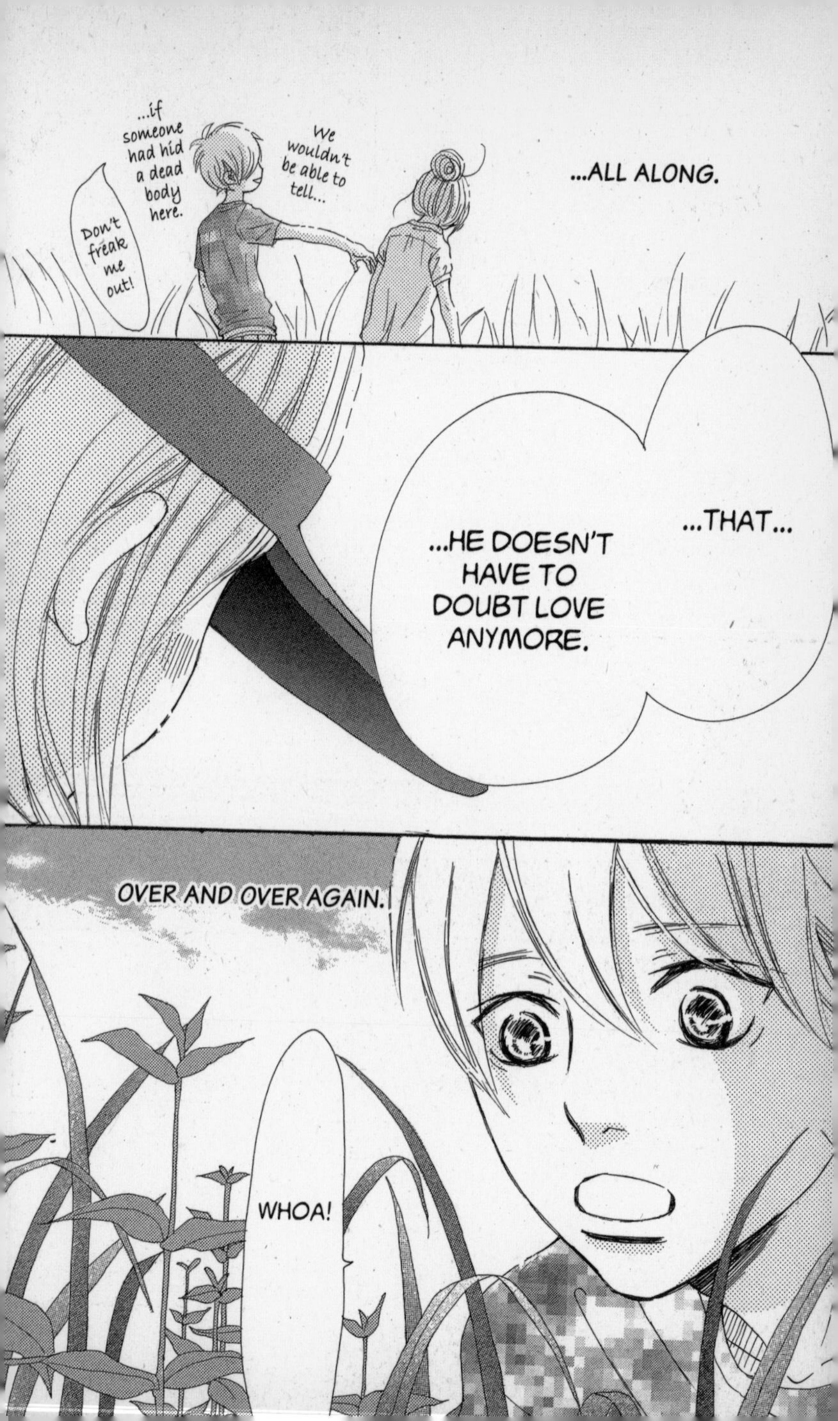
...ALL ALONG.
We wouldn't be able to tell...
...if someone had hid a dead body here.
Don't freak me out!
...THAT...
...HE DOESN'T HAVE TO DOUBT LOVE ANYMORE.
OVER AND OVER AGAIN.
WHOA!

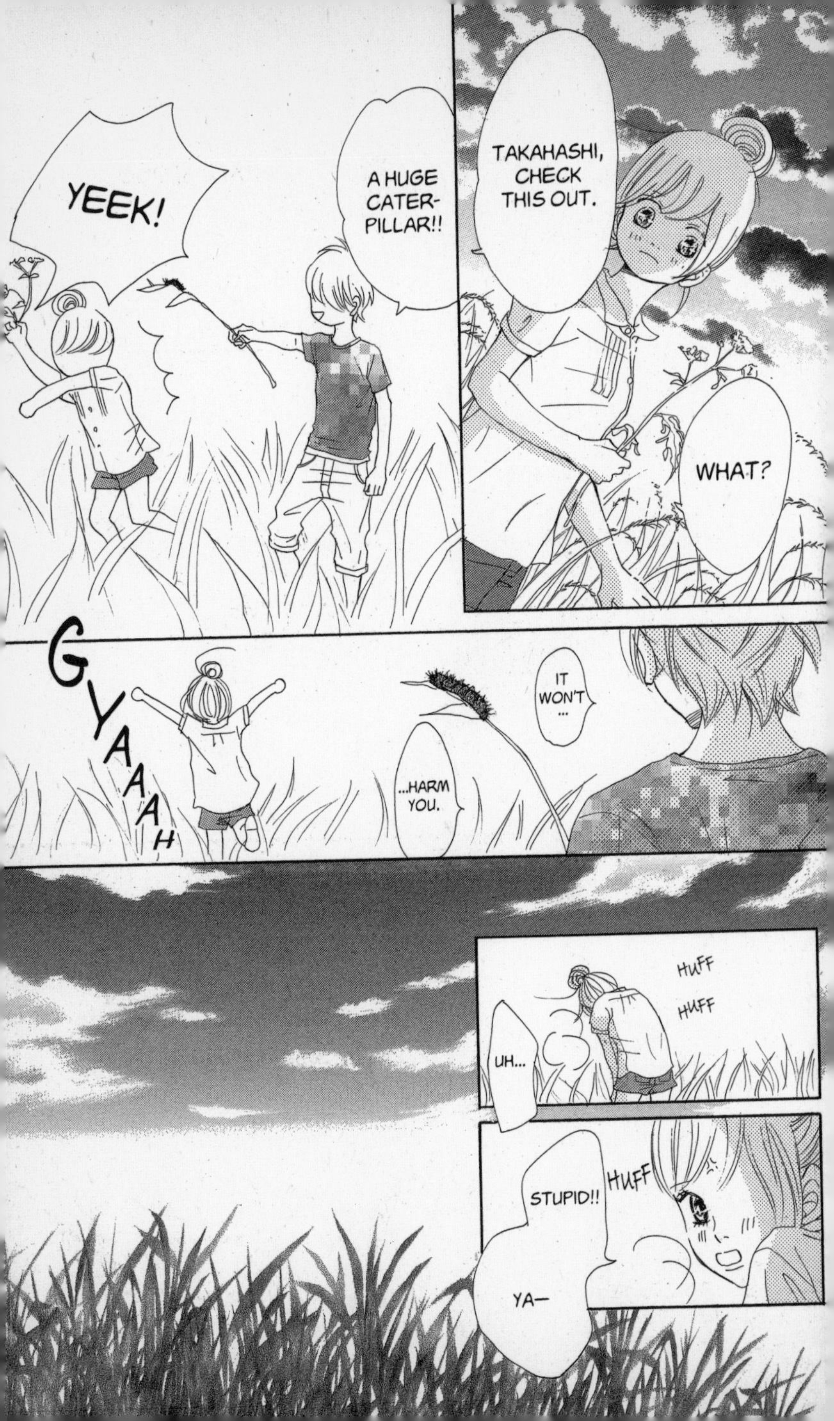
TAKAHASHI, CHECK THIS OUT.
WHAT?
A HUGE CATER-PILLAR!!
YEEK!
IT WON'T ...
...HARM YOU.
GYAAAAH
HUFF
HUFF
UH...
HUFF
STUPID!!
YA—

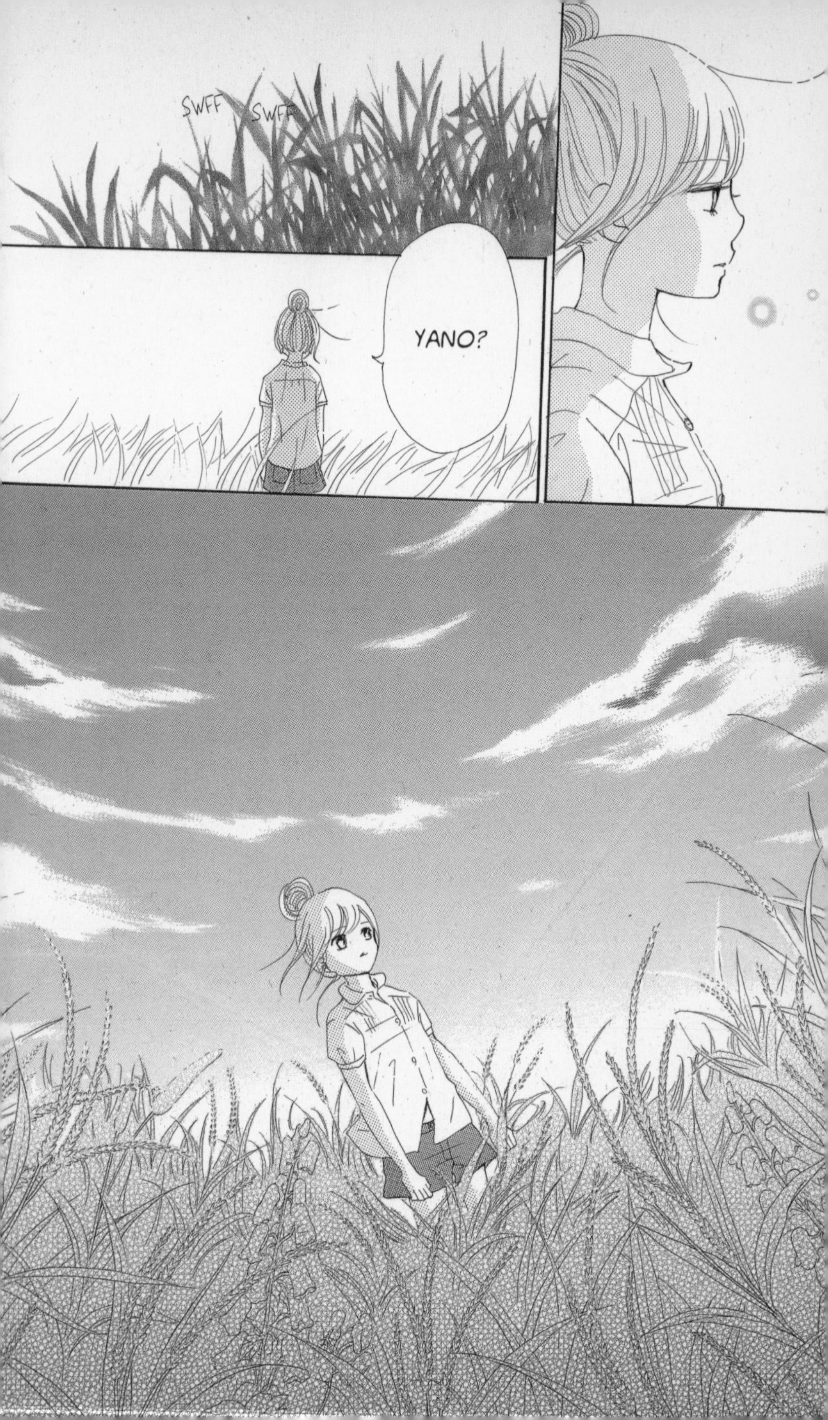
SWFF SWFF
YANO?

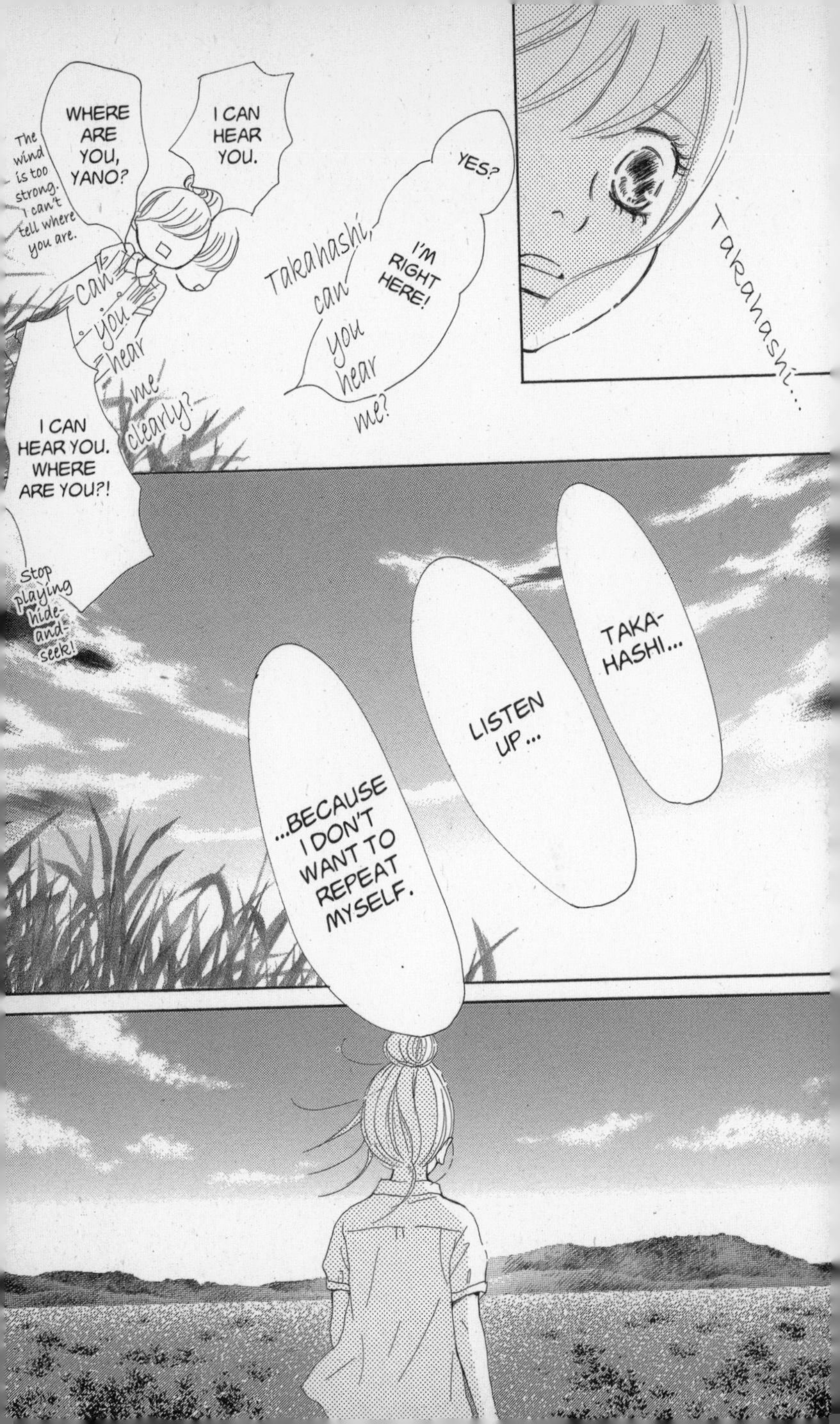
Takahashi...
YES?
I'M RIGHT HERE!
Takahashi, can you hear me?
I CAN HEAR YOU.
WHERE ARE YOU, YANO?
The wind is too strong. I can't tell where you are.
Can you hear me clearly?
I CAN HEAR YOU. WHERE ARE YOU?!
Stop playing hide-and-seek!
TAKA-HASHI...
LISTEN UP...
...BECAUSE I DON'T WANT TO REPEAT MYSELF.

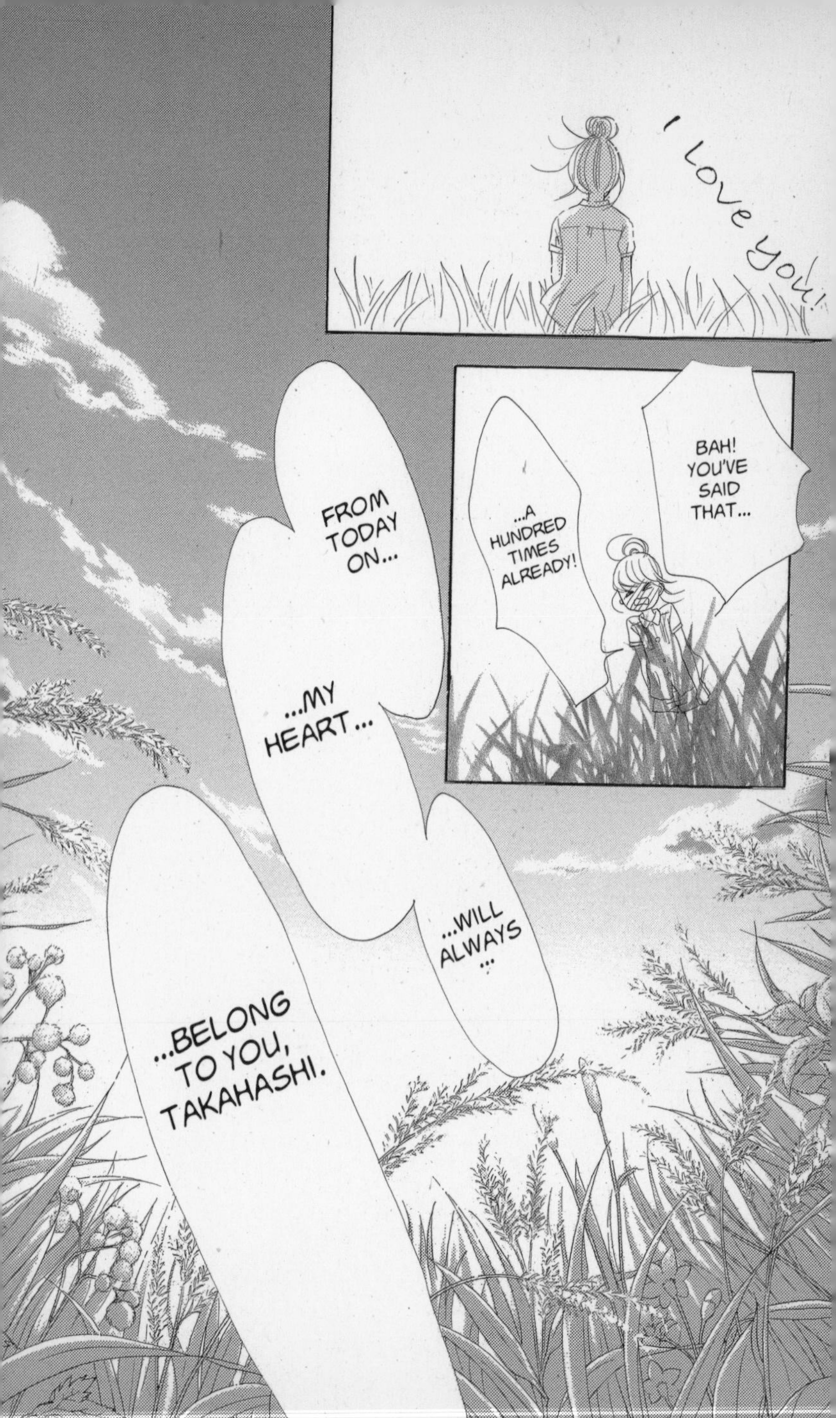
I love you!
BAH! YOU'VE SAID THAT...
...A HUNDRED TIMES ALREADY!
FROM TODAY ON...
...MY HEART...
...WILL ALWAYS ...
...BELONG TO YOU, TAKAHASHI.

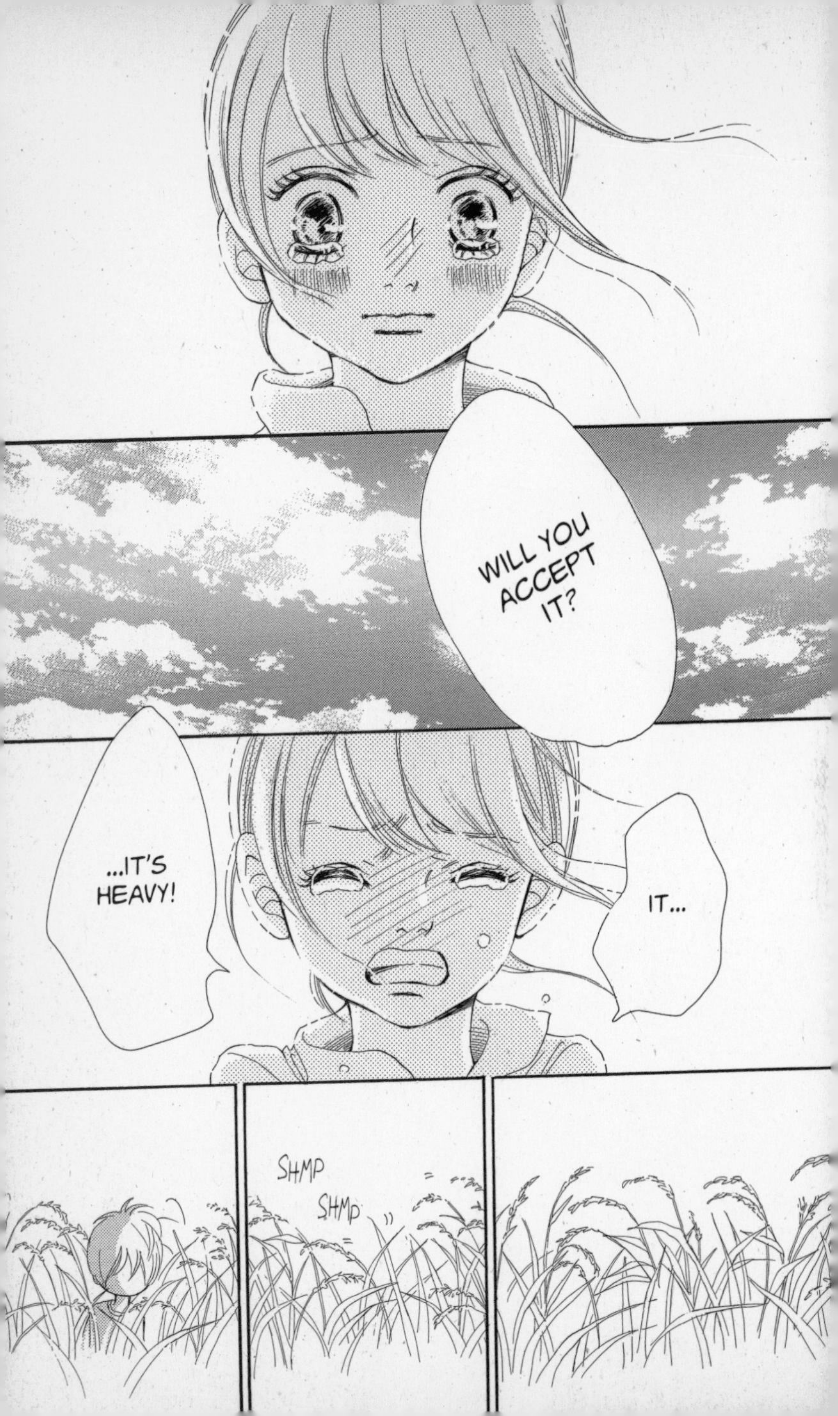
WILL YOU ACCEPT IT?
IT...
...IT'S HEAVY!
SHMP
SHMP

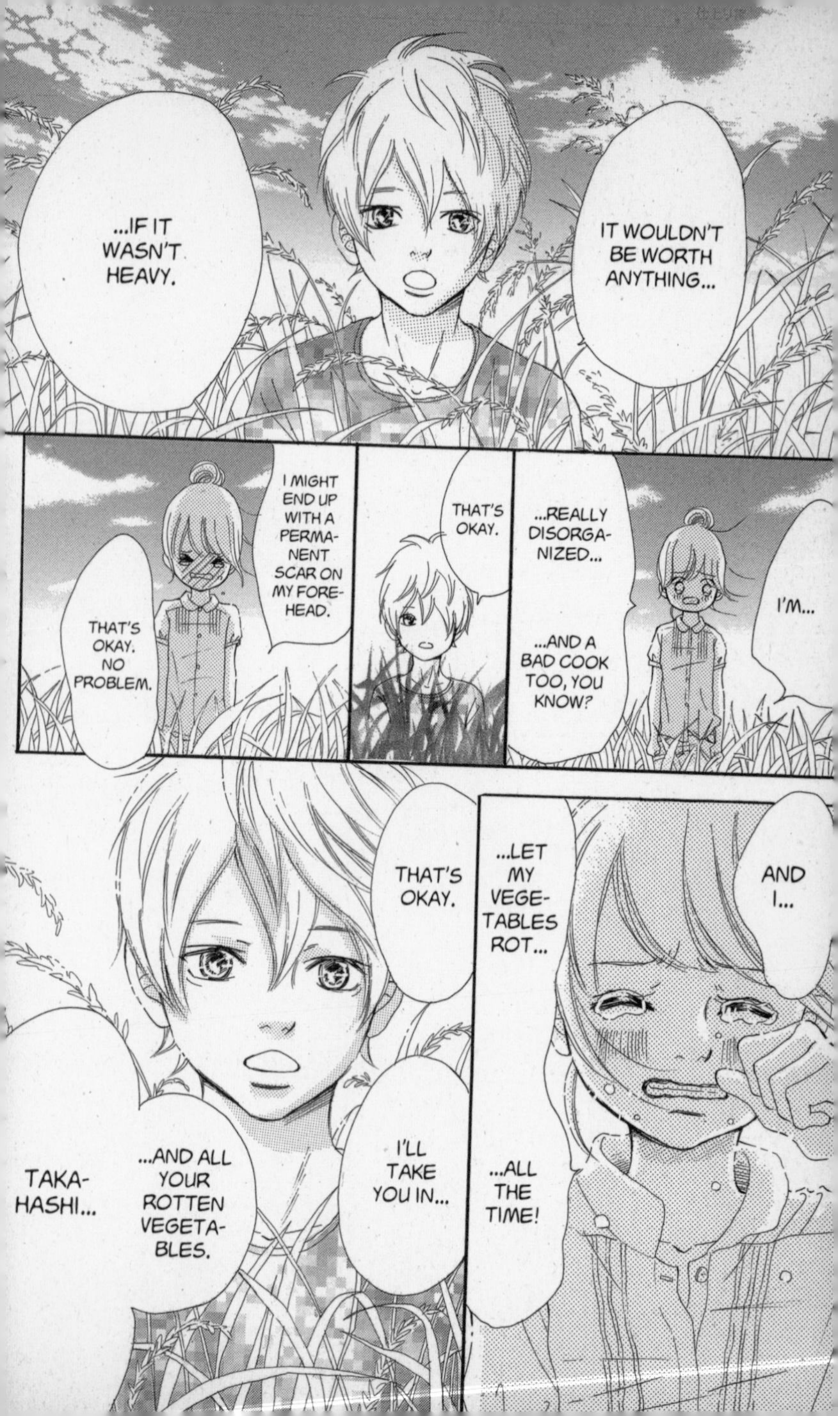
IT WOULDN'T BE WORTH ANYTHING...
...IF IT WASN'T HEAVY.
I'M...
...REALLY DISORGANIZED...
...AND A BAD COOK TOO, YOU KNOW?
THAT'S OKAY.
I MIGHT END UP WITH A PERMANENT SCAR ON MY FOREHEAD.
THAT'S OKAY. NO PROBLEM.
AND I...
...LET MY VEGETABLES ROT...
...ALL THE TIME!
THAT'S OKAY.
I'LL TAKE YOU IN...
...AND ALL YOUR ROTTEN VEGETABLES.
TAKAHASHI...

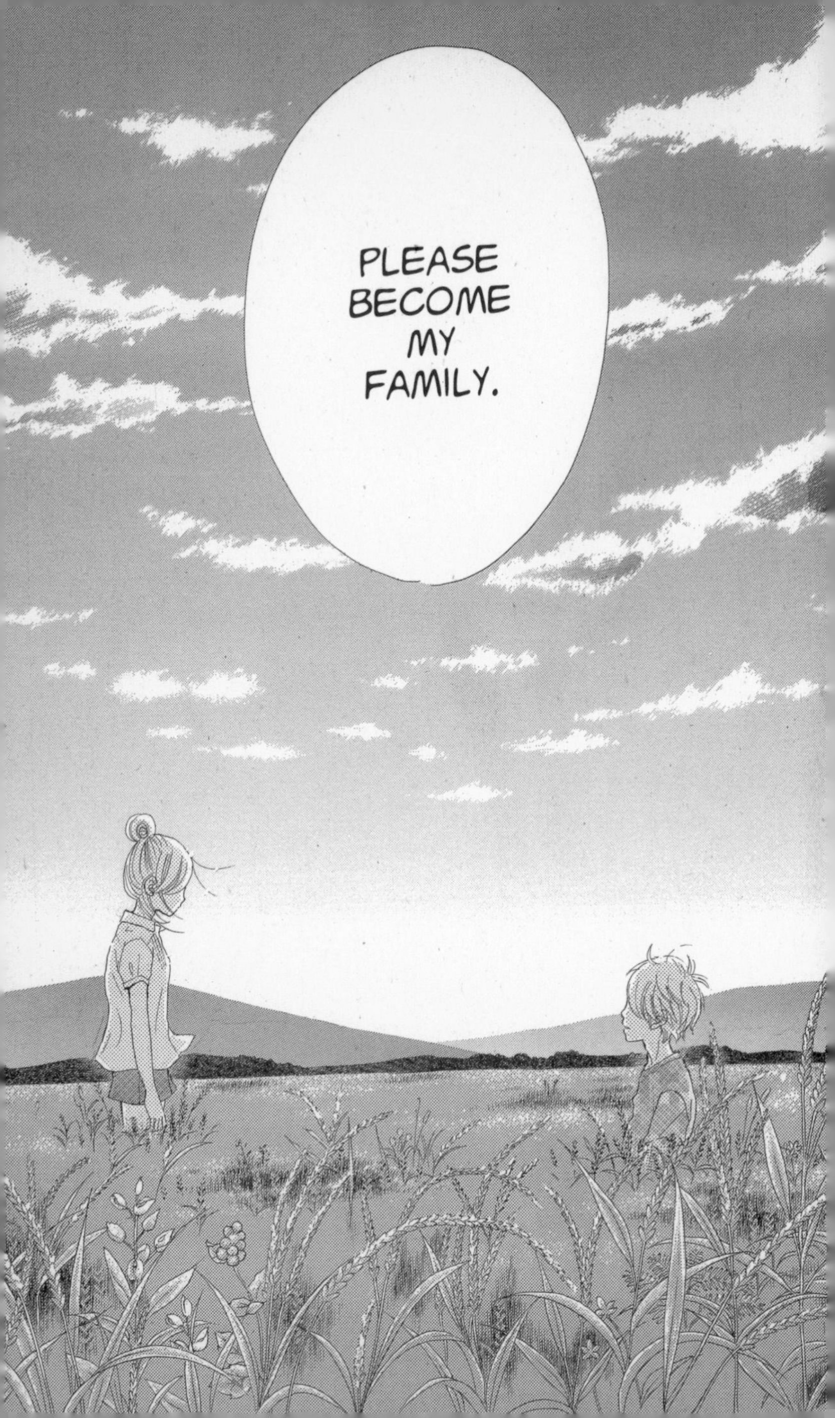
PLEASE BECOME MY FAMILY.

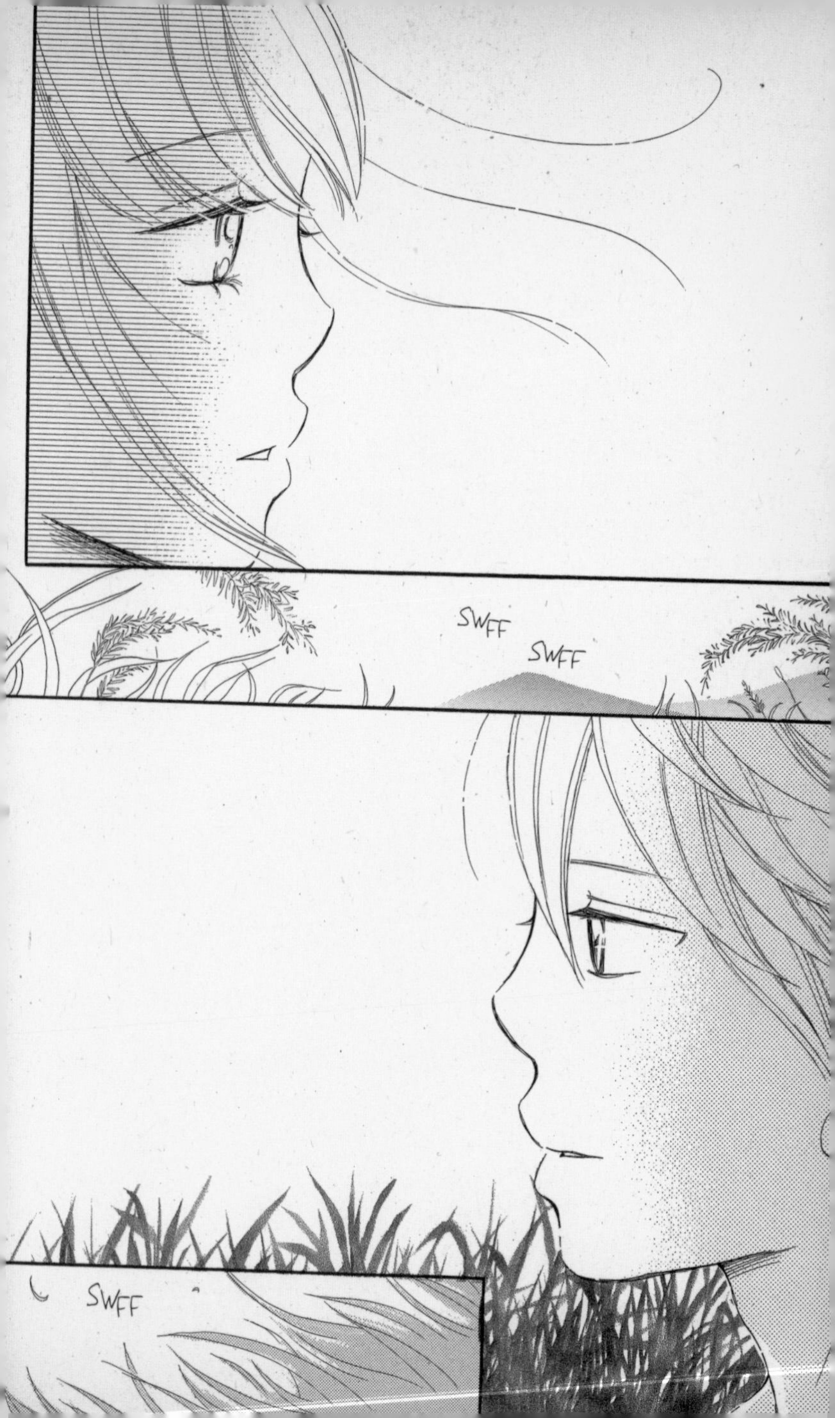
SWFF
SWFF
SWFF

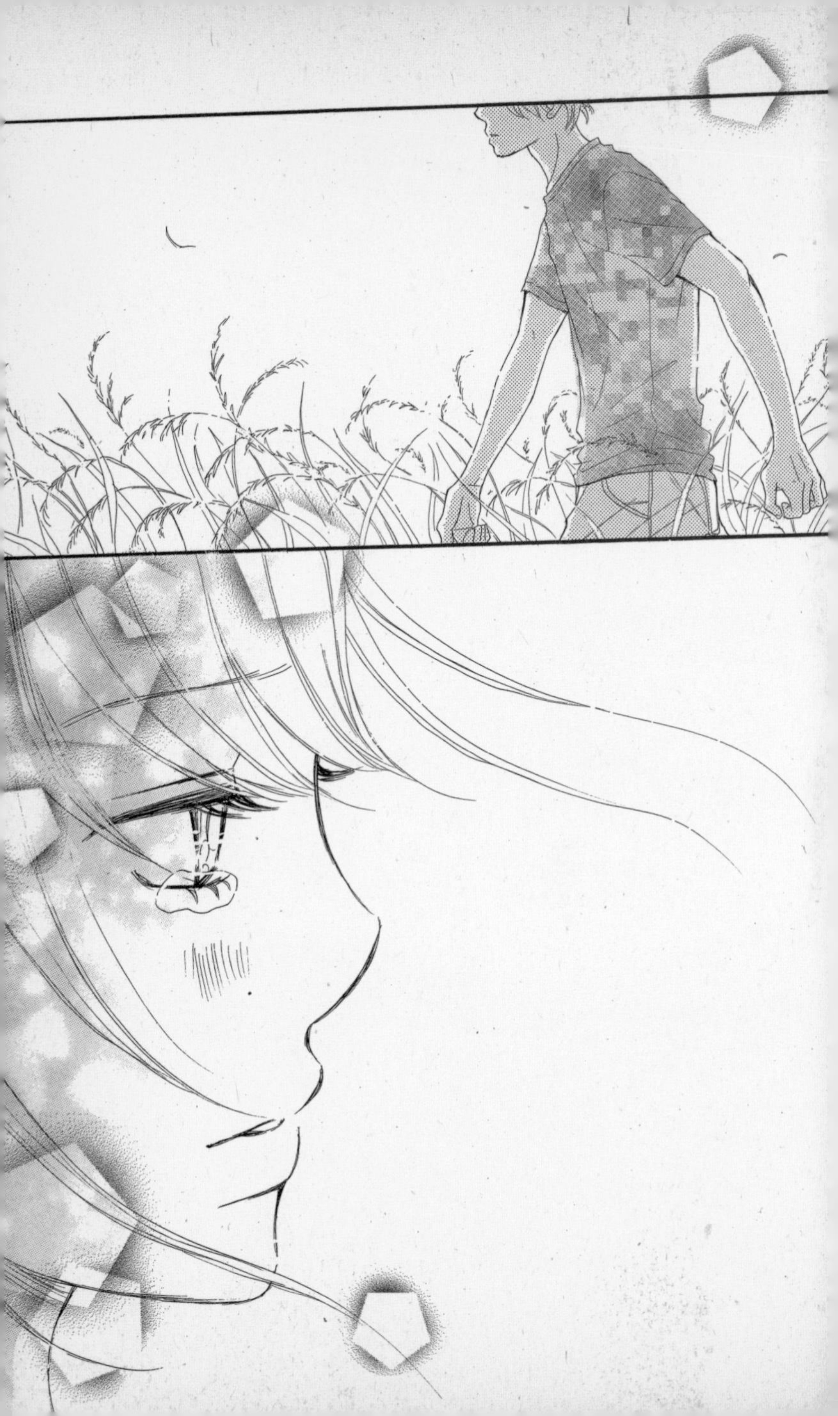

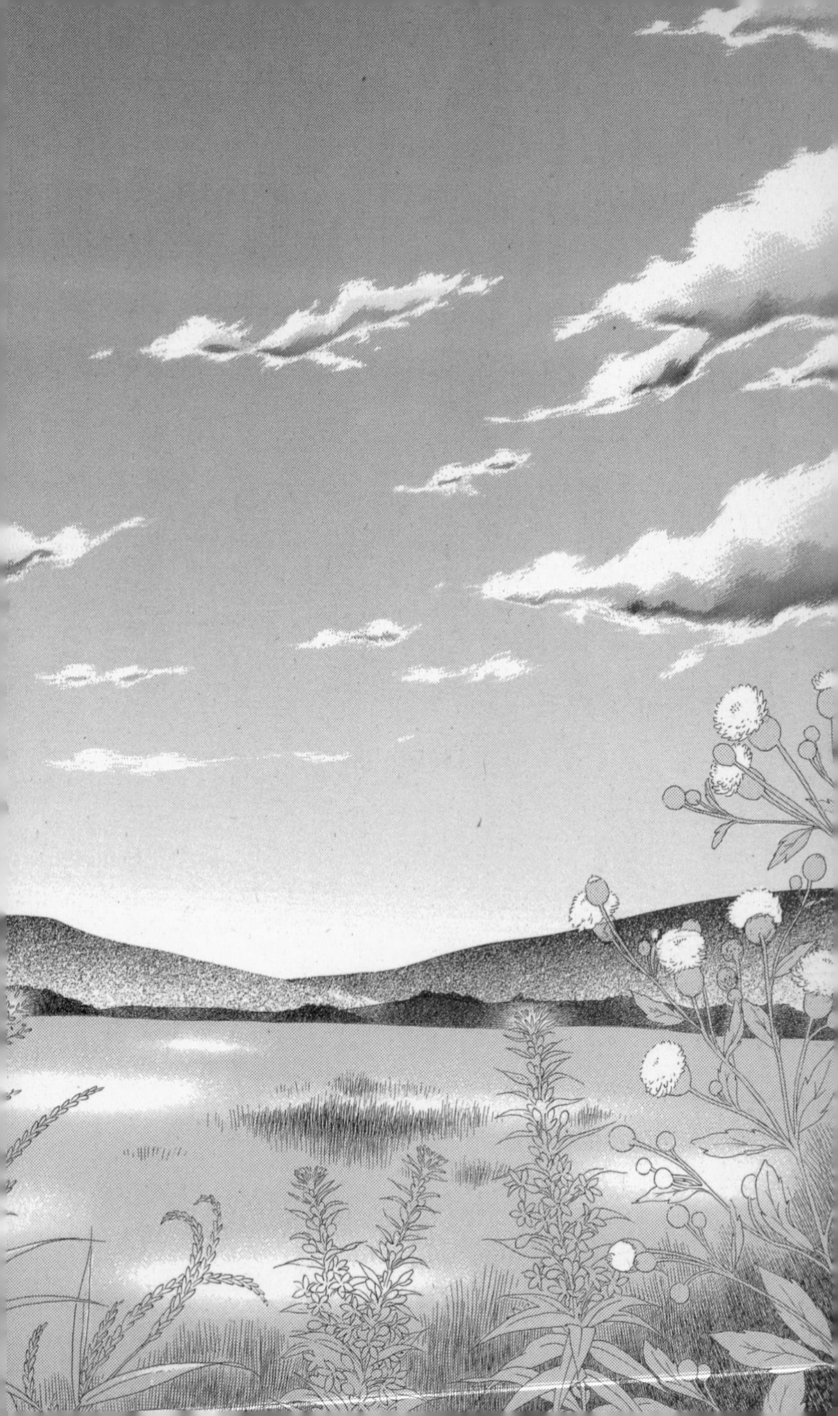

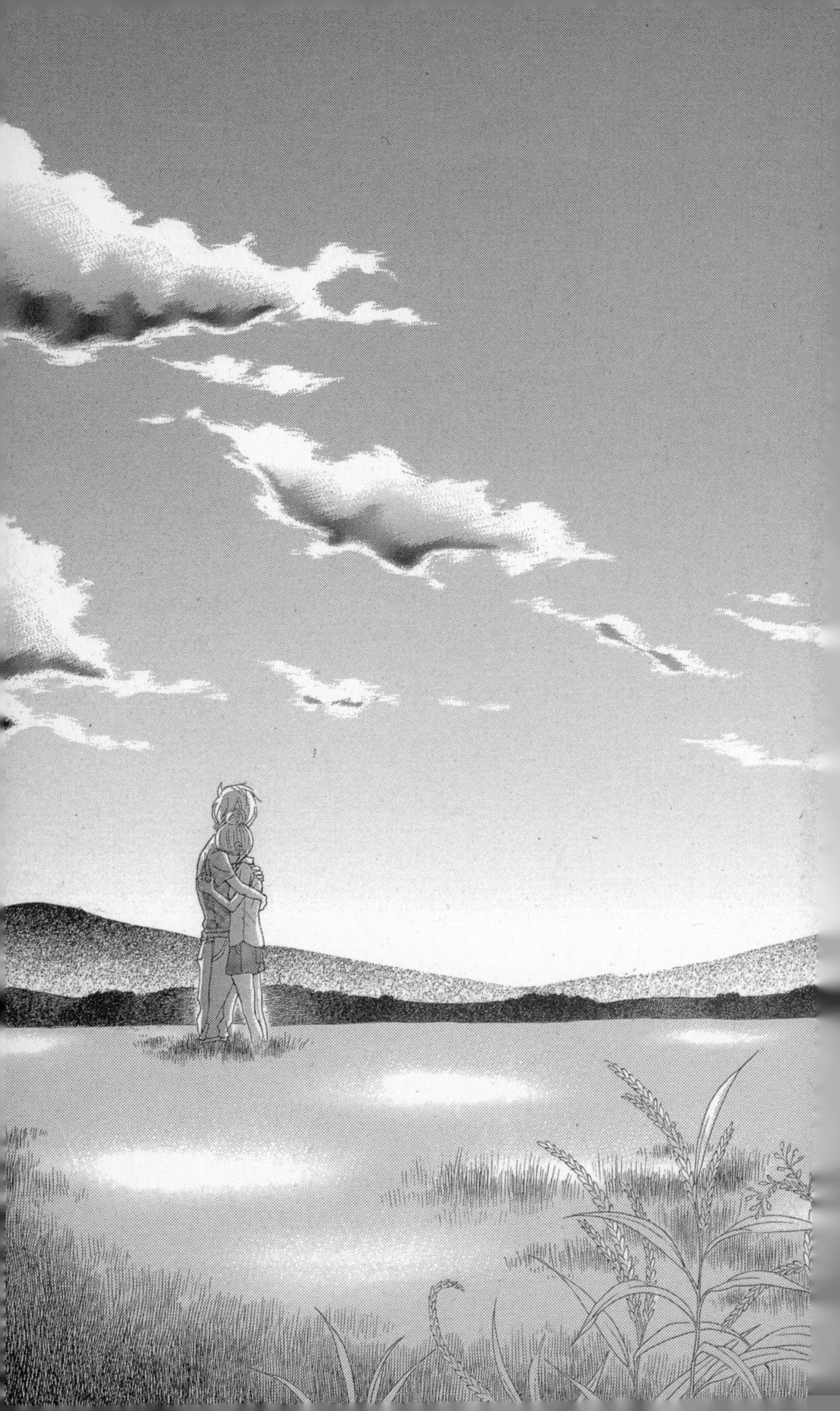

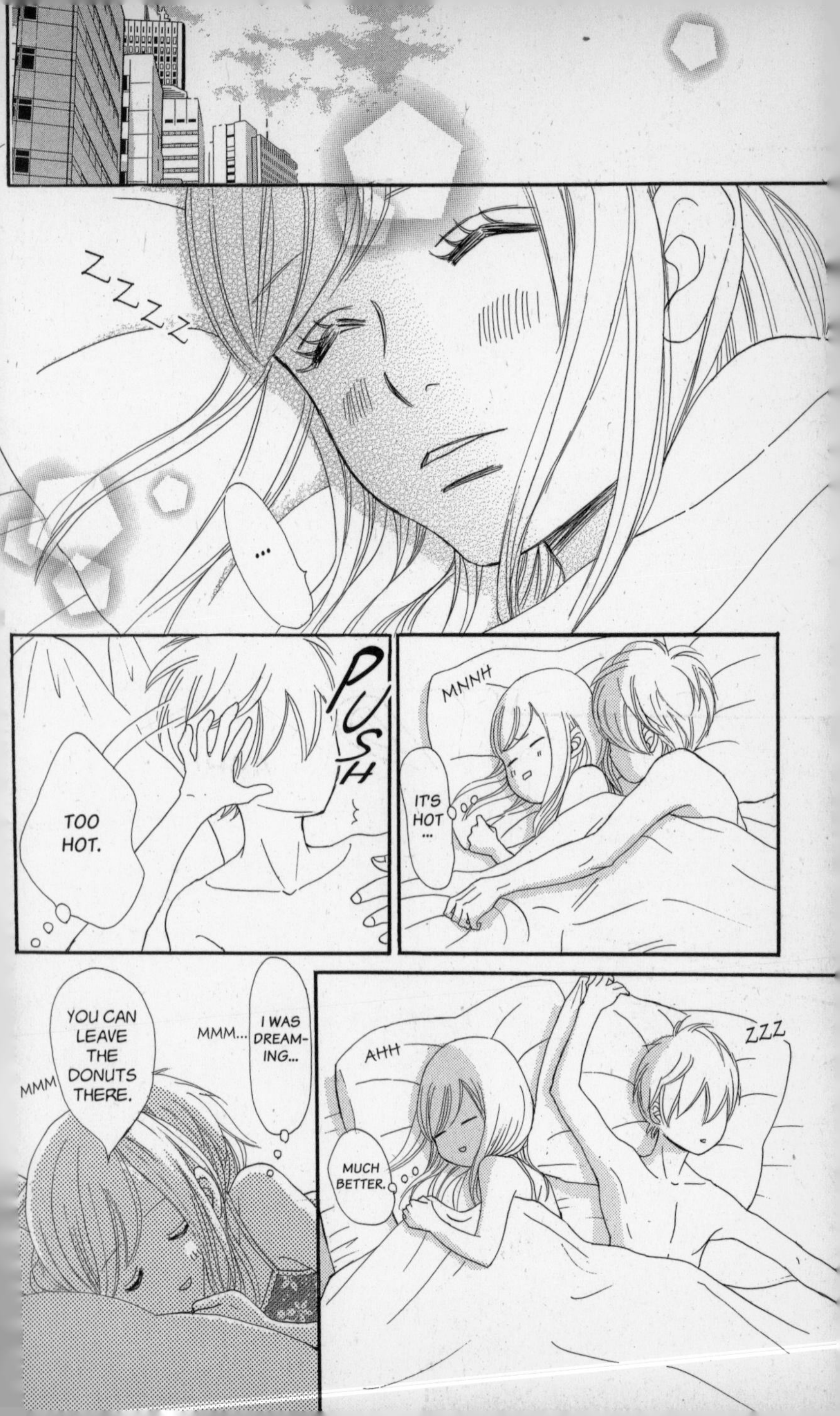
ZZZZ
...
MNNH
IT'S HOT ...
PUSH
TOO HOT.
ZZZ
AHH
MUCH BETTER.
I WAS DREAMING...
MMM...
YOU CAN LEAVE THE DONUTS THERE.
MMM

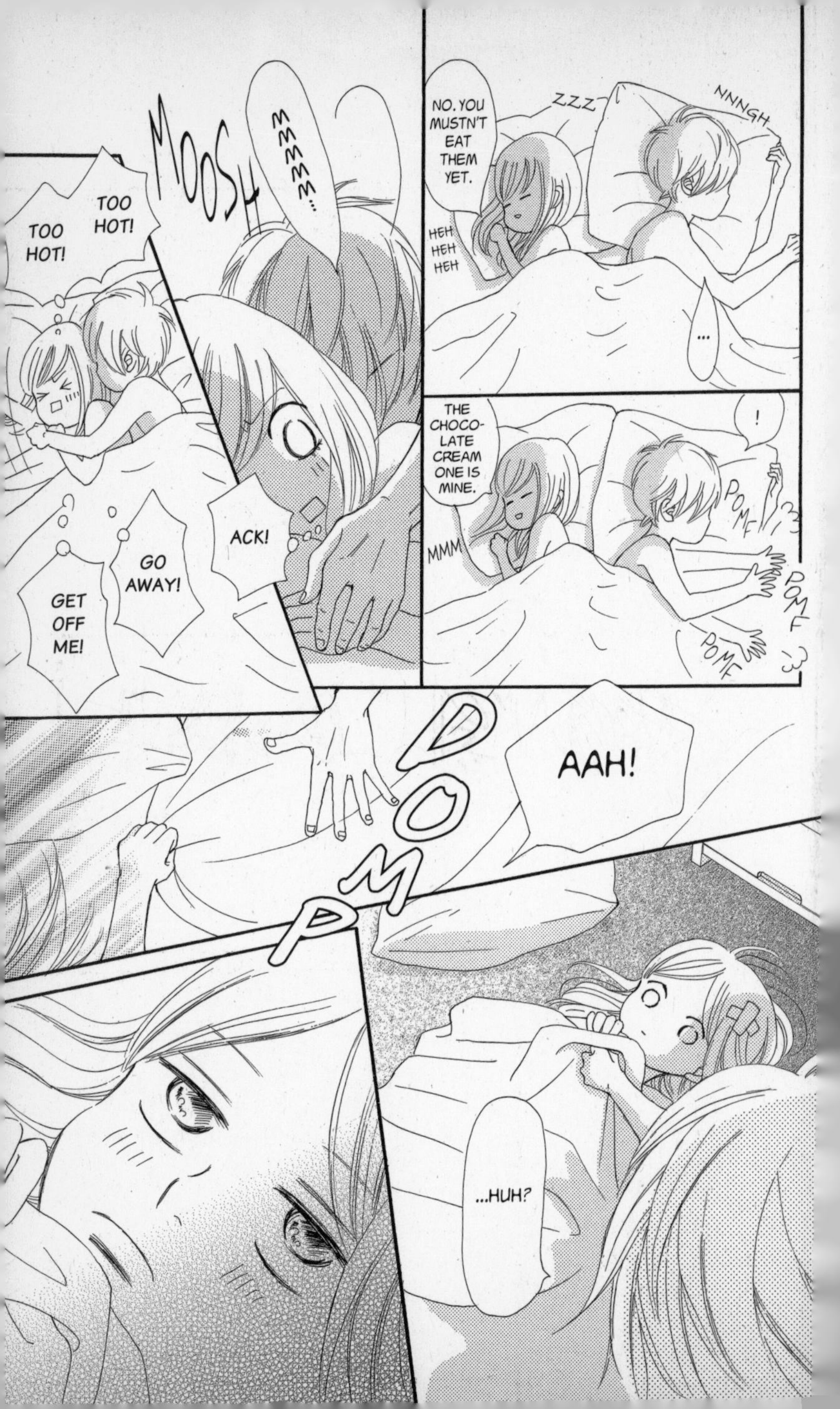
NNNGH
ZZZ
NO. YOU MUSTN'T EAT THEM YET.
HEH HEH HEH
...
!
THE CHOCO-LATE CREAM ONE IS MINE.
MMM
POMF
POMF
POMF
MMMMM...
MOOSH
ACK!
TOO HOT!
TOO HOT!
GO AWAY!
GET OFF ME!
AAH!
DOMP
...HUH?

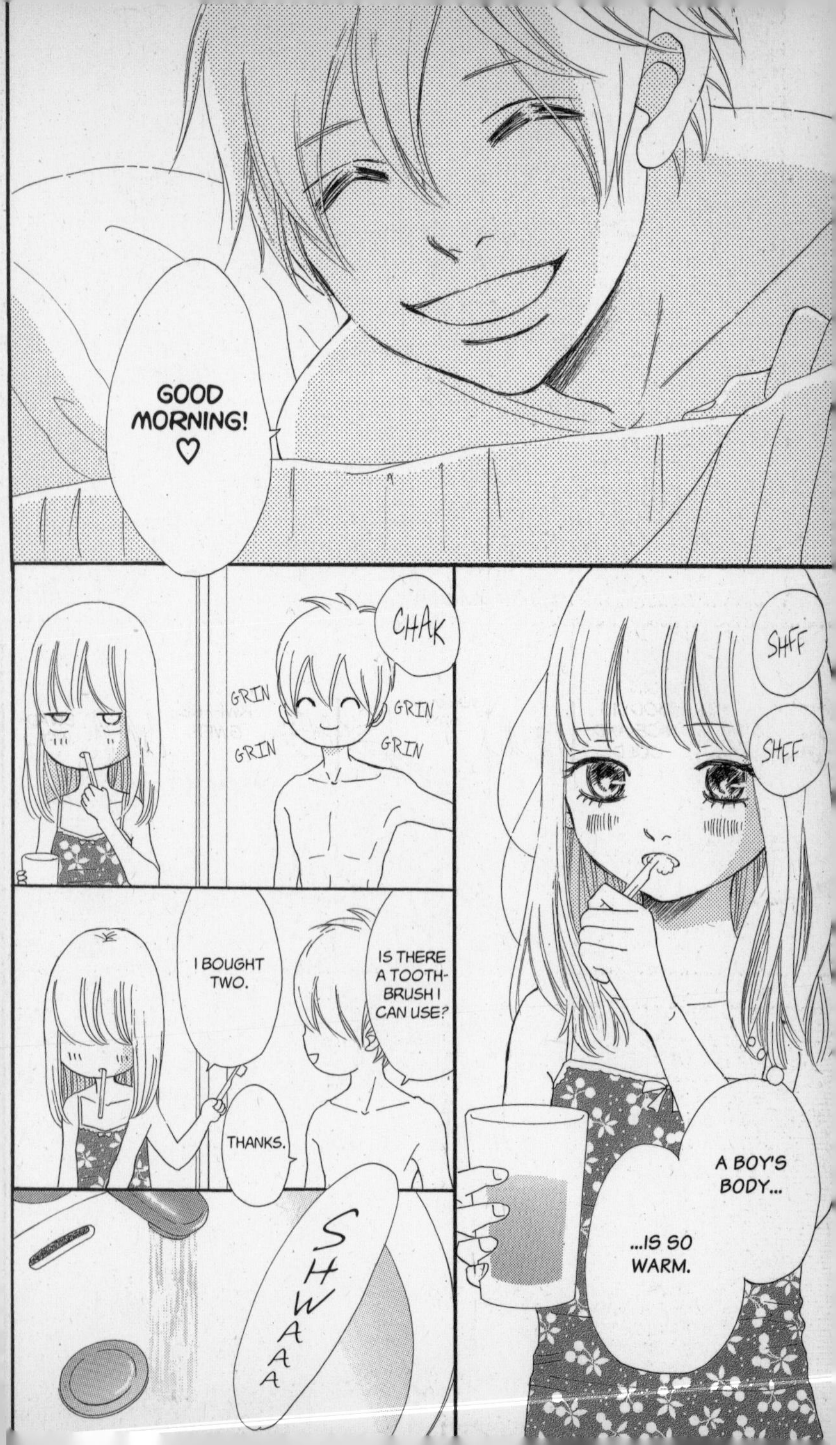

GOOD MORNING! ♡
SHFF
SHFF
A BOY'S BODY...
...IS SO WARM.
CHAK
GRIN
GRIN
GRIN
GRIN
IS THERE A TOOTH-BRUSH I CAN USE?
I BOUGHT TWO.
THANKS.
SHWAAAA

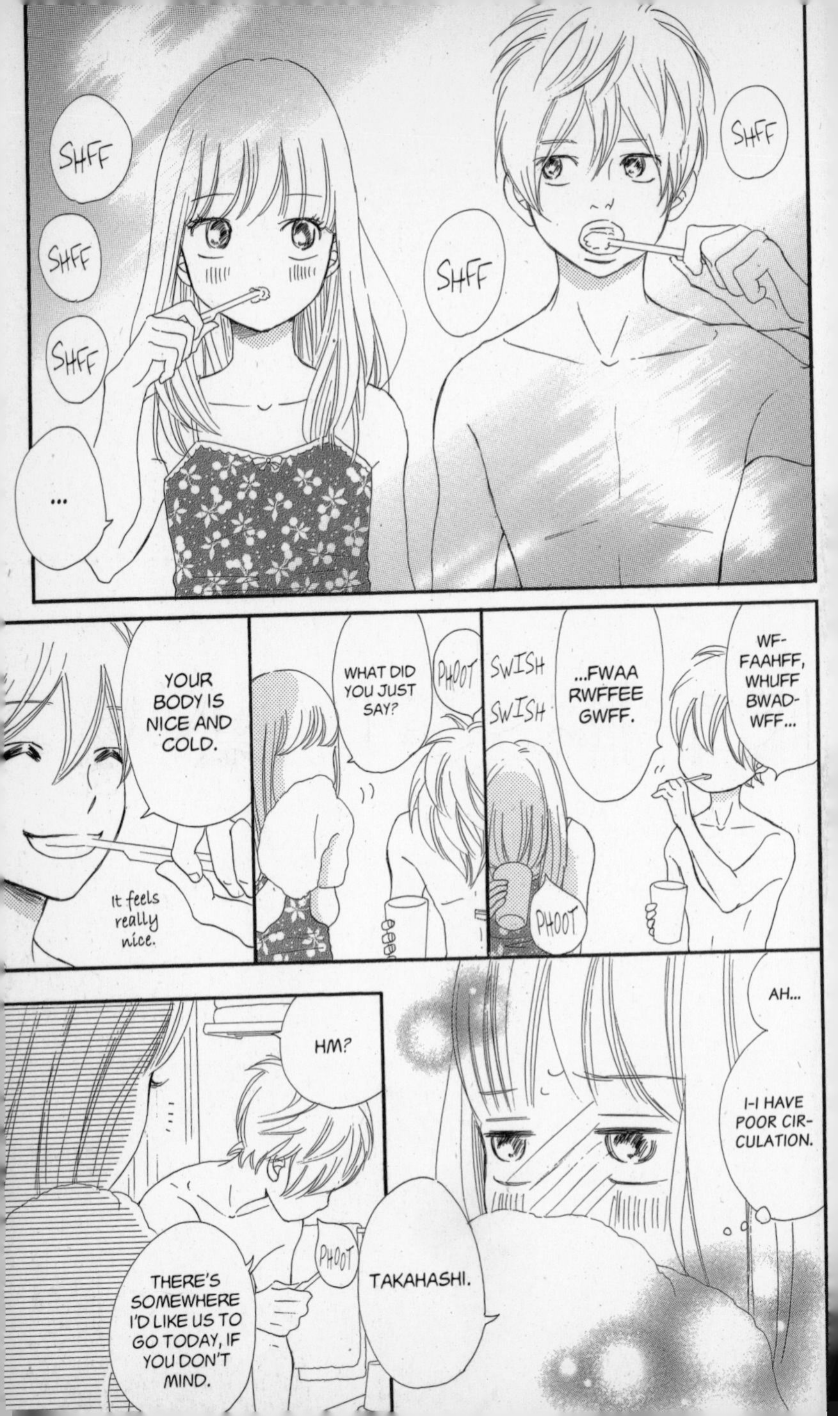
SHFF
SHFF
SHFF
SHFF
SHFF
...
WF-FAAHFF, WHUFF BWAD-WFF...
...FWAA RWFFEE GWFF.
SWISH
SWISH
PHOOT
PHOOT
WHAT DID YOU JUST SAY?
YOUR BODY IS NICE AND COLD.
It feels really nice.
AH...
I-I HAVE POOR CIR-CULATION.
HM?
TAKAHASHI.
PHOOT
THERE'S SOMEWHERE I'D LIKE US TO GO TODAY, IF YOU DON'T MIND.

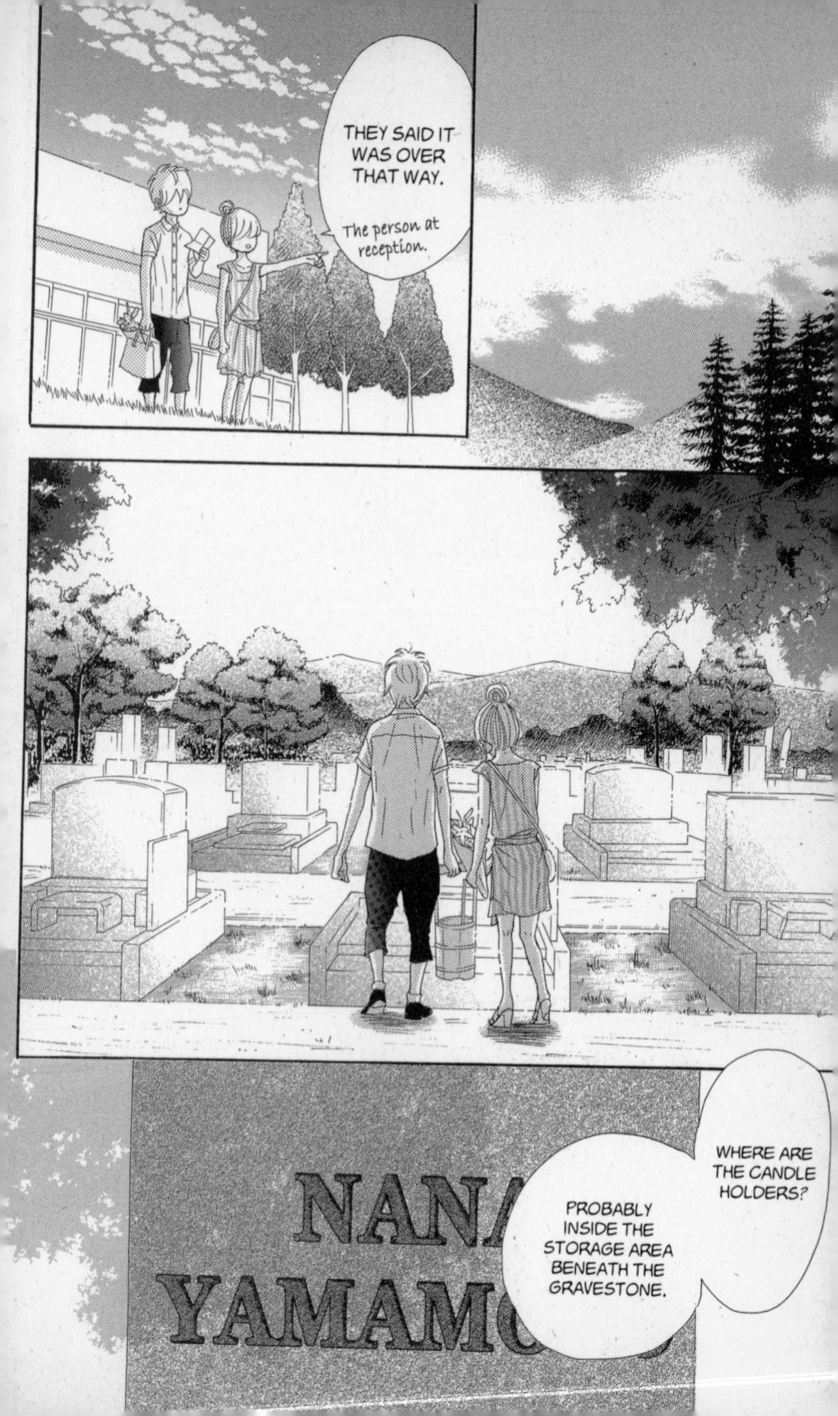
THEY SAID IT WAS OVER THAT WAY.
The person at reception.
WHERE ARE THE CANDLE HOLDERS?
PROBABLY INSIDE THE STORAGE AREA BENEATH THE GRAVESTONE.

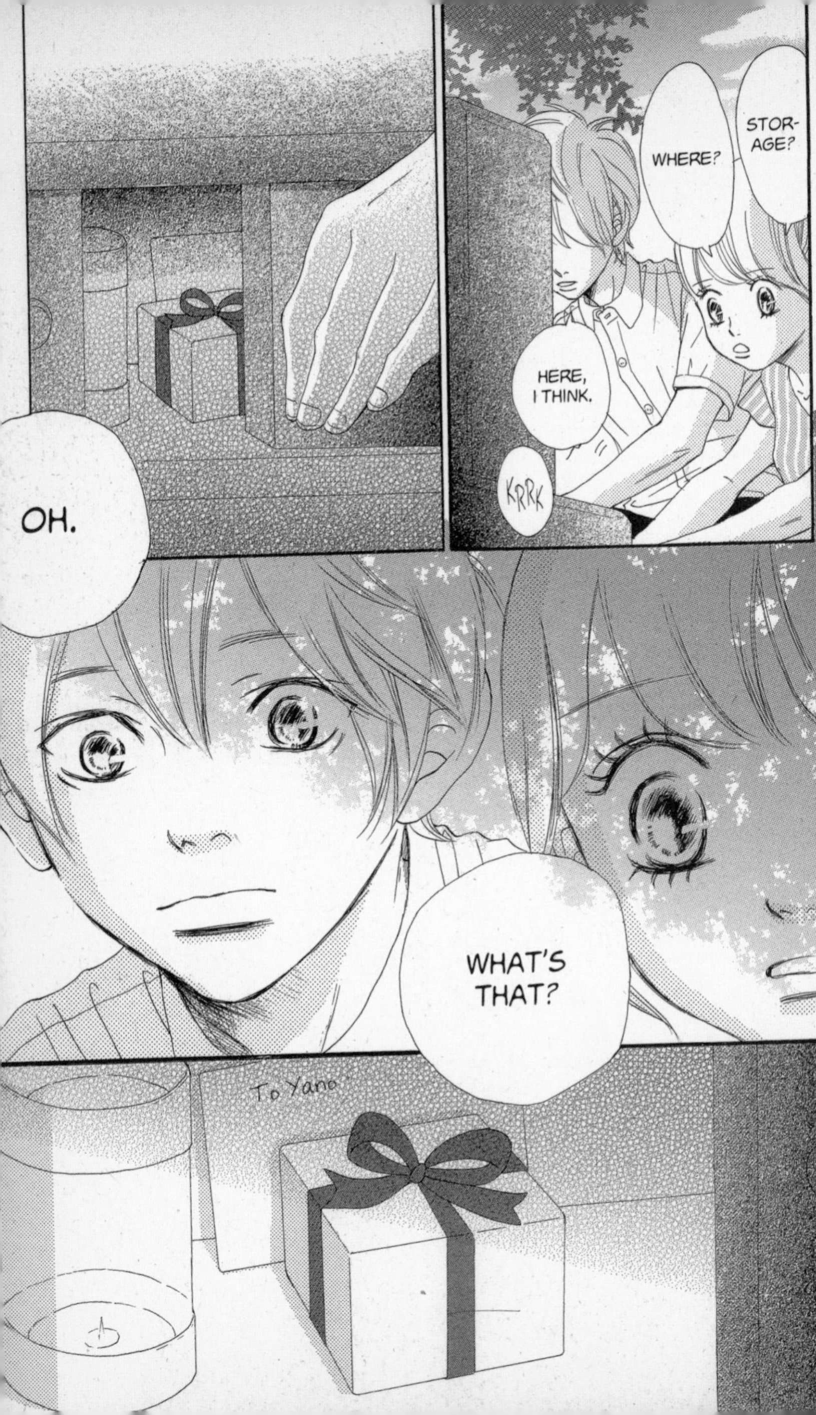
STOR-
AGE?
WHERE?
HERE,
I THINK.
KRRK
OH.
WHAT'S
THAT?
To Yano

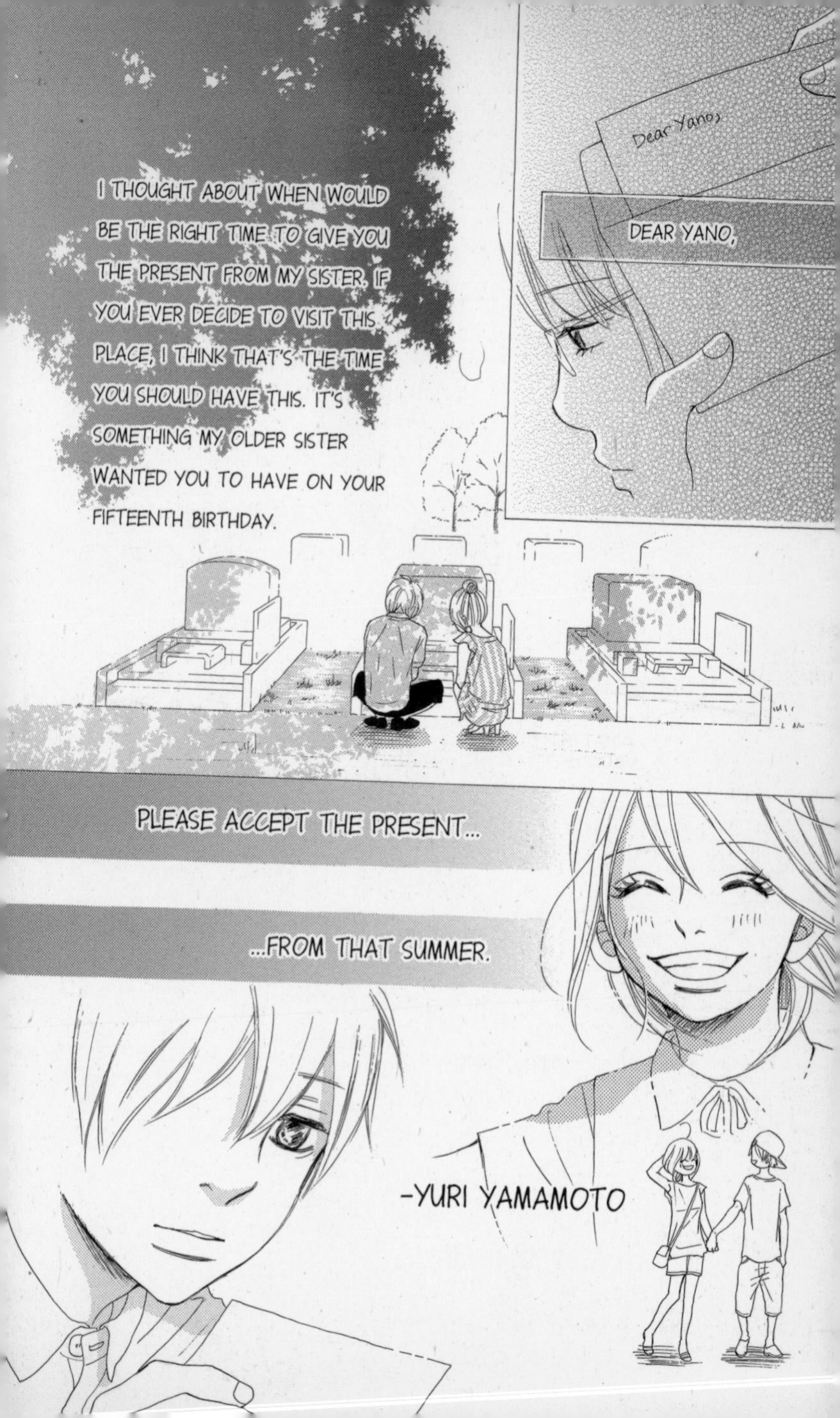
Dear Yano,
DEAR YANO,
I THOUGHT ABOUT WHEN WOULD BE THE RIGHT TIME TO GIVE YOU THE PRESENT FROM MY SISTER. IF YOU EVER DECIDE TO VISIT THIS PLACE, I THINK THAT'S THE TIME YOU SHOULD HAVE THIS. IT'S SOMETHING MY OLDER SISTER WANTED YOU TO HAVE ON YOUR FIFTEENTH BIRTHDAY.
PLEASE ACCEPT THE PRESENT...
...FROM THAT SUMMER.
-YURI YAMAMOTO

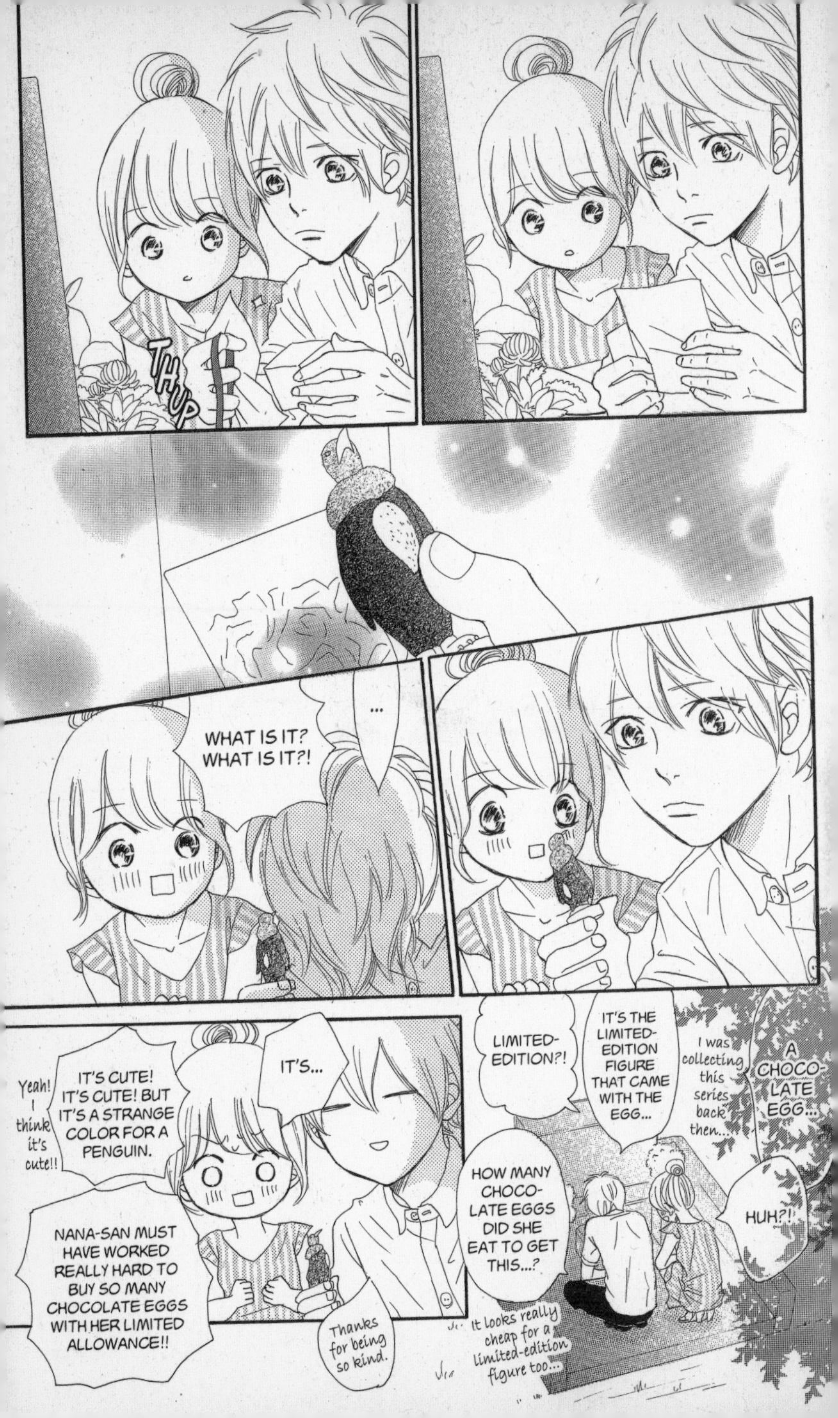
THUP
...
WHAT IS IT? WHAT IS IT?!
A CHOCO-LATE EGG...
I was collecting this series back then...
IT'S THE LIMITED-EDITION FIGURE THAT CAME WITH THE EGG...
LIMITED-EDITION?!
HUH?!
HOW MANY CHOCO-LATE EGGS DID SHE EAT TO GET THIS...?
It looks really cheap for a limited-edition figure too...
IT'S...
IT'S CUTE! IT'S CUTE! BUT IT'S A STRANGE COLOR FOR A PENGUIN.
Yeah! I think it's cute!!
NANA-SAN MUST HAVE WORKED REALLY HARD TO BUY SO MANY CHOCOLATE EGGS WITH HER LIMITED ALLOWANCE!!
Thanks for being so kind.

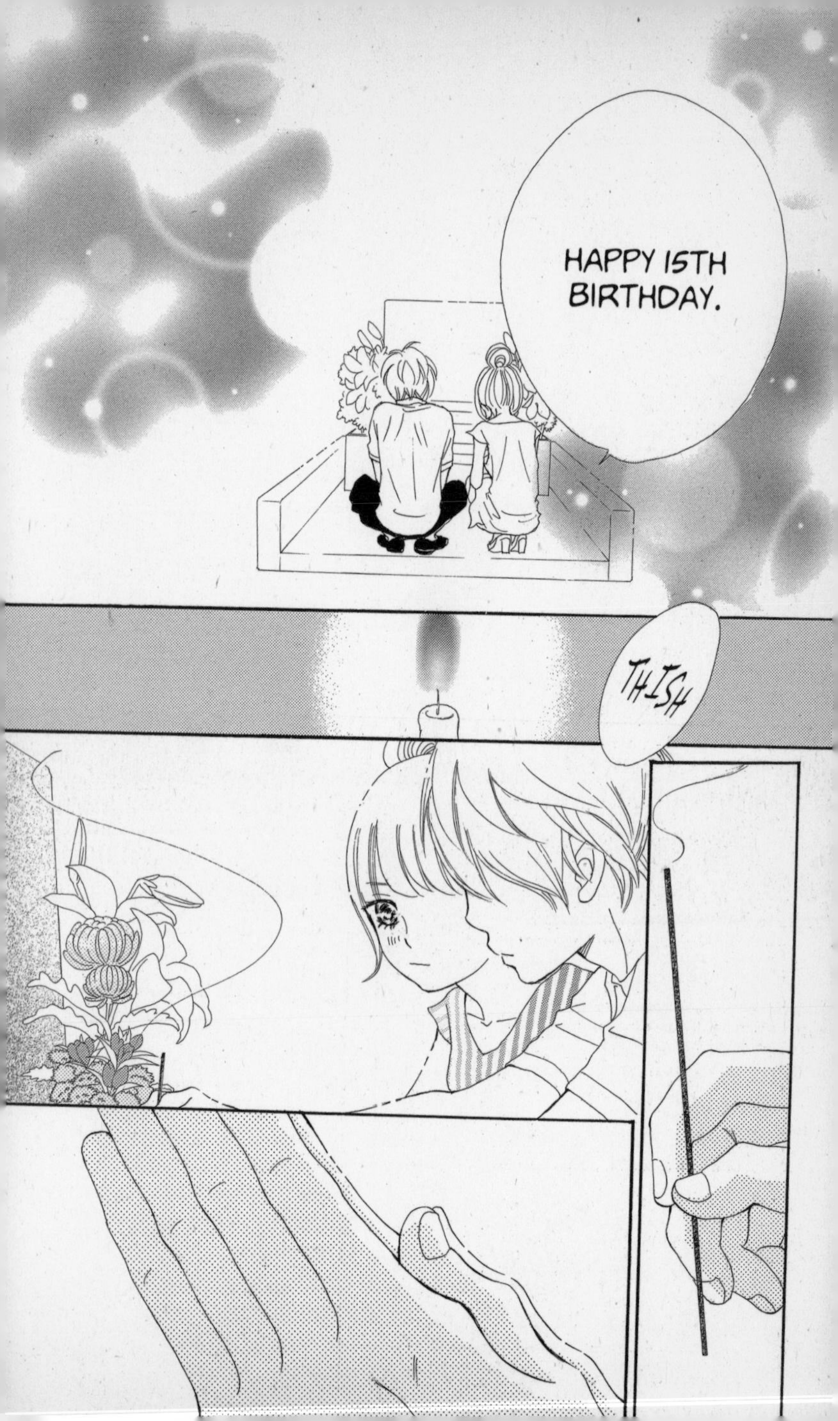
HAPPY 15TH BIRTHDAY.
THISH

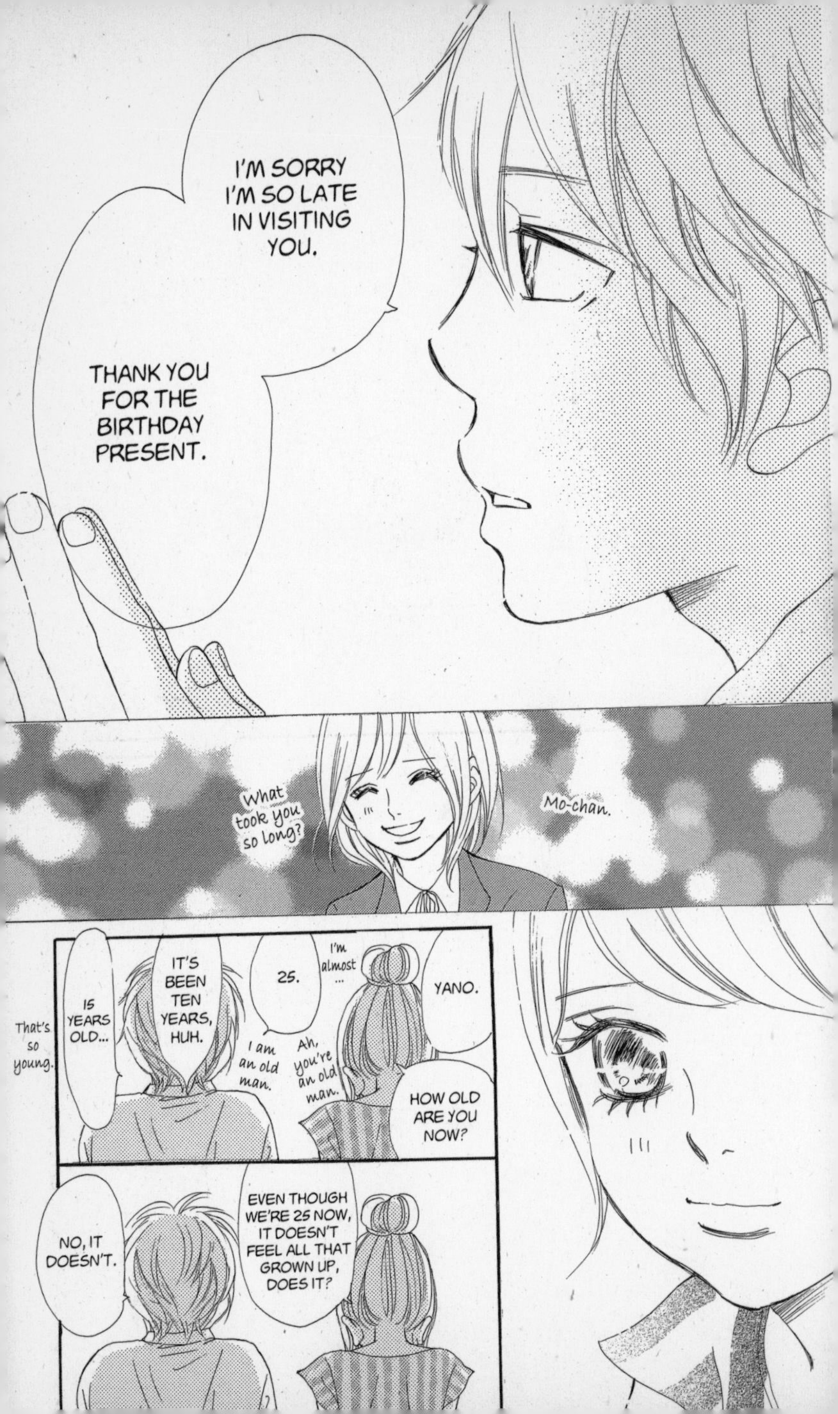
I'M SORRY I'M SO LATE IN VISITING YOU.
THANK YOU FOR THE BIRTHDAY PRESENT.
Mo-chan.
What took you so long?
YANO.
HOW OLD ARE YOU NOW?
I'm almost ...
25.
Ah, you're an old man.
I am an old man.
IT'S BEEN TEN YEARS, HUH.
15 YEARS OLD...
That's so young.
EVEN THOUGH WE'RE 25 NOW, IT DOESN'T FEEL ALL THAT GROWN UP, DOES IT?
NO, IT DOESN'T.

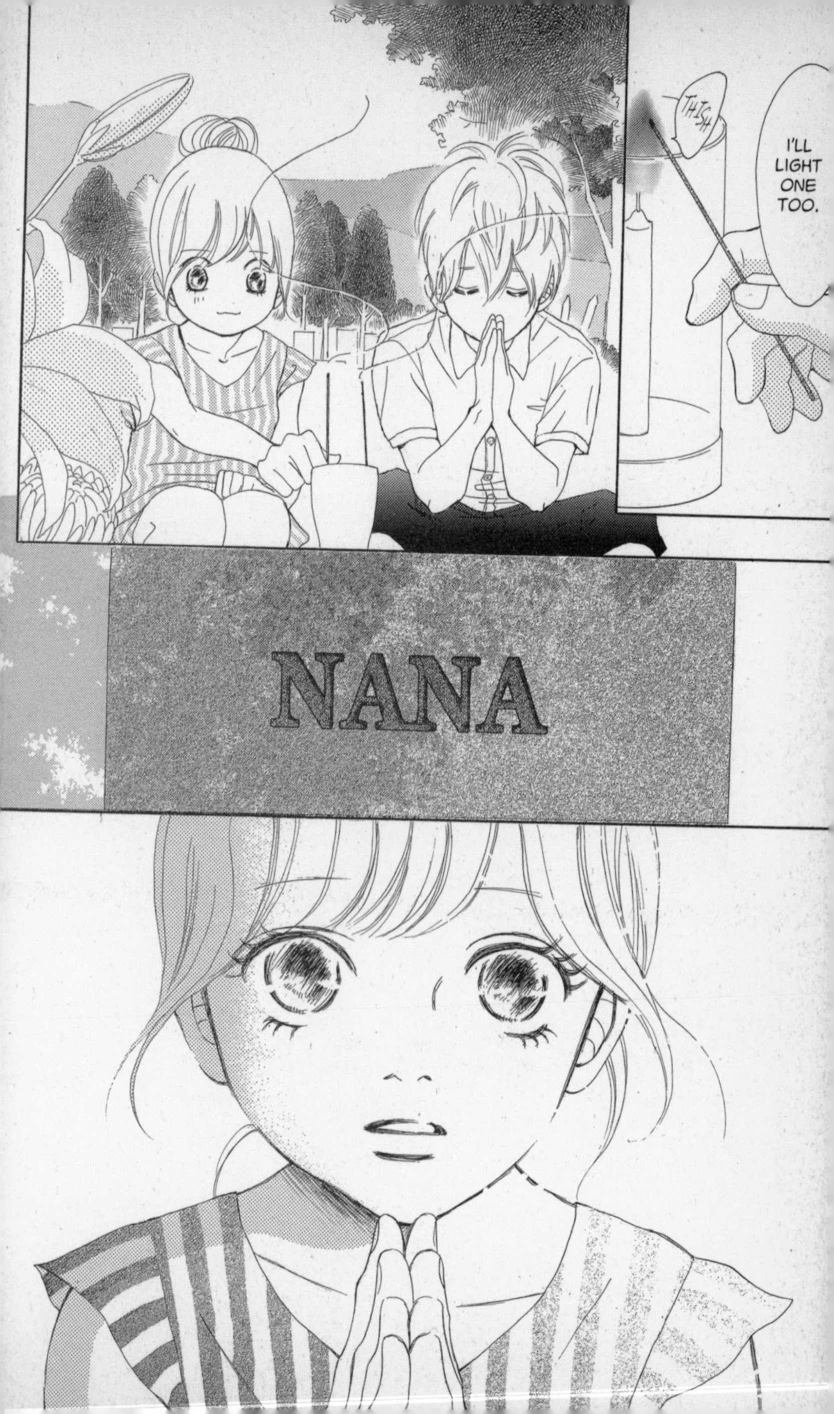
I'LL LIGHT ONE TOO.
THISH
NANA

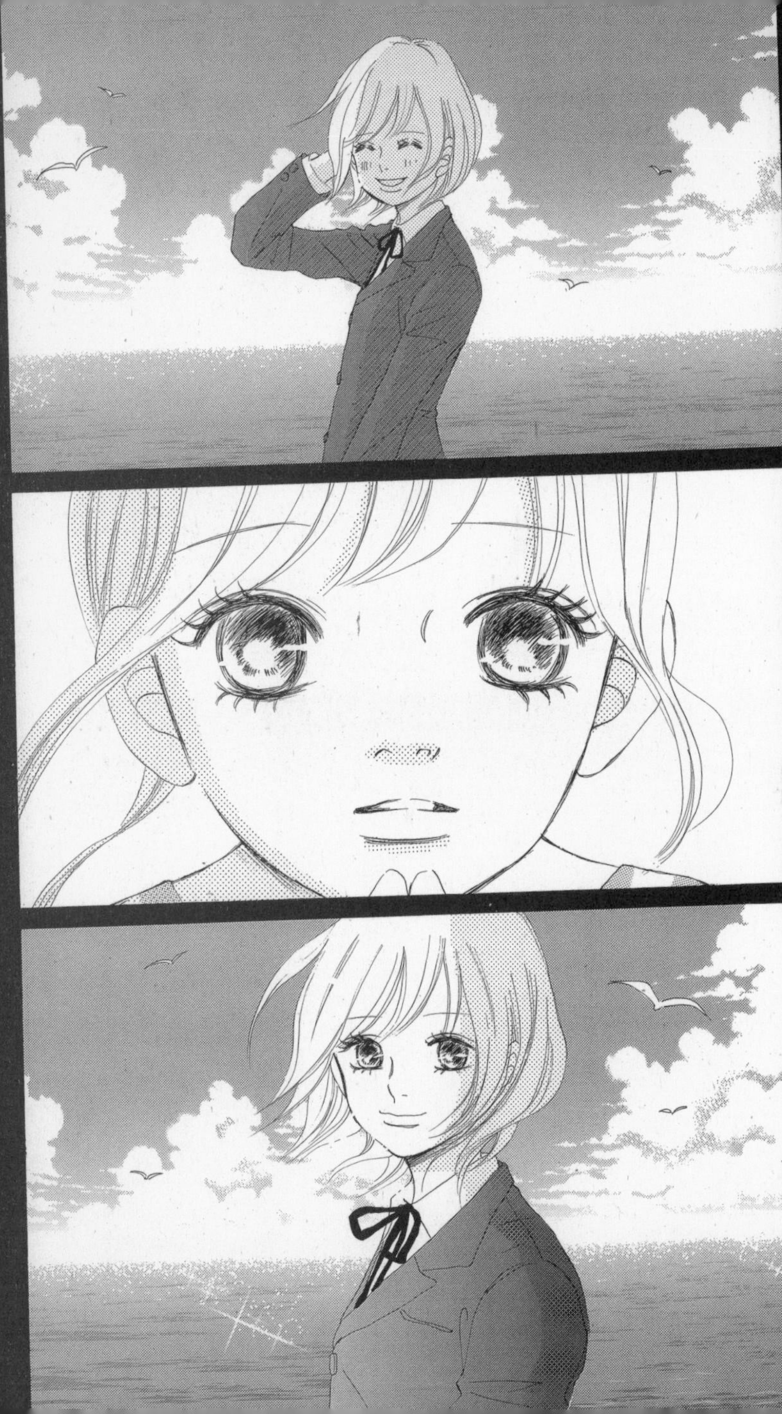

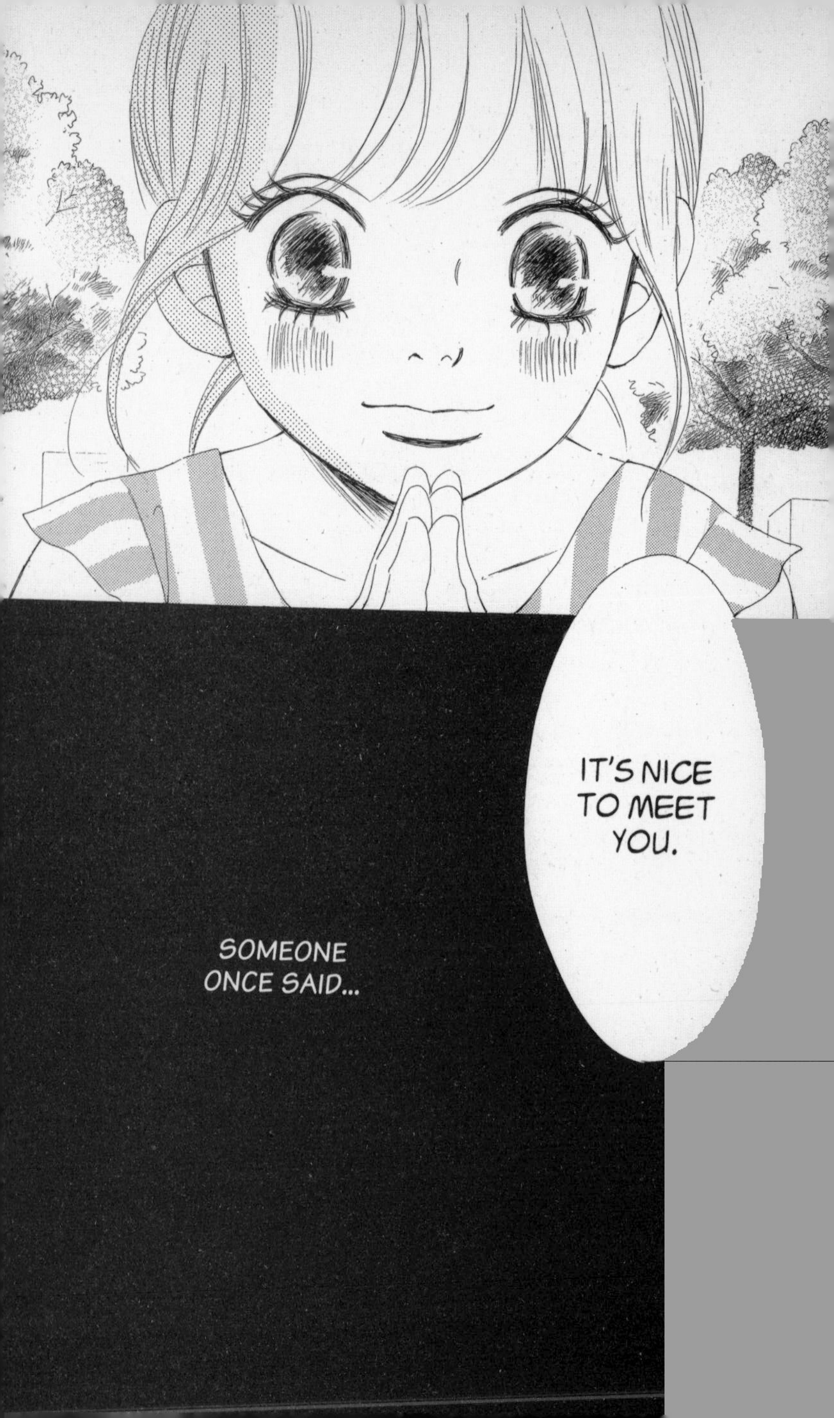
IT'S NICE TO MEET YOU.
SOMEONE ONCE SAID...

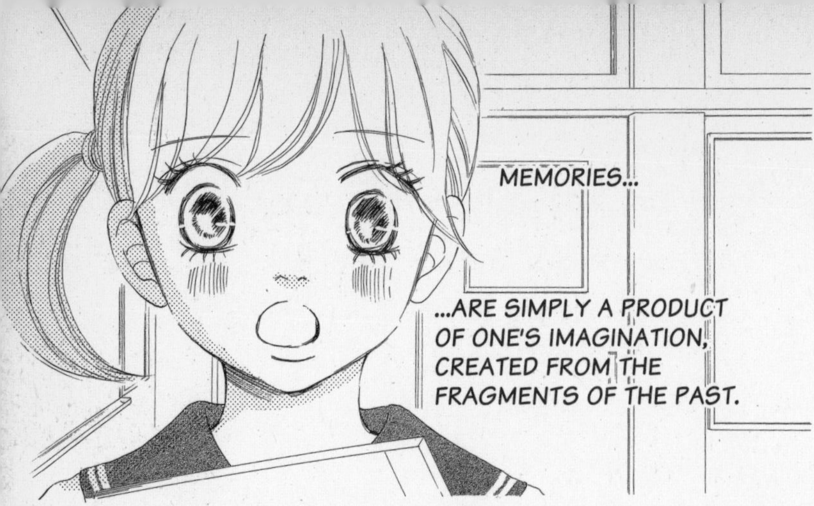
MEMORIES...
...ARE SIMPLY A PRODUCT OF ONE'S IMAGINATION, CREATED FROM THE FRAGMENTS OF THE PAST.

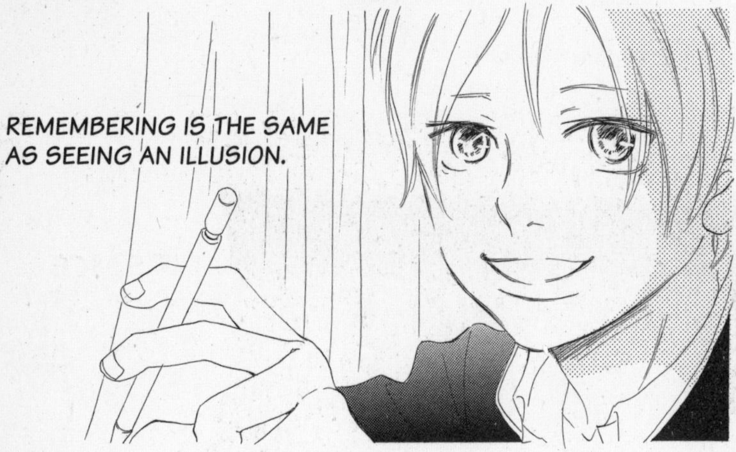
REMEMBERING IS THE SAME AS SEEING AN ILLUSION.

SO WHAT DOES IT MEAN TO LIVE?

WHAT IF I HAD STOPPED THERE...

IF I HAD TAKEN A TURN...

IF I HADN'T COME ACROSS THAT
BUMP IN THE ROAD...

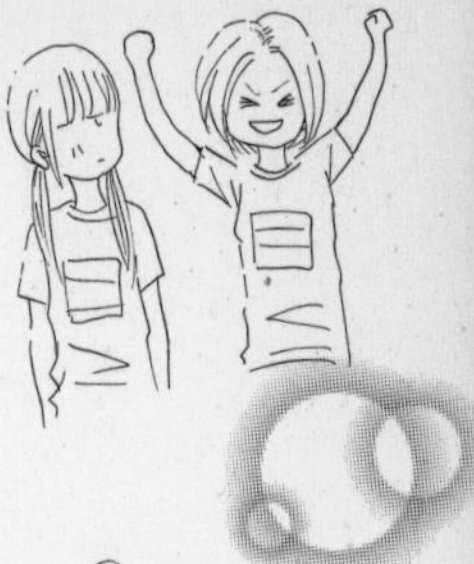

IF I HADN'T TAKEN A DETOUR...

IF I HAD NEVER STOPPED...

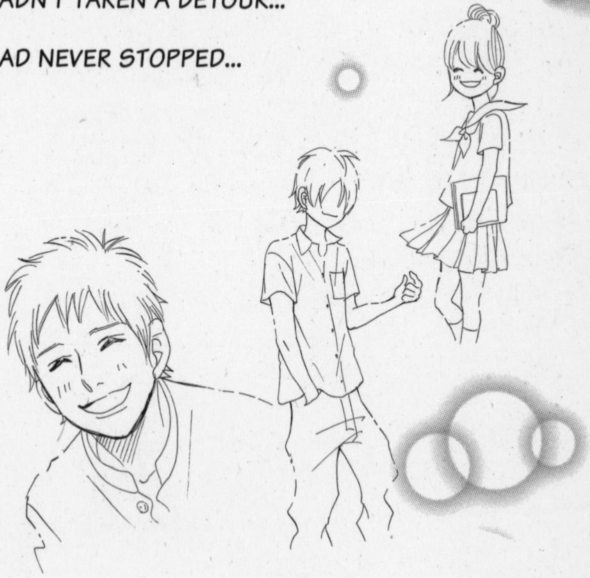

WHAT IF, BACK THEN...

WHAT IF...?

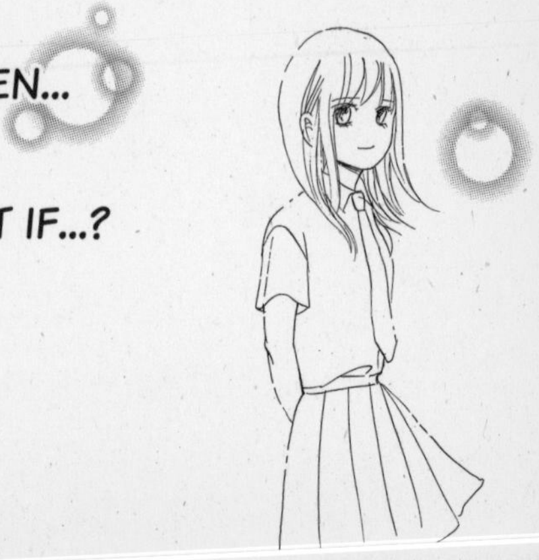

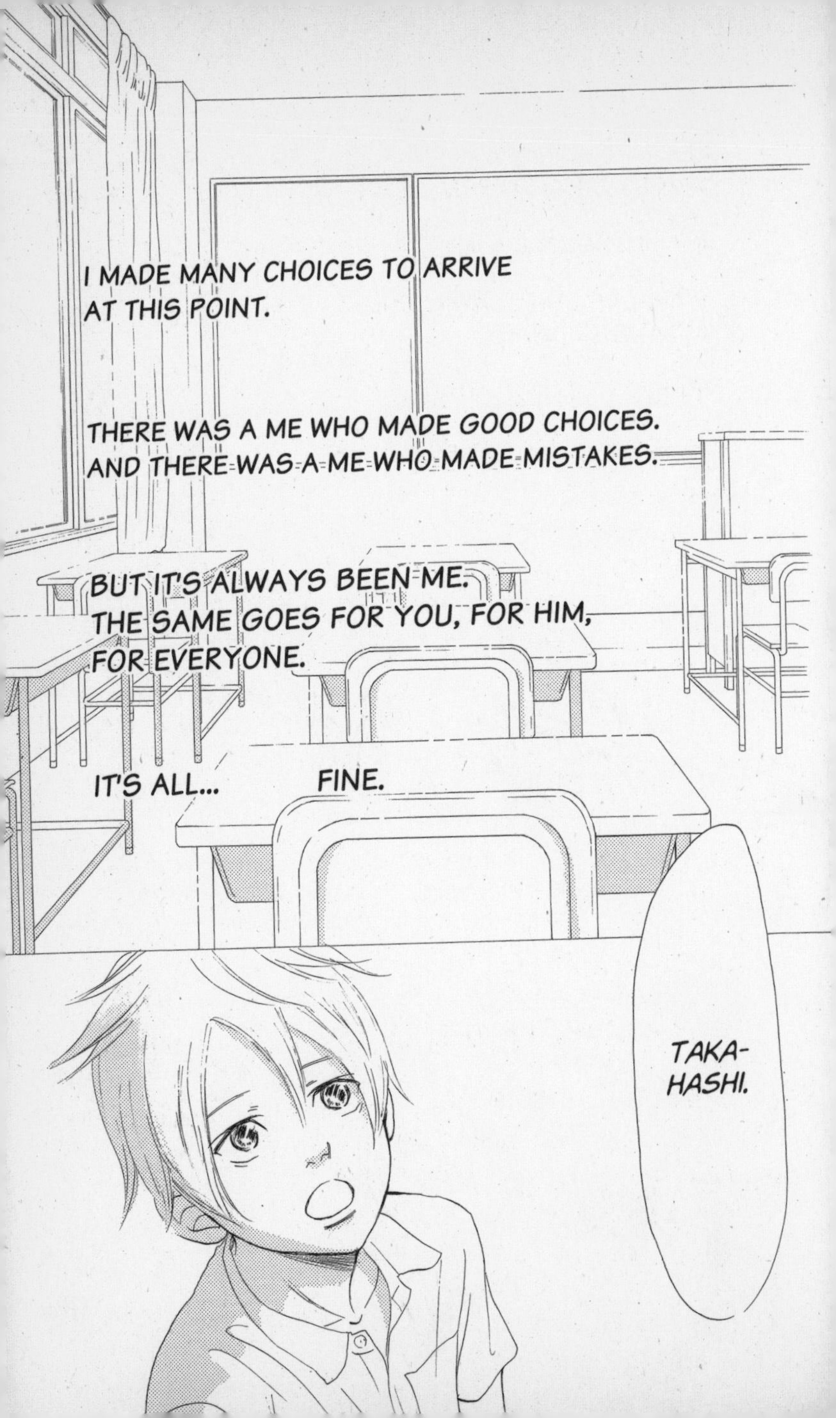
I MADE MANY CHOICES TO ARRIVE AT THIS POINT.
THERE WAS A ME WHO MADE GOOD CHOICES. AND THERE WAS A ME WHO MADE MISTAKES.
BUT IT'S ALWAYS BEEN ME. THE SAME GOES FOR YOU, FOR HIM, FOR EVERYONE.
IT'S ALL... FINE.
TAKA-HASHI.

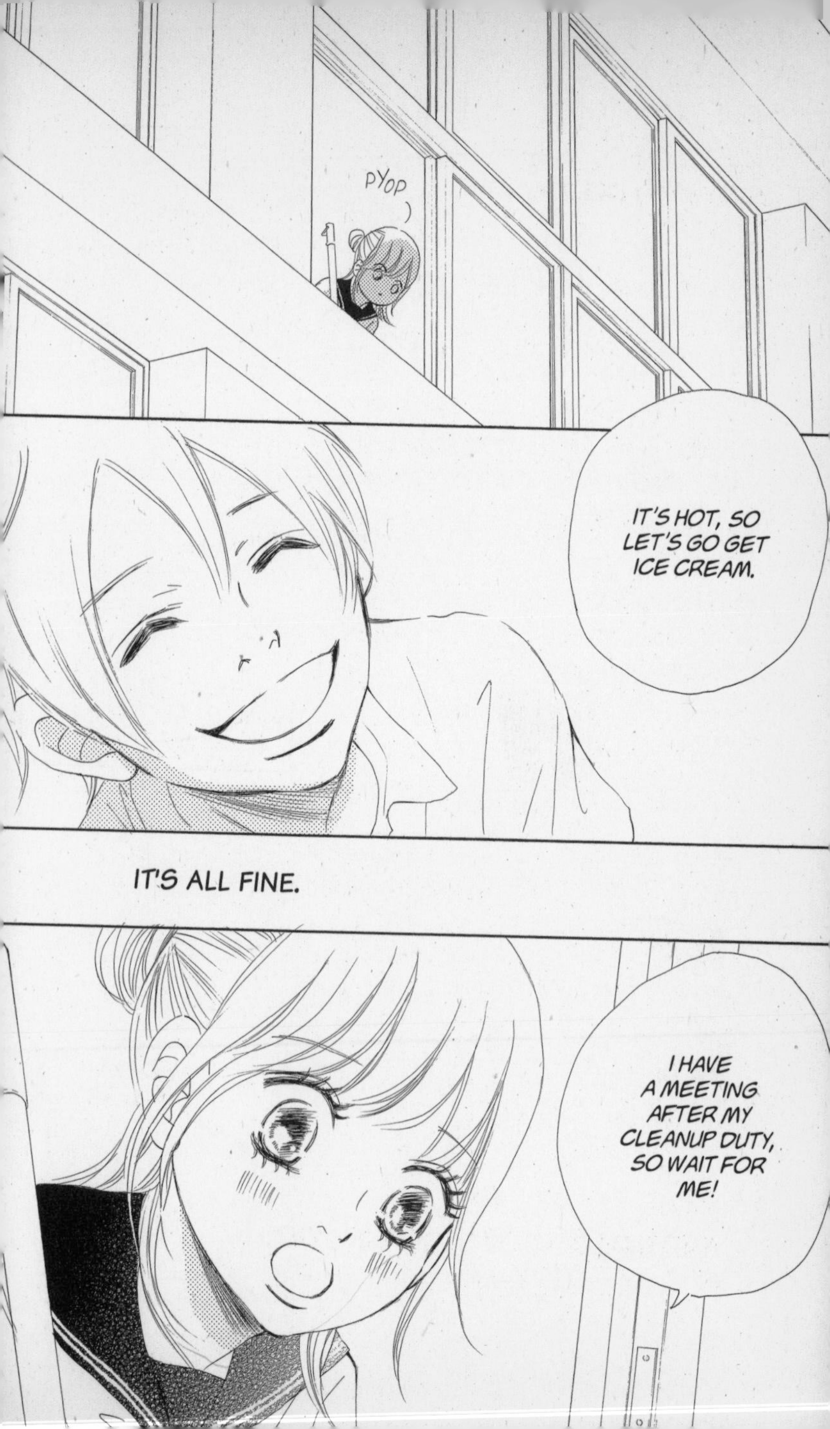
PYOP
IT'S HOT, SO LET'S GO GET ICE CREAM.
IT'S ALL FINE.
I HAVE A MEETING AFTER MY CLEANUP DUTY, SO WAIT FOR ME!

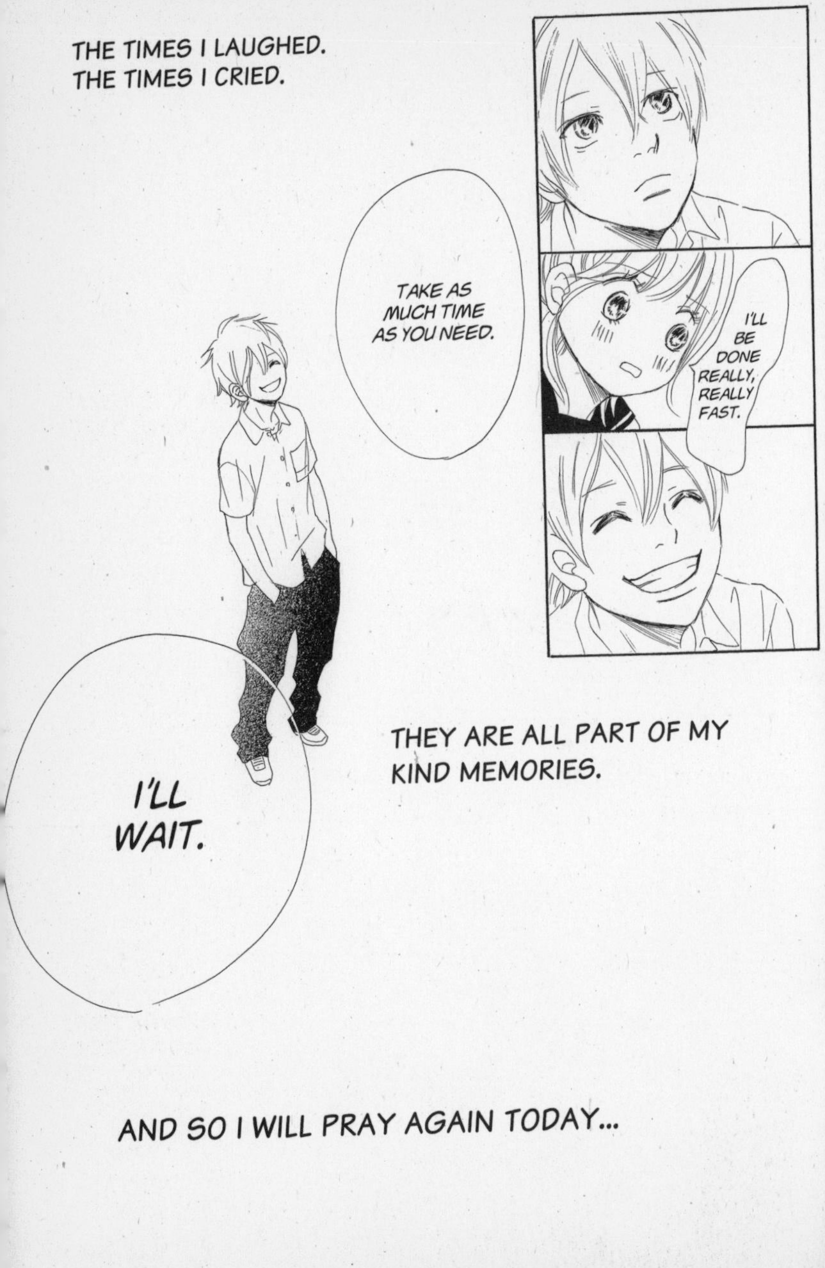
THE TIMES I LAUGHED.
THE TIMES I CRIED.
I'LL BE DONE REALLY, REALLY FAST.
TAKE AS MUCH TIME AS YOU NEED.
I'LL WAIT.
THEY ARE ALL PART OF MY KIND MEMORIES.
AND SO I WILL PRAY AGAIN TODAY...

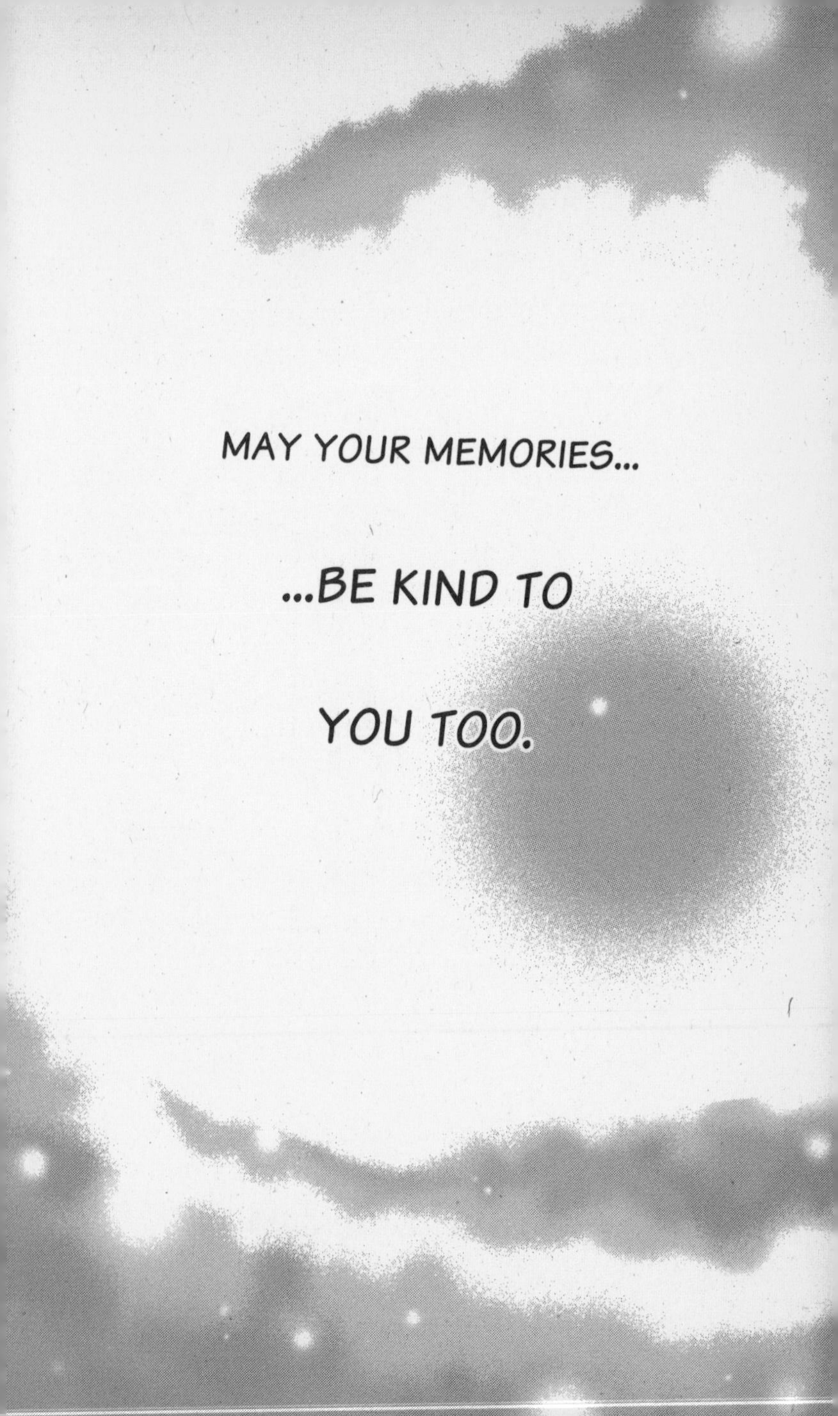
MAY YOUR MEMORIES...
...BE KIND TO
YOU TOO.

Bye-bye.

WE WERE THERE/END

Transferring one's dream and the images from one's brain onto a piece of paper is a fun and simple task, but when you add a story as well, you suddenly end up wandering into a labyrinth of eternal suffering. I am a wanting manga creator, and I have made these characters wander about a lot. Even as I write this, I still do not know if this was the right way. Maybe there was a different way—a better way around it? So I hope we will meet again in my next work with all these questions to solve piled up in front of me. This series went on for ten years if I include the time I was on hiatus. Thank you very much for supporting this series for such a long time.

–Yuuki Obata

Yuuki Obata's birthday is January 9. Her debut manga, *Raindrops*, won the Shogakukan Shinjin Comics Taisho Kasaku Award in 1998. Her current series, *We Were There (Bokura ga Ita)*, won the 50th Shogakukan Manga Award and was adapted into an animated television series. She likes sweets, coffee, drinking with friends, and scary stories. Her hobby is browsing in bookshops.

WE WERE THERE
Vol. 16
Shojo Beat Edition

STORY & ART BY
YUUKI OBATA

BOKURA GA ITA Vol. 16
by Yuuki OBATA
© 2002 Yuuki OBATA
All rights reserved.
Original Japanese edition published by SHOGAKUKAN.
English translation rights in the United States of America
and Canada arranged with SHOGAKUKAN.

Adaptation/Nancy Thistlethwaite
Translation/Tetsuichiro Miyaki
Touch-up Art & Lettering/Inori Fukuda Trant
Design/Yukiko Whitley, Jodie Yoshioka
Editor/Nancy Thistlethwaite

Printed in Canada

Published by VIZ MEDIA, LLC
P.O. Box 77010
San Francisco, CA 94107

10 9 8 7 6 5 4 3 2 1
First printing, May 2013

www.viz.com

www.shojobeat.com

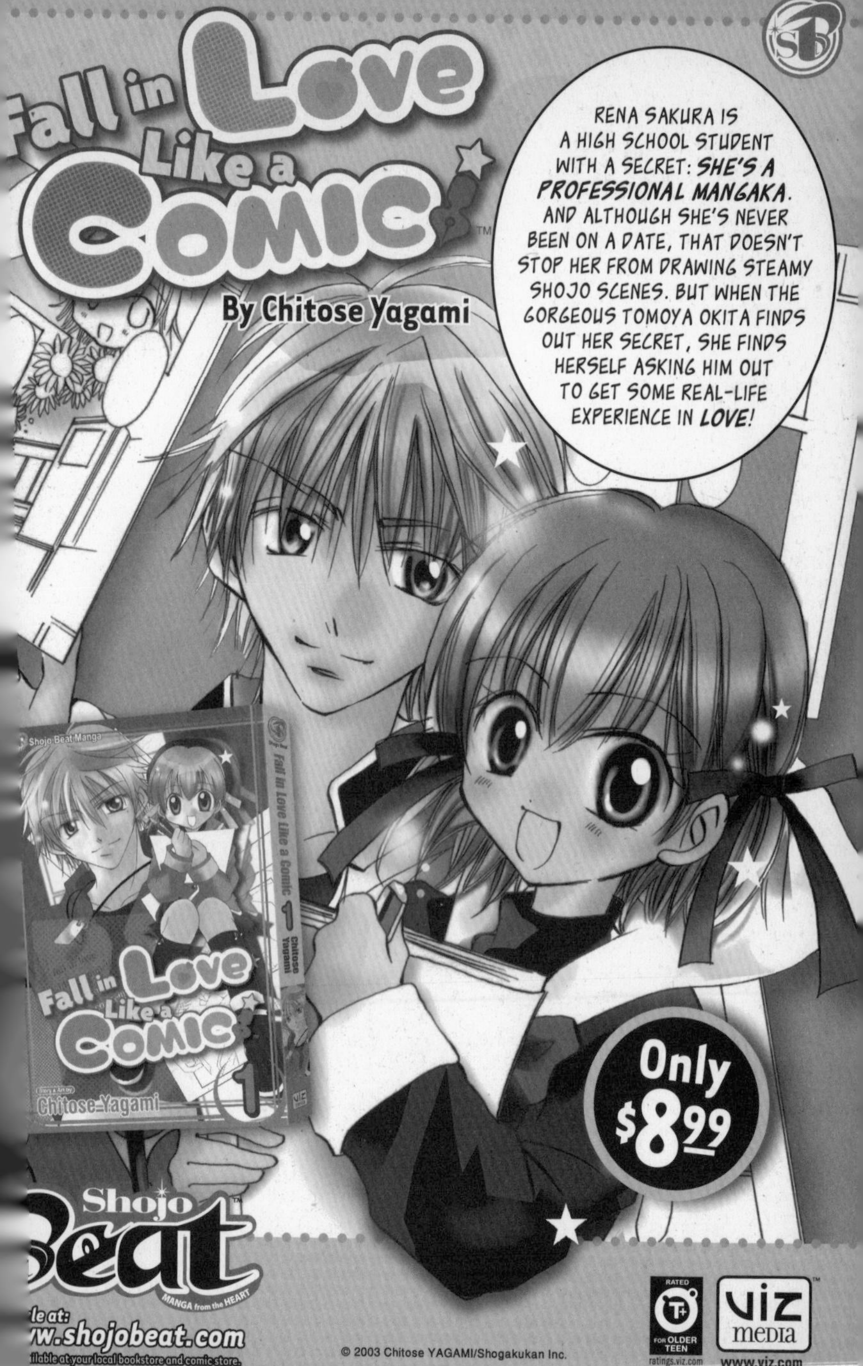

Fall in Love Like a Comic™
By Chitose Yagami
RENA SAKURA IS A HIGH SCHOOL STUDENT WITH A SECRET: SHE'S A PROFESSIONAL MANGAKA. AND ALTHOUGH SHE'S NEVER BEEN ON A DATE, THAT DOESN'T STOP HER FROM DRAWING STEAMY SHOJO SCENES. BUT WHEN THE GORGEOUS TOMOYA OKITA FINDS OUT HER SECRET, SHE FINDS HERSELF ASKING HIM OUT TO GET SOME REAL-LIFE EXPERIENCE IN LOVE!
Shojo Beat Manga
Fall in Love Like a Comic 1
Chitose Yagami
Story & Art by
Only $8.99
Shojo Beat™
MANGA from the HEART
le at:
w.shojobeat.com
ilable at your local bookstore and comic store.
© 2003 Chitose YAGAMI/Shogakukan Inc.
RATED
T+
FOR OLDER TEEN
ratings.viz.com
VIZ media
www.viz.com

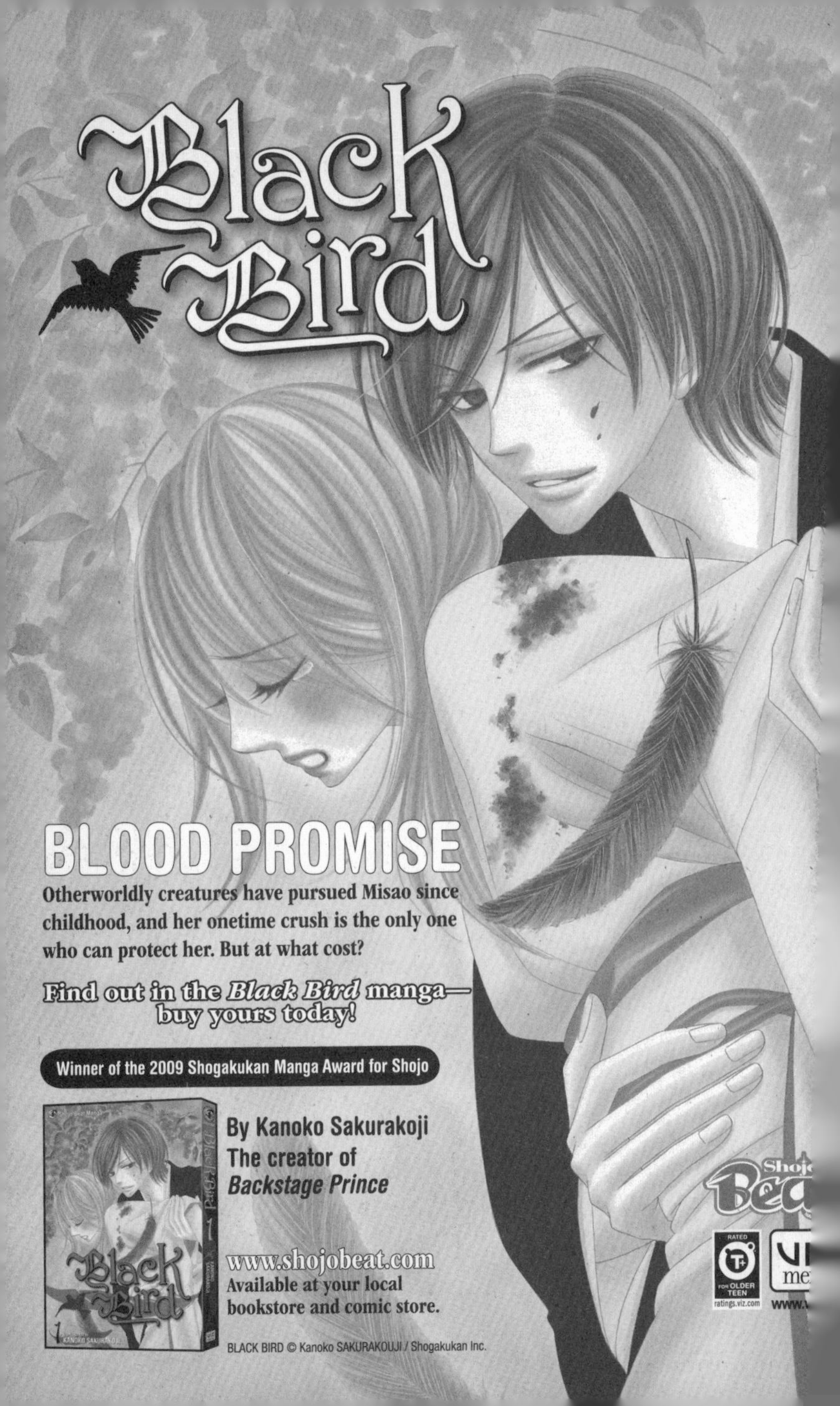
Black Bird
BLOOD PROMISE
Otherworldly creatures have pursued Misao since childhood, and her onetime crush is the only one who can protect her. But at what cost?
Find out in the Black Bird manga— buy yours today!
Winner of the 2009 Shogakukan Manga Award for Shojo
By Kanoko Sakurakoji
The creator of Backstage Prince
www.shojobeat.com
Available at your local bookstore and comic store.
BLACK BIRD © Kanoko SAKURAKOUJI / Shogakukan Inc.
RATED T+ FOR OLDER TEEN
ratings.viz.com

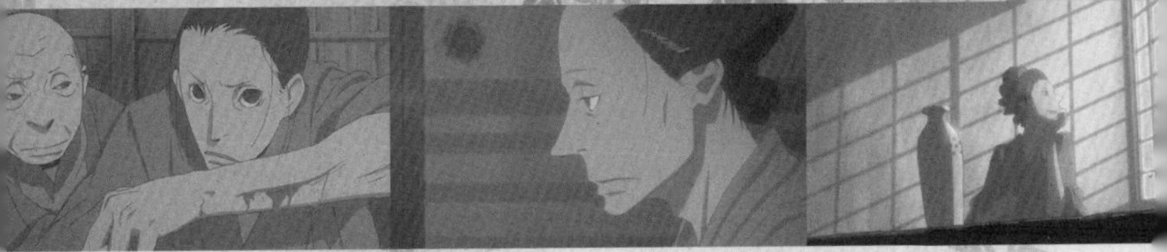

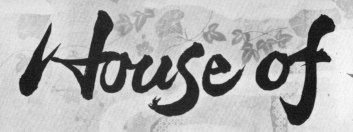

House of

from groundbreaking manga creator
Natsume Ono!

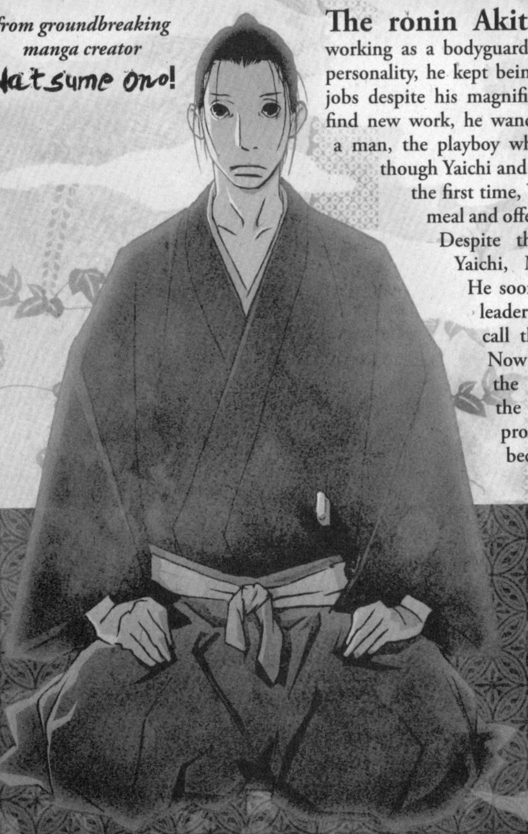

The ronin Akitsu Masanosuke was working as a bodyguard in Edo, but due to his shy personality, he kept being let go from his bodyguard jobs despite his magnificent sword skills. Unable to find new work, he wanders around town and meets a man, the playboy who calls himself Yaichi. Even though Yaichi and Masanosuke had just met for the first time, Yaichi treats Masanosuke to a meal and offers to hire him as a bodyguard. Despite the mysteries that surround Yaichi, Masanosuke takes the job. He soon finds out that Yaichi is the leader of a group of kidnappers who call themselves the "Five Leaves." Now Masanosuke is faced with the dilemma of whether to join the Five Leaves and share in the profits of kidnapping, or to resist becoming a criminal.

Shojo Beat Manga
TOKYO BOYS & GIRLS
1
Shojo Beat Manga
TOKYO BOYS & GIRLS
5
Miki Aihara

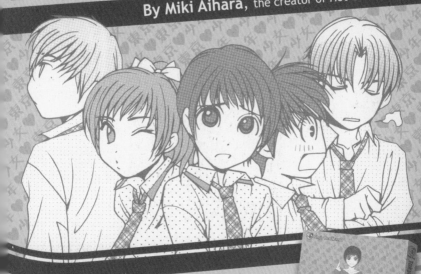

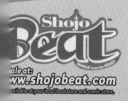

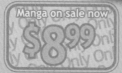

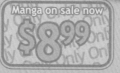

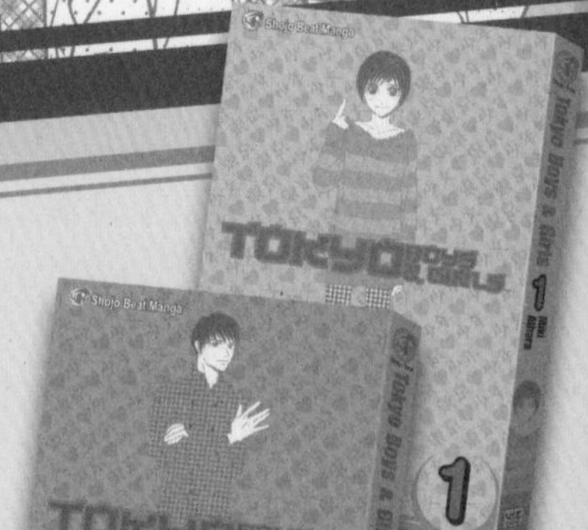